# Policymaking and Peace

STUDIES IN PUBLIC POLICY

**Series Editor: Paul J. Rich, Policy Studies Organization**

Government in the new millennium demands creative new approaches to managing change. Faced with the impact of globalization, technological revolution, and political reform, what can be done to encourage economic growth, develop more effective public administration at home, and forge strong and lasting relationships abroad?

Lexington Books and the Policy Studies Organization's **Studies in Public Policy** series brings together the very best in new and original scholarship, spanning the range of global policy questions. Its multi-disciplinary texts combine penetrating analysis of policy formulation at the macro level with innovative and practical solutions for policy implementation. It provides the political and social scientist with the latest academic research and the policy maker with effective tools to tackle the most pressing issues faced by government today.

### Titles in the Series

*Public Policies for Distressed Communities Revisited*
Edited by F. Stevens Redburn and Terry F. Buss

*Analyzing National and International Policy: Theory, Method, and Case Studies* by Laure Paquette

*Developmental Policy and the State: The European Union, East Asia, and the Caribbean* by Nikolaos Karagiannis

*Policymaking and Democracy: A Multinational Anthology*
Edited by Stuart Nagel

*Policymaking and Prosperity: A Multinational Anthology*
Edited by Stuart Nagel

*Policymaking and Peace: A Multinational Anthology*
Edited by Stuart Nagel

# Policymaking and Peace

## A Multinational Anthology

Edited by
Stuart Nagel

LEXINGTON BOOKS
*Lanham • Boulder • New York • Oxford*

LEXINGTON BOOKS

Published in the United States of America
by Lexington Books
A Member of the Rowman & Littlefield Publishing Group
4720 Boston Way, Lanham, Maryland 20706

PO Box 317
Oxford
OX2 9RU, UK

British Library Cataloguing in Publication Information Available

**Library of Congress Cataloging-in-Publication Data**

Policymaking and peace : a multinational anthology / edited by Stuart Nagel.
    p. cm.—(Studies in public policy)
    Includes bibliographical references and index.
    ISBN 0-7391-0461-6 (hardcover : alk. paper)
    1. Peace. 2. Conflict management. 3. International relations. 4. Policy sciences.
I. Nagel, Stuart S., 1934– II. Studies in public policy (Lanham, Md.)

 JZ5538 .P65 2002
 327.1'72—dc21

                                                                2002009877

Printed in the United States of America

&#9854;<sup>TM</sup> The paper used in this publication meets the minimum requirements of
American National Standard for Information Sciences—Permanence of Paper
for Printed Library Materials, ANSI/NISO Z39.48-1992.

For Alex Inkeles, scholar of peace and democracy

# Contents

**Part IV  Dispute Resolution**

6  Contemporary Diplomacy and Conflict Resolution:
       The Intertwining                                          159
       *John D. Stempel*

    7  Yugo-Nostalgia, Pragmatism, and Reality: Prospects for
       Inter-Republic Cooperation                                181
       *James H. Seroka*

**Part V  International Crime**

    8  Dunblane and the International Politics of Gun Control     193
       *Aaron Karp*

    9  Domination, Quiescence, and War Crimes                     213
       *John Braithwaite*

   10  The Threat of Terrorist Exploitation of Nuclear Smuggling  227
       *Gavin Cameron*

**Part VI  International Law and Order**

   11  International Legal Harmonization: Peace, Prosperity,
       and Democracy?                                             245
       *Jarrod Wiener*

   12  Lawyers as a Commodity in International Trade              269
       *Timothy J. O'Neill*

**Part VII  Peace, Prosperity, and Democracy**

   13  Violent Conflict, Security, and Development                285
       *Yannis A. Stivachtis*

   14  Democracy, Diversion, and the News Media                   311
       *Douglas A. Van Belle*

   15  Institutional Constraints, Political Opposition, and
       Interstate Dispute Escalation: Evidence from
       Parliamentary Systems, 1946-89                             335
       *Brandon C. Prins and Christopher Sprecher*

Index                                                             359

About the Contributors                                            375

# Introduction—Policy and Peace: Prospects and Prejudices

*Paul J. Rich*

Peace is obviously an international issue, and perhaps the most international of all issues. The fourth article of the Policy Studies Organization constitution reads, "The word 'American' is not used since the organization is open to members and is concerned with policy problems throughout the world."

We live, as all of us with an interest in political science know, in a time when completely contrary movements seem to simultaneously gather strength, including globalization and nationalism. So, to speak about a common scholarship is immediately to bring to mind such disturbing and valid challenges to academic ecumenicism and to peace as the demands for recognition of those struggling for autonomy in Quebec and Chiapas, of native peoples throughout the continent, and of strong but still frustrated movements for the overdue revision of the academic record to include women, gays, and ethnic groups. In those areas we are still, to paraphrase Winston Churchill on World War II, not at the end but perhaps at the end of the beginning.

We are certainly not going to have peace without more attention to minorities like the Palestinians, the Tamils, the Kurds—it's a long list. Proponents of a world focus for scholarship have to take very seriously the concerns of those who feel that research has ignored their identity, some of whom now fear that our enthusiasm for a new world approach inadvertently will leave them out. Looking back over past publications, only a small amount of the work, although undoubtedly good work, has been concerned with peace and gender, or peace and indigenous peoples, or with policy studies regarding, for example, peace in Canada and Mexico.

Perhaps it would in this respect be appropriate to mention specifically the need for more policy studies regarding separationist movements such as in

Chiapas and Quebec. In the Chiapas case, while it is the most widely known of Mexican internal problems,[1] it is only indicative as the demands of minority cultures are growing elsewhere in Mexico.[2] In an era that has seen the revival of the Scottish parliament, the excesses of Basque insurgents, and the revival of Hawaiian nationalism, not to mention casinos on Indian reservations, it would be the brave student of policy studies who would see anything but eclecticism on the horizon. Tom Nairn enjoins:

> Critics love fulminating about the distortions and phoniness which so frequently blight such transpositions, forgetting the hopeless or totally daft mythologies which held all previous *mentalities* down into status clamps . . . the cankered, one-off, lop-sided, ham-fisted, half-baked, one-eyed trajectory of actual modernisation led to rough justice. That was still better than what preceded it—no justice whatever, and forever. It also led to an ascriptive equality of pasts: the Irish, the Serbs, the Tibetans, the Inuit and the Micronesians will not be left out, and stake their claims like everyone else . . . having been startled into memoriality, they are damn well not going to subside again. Before industrialization, this happened all the time: cultures, peoples, traditions would just 'go under,' leaving a few puzzling bricks or stones behind if they were lucky. Even at the very end of the twentieth century, metropolitan blueprinters come out every other week with new plans for improved or graceful subsidence in the best interests of 'everyone.'[3]

Many in the policy studies field are familiar with the enormous amount of traveling that the late Professor Stuart Nagel did in his hopes of extending PSO globally and in inspiring peace studies. He was perennially disappointed about the lack of articles and books generated as a result. Perhaps one lesson arising out of that is that people cross boundaries with more ease sometimes than scholarship does.[4] The number of American and Canadian academic books and articles, for example, regardless of subject, which reveal a familiarity with Mexican scholarship in the same field is limited.[5] The construction of a world scholarship is still in the future and is going to require several generations of energetic bridge building and revisionism.[6] For instance, if there is a North American community already, it is spelled with a small "c" and not a large "C" as in the European Community.[7]

The readers of this volume will note a preponderance of citations of American work. This academic dominance of the Americans suggests the famous remark of the Mexican president Porfirio Diaz: "Poor Mexico. So far from God and so close to the United States!" The Canadian journalist Thomas Walkom recently wrote in the *Toronto Star:*

> We are in danger of becoming a nation whose time has gone. . . Already, almost all Canadian institutions designed to express national sensibilities are under attack as impediments to world trade—by the WTO or the North American Free Trade Agreement or just by the Americans. We cannot protect our magazines or

books; we cannot demand distribution of Canadian films. We have been a nation for 132 years. Unless we wake up, we will not keep going for another 50. Death will come slowly—a privatization here, a trade agreement there. Maybe there will be a currency agreement with Washington. For reasons of efficiency, we will put our cash-starved armed forces under American command. And finally, to give all Canadians a crack at the big apple, will come a common North American citizenship. The withering of Parliament will take longer, for politicians are adept at holding on to their jobs. In the new North America, Parliament might even survive intact, as a quaint, powerless regional body charged with matters that are not deemed too important. You want to know Canada's situation as the last embers of the twentieth century flicker and die? This is it: We are not exactly being murdered. Call it, rather, assisted suicide.[8]

Canadians are often their own severest critics, and not all of them see an emerging North American or global community as a threat. The Canadian Minister of Foreign Affairs, Lloyd Axworthy, has pressed for further integration, including the so-called Murmansk to Monterrey corridor that would dramatically integrate transportation. He writes, "This interaction may also point the way to a wider sense of community and help shape a shared sense of 'North American-ness.' Mexicans, Americans and Canadians already have a strong sense of their own identity. The challenge will be to develop a North American 'footprint' that treads lightly enough that it does not crush the existing landscape formed by distinctive histories and cultures." He then adds, "Our aim should be to construct a community that serves North Americans but that is also open to the world—a community, for example, that is open southward to the rest of the Americas or northward to the Arctic region."[9]

In my judgment, the key to peace is a heightened appreciation of pluralism and, way down the road one should add, of its close cousin, federalism. (There is not enough space to comment on how closely these two ideas are connected, but events on September 11, 2001 have surely made everyone aware of the need to think about federal structures that can accommodate minorities.)

This however is not the place for a lengthy discussion of world federalism, which is often denounced as encouraging political fragmentation.[10] Religious and ethnic pride rouses fears of "heading down the road to another Bosnia."[11] We share a need for policies friendly to political and cultural pluralism, a fact sometimes ignored or neglected, but important as we enter the uncharted waters of the twenty-first century. The Canadian political theorist Reg Whitaker remarks in his useful book *A Sovereign Idea: Essays on Canada as a Democratic Community*, "Is one acting as an Albertan or as a Canadian? If the answer is 'both,' as it usually will be in a functioning federal society, the question of community has, in effect, been opened up again . . . That may be very untidy and for the bane of rationalists, it may make federations difficult to operate, but it demonstrates that federalism isn't merely compatible with (representative) democracy, but may offer one of the better institutional frameworks for coping with some of the inherent problems of democracy."[12]

He might well have added that citizens in any democracy need an education which makes them aware of the pluralism inherent in the world, and of the practical necessity of respecting that pluralism. John Raulston Saul cautions:

> An educational or social system that defines progress as the total of a myriad of more or less water-tight compartments denies the possibility of a citizen-based society. It therefore denies the individual as the source of legitimacy. However fine the abstract intentions of professionalism and expertise may be, the net result of this approach is a mechanistic view of men and women. Knowledge and understanding in their real sense—as the foundations of consciousness—become impossible. Society conceived in this way is viewed through corporatist eyes and denies both the complexity of the human and the complexity of human society.[13]

As students of policy studies, it is one of our jobs to point discussion towards the ways to handle the pluralities of a troubled world. Someday, we hope, there will be a more sympathetic political environment for all. This book, in its diversity, is a real step in that direction.

## NOTES

1. Free market initiatives, privatization schemes, and NAFTA-sponsored lowering of trade barriers have meant that the poor states of Mexico, those that are largely rural and made up of the campesinos face direct competition with Canadian and American industry and agribusiness.

2. In Chiapas, an entire farming culture feels abandoned by Mexico City.

3. Tom Nairn, *Faces of Nationalism: Janus Revisited* (Verso, London and New York, 1997), 5.

4. See Noel F. McGinn, *Towards International Cooperation in Education for the Integration of the Americas* (Washington, D.C.: Inter-American Council for Integral Development, 1999), 23.

5. The reverse is equally true. See John Reid, *Spanish American Images of the United States, 1790–1960* (Gainesville: University Press of Florida, 1977).

6. Allen Hammond, *Which World? Scenarios for the 21st Century* (Washington, D.C.: Island Press, 1998), 255 *ff.*

7. See John D. Wirth, "Advancing the North American Community," *The American Review of Canadian Studies* Summer 1996: 261–273, available at www.northamericaninstitute.org/na_community/advancing.html. A mainstay of the North American Institute, Professor Wirth has been one of the early pioneers in post NAFTA North American integration studies.

8. Thomas Walkom, "A Canadian Call to Arms," *Toronto Star,* 24 December 1999, available at www.flipside.org/vol3/jan00/00ja29b.htm.

9. Lloyd Axworthy, "Notes for an Address," Canadian Institute of International Affairs 1998 Foreign Policy Conference, 16 October 1998, available at www.dfait-maeci.gc.ca/engli...ws/statements/98_067e.htm.

10. See Alan Freeman and Patrick Grady, *Dividing the House: Planning for a Canada Without Quebec* (Toronto: HarperCollins, 1995).

11. Larry Rohter, "Maya Renaissance in Guatemala Turns Political," *New York Times*, 12 August 1996, A5.

12. Reg Whitaker, *A Sovereign Idea: Essays on Canada as a Democratic Community* (Montreal and Kingston: McGill-Queen's University Press, 1992), 199.

13. John Ralston Saul, *The Unconscious Civilization* (New York: The Free Press, 1995), 164.

# I

## THE NATURE AND END OF THE COLD WAR

# 1

# Politics of the 'State' in the Cold War

*Richard Saull*

## REALISM, THE STATE AND INTERNATIONAL RELATIONS THEORY

Realism is, and has provided the dominant focus for International Relations (IR) scholarship and discussion of the Cold War. To discuss the politics and history of the Cold War without an explicit reference and discussion of the state in international relations, and the currency of the state, would be to not only ignore the import of the changing nature of state action in international relations that the Cold War witnessed, but also to avoid the role of what *appeared* to be the dominant actor in this period of world history. I stress "appear," because it is my contention that the discussion of the state, and the nature of the state in most Cold War literature has taken an all too problematic conceptualization of the state, which lacks sociological content and adequate historicization. What I mean, and this will become clearer, below, in the substantive argument of this paper, is that we need to reconceptualize the state if we are to properly understand the historical specificity of the Cold War in IR.

The Cold War saw the emergence of the "state," as a product of the globalization of the international system, as a universalized political form. This was in legal-diplomatic terms *only*. Although the state has become globalized, what this actually witnessed was the emergence of distinct forms of political community that have representation as states in international relations, but whose content has varied greatly. What this means is that, in political terms, the notion of the state must be contested. This contestation relates to the process of the emergence of new "states" in the international system, and their effect on that system, and how they have related to the pre-existing forms of state. However, it does not relate only to the proliferation of states, but also the changing nature, both domestic and international, of the dominant states in the international system. The state is not only an abstract concept, and if we conceive of it only in the abstract we end up with a rather vacuous social/political category. Although we can identify attributes of a "state" or more historically accurate, "political rule" in the abstract, we need to investigate the peculiarities of states or *political forms* if we are to provide any historical explanation of them. Thus, the state obviously played a significant role in the international relations of the Cold War, roles that were specific to the historical and social content that they existed within. The state was not an "abstract actor," but rather an historical agent, which through the processes of historical development, changed. Through its actions it changed the situation, both internally and internationally, which served to facilitate a change in its own nature. The state then, helped change the politics of the international and was itself changed by it. This was what the Cold War was about and it is this that this paper seeks to investigate.

The state in international relations is the instrument of a currency of relations based on politics. This understanding relates directly to the conception of the state as traditionally understood. Instead of understanding international relations as being confined to the state and politics, we should seek to understand international relations as the external projection of the processional developments and conflicts within and between different social formations. In such terms one could identify, *empirically*, that all states have different international relations as they reflect different processional forms of political rule related to developments in class conflict within capitalism and those social formations that are not fully capitalist, (i.e. where other mode[s] of production are dominant). However, that is not the task at hand here, but rather to suggest and outline some theoretical points that reflect the specificity of forms of international relations that reflect different forms of political rule.

Nuclear weapons, and the arms race between the superpowers provide the most graphic aspect of the logic of the state in international relations during the Cold War, and the literature of both IR and the Cold War reflect this.[1] This literature has been the focus of the critical pen during the closing stages of the Cold War and subsequently.[2] This, in many respects, justified attack on the dominance of a particular "security paradigm" in IR has to be welcomed, but it should not lead us to either associate realism *tout court* with security in its nuclear or purely "hard" form, and neither should it lead us to a marginalization of the role of the state in IR and especially the Cold War. For it was in the Cold War where we were to see the triumph of state power, or more accurately, specific forms of state power, as the means of realizing political objectives in international relations. This is not only about the political-military formations that dominated the divided Europe for nearly half a century, but also the ways in which the state sought to maximize its leverage and

*Politics of the 'State' in the Cold War* 5

scope for action and influence in international relations during the Cold War. What this involves is that the nature of the state needs to be problematized, so that instead of treating it as a given form, we focus on the specific content of "the relations between states" that the Cold War appeared to reflect. Only if we do this will the uniqueness of the "political-military relations" and conflict of the Cold War be visible. This will be the dominant concern of this paper, the nature of the state, and the specific kind of "politics" in the Cold War. Realism only provides a starting point here, and it will be the purpose of this paper to criticize Realism's ontology and epistemology of the state and international relations, and replace it with one derived from an Historical Materialist understanding.

This paper will seek to reconceptualize the role and place of the state in the Cold War, and the politics of the state. This will be achieved through a discussion of the social essence of the state, and the different logics of types of state, based on the illustration provided by the Cold War. This will be highlighted by the impact of social revolutionary states in the international system and how these provide a focus for alternate appreciations of the state-(society) relationship in international relations, and where and how the two dominant but different state forms of the Cold War, the Soviet Union and the United States, fit into this conceptualization.

Realism, as a theory of International Relations, is mainly concerned with a focus on the state and the political relations between states. Both the units or agents of international relations and the currency of those relations are identified with politics, and more specifically, the politics of power.[3] Although one can find distinct cleavages within the Realist corpus, the ontological focus on the state pervades *all* Realist work.

For Realists the state or the nature of the state is something that is fixed in the realm of international relations. Quintessentially the state is the state, as it has always been. A state in international relations is a means of organizing a people in a limited territorial entity based on the internal supreme political authority of sovereignty, and externally the physical ability to preserve that internal authority from external threats. For all intents and purposes the state in IR then, is an agent of political violence, a shell for controlling and directing political violence against other states. In this respect, the "state" or political community of classical Greek civilization is no different to the state of nineteenth century Europe, and the United States and the Soviet Union during the Cold War. In essence they are the same.[4] They have the same functions; they confront the same internal and external limitations. The only things that have changed, historically, are the means and how the means to achieve the goals end up inflecting or determining the system/structure in which these states exist within. This is obviously the case for nuclear weapons. Explanation then, is ontologically limited to the role of the means of political violence on the system.

In ontological and explanatory terms the substance of Realism amounts to an understanding of politics that is obviously very limited. It screens out other actors, it screens out other obvious definitions or logics of politics and it treats the political actors (states) as absolute and autonomous entities, at the least in the abstract. Another problem is that it reduces all change or actions to the political. This is not a problem with the identification of the "political" but becomes one with the rather narrow and barren nature of the political in Realism.[5] Power is the political. In seeking to explain everything through the interests of power, we end up obscuring or tarnishing everything with the brush of power politics that is only recognized in its appearance of military and strategic competition. Politics is taken as a recognized uncontested categorization,[6] a concern that is separate from economics and normative content. However, the "politics" of Realism is extremely problematical because it fails to actually discuss what politics is in IR. This again is something that I will develop later, below.

What remains in this understanding of Realism, IR theory and the Cold War, is that Realists have a particular focus and understanding of the state. It is this ontological focus that provides Realism with its elegance of explanation but also its fundamental limitation of explanatory power. This is for two interwoven reasons. One is the "reductionist," to use a Waltzian term, notion of the state in Realism, which partly explains the silence on other aspects of international relations that either alter the Realist conceptualization of the state and/or actually work from a completely different ontology. The other is related to the understanding of the state, which remains wedded to the conceptual and political separation from the economic, which serves to sever the bond between the modern state and its structural position and role in particular strategies of accumulation that are part of a specific politics. Thus, the type of politics of the state in this respect (a Marxist understanding) will seek to explore the unity of the political and the economic, to give the politics of the state a more materialist orientation, but more importantly, to raise specific and important *political* questions that Realism as a whole either completely ignores or treats as a separate phenomena.[7]

## RECONSTRUCTING A POLITICS OF THE STATE IN THE COLD WAR

Realism fails to provide an adequate conceptualization of the state, and thus fails in its explanation of the Cold War. This section of the paper will attempt to go beyond the Realist notion of the state in the Cold War and endeavor to provide a Historical Materialist conceptualization of the state in the Cold War. This will be achieved by renegotiating the boundaries and terrain of politics. In a precursor to what follows, politics *qua* the state will be reconstituted in terms of social relations. What this means is that the bourgeois separation of politics (the state) and economics (the market) will be replaced by the conceptualization of politics as "the unity in the separation"[8] of the political/public sphere of the state and the private/economic sphere of production.

Such a conceptualization of politics is drawn from the work of Marx and Engels, a conceptualization that begins with the politics of "man's interaction with nature," (i.e. the material *and* social relations of production which lie at the heart of any understanding of human/social relations). For people to make history they need to be able to produce. This is the first act of any society.

> the first premise of all human existence and, therefore, of all history . . . is the premise . . . that men must be in a position to live in order to be able to make history . . . . the production of material life itself . . . is . . . a fundamental condition of all history.[9]

The act of production is a material *and* social act to the point that the individuals cooperating in production are in themselves a *productive force*. What this means is that production is a social activity that does not concern only what is usually identified with the "material base" of a society.[10] Following this is the fact that both the nature of production and the social relations corresponding with this, change. Thus, production is an evolutionary form, and it is the evolution, *through struggle*, that is the basic explanatory feature of all human societies,[11] and we are to understand these changes as deriving from social relations of production.

The state or the public, political sphere that appears as separate or autonomous is seen as an historical and social phenomenon, which cannot be treated, analytically or otherwise, as separate from the social relations that stem from human's interaction with nature, which is the basis of the production and reproduction of social life. I will not be addressing the historical evolution of the state form.[12] I have already alluded to this need for historicization in my critique of existing realist knowledge. Instead, I will discuss the nature and politics of the state, as a political form in the Cold War.

What does this entail? Primarily, it entails a brief discussion of the state as a nonstatic political-spatial form. What this means is that we need to see the state, not in the rather a-historical and static terms of Realism nor in the hyperbolically charged terms of Liberals and Transnationalists who talk of the "death of the state," but rather as a particular and evolving social-historical form that has centralized political *class* power. The history of international relations, no less typified by the history of the Cold War is one of the changing, evolving and conflicting development of the state.[13]

The state is only a state in terms of history, in terms of politics. The Cold War more than any period of world history reflects this. This brings me on to the second point, and that is the need to address and discuss the politics

and/or political logic of different types of "state" and, between these two issues, is the need to trace the historical development of the state in both domestic and international terms as part of a social totality which is only reducible to the expansion of capitalism and the international social conflicts
wrought in the wake of this expansion. It is these conflicts located, both
within the territorial confines of the state, but also beyond and between
states that have involved the state and transformed it, and in so doing have
altered the social relations that realize a particular type of state form.

The "hard," "outer" shell of the Realist state obviously plays a part in this
history, but not in the terms set out by Realists. The currencies of nuclear
weapons, conventional forces and other forms of the state, are present, but
only in a social context.[14] The prosecution of organized political violence by
the state is not separable from the strategies of the social reproduction of that
state. Thus, the state in these terms, and its military or political expansion, in
Realist terms, is transformed to reflect the actual social characteristics of
states. The state is not seen as reacting according to the laws of anarchy that
appear to ensure a uniformity of political outcomes *à la* Waltz, but rather, the
state reflects domestic and international class conflict derived from the contradictions of the expansion and consolidation of capitalist social relations
and the peculiar types of political-state forms that such a process and conflict throws up.

## The State as a Contested Political Form

In the Realist account of politics, the state is seen as a given, a natural form
that is part of the conscious makeup of contemporary, and more importantly,
historical civilization. What matters in their discussion of the state is the rather
barren legal-territorial concern with political authority based on the monopolization of physical violence, alone. This is obviously important in recognizing the emergence of the state, but cut adrift from the social relations between people, it parcels out politics to a public sphere that is removed from
the privatized or (relatively) autonomous realm of socioeconomic production. Once this occurs, politics and history become enshrined in the separate
public authority of the state, which relegates the actual history of people to
the private sphere or civil society. The history of social struggles involving
class(es) is airbrushed from the historical record.

The state is not embodied with agency, rather, it is purely an organizational form of power.[15] What is obviously missing in this account of the state,
and its emergence is the fact that the actual historical presence of the state
within a society or social totality is a product of a particular social-historical
process, which can only be associated with the unfolding of the logic of a
capitalist modernity. If this is the case, then the state that Realism talks about
is the capitalist state. For Realism, the state is a category or an ideal-type, in

the sense of the state being a general political form endowed with general organizational attributes that make it act in a general way. What this means, is that the state is treated as an historical subject, when according to analysis of what the state actually is, it is an abstract general category, (i.e. an organizational form which enforces a form of rule through its monopoly of physical violence). On this reading we are not dealing with anything that in reality exists, but in something that only exists in reality as an abstraction.

The alternative to this from a Historical Materialist perspective is to treat the state, as an existing social and historical form.[16] What this means is that we must obviously have abstract categories and criteria for talking about something, concepts that furnish meaning to a theory, but that we must apply these concepts and ultimately realize them through an historical and specific understanding of types of state or *forms of political rule*. This is an historical investigation and it implies change and agency. Ergo, Historical Materialism is not concerned with a *general* theory of history or society but rather about:

> definite individuals who are productively active in a definite way enter into these definite social and political relations. Empirical observation must *in each separate instance* bring out *empirically*, and without any mystification and speculation, the connection of the social and political structure with production.[17]

Therefore the notion of the state in IR needs to be seen in "processional" terms, that is, as something that has emerged because of the presence and operation of particular kinds of agency, and something that has been subject to change as well as initiating change. The history of the state is thus contingent and alive. The state from this perspective is not reducible to "politics" as conventionally understood, and it is not reducible to an idealized form separate from society or the social relations between people. Rather, the state should be seen as a "processional form," an institutional mechanism associated with the emergence of capitalist social relations that saw an apparent separation of the public power/authority and material production with the dissolution of feudal forms of political rule that incorporated the direct, political extraction of the surplus of the direct producers. Whereas feudal politics incorporated public authority and political rule with material production, the emergence of capitalist social relations saw the emergence of a separation between the form of political rule and the indirect, purely economic forms of surplus extraction from the direct producers.[18]

However, although the state, as it emerged as a separate and public source of authority that was able to incorporate aspects of social struggle through the expansion of the franchise (making people in society "politically" equal), the state as politics could not incorporate a politics derived from the social relations of production. The production and reproduction of the materials and ideas of social life was privatized. Appearing separate, however, the form of political rule and the means of appropriation have been coupled together, in the sense that although they appear separate, and because there is a *real* difference between capitalist social relations and forms of surplus extraction from pre, and noncapitalists forms, they cannot be *comprehended* separately. Without the capitalist state there would be no "market relations," without capitalism there would be no capitalist form of political rule *qua* state.[19]

The state through law, and its strategic deployment of political power and coercion, acts as a *relation* of capitalist production.[20] In this sense then, the state and thus the politics identified with the state or the public sphere, is not limited to the traditional understanding of politics associated with Liberal conceptions. Rather, politics must include the state, but not as a separate sphere of authority, but as it relates to the "production and reproduction of social life," (i.e. capitalist social relations). Politics is thus about how the state helps shape and is itself shaped by the ongoing conflicts and contradictions associated with the preservation and expansion of capitalist social relations, both within the limits of territorial states, and at the international level between states, and within the capitalist social relations that traverse the territorial boundaries of states.

On two levels we can see, following the argument above, that the *state is a contested form of political rule.* On one level the state is a contested political form in terms of its role as a relation of capitalist production. The form of the state is bound up with its relationship with capital, in the sense that it acts both as a guarantor of capitalist social relations and acts within those social relations through forms of lawmaking, and other aspects normally associated with the "soft" or welfare state. On another level the state is contested not within the social relations of capitalism, but as an objective for the overthrow of the specifically capitalist form of political rule. Thus, the social struggles within capitalism between those who sell their labor and those individuals and institutions that exist on the basis of the appropriation of that labor do not always stop at the door of the work place. Historically this has been the case; social struggle has been perceived and practiced purely in economic terms, at the apparent source of the inequality. However, for a frontal assault on the social relations themselves the social struggle of the proletariat must go beyond the economic source and seek the overthrow of the political power behind the form of exploitation. Therefore the state has been historically contested as a specific form of political rule through social revolution whereby revolution seeks to overthrow the state and transform the form of political rule by reconstituting the state (and society). Thus, the reconstitution of the state sees a direct transformation of the social relations previously existing.

Seeing the state as an essentially contested political form opens up the state both to further intellectual inquiry, but also social *as* political strategies for its overthrow and replacement. It suggests that the state is a historically recent form of political rule in global terms, even to the point where the state as a capitalist state *par excellence,* is still not a fully global form. This, in one sense, is the history of modernity in its capitalist incarnation, the struggles both within developing or existing capitalist states and between capitalist forms of rule as they have internationally expanded through the classical stages of imperialism associated with the European great powers, and the "colonial experience" to the more recent forms of political rule that do not have an obviously political form. What this last point entails is that capitalism, to maintain itself and expand, changes in *form.*[21]

Thus, the end of colonial rule after World War II reflected the changing nature of capitalism as a global social relation. It no longer required colonial state forms or direct forms of political rule to secure its self-valorization.[22] Capitalism expanded with, but for the most part without the requirement of a direct international state expansion.[23] What this means is that the Cold War saw the end of the colonial period, which reflected the directly coercive form of expansion. Decolonization and the emergence of new state forms/forms of political rule allowed for the expansion of capitalist social relations *qua* the law of value and indirect surplus appropriation, rather than securing this through an "imperial system." Capitalism expanded with the proliferation of the state form, in particular after the Second World War. With the emergence of proto-capitalist state forms in the former colonies, and the U.S. attempts to open up the international economy, capitalism could valorize itself and the projects of American capital could be realized without the need for direct forms of political control. The colonies became politically "independent," but they were also tied to the expanding international capitalist system that allowed increasingly freer movement of capital, and the ability of capitalist social relations to penetrate the former colonial areas without the need for direct forms of imperial control. I do not want to suggest that this was a smooth, inevitable process, which many caricatures of Marxism suggest. This is not teleological, but rather highlights the fact of the Cold War as struggle within and between different social forms. The revolutionary changes and conflicts in the former colonial and "Third World" reflect this history as a processional historical development based around social conflict.

This point applies equally to the advanced capitalist states. Prior to American hegemony international capitalism was based around British "political" dominance through its imperial system. The other capitalist states mirrored this through the need for direct-political, "state" involvement in strategies of surplus extraction most visibly under Fascist regimes. American capitalist predominance revolutionized the international relations of capital, by providing through Bretton Woods and a dominant American economy, indirect or *visibly* nonimperialist forms of capitalist expansion. Capitalist social relations could expand through their own self-valorization, rather than through the functional use of war and colonial conquest, because of the American international dollar economy helped by the proliferation of "independent" states that did not need to be occupied to be capitalist. This is not to suggest that there was no use of force or projections of direct American capitalist state power in the post-war era, there patently were. The Bretton Woods system of international capitalism like the rule of capital in any social formation ultimately rests on the monopolization of class power in the form of the state and its ability to use force. This happened in numerous occasions during the Cold War. When the expansion of the rule of capital was being contested or abolished the United States acted through military force to either prevent or overthrow such projects. However, the era of *systematic* direct political control as a means to expand capitalism was replaced by more indirect or "privatized" forms.

Thus, the state emerges as a global or at least potentially global form of limited political rule through the expansion of capitalism, and how this process, subverts, destroys and incorporates aspects of previously existing and noncapitalist forms of rule. These can only be explained in terms of social-class struggle concerning how the forms of political rule within a society are related to, or fused with forms of social relations of production. Thus, feudal production was associated and related to distinct forms of political rule, as is capitalism, and as are socialist or revolutionary societies.

The contestation of forms of political rule, which the state is but one, and the most important (because of its global pretensions and possibilities as a phenomenon associated with capitalism), provides the backdrop for international relations and the Cold War. The history of the state as a form of political rule is not separable from the international. That is, international relations determine the domestic configuration of capitalist social relations and is in turn determined by them. They are not separable. The state cannot be detached from its position embedded within a particular social context that is not limited to the territorial boundaries of the state. The state as a contested form of political rule is also contested in international terms. Again this works both ways. The state facilitates forms of international relations connected with specific forms of political rule, and is partly shaped by international forces. We have an interrelationship between the domestic and international spheres, which shapes the form of the state, and which the state partly shapes as well.[24] The contestation derives from the conflict between different forms of political rule.

Thus, capitalist states as forms of political rule are characterized by particular forms of international relations. This obviously leads to a different type of international relations between these forms of political rule as we can identify the similarities *within* a society relating to political rule, concerning the nature of the state, and how this relates to the other institutions within society. What characterizes relations between capitalist states is the currency of capitalist social relations, which are "relatively autonomous" from the relations derived from the form of political rule. What this means is that the relations between these "states" rests on social relations derived from capitalism. In this sense the relations between these types of states relate to contradictions and conflicts fundamentally concerned not with the state as such or forms of political rule, but rather, with the nature and dynamic of capitalist social relations. Conflict in political terms, as described by Realists, does not have a currency, instead, politics only "appears" when these conflicts and contradictions relate to social relations that interfere with the political rule of the state.

Thus, the international relations/politics of capitalist states are qualitatively different to those between noncapitalist "states," and capitalist and noncapitalist "states." This is quite clear, even with more orthodox interpretations of international relations. In terms of the international society approach the relations between "Christendom" and the Islamic world were different from intra-Christian relations.[25] However, in terms of an "international society," (i.e. a global system represented by sovereign nation-states as the forms of political rule) we can go beyond the distinctions recognized by orthodox approaches to IR, and conceive of the relations between political forms *qua* states as being derived from their social relations. What this means is that the political form, in terms of the nature of the state (political rule within a given society/territorial entity), is only explicable in terms of how this political form reflects and is part of the social relations of production. Thus, during the Cold War international relations was not about the political relations between states, but about the *forms* of political relations between different forms of political rule, which reflected differing ways of organizing social life based on different ways of organizing a society's reproduction of social life through its interaction with nature.

The way that societies reconstituted themselves, altering their ways of organizing social life have been through social revolution. It was these developments in the Cold War that provided the currency of the political relations of the Cold War that the United States and the Soviet Union were part of. It is to the currency of the social revolutionary state, as a form of political rule in the Cold War, and the conflict that stemmed from this with capitalist forms of political rule, that the source of the explanation of the Cold War is to be found.

## The Revolutionary "State" as an Alternative Form of International Politics

Revolutionary "states" have provided the discipline of IR with its most visible case of both the contestation of the state as a form of political rule, and its transformation through a reconstitution of social relations. Although on one level, the level of appearances, these forms of political rule assume the form of the state, they are qualitatively different, and realize an alternative form of political rule derived from a different set of social relations. Thus, in these political entities the form of political rule, and following this, international relations is different to that of the state as previously understood.

In orthodox IR revolutions are largely seen as domestic concerns that see a change in the form of legitimacy of a state. Although there may be recognition of the *attempts* to revolutionize foreign policy and the international domain[26] this is soon replaced by a return to the "bread and butter" of *Realpolitik*. The form of the state only changes to the extent of personnel; as a participant in international relations, as a political authority occupying a piece of the world's territory, such states confront and reflect the exigencies that all states reflect in the international system. This, in one respect is true. The physical survival of any state, as a form of political rule, cannot be taken for granted. A revolutionary form of politics and the institutions that it creates and attempts to consolidate and expand is obviously aware of the physical threats to its existence through the application of internal and/or international counter-revolutionary force to quash a revolution. The fact that all states confront a "security dilemma," to borrow Waltz's phrase, should not lead us to assume, as Waltz and Realism does, that one, this provides the determining logic of world politics, and second, that this logic is acted on in the same way by all types of state.

Revolutionary forms of political rule as suggested by Halliday through his conceptualizations of "state-society relations"[27] and "heterogeneity and homogeneity,"[28] more than any other form of state confront this threat in the most acute dimensions than other types of state. Indeed, social revolutions have not been able, historically, as the history of the Soviet Union suggests, to overcome the dilemma posed by existing within a hostile and predatory international environment. What we can say, however, is that because a revolution overthrows a type of political rule; in the Cold War period, forms of political rule imbricated with the consolidation and expansion of capitalist social relations, the nature of the relations between different states are different despite appearing to mirror international relations as conventionally understood. What then is the currency of these international relations that relate to a distinctly different form of political rule?

On the level of appearances, as is clear from the orthodox-Realist scholarship on the Cold War, the politics that constituted the Cold War was reflected in bipolarity, the superpower relationship manifested in the competition for strategic influence and military advantage. This analysis fails to question, let alone identify a different logic of politics, and political expansion between the different forms of political rule that the United States and the Soviet Union affected. On one level it is without doubt that the Soviet Union like other revolutionary forms of state has had to adapt to a logic of security when confronted with numerous military threats to its physical existence.

Trotsky's organization of the Red Army after the revolution, and the subsequent "bloodying" of the Red Army in the "civil war" and in the defeat of the Wehrmacht in 1941–1945, ultimately revolved around a logic of military efficiency. This was about the defense of the physical space of the revolution, and the institutions, the form of political rule under the dictatorship of the Communist Party and the social relations that had, and were in the process of being constructed. In this sense the logic of military power was clearly evident. For it to have been absent would have been foolhardy, and to suggest that this reflects the enduring nature of "anarchy" *qua*, all states are the same, is essentially a crude form of *reductionism*.

If we ask why the Bolshevik revolution and other social revolutions have confronted these "military" or "security" threats they obviously imply a threat to what and why. In this sense the Bolsheviks were a threat because of their institutional and social form. It was not only the form of the Bolshevik state and the society it claimed to reconstitute, based on a particular class constituency, but also the fact that such a conception was based on a distinctly different logic of politics derived from socialism. It was this politics and, its international potential to penetrate other states, and its realization that provided the distinct logic of a conscious potential human agency, and how this agency sought to transform, internationally, capitalist-based forms of political rule. If we follow this line of argument, then the concept of military competition or strategic interest becomes enriched with something more than just the enduring competition between states derived from balance of power equations. Instead we relate military conflict to attempts at social transformation and their suppression.

However, as in the case of capitalism, revolutionary-socialist social formations reflected the contradictions of particular forms of struggle both internal and international that related to the pressures within each social formation.[29] Similar to capitalist social formations, though reflecting different forms, revolutionary social formations were determined by the outcome of struggles related to the social relations of production.[30] Thus, Stalin's determination to deal with the "peasant problem" reflected the conflict of different production and thus class projects in the countryside. The forced collectivization of agriculture after 1928, and the brutal way it was implemented reflected a particularly brutal form of class conflict that saw the destruction of the *Kulak* class. In this case, both the international and internal sources of conflict were present. Internally, the Soviet Union faced food shortages and the conflict in the countryside over the role of private property and the distribution of peasant produce to urban areas. This was problematic for the Bolsheviks in terms of their socialist project of socializing the means of production and abolishing private property, but became increasingly acute with respect to the perceived *need* to modernize and industrialize. This need, which Stalin was clearly aware of, related to the international threats to the Soviet Union, which derived historically from Russia being a victim of its own social and

industrial backwardness.[31] It was not only the international pressure that was
to force the Soviet Union to pursue a strategy of rapid and intense (and
costly, in human and social terms) industrialization and modernization. It
also originated from the project that the Bolsheviks had based their revolution on; to make the Soviet Union socialist. For the Bolsheviks this required
the development of the Soviet Union's productive forces. As they stood after
1917, and with a backward agricultural sector and distorted, fractured industrial base, the productive forces could not, according to the Bolsheviks, sustain or support socialism. The productive base of the social formation required development, thus allowing the realization of socialism as perceived
to be a social formation founded on a productive base superior to that of
capitalism.[32] On this reading the project of the Soviet Union was identified
with the surpassing of the existing capitalist social formations[33] in terms of
production. Such a project inevitably led to forms of state coercion to develop the productive forces. Although property was socialized, and the rule
of capital had been abolished, the social relations that came to the fore under the Bolsheviks reflected the contradictory nature of being socialist in the
terms already described, but also reflecting a project that required the socialist state to enforce particular coercive, quasi-*capitalist* techniques to ensure a rapid development of the Soviet Union's productive base. As Engels
stated:

> it remains the case that to socialize the means of production does not *ipso facto*
> do away with all the social relations upon which capitalism rests; its division of
> labour . . . may well remain intact.[34]

Thus, this explains, but in a different manner, the analysis of the Soviet
Union and Stalinism in particular as "revolution from above." The party-state
through its control of the coercive apparatus and its domination of society
ensured the top-down implementation of modernization whilst preserving
the socialist gains of the revolution.[35] Although coercive techniques were
used to ensure increases and expansions in production, these methods and
instruments did *not* amount to a form of capitalism or state capitalism in the
Soviet Union. However, they did lead to the development of forms of alienation that were similar to those found under capitalist social relations due to
the presence of particular methods employed.[36]

The Soviet Union like most of the other revolutionary social formations,
which in many respects adopted aspects of the "Soviet model," was characterized throughout its existence with this tension located in its contradictory
and tension induced form of social relations. Because of the Bolshevik
determination to modernize and "out produce" capitalism, the Soviet Union
located itself in a frame of reference that identified with capitalism, as the object of its project. The history of the Soviet Union, which climaxed with the
perestroika of Gorbachev, reflected this tension, and the dominance of a the-

oretical and practical paradigm based on the belief that socialism would be realized with the fullest development of its productive forces. The Soviet Union, as a social formation, and as a mode of production was trapped in the shadow of capital. Its productive strategy was in effect, an attempt to emulate or use techniques, forms of technology and foreign expertise, with which to "perfect" socialism. Social relations, (i.e. the political and social relations of the direct producers at the source of production) were not recognized as in themselves being a productive force. Instead, in practice, labor power was treated as a tool of production,[37] rather than as the means with which to revolutionize the social relations of production.

The consequences of this for the "Soviet type" of social formation became apparent with developments in the late 1980s in the Soviet bloc. *Solidarnosc* in Poland is exemplary here. This social-class movement was a product of a history of class struggle within Poland between the workers and the political authorities, the institutions that claimed to be the political expressions of working class rule. From the 1950s onwards, crystallizing in 1980–1981, the Polish working class confronted the political institutions on material *qua* class questions. The outbreaks of social unrest directly related to the ability of the "state" to adequately provide goods for society, be it through price subsidies or the availability of certain consumer goods. Under state-socialism the working class identified the institutions of the party-state as being responsible for these material provisions not the market. This being the case, the protests by *Solidarnosc* can be seen in class terms. The protests were a reaction against the failure of a "socialist state" to provide for its people, a failure of its fundamental *class* role. Such an argument has major ramifications for our understanding of the collapse of communism and the end of the Cold War.

This problem was reflected in the conflicts amongst revolutionary-socialist states, notably the Sino-Soviet conflict. This needs to be seen from the perspective of the evolution and dominance of the Soviet model, and how this related to other revolutionary social formations, rather than the pervasive assumption that these states were just like any other in their relations with each other. Soviet experience and the Soviet "way of doing things" through its form of socialist construction became, in effect, the established path of development and class struggle through political institutions. Bolshevism or the Soviet model, just as it had managed to silence (and liquidate) any opposition, both capitalist and socialist, in the Soviet Union, it could not tolerate international socialist opposition. International socialist opposition or rivalry, be it Chinese, or Dubcek's "socialism with a human face," threatened to undermine the delicate relationship between the party-state as the agent of socialist transformation, and international revolution, with the working classes in the Soviet Union. This became increasingly problematic for the relations between the Soviet Union, and other socialist social formations, because each could not tolerate an alternative or different path. Such a situation would have obviously undermined the form of political rule within each respective socialist state, because all of the social formations concerned had not resolved the contradictions of the relationship between the political institutions and the development of productive forces. The Soviet withdrawal of advisers in 1960, which was a major blow to the Chinese development project revealed these tensions. Soviet actions were based on Chinese criticism of the internal and international developments of the Soviet Union under Khrushchev.[38] But it was more than just rhetorical jousting between the two Communist Parties. The hostility struck at the heart of the contradictory nature of both social formations, which related to the incomplete nature of their respective revolutions.[39]

Such a conceptualization helps to illuminate the international relations of socialist states, and support for particular forms of socialist construction/ transformation. Because of the particular relationship between politics and economics in these social formations, international relations reflected the internal tensions of socialist construction and class struggle. The Sino-Soviet split then, and how this was mediated in international relations to the point of military conflict in border clashes and support for rival factions in national liberation struggles, was part of the conflict over rival forms of socialist construction that the Soviet Union and China pursued. The conflict concerned the role of the institutions of political rule, the party-state, as the agency of class struggle and socialist construction rather than the working class.

This was as much an international problem as it was a domestic one. In the Soviet Union and China the respective Communist Parties were the forces of class struggle, but in international terms, the Soviet Union regarded itself as the "agent of the international communist movement." Because of the centralization of the political power of Comintern in Moscow partly explained *and* caused by the lack of Soviet support for social revolution after the aborted revolutions in Central Europe after the early 1920s, international revolution became identified with the international relations of the Soviet Union. Just as in the Soviet social formation the institutions of party-state directed and determined the class struggle and the nature of socialist transformation (in effect, by definition they limited it, by not fully abolishing the separation of politics and economics, and not basing socialist construction and politics on the social relations of production), so, in international relations, by taking it upon themselves to be the agent of international revolution, and enforcing a policy of *rapprochement* with bourgeois nationalists, the Soviet Union ended up stifling international revolution. The international relations of the Soviet Union then, reflected the contradictory position of its social formation whereby capitalism had been abolished, and where the project of socialist transformation was being stifled by the separation of politics and economics, and the fact that politics, institutionalized in the form of the coercive-dictatorial authority of the party-state, as a separate sphere and set of institutions had not been abolished.

China, and subsequently other revolutionary movements, were the victims of this instrumental approach to socialism that ended up basing its politics, internal and international, on a "productivist" logic. Just as the Soviet Union confronted the problems of constructing socialism from an underdeveloped base, and the way in which Bolshevism approached this, so did the USSR's international relations. The critique of the Soviet model, and its international relations by China obviously corresponded to the manifestations of the contradictions of the Soviet social formation. Because of its productivist orientation in international relations, the Soviet Union was not, according to the Chinese, sufficiently supportive of international revolution.[40] The accusation of revisionism was connected to the Soviet Union's continuation of an international relations that was *reducible* to a domestic politics of the development of productive forces, *above all else*. This was obviously a class-based project, the goal of housing, feeding and providing employment and improved living standards for Soviet people, but it was pursued in a manner where political power was increasingly alienated from the social relations of production. The internationalization of socialism was reduced to a politics of the Soviet state in its relations with other states and revolutionary movements. But because of the domestic goals and thus constraints, the Soviet Union ended up being passive in terms of the sponsorship of international revolution, and positively counter-revolutionary when the international situation or when the actions of Third World revolutionaries or Communists in the West threatened to jeopardize the domestic construction of "socialism." China though in many respects a form of the Soviet model was different due to the nature of its revolution and the circumstances of China, and because of its international position saw social revolution and a more hostile policy towards international capital as a better way forward than moderation at the particular conjuncture of the 1960s. Though China was right to attack the USSR's passivity towards bourgeois states, and its links with them, it ultimately followed the pattern set by Moscow.[41]

How these social projects actually had an impact on international relations is clear from the subsequent development of both the Soviet Union and China. Both failed to fully resolve the contradictions in the relationship between the form of political rule and how this related to production and the social relations of production. Both failed to overcome the "productivist" orientation of their respective strategies of social transformation.[42] Both became increasingly dependent on external and capitalist forms of production through the import of technology and following Western methods. It was only a case of timing. China in many respects, as is the case today, with the capitalization of China under the auspices of the "Communist Party," merely followed on from the Soviet Union. The conflict in the 1960s

to the American *rapprochement* with China with Nixon's visit in 1972, all reflected the unfolding of the contradictions within these social formations.

## The Real Politics of the Cold War

The capitalist form of political rule based on the apparent separation of the
forms of politics and economics, but the actual "unity within the capital social
relation of the spheres of economics (production) and politics (the legal and
property framework of production)[43] lies hidden within the orthodox account
of "politics." The form that politics appears as amounts to a politics confined
to the state, both domestically and externally, manifested in foreign policy.
Like the "privatization of economics" or production within the domestic
realm, international relations, it is suggested, relates to a politics confined to
the state. The reality, however, of both politics at the domestic level and in international terms is that politics reflects the parcelization of power relations
between the form of the state and the form of production *derived* from the
capitalist social relation.[44] Thus, the system of nation-states is, ultimately, a reflection of the globalization of the capitalist social relation. The system of
states and the world market of capital are thus dual and co-terminus developments.[45]

In terms of the Cold War and the role of the United States, the politics of
the United States in the Cold War reflected the division found in the capitalist social relation. What this means is that the "policy" of the United States, in
terms of economic policy, arms production, military interventions and
strategic nuclear policy was a reflection of both the internal and international
contradictions located in the class struggle associated with capitalist modernity. However, what needs to be made clear, especially in comparison to the
Soviet Union, is that the United States as a social formation, a capitalist form,
had a distinct form of international relations. It was not only the American
projection of "hard" military power into Indochina that the Cold War was
about, though this was obviously important for a number of reasons, but the
fact that the capitalist social relation is international. Although refracted
through particular social formations, this form of social relations is such that
it does not recognize the limitations of state space. Thus, capitalism is an international relation that is obviously linked to the state, but that is also relatively autonomous. As long as there is a legal and political framework in
place capital can inhabit any social space regardless of the politics of states.
The only forms of political rule that have successfully limited its movement
and penetration have been revolutionary socialist states.

Following this, the Cold War saw a correspondence between the expansion of capitalist social relations as a politics of expansion. Whereas Realists
talk of the expansion of power and securing advantage at the level of appearances or on the surface related to forms of state, what was really hap-

pening, ultimately, with or without nuclear weapons, was a politics of expansion based on capitalist social relations. What was and is particular about this politics of expansion, is that it was different in *form* to that of the earlier means of expanding capitalism.

The Cold War then, saw social struggles within particular social formations over the form of political rule *qua* state. The struggles over forms of political rule related to the nature of social relations were not limited to the new "states" of the Third World. Even within the social formation of advanced capitalism the contradictions of the capitalist social relations, and the particularities of forms of class struggle were prevalent and help us to understand the nature of these social formations and their international relations. However, the intensity and results of class struggle were most apparent in the Third World where new states emerged that were characterized by a structural presence in the global economy and weak state form. These "states" were weak in the sense that they were prone to crisis from both internal and external sources. All forms of political rule when based on forms of class domination which in turn rests on forms of exploitation are subject to social crisis, and the evolution of the relationship between the form of political rule and the form of surplus extraction derives from the changing nature of this relationship.[46]

The institutions of the state obviously behave according to a particular crisis in the capitalist social relation, but their scope for action is obviously limited by their structural imbrication within that social relation. There are certain things ultimately, that the state will not or cannot do. The weakness of the state as a form of political rule depends, obviously, on the nature of the crisis involving class struggle, and the capacity of the state to address it. Capitalist states, those states that have secured the apparent separation of politics and economics where the sphere of production, and the social relations between people flowing from that have been privatized, and in effect depoliticized, can deal with a crisis in the capitalist relation more easily than other forms of state. This is because of the fact that economic struggle as class struggle appears, and in practice is not about changing the state, but rather about the "private" economic relationship between labor and capital. The state does not appear to be involved, it is a matter for the private sphere.[47] The states of the Third World were weak precisely because they continued to rely on a form of political rule directly involved in maintaining economic as political relationships. The economy in these social formations had not been fully privatized, and surplus extraction was not "autonomous." These states were weak then, because of the contradictions present in the sense of the conflicts involved in the transition from one or a number of modes of production to that of the capitalist mode of production and the role of the state in this process of class conflict. Moreover, these processes occurred within an international context of international capitalist penetration, and in a number of instances, the identification of the state with a comprador bourgeoisie.

What characterized these social forms above all was their differentiated or hybrid nature. They were not fully capitalist but had been, and were being penetrated both from indigenous sources and international sources of capital. Because of this, and the historical role of the imperial form of state, and its subsequent post-colonial form, as a facilitator of certain forms of social relations, pre-capitalist and capitalist, these social formations were to be pregnant with a tissue of social contradictions identified with the form of the political rule, the state. Thus, in anti-colonial and post-colonial struggles the state was the focus of social as political conflict. What this meant was that social revolution became the currency of politics as revolutionary coalitions based on class configurations targeted the state as the *means* to alter their social relations of production, because capitalist social relations were not fully developed, (i.e. the form of political rule was such that there was *no* clear or apparent separation of the spheres of the political and the economic). This being the case, the state was seen as repressive and was seen as being tied to a particular form of class domination, be this the *latifundia* of Latin America or a comprador bourgeoisie.

The conflict between the United States and the Soviet Union needs to be seen in this much broader context, involving a *processional* development, based around the two very different and antagonistic forms of political rule that each represented. The Cold War needs to be seen in terms of the *totality* of relations between different, conflicting forms of political rule, which were expressions of different forms of social relations. Thus, the Cold War involved the Soviet Union and the United States, but it was *not* about these states as such.

The differences in terms of social relations, and forms of political rule derived from the fact that these two states were reflections of different social formations reflecting the dominance of different modes of production and different forms of politics. The United States, as a social formation, represented and represents, *par excellence*, the dominance of the capital social relation with the separation of the spheres of "politics" into the political, the capitalist state, and the economic, the market and civil society. The Soviet Union on the other hand exemplified a form of political rule based on a specific form of social relations. What this amounted to was that the sociopolitical contradictions within Russia were overcome by the overthrow of Czarist attempts at capitalist modernization and its replacement through revolutionary transformation. Private property was abolished, labor became decommodified, and production was planned. All this reflected a class project where the social gains of the proletariat and the radical peasantry was institutionalized in the form of political rule of the state. Bolshevik state power determined both the realms of state and society.

The United States and the Soviet Union obviously reflected in many respects the global tensions and the configurations of social struggles in world politics. Through their different forms of international relations they also helped determine the outcomes of social-class conflict in other social formations. They did this through the applications of military power, and the export of particular forms of political rule.[48] Orthodox accounts in IR, as I have discussed above, give preference to the "hard" or traditional concerns of IR, foreign policy of the state, and projections of military power according to the logic of *Realpolitik*. My argument thus far, has been that such focus on the state, for a number of reasons, is misplaced and limited. The state, both domestically and internationally, is a specific form of political rule, and the United States and the Soviet Union, as different forms of political rule, reflected different international relations *derived* from their different social relations of production.

Despite the fact that in many respects, and cited by Realists as explanatory, that the Soviet Union and the United States employed similar instruments of international relations, for example military interventions, arms shipments, and economic aid and the use of diplomatic forums as "states," and also appeared to be inconsistent in their support for particular types of "state," crudely put: capitalist states for the United States and social revolutionary states for the USSR, respectively; these instances do not provide evidence of the operation of a timeless *Realpolitik*. To suggest that because the Soviet Union did not send the Red Army overseas at every opportunity to support communist revolutionaries or that it engaged with, politically and economically, states that persecuted communist parties does not prove that the Soviet Union was like any other state. It does violence to the complexity of the Soviet Union as a particular type of social formation and the contradictions of its form of political rule both in domestic and international terms.

The contradictions of such a social formation saw it play in many respects a "counter-revolutionary" role in its international relations whilst at the *same* time supporting a social system that was on the whole, anti-capitalist, and internationally, expediting the expansion of social revolution. What needs explanation then, are the manifestations of these contradictions, and the consequences of these forms of *political* action for the Soviet social formation. They should not be seen purely in terms of Realist "zero-sum" calculations or as static or fixed. Rather, the politics of the Soviet Union, as a presence in the international system up to its dissolution, should be seen as reflecting, in processional terms, domestic and international developments. This was reflected in the evolution of the Soviet development project and its controlled links with international capital, and how this was influenced by, and qualified the international relations of the Soviet Union. This is especially important when we consider the fact that the international relations of the Soviet Union were unified in the form of political rule unlike capitalist forms of international relations. The selection of "facts" to suggest that the Soviet Union was a normal state or not on the criteria of how the Soviet Union applied support or not to anti-capitalist states merely serves to obscure the *problematique* of the Soviet Union.

What then, were the differences in the forms of international relations between the superpowers despite the *appearances* of similarity? The differences stemmed from the forms of political rule, and how these forms were derived from social relations of production. Because of the abolition of capitalism *as a mode of production* in the Soviet Union (and other revolutionary social formations), the relationship between state and society was redefined. Instead of having a relatively private sphere of the reproduction of social life, that is the "economy," the form of political rule *directly* organized production. Thus, the political sphere, the state form was identified and indeed was fully part of production relations, and this was evidently formative in the form of international relations of such a state. There was no logic of expansion comparable to capitalist states. Whereas capitalist states expanded through the expansion of capitalist social relations, and the political structures derived from such expansion, the Soviet Union and other revolutionary states did not. Instead, the Soviet Union was limited to a form of expansion confined to the political form. The Soviet Union, then, did not expand, at least in a way comparable with capitalist forms of political rule. The Soviet Union was limited to either the direct political control through a direct physical presence, as in East-Central Europe or through supporting *local* revolutions, externally. It did not, it could not, expand politically beyond what I have described. This being the case, the social relations of socialism, the abolition of capitalism; if they were not to be overthrown by the Red Army directly, were limited in their manifestation to the specific politics of each social formation and would expand only through local class struggle.

The contrary was the case in the United States. Here as elsewhere, though to varying degrees, the state appeared separate from civil society and production relations. As is clear from what I have said already, based on Marx's *critique* of the categories of political economy, this separation is a form of the appearance of the capitalist social relation. What this entails is that the "economy" functions autonomously according to the pristine logic of capital, but its operation is within a framework where the state acts and is a social relation of production. It is this specific feature of the form of the capitalist state that provides for a logic of domestic politics *and* international relations. Thus, the international relations of the United States during the Cold War (and beyond), is that of the state form as an international relation of *capitalist* production relations.

The United States and capitalist states in general operated according to a very different logic, and form of political expansion that was not limited to a direct physical presence within a particular area. Because of the separation of the spheres of social life, capitalism, as a social relation, and the politics that derive from this can expand autonomously without the need for a direct physical-political form of agency. Rather, the rule of capital, and capitalist social relations expand through commodities and the exchange of commodities and the relations and politics that follow from the "mutual dependence mediated by things." The form of political rule of capitalism is reflected in separate states, but which capital does not recognize or is not limited by. The separation of the spheres of social life under capitalism allows forms of expansion to take on an apparently nonpolitical form when the consequences and actual process of that expansion *are* political. The United States or American capitalism expanded prodigiously without appearing as such, because it expanded into forms of political rule that did not regard such social relations as directly political, though in practice they certainly were. This form of political expansion only became contested by revolutionary social formations or those social formations that were capitalist, but were experiencing particularly intense forms of class struggle. Politics, following this interpretation, becomes broader and deeper, and it provides the defining logic of the Cold War and the conflict reflected in the conflicting forms of politics of the Soviet Union and the United States.

International relations then, *is* capitalism. The form and currency of the international relations of the modern era are those of a capitalist modernity based upon the separation of the spheres of the political and the economic that are the defining features of capitalism. However, as within the capitalist social relation, as a unique form of the appropriation of labor power historically distinct from other forms, this social relation is based upon *class struggle*. Both in terms of its emergence and expansion this social relation is characterized by the class struggle between appropriators and appropriated. International relations is this struggle, the social struggle revolving around strategies of accumulation based on appropriation and the contradictions and conflicts that this process creates. Again we return to history and politics as *process* involving particular forms of human agency within specific forms of relations.

This social struggle is not something germane to capitalism alone; it also features within revolutionary social formations. Revolution does not abolish class conflict it merely changes the terrain of that conflict and the structure of that conflict.[49] For within the Soviet Union it was quite clear that the proletariat did not *rule*. Although the gains of working class victories after 1917 were institutionalized within the Soviet social formation, because of the contradictory nature of that social formation; a statist form of social relations, there was class conflict between the direct producers and the state. It was this conflict that was also reflected in the international relations of the Soviet Union. And, ultimately, it was these contradictions of the Soviet form of political rule that explain the apparent inconsistencies and "state-like" relations of the Soviet Union. Thus, the Soviet Union was not fully socialist, and thus its social relations reflected this contradiction. Because of its forms of political rule it had international relations of a contradictory social formation, one that was socialist in the sense that capitalism had been abolished, and other social features were present, but that also was characterized by a form of political rule that had aspects of capital present.[50] This derived from its project of the development of productive forces where the state or the political institutions were used as instruments to accelerate the development of productive forces. Because the aim was to reach the level of capitalist development and then surpass it, the Soviet Union or Bolshevism as a paradigm failed to focus on a socialism located in social relations, (i.e. *how* we actually reproduce ourselves), and instead focused on a project that emphasized the maturation of the material forces of production as *things*, rather than the more humanist version of social relations. Thus, Soviet foreign policy did seek relations with capitalist states if it was a means to secure material improvement and economic advantage, and the problems that this caused the Soviet social formation came to a head under Gorbachev where the creeping "capitalization" of the Soviet Union was finally given party sanction, and the logic or the contradictions of Bolshevism were finally played out.

As for the United States, the projection of military power and influence went alongside each other; it was the other side of the coin of the American led international capitalist system. American order preserved capitalist global social relations. Thus, as in the domestic realm the State or political form is a form of the capitalist social relation, and acts within the constraints of that relation based on class conflict as process, so in international relations the United States provided the legal and political framework for the expansion of capitalist social relations. The United States did not determine these developments, because, as I have already mentioned, capitalism has a logic of its own, and it was the agency of change, rather than the state. But the realization of the globalization of capital, which provides the basis of the neoliberal onslaught against the hard-won gains of post-war collectivism, would not be as it is now without the state and capitalist states as particular forms of political rule derived from capitalist social relations. The development of the world market reflects, then, in the Cold War, the international expansion of and struggle involving the two aspects of the form of the capitalist social relation, state and market.

## CONCLUSIONS

The argument I have presented here has made the claim that state as traditionally understood within political science and IR needs to be replaced. Drawing on an Historical Materialist approach I have tried to outline an alternative conceptualization of the "state" or politics based on the historical experience of the Cold War, and the forms of political rule that this period in the history of capitalist modernity and its "contesters" has thrown up. The state, as a concept and actuality, needs to be grounded within a specific historical and social experience. Though we can identify common attributes of, and concepts for understanding forms of political rule, and how these have an impact on international relations, only an open-ended ontology can provide the means with which to explain the role of the state in the Cold War. If, as orthodox scholars claim, that all states are more or less the same, and act according to the imperatives of anarchy, then intellectual inquiry and political choices are foreclosed. If, however, one's intellectual position is more contingent and open to the possibilities of change and reformulating a "politics," then history is theirs to be made and studied in a much more rewarding way.

What this means for the Cold War is that the forms of political rule and the agency associated with specific forms of political rule need to be scrutinized and understood, not as products of a teleological progression, nor a static time-space continuum, but rather as the processional developments related to and part of the expansion of a specific form of social relations based on capitalism. This is not to suggest that capital has a pristine logic which pervades the world over, but rather, to suggest that the expansion of capitalist social relations as *the* international relations of modernity reflects both the existence of previous noncapitalist forms of reproducing material (and ideal life) which have either been abolished or incorporated, in a bastardized form, into a globalized system. This is not only an economic phenomenon, but is reflected in the totality of social relations within each social formation.

The form of politics, the form of the institutions and administration of social life within a given territory reflects this incorporation of noncapitalist political forms into an "international society" of states. The experience of historical communism or state socialism is part of this experience. Although these were conscious attempts by specific forms of social agency to pioneer an alternative political path, and create a different new form of history, their history is undeniably tied up with the experiences of capitalist modernity, as providing the source of contradictions and conflicts and the concepts and praxis of that alternative. The Bolshevik revolution, and the formation of noncapitalist forms of political rule and politics emerged out of the contradictions of capitalism as a global system. Were this not the case we would not be talking about revolution or international relations as something concerned with the relations between different forms of politics. It is our understanding of the international as a sphere of politics that is united by the totality of capitalism, in all its myriad forms, that provides the empirical terrain of any understanding of the forms of political rule.

This empirical landscape is characterized by the social struggles of people as classes revolving around how they produce and reproduce their social life, and the social relations that follow from this. Politics or the form of political rule is fundamental to any understanding of this, and how this affects international relations. Ultimately, because of the nature of the social relations in question, those of an expanding capitalism, social relations cannot be theoretically understood in terms of the domestic-international separation. However, in empirical terms, we can identify distinctions between social formations and peoples who inhabit different parts of the world, in terms of the social relations of production and the corresponding forms of political rule. What defines these forms of politics, of production and rule, the bourgeois forms of economics and politics, are forms of social struggle. What characterizes capitalism is that this struggle is one of class, both in terms of the emergence of, within it, and to promote its transformation. It is the level and form of class struggle that determines the form of political rule and thus the actual configuration of the state.

International relations then, as a reflection of the relations between forms of political rule, ultimately, is reducible to the level of class conflict within each social formation. This is something that is pertinent in terms of those forms of political rule subject to intense, revolutionary struggle, as much as it is to those social formations characterized by low or passive forms of class conflict that do not raise the issue of the form of political rule. This is also pervasive for those social formations that are not capitalist. The Soviet Union, and other state-socialist forms of political rule did not manage to resolve or overcome the contradictions related to the form of political rule and the social relations of production. And, as I have argued, the nature of the problems derived from these peculiar social formations, and the particular social struggles based upon the institutional conflation of the spheres of the economy and political rule, that saw social contradictions being identified with the form of political rule, rather than the form of production, alone. It was this form of politics, distinct from capitalist forms that explain the international relations of historical communism.

Thus, international relations is concerned with the relations between different forms of political rule. During the Cold War the forms of conflict related to struggles within certain social formations about the contestation of the form of political rule, and the involvement of other social formations in these struggles. The "politics of the state" in these terms is reconstructed to identify the different forms of politics in international relations that reflect the different levels and forms of class struggle, and the different ways in which these different forms of political rule *qua* states related to each other. The logic of anarchy and its appendages of the arms race and nuclear deterrence as the "long peace" are replaced by a politics of social struggle, which is influenced by the balance and application of military power, but is not reducible to it. Rather, the reduction lies at the heart of how human beings relate to each other, socially, and the conflicts that flow from such social configurations.

## NOTES

1. See the general works on the Cold War and IR as exemplified by: G. Kennan, "The Long Telegram," in *The Foreign Relations of the United States, 1946 Volume VI* (Washington D.C: U.S. Government Printing Office, 1969), 696–709; *American Diplomacy* (Chicago: University of Chicago Press, 1984); *Memoirs, 1950–63* (London: Hutchinson and Co., 1972); *Soviet Policy, 1917–1941* (Princeton, N.J.: D. Van Nostrand Co., Inc., 1960); *Russia and the West under Lenin and Stalin* (Boston: Little Brown and Co., 1960); *The Nuclear Delusion: Soviet-American Relations in the Atomic Age* (New York: Pantheon Books, 1982); "X" The Sources of Soviet Conduct" in *Foreign Affairs,* July 1947, 566–82; "In Conversation with Fred Halliday" *From Potsdam to Perestroika: Conversations with Cold Warriors* (BBC News and Current Affairs: BBC Radio 4, April 1994); H. Kissinger, *Diplomacy* (New York: Simon and Schuster, 1994); G. Liska, *Russia and World Order: Strategic Choices and the Laws of Power in History* (Baltimore: The Johns Hopkins University Press, 1980); *Career of Empire: America and Imperial Expansion over Land and Sea* (Baltimore: The Johns Hopkins University Press, 1978); *Rethinking U.S.-Soviet Relations* (Oxford: Basil Blackwell, 1987); J. Lewis Gaddis *Strategies of Containment: A Critical Appraisal of Postwar American National Security Policy* (New York: Oxford University Press, 1982); *The Long Peace: Inquiries into the History of the Cold War* (New York: Oxford University Press, 1987); "The Emerging Post-Revisionist Synthesis on the Origins of the Cold War," in *Diplomatic History* 7 Summer 1983: 171–204; *The United States and the End of the Cold War: Implications, Reconsiderations, Provocations* (New York: Oxford University Press, 1992); "The Cold War, the Long Peace and the Future," in M. Hogan, ed., *The End of the Cold War: Its Meaning and Implications* (Cambridge: Cambridge University Press, 1992) 21–38; "International Relations Theory and the End of the Cold War," in *International Security* 17(3) Winter 1992–1993: 5–58.

2. See R. Ned Lebow and T. Risse-Kappen, ed., *International Relations Theory and the End of the Cold War* (New York: Columbia University Press, 1995).

3. H. Morgenthau, *Politics among Nations: The Struggle for Power and Peace* 6th Edition (New York: Alfred. A. Knopf, 1985), 5–12; 22; 25–35. Although Waltz does not use Morgenthau's understanding of power, at least explicitly, his concern with security, its military definition and projection in a "self help" system obviously relates to power or more explicitly for Waltz, the balance of power. See Waltz's discussion of the balance of power in 102–28; and the military definition of power in 161–93 in *Theory of International Politics* (Reading, Mass.: Addison-Wesley Publishing Co., 1979) and K. Waltz *Man, the State, and War: A Theoretical Analysis* (New York: Columbia University Press, 1959) 159.

4. See Morgenthau *Politics among Nations,* 5, 8; Waltz *Theory of International Politics,* 66; and *Man, the State, and War,* 80–123.

5. For a critique of this, see J. Rosenberg *The Empire of Civil Society: A Critique of the Realist Theory of International Relations* (London: Verso, 1994), 11–12; 18–19.

6. Rosenberg *The Empire of Civil Society,* 4, 6.

7. Marx's work has been open to historical interpretation that has "reified" the separation of the political sphere from the economic sphere which is taken from a literal reading of the "base/superstructure" dichotomy. An alternative reading would use these concepts, not as such, but as metaphors that have an existence only in abstract

or ideational forms, *qua* they have no *real*, concrete existence in separation. This will become clearer when I discuss a materialist understanding of the politics of the state below. For discussions of the "base/superstructure" metaphor, see Derek Sayer, *The Violence of Abstraction: The Analytical foundations of Historical Materialism* (Oxford: Basil Blackwell, 1987).

8. Ellen Wood's discussion of the "separation of the political and economic in capitalism" provides an excellent account of the historical specificity of capitalism, but also delivers a devastating broadside against those Marxists who have reproduced this separation and thus implicitly adopted bourgeois categories. See 19–48 in *Democracy against Capitalism: Renewing Historical Materialism* (Cambridge. Cambridge University Press, 1995).

9. K. Marx and F. Engels *The German Ideology* Part 1, (1846), 39

10. Marx makes this clear in volume 4 of *Capital*, (1863), 288:

it can in fact be shown that *all* human relations and functions, however and in whatever form they may appear, influence material production and have a more or less decisive influence upon it.

Derek Sayer has attacked the "orthodox" understanding of Marx's work on this point, by attacking those Marxists who have sought to limit the notion of productive forces to "material things," by making a clear distinction over what constitutes the material base and the ideological/political superstructure. See *The Violence of Abstraction: The Analytical Foundations of Historical Materialism* (Oxford: Basil Blackwell, 1987), 15–49.

11. P. Corrigan, H. Ramsay and D. Sayer, "The State as a Relation of Production," in P. Corrigan, ed., *Capitalism, State Formation and Marxist Theory: Historical Investigations* (London: Quartet Books, 1980), 10.

12. For a historical materialist discussion of the evolution of the state, and the expansion of this particular social form, see H. P. Lacher, *Historicizing the Global: Capitalism, Territoriality and the International Relations of Modernity* Ph.D Thesis, University of London (2000) and M. Turner, *The Expansion of International Society? Egypt and Vietnam in the History of Uneven and Combined Development* Ph. D Thesis, University of London (2000).

13. Therefore to talk of the state in *a priori* terms can be problematic. Instead, a Marxist formula would attempt to leave the state empirically open-ended and not preclude discussion of the state with definite, transhistorical features. Rather, following P. Corrigan, et al. we should see the state as "empirically open-ended":

The state is thus . . . the entire repertoire of activities by means of which a ruling class endeavors to secure its collective conditions of production. This concept (like those of the productive forces and relations of production). . . . is an empirically open-ended one. What defines the State is not any set of concrete institutions. These in fact vary historically, State forms being constructed continuously in the course of class struggle. The State is defined by a (productive) *function*: it is this, and this alone, that enables us empirically to identify in any particular context a particular institutional arrangement as the "State."

*Socialist Construction and Marxist Theory: Bolshevism and Its Critique* (London: Macmillan, 1978), 9 (emphasis in original).

14. To treat these forms of political power in their own terms, detached from anything apart from the "logic of anarchy" exposes the poverty of what constitutes "International Theory." The case should be, instead, to treat these forms of politics within the wider world with which they exist within and are shaped by. For example nuclear weapons are constantly discussed purely in terms of the operation of deterrence. A much richer understanding of the historical notion of these forms of politics could be derived from specifying the historical uses of such weapons. See for example, on this point D. Ellsberg "Introduction: Call to Mutiny," in E. P. Thompson and D. Smith, eds. *Protest and Survive* (New York: Monthly Review Press, 1981), i, v–vi.

15. What this means is that the state is de-socialized and de-historicized. Instead of seeing the state as a contingent institutional form, which *can* be changed or abolished, because of the states system, all forms of "political rule/administration" become states, despite the fact that we can identify, empirically, that "states" come in myriad forms reflecting different histories and social forces.

16. Marx was clear on this. His project and focus of historical and critical investigation, was not society, but rather a particular society, capitalism, and the existing categories and forms associated with such a society. This being the case, he was not concerned with abstract notions of society in general, but developing the conceptual tools and apparatus of a specific form of society, to change it. See "K. Marx Letter to Lassalle February 22, 1858," in D. Sayer, ed., *Readings from Karl Marx* (London: Routledge, 1989), 50.

17. K. Marx and F. Engels, *The German Ideology* Part 1 (1846): 36 (emphasis in original).

18. See E. Wood, *Democracy against Capitalism,* 36–44.

19. See P. Corrigan, H. Ramsay and D. Sayer, "The State as a Relation of Production," in P. Corrigan, ed., *Capitalism, State Formation,* 11, and J. Holloway and S. Picciotto, eds., *State and Capital: A Marxist Debate* (London: Edward Arnold, 1978), 2; 7; 16.

20. See E. Wood, *Democracy against Capitalism,* 59–67, and D. Sayer, *The Violence of Abstraction,* 52–53; 89; 98.

21. See L. Trotsky, *The Permanent Revolution and Results and Prospects* (London: New Park Publications, 1962).

22. For a related discussion, see R. Pollin, "Contemporary World Economic Stagnation in World Historical Perspective," in *New Left Review* no. 219 September–October 1996, 109–18.

23. By the end of World War II, capitalist social relations within most of the colonial area and within the "informal" colonies (or those areas subject to only American and European "economic" penetration), had forms of political rule that were beginning to facilitate the self-valorization of capital. What this meant, was that a direct, formal imperialist presence within the colonial social formation was not required to sustain the presence and expansion of capitalist social relations. I am not suggesting that these social formations were capitalist, (i.e. dominated by a capitalist mode of production), but that the formal colonial experience and the "informal" or nonpolitical capitalist penetration of many formerly "independent" states, saw the development through social struggle of political forms of rule that facilitated the emergence and expansion of capitalist social relations of production. Struggle, and *class* struggle provides the explanatory formula for an understanding of these developments, the development of bourgeois

forms of rule, that was an international as much as an internal process. The Cold War and American involvement being formative. The post-war era then provided the political-institutional forms for the globalization of capitalism as a world system. Up to this point, the world was *not* capitalist in system terms. Rather, capital, through imperialism, and the occupation and penetration of noncapitalist/precapitalist social forms through types of physical conquest, was dependent on the physical presence of capital as an armed force to subdue indigenous group hostility. With pacification came the emergence and creation of political institutions derived from the capital relation, what are inappropriately described as states, were in fact forms of political rule that became states, but through class conflict. This process was "finalized" or reached a stage of qualitative transition with de-colonization and the incorporation of waves of new "states" into international society. This was the *realization* of the colonial project. Capital, ultimately, did not need a direct political, physical presence to maintain itself through self-valorization. The colonial "exchange of non-equivalents" meditated by direct forms of appropriation, based on coercion had become the rule of the "exchange of equivalents," the rule of commodity production.

24. Thus the state is deeply imbricated in strategies of accumulation. It provides the basic resources for capitalist production, both directly through education, welfare provision and other technical "functions." Through this, the state can initiate changes that will influence particular fractions of capital, which ultimately will serve to alter the nature of capitalist production within a given social formation. The 1979–1983 Thatcher administration is an obvious example of such state initiatives and the impact it had on British capital. However, we cannot remove these developments from international changes, in particular the profitability of sections of British capital, which were significantly damaged by the increase in intensity of class conflict in the 1970s. In many respects the Conservative class project reflected this concern to attack collectivist institutions and organized labor power. See J. Holloway and S. Picciotto, eds., *State and Capital*, 13; 16; 25, for a more detailed discussion.

25. See H. Bull and A. Watson, ed., *The Expansion of International Society* (Oxford: Clarendon Press, 1985), 1–9.

26. See the work of David Armstrong, *Revolution and World Order* (Oxford: Clarendon Press, 1993) in this regard.

27. See F. Halliday, *Rethinking International Relations*, chapter 4.

28. See F. Halliday, *Rethinking International Relations*, chapter 5.

29. Thus, revolutions do not abolish the social tensions within a social formation; if anything they intensify them, as particular classes are appropriated, through class conflict, and the conflicting social projects of the different classes involved in the revolution compete for political leadership. The most obvious example in Russia after 1917 concerned the peasantry and their goal of private property, which went against the project of the Bolsheviks. See C. Bettelheim, *Class Struggles in the USSR, Volume One, 1917–23 and Volume Two, 1923–30* (Hassocks: Harvester Press, 1977/78).

30. The outcome (of revolution) depends upon further struggle; the struggle to build the socialist mode of production, socialist construction, which is necessarily a class struggle. P. Corrigan et al., *Socialist Construction and Marxist Theory*, 38.

31. Stalin was fully aware of Russian history, as were *all* of the Bolsheviks, that Russian backwardness had been responsible for the military debacles in the Crimea in 1854–1855, the Far East in 1904–1905, and on the Eastern Front between 1914–1917:

We are going full steam along the road of industrialization to socialism, leaving behind our age-long "Russian" backwardness. . . . We are becoming a country of metal, a country of the automobile, a country of the tractor. And when we have seated the USSR in an automobile, and the peasant on a tractor, then let the honourable capitalists, who plume themselves on their "civilization," try to catch us up. We shall see which countries can then be counted as advanced. . . . We have lagged 50 to 100 years behind the advanced countries. We must close this gap in ten years. Either we shall do it, or they will crush us.

Stalin "The Year of the Great Breakthrough," November 1929 cited in E. H. Carr, *The Russian Revolution from Lenin to Stalin (1917–1929)* (London: Macmillan, 1979), 170–171.

32. See P. Corrigan et al., *Socialist Construction and Marxist Theory,* 24–50 for an excellent survey of how modernization or "capitalist tendencies" based on a development project defined in terms of materially outproducing capitalism, by "catching-up and overtaking" dominated Bolshevism and the Soviet model.

33. Khrushchev's often misquoted speech at the UN in 1960, specifically the "we will bury you . . ." remarks referred to his belief that the Soviet Union would out produce the United States and thus "bury capitalism to history." See the work of Isaac Deutscher for an illuminating discussion of these themes of modernization and development in Bolshevism, in particular *Ironies of History: Essays on Contemporary Communism* (London: Oxford University Press, 1966).

34. F. Engels cited in P. Corrigan et al., *Socialist Construction and Marxist Theory,* 39.

35. Thus, for the Bolsheviks, Lenin as much as Stalin, the state was conceived as the major agency of socialist construction:

in both its production and political facets. It was both the motor of construction and the instrument of class struggle developing the forces and revolutionizing the relations of production through its fiscal and planning machinery, whilst securing the political conditions for this stratagem through its repressive and ideological apparatuses.

P. Corrigan et al., *Socialist Construction and Marxist Theory,* 44.

36. See P. Corrigan et al., *Socialist Construction and Marxist Theory,* 42–43.

37. See P. Corrigan, ed., *Capitalism, State Formation and Marxist Theory,* 2.

38. See I. Deutscher, *Ironies of History,* 136.

39. Incomplete, not in the sense that these revolutions had been stopped prematurely, but rather, that the form of politics in these social formations reflected the limited stage of class struggle where the revolutionary political leadership had not facilitated forms of class struggle that would have abolished, completely, through an ongoing process the separation of the spheres of social life, which was partially resolved by Bolshevism and Maoism. Because of the productive project, and the need for rapid development, these social forms continued to reflect a partial separation of economics and politics in the sphere of the social relations of production.

40. This was related to Bolshevism's (Lenin's) theory of colonial revolution, in that Lenin saw a progressive role for the respective national bourgeoisie in the colonial revolution if it was sufficiently anti-imperialist. This, however, was not only a political question, but also concerned the notion of development and the role that the national bourgeoisie could have in the progressive development of productive forces in

underdeveloped states. See M. Carnoy, *The State and Political Theory* (Princeton: Princeton University Press, 1984), 179.

41. Just as Comintern had suggested to the CCP to join with the KMT, which had disastrous consequences for the former, so did Zhou-Enlai advise the Indonesian Communists to remain a civilian party in alliance with bourgeois nationalists. The result of this strategy, mirrored, though was much bloodier, that of the catastrophe that befell the CCP in the 1920s, with the annihilation of the PKI in 1965.

42. See P. Corrigan, H. Ramsay, and D. Sayer, *For Mao: Essays in Historical Materialism* (London: Macmillan, 1978) for a more in-depth discussion of this.

43. What this separation hides is the actual *source* of politics derived from the capitalist social relation that appears in an economic and political form. This relates to a specific form of class rule/domination. Thus the state in capitalism reflects a particular *form* of class struggle. This manifests itself, according to Holloway and Picciotto into:

> particularisation of the two forms of domination finds its institutional expression in the state apparatus as an apparently autonomous entity. It also finds expression in the separation of the individual's relation to the state from his immediate relation to capital, in the separation of the worker and the citizen, in the separation of his struggle into "economic struggle" and "political struggle"—whereas this very separation into forms determined by capital, involves therefore an acceptance of the limits imposed by capital.

"Capital, Crisis and the State," in S. Clarke, ed., *The State Debate* (Basingstoke: Macmillan, 1991), 114.

44. Holloway and Picciotto, eds., *State and Capital,* 2

45. Thus, as Holloway and Picciotto make clear:

> The development of the state must rather be seen as a particular form of manifestation of the crisis of the capital relation . . . the state must be understood as a particular surface (or phenomenal) form of capital relation, i.e. of an historically specific form of class domination.

S. Clarke, ed., *The State Debate,* 110.

46. See Holloway and Picciotto, *The State Debate,* 110–11 and M. Carnoy, *The State and Political Theory* (Princeton: Princeton University Press, 1984), 254–55.

47. See Wood, *Democracy against Capitalism,* 44–48 on this point.

48. Fred Halliday has been the most consistent voice on the role of the "superpowers" in world politics, fashioning support for particular types of states, that reflect each one's internal constitutive form. See his *Making of the Second Cold War: Rethinking International Relations*; and *From Kabul to Managu.*

49. See Corrigan et al., *Socialist Construction and Marxist Theory,* 38.

50. According to Corrigan et al., *Socialist Construction and Marxist Theory,* xvi:

> Central to Bolshevism is a struggle between two roads and two lines. Socialist construction was hampered in so far as certain clearly capitalist techniques and relations (i.e. forces) were considered necessary to create the material basis for socialism. Socialist construction was liberated and accelerated in so far as its resources were coherently and consistently recognized to be particular productive collectivities (i.e. relations), that is to say, when socialist construction was seen to turn on the simultaneous conscious, collective and thus egalitarian transformation of circumstances and people.

# II

## THE UNITED NATIONS AND WORLD PEACE

# 2

# Reforming the United Nations Security Council: A Decision-making Analysis

*Courtney B. Smith*

The United Nations has found itself thrust into the spotlight of global politics as never before in its tumultuous history. The end of the Cold War and the accompanying breakdown of superpower rivalry has resulted in a dramatic increase in the demand for multilateral management of a growing range of transnational problems.[1] As the world's only universal membership and general purpose international organization, it is clear that much of this demand will be directed towards the institutions of the UN System.[2] Unfortunately, these pressures for increased activity come at a time of shrinking resources and financial uncertainty such that the UN may find itself overstretched to the point where all of its programs are compromised.[3] Furthermore, in the midst of these contradictory challenges and opportunities, the UN finds itself undergoing a reform process that has the potential to fundamentally alter the manner in which the organization has functioned over the past fifty years.

Reform has been mentioned, at least to some extent, in regards to almost every aspect of the UN's structures, processes, and mandates; however, the issue of restructuring the Security Council has become of central importance to the overall reform effort.[4] This is true because much of recent UN activity has been centered on the Council and because membership in the Council represents an important source of power and influence, both within and beyond the UN System. As a result, many of the UN's 185 member states have used this opportunity to express their dissatisfaction with the Council's unrepresentative character and its rather secretive way of conducting business.[5]

These concerns have led to considerable debate in the Plenary of the General Assembly and resulted in the creation of an open-ended working group to focus specifically on the composition and working methods of the Security Council.[6] While some significant breakthroughs have been achieved, progress on the most important issues remains elusive. Therefore, as these reform efforts enter their fourth year, a reassessment of the procedures and methods used to build agreement on Security Council reform is required.

Unfortunately, there are two difficulties that complicate our efforts to understand decision making regarding Security Council reform. First, scholarly understanding of the internal processes of international organizations is arguably less developed and nuanced than it was twenty-five years ago.[7] While it is certainly possible to argue that this relative neglect of formal international organizations has been corrected, at least to some extent, with the growing focus on the United Nations across the past six years, it is also becoming clear that this new scholarship has only served to further illuminate some glaring shortcomings that must be addressed. For example, recent research has centered on the nature and effects of the decisions made by these organizations, but little attention has been paid to the process by which the decisions are made. In other words, scholars have been content to look solely at the outputs of the global policy process rather than investigating the how and why of the dynamics underlying these processes.

Second, during this period of scholarly neglect, the internal structures and procedures of the United Nations have changed. Not only has its membership increased, but there has also been a gradual shift from majority voting towards the use of consensus procedures in the General Assembly and other UN bodies.[8] Since these procedures structure all subsequent interaction and help to specify how much influence each member will have over the content of the decision,[9] their impact on the processes of the UN can be significant. In the case of Security Council reform, there have been some indications that majority rule would be used in the Assembly; however, it is much more likely that consensus will be the decision rule of choice.[10] This is true because reforming the Council would require amending the Charter and because all members want to avoid restructuring the Council in a manner that enjoys anything less than near universal support.

Therefore, the primary goal of this paper is to examine the consensus building process underlying efforts to reform the UN Security Council. This will be achieved by examining fourteen propositions regarding those factors that are argued to cause consensus to be possible in the case of certain decisions and not others. The factors and propositions used in this study also relate to the second goal, developing and refining a decision-making framework that can be used to study the internal processes of a wide variety of international organizations in a systematic fashion. The absence of such a theoretical foundation remains a critical lacuna in the study of international organizations and a series of scholars have called for an analytical framework to rectify this shortcoming.[11] A third and final goal of this paper is to use a case study on Security Council reform to assess the validity and generalizability of the framework itself. This is an important preliminary application of the framework that may offer useful insights for future research on consensus building processes in international organizations.

In order to meet these goals, the paper will provide a brief review of existing literature on decision making in international organizations. Next, the study will design a framework that can be used to study consensus building in a systematic fashion. This framework will then be used in a preliminary case study focusing on Security Council reform. Finally, the conclusion will assess the prospects for Council reform and evaluate the framework that was designed.

## RELEVANT LITERATURE

The study of international organizations dates back almost as far as the organizations themselves. Unfortunately, much of the early writings were descriptive treatments that provided useful information but offered little in the way of theory.[12] However, the study of international organization has given rise to several important theoretical traditions such as functionalism, neo-functionalism, transnational relations, complex interdependence, and regime analysis.[13] These efforts have had some notable success in trying to push scholars beyond the state-centered and conflict-based realist paradigm; but unfortunately, their utility for the purposes of this study remains limited due to their neglect of the formal and informal structures and procedures that characterize the consensus building process in international organizations.

Just as the United Nations emerged from four decades of Cold War paralysis in the late 1980s, the international organization subfield began to move beyond the confines of regime analysis which had dominated this area of scholarship for nearly a decade.[14] Scholars began to offer new theoretical perspectives that tried to overcome some of the most glaring limitations of this previous writing.[15] And while these efforts have yet to fully embrace the call for research focused on the internal political processes of international organizations,[16] they do offer some insights for the propositions contained in the analytic framework outlined in the following section.

In addition to this general literature on international organizations, there are three areas of research which have focused more directly on the UN and are thus also relevant to this particular study. The first is empirical studies which have addressed certain aspects of the internal workings of the organization.[17] While these efforts were largely completed nearly thirty years ago and none of them focused specifically on decision making, they did address relevant issues such as influence and participation. The second area of scholarship includes decision-making studies written by former participants in the political processes of the UN.[18] Some of these have focused exclusively on the principle organs of the UN, while others have addressed conference diplomacy more broadly. The only disadvantage to these approaches is that they were not guided by a systematic framework. The third area of scholarship includes studies which specifically focus on the General Assembly.[19] These efforts have provided a wealth of information about its functions, procedures, and processes, but again, the analysis was not guided by a systematic framework.

Despite the fact that much of this literature was written at a time when the United Nations was a much different place than it is today, it nonetheless continues to provide concepts that are relevant for present day studies of the UN. Finally, there is one last area of scholarship which will be used in developing the decision-making framework which will serve as the basis for this research—the work on decision units found in the foreign policy literature.[20] Therefore, the propositions and framework used in this study find their roots in five distinct areas of scholarship, all of which have significant insights to offer. However, the key contribution of this particular project will be to synthesize these concepts into an integrated framework that can be used to identify and understand the factors that cause consensus to be possible within the complex dynamics of the UN System.

## THE FRAMEWORK

The focus of the first part of this paper is to propose a framework that can be used to analyze the consensus building process found in the General Assembly by drawing on the literature identified above. The purpose of the framework is to identify the factors that cause consensus to be possible in the case of some decisions and not others. Therefore, the dependent variable of this study is the presence or absence of consensus regarding Security Council reform. Furthermore, the definition of consensus that will be used is that the decision was made without objection from any voting member of the Assembly.[21] The propositions discussed below will argue that certain variables make this consensus more or less likely because they either facilitate or inhibit the consensus building process.

The framework includes five factors: decision unit, interests, leadership, strategic interaction, and networking.[22] These factors draw on the characteristics of the actors involved in the Assembly as well as on the characteristics of the consensus building process itself. As a result, it is the basic premise of this paper that these five factors influence whether or not consensus will be possible, what degree of consensus is ultimately achieved, and the speed with which this outcome is obtained. These five factors, and the accompanying propositions, are designed to be applied to a particular case in the order they are presented. In other words, the first step in using the framework is to determine the decision unit, then consider interests, and so on.[23] The components of the framework are outlined in table 2.1 and briefly introduced in the following paragraphs.

**Table 2.1.  The Decision-Making Framework**

| Factor | Variable | Proposition |
|---|---|---|
| | Size | 1) The smaller the number of participants in the decision unit, the greater the likelihood of consensus. |
| | Procedure | 2) The greater the flexibility of the procedures used in the decision unit, the greater the likelihood of consensus. |
| | Nonstate actor | 3) The greater the involvement of non-state actors in the decision process, the greater the likelihood of consensus. |
| Interests | Convergence | 4) The greater the degree of convergence in the goals of the actors in the decision unit, the greater the likelihood of consensus. |
| | Minority salience | 5) The less salient an issue is to the actors in the minority position, the greater the likelihood of consensus. |
| | Formal leadership | 6) If the formal leadership is sanctioned through established procedures is present, then there is a greater likelihood of consensus. |
| Leadership | Ad hoc leadership | 7) If ad hoc leadership is provided by one or more actors in the decision unit, then there is a greater likelihood of consensus. |
| | Legitimate leadership | 8) The more legitimate, credible, and respected the leadership that emerges, the greater the likelihood of consensus. |

*continued*

**Table 2.1.    The Decision-Making Framework** *(continued)*

| Factor | Variable | Proposition |
|---|---|---|
| Strategic interactions | Middle powers | 9) The more active the representatives of middle powers in the decision unit, the greater the likelihood of consensus. |
| | Autonomy | 10) The greater the degree of autonomy of the participants in the decision unit, the greater the likelihood of consensus. |
| Networking | Formal groups | 11) If formal ad hoc negotiating groups are established by the presiding officer, then there is a greater likelihood of consensus. |
| | Broad perspective | 12) If the members of negotiating groups look beyond their narrow interests with the support of those they represent, then there is a greater likelihood of consensus. |
| | Informal networking | 13) If informal networking is present on an issue, then there is a greater likelihood of consensus. |
| | Working relationship | 14) The better the working relationship between the members of the decision unit, the greater the likelihood of consensus. |

## DECISION UNIT

The first factor in the decision-making framework relates to identifying the decision unit in regards to each particular issue or case. This is a concept developed specifically for studying foreign policy decision making,[24] but it also appears relevant to the study of consensus building in international organizations. One of the key contributions of this concept is to stress the importance of identifying the actors and arenas that will be most relevant in a given situation.[25] This is true in the case of foreign policy because authority can be exercised in a wide range of arenas by a potentially diverse range of actors. It can be argued that this realization is even more important in the case of international bodies such as the UN System because they are composed of a whole series of somewhat autonomous organizations.

Even with the case of the General Assembly alone, the range of potential decision units is quite large. In terms of actors, there are many which can play a role: representatives of member states, representatives of groups of states functioning as a bloc, executive heads including the Secretary-General, secretariat staff, presiding officers who are elected each session, representatives from nongovernmental organizations (NGOs), representatives from other international governmental organizations (IGOs), of arenas, three types must be considered: the Plenary, the six main committees of the Assembly,[26] and working groups created to deal with specific issues.

As a result of this complexity, the first step in understanding consensus building is to identify the set of actors and arenas that will form the decision unit on a particular issue. This provides the first propositions for the study:

*Proposition 1:* The smaller the number of participants in the decision unit, the greater the likelihood of consensus.

*Proposition 2:* The greater the flexibility of the procedures used in the decision unit, the greater the likelihood of consensus.

*Proposition 3:* The greater the involvement of nonstate actors in the decision process, the greater the likelihood of consensus.

The rationale behind these propositions is quite straightforward. The first two are drawn from the public choice and cartel literature.[27] In terms of size, large groups make consensus less likely because there is often a greater diversity of interests and a more complex pattern of interaction. On the other hand, smaller groups can facilitate the process of building trust and friendship, both of which can encourage consensus. In terms of procedures, greater formality often leads to increased rigidity and the possibility of the rules themselves becoming the subject of dispute. On the other hand, flexible procedures can provide the necessary coordination and interaction to allow for collective problem solving without generating these possible side effects.[28] Finally, in terms of nonstate actors, it is important to realize that while these actors may lack formal voting power, they can nonetheless facilitate consensus building by helping to smooth over the differences between states.[29]

## INTERESTS

The second factor in the framework involves an exploration of the interests of the actors included in the decision unit in regards to a specific issue. Identifying these interests can be difficult;[30] however, interests are crucial determinants of behavior and must be included in the framework. There are two primary ways in which actor interests influence the consensus building dynamics of the Assembly. First, the salience of an issue to the actors involved will help to determine their behavior.[31] This is true because the influence of an actor depends less on its overall resources than it does on the actor's willingness to commit these resources. For instance, an otherwise influential actor who is not interested in an issue will probably have a lesser role in the decision-making process since they will not want to expend scarce resources and effort. However, if an otherwise marginal actor takes an interest in an issue, their willingness to commit their limited resources may have surprising results.

Second, the presence or absence of common ground between the interests of the actors at the outset of Assembly debate on an issue will influence the subsequent dynamics of the political process.[32] The absence of common ground will result in a more conflictual and complex process just as the presence of common ground that crosses traditional lines of cleavage can help prevent conflict and paralysis. Based on these two relationships between interests and the decision-making process, it is now possible to offer two additional propositions on consensus building:

*Proposition 4:* The greater the degree of convergence in the interests of the actors in the decision unit, the greater the likelihood of consensus.

*Proposition 5:* The less salient an issue is to the actors in the minority position, the greater the likelihood of consensus.

These two propositions are rather obvious in that their logic is based on common sense. Since any participant can block a decision in the case of consensus, the interests of each and every actor can have an impact on the outcome.[33] However, despite the fact that these propositions are probably less innovative than some of the others, they are nonetheless important and must be included in the analysis.

## LEADERSHIP

The third factor in the framework focuses on the importance of leadership in the consensus building process. Effective leadership is crucial in international organizations because it can get the decision-making process moving and keep it running smoothly.[34] For instance, leadership is needed to decide how meetings will be structured, how work will be organized within the given time constraints, and how the work of different bodies will be coordinated. In addition, leadership is required to allocate speaking time, rule on procedural questions, assign issues to the appropriate body, and allow time for behind the scenes negotiation.

This leadership can be provided by almost any of the actors active in the Assembly; however, there are two types of actors which consistently receive the most attention in terms of leadership: executive heads and presiding officers. Executive heads can play an important role in the internal processes of their organizations by facilitating compromise, taking initiatives, issuing reports, and suggesting agenda items.[35] Likewise, the presiding officers which are elected each session play roles which help provide important leadership in the Assembly.[36]

These functions include allocating speaking time, organizing informal consultations, and starting/ending meetings.

How effective an actor is at providing this leadership often depends on their own personal attributes. In fact, the personal attributes discussed here can be important in the case of any participant in the decision unit, a point which will discussed in more detail under networking. The characteristics argued to be important in the Assembly are diverse including intelligence, tolerance, charisma, reputation, experience, patience, negotiating skills, flexibility, creativity, honesty, loyalty, stamina, and linguistic versatility.[37] It should be immediately clear that no single individual can combine all of these different, and even contradictory, attributes. However, the key for a successful participant is to possess as many of these as possible, and even more importantly, to recognize their own limitations. As a result, it is now possible to offer three more propositions:

*Proposition 6:* If formal leadership sanctioned through established procedures is present, then there is a greater likelihood of consensus.

*Proposition 7:* If ad hoc leadership is provided by one or more actors in the decision unit, then there is a greater likelihood of consensus.

*Proposition 8:* The more legitimate, credible, and respected the leadership that emerges, the greater the likelihood of consensus.

The idea behind propositions six and seven is that formal leadership provided by the President of the Assembly, a committee Chairperson, or the appointed leader of a negotiating group can facilitate the consensus building process.[38] Furthermore, this holds true even when no formal leadership is sanctioned and yet one member (or members) of the decision unit takes it upon him/herself to fill this role. Finally, the quality of this leadership can vary, with leadership that is seen as legitimate and credible having the most helpful impact on the consensus building process.[39] This legitimacy and credibility, in turn, stems from some of the personal attributes discussed above such as expertise, reputation, and negotiating skill.

## STRATEGIC INTERACTIONS

The fourth factor in the framework directs attention toward the bargaining and interaction that occurs within the decision unit. It involves identifying the strategies available to each participant and assessing their implications for consensus building. One relevant issue concerns the formal voting procedures that will be used to make decisions.[40] The two main options in the UN context are majority rule and consensus, each of which has advantages and disadvantages.[41]

Although the arenas relevant to the Assembly can employ majority rule, consensus is becoming the decision rule of choice.[42] As a result, the framework developed here must take into account the potential influence of all participants in the decision unit since any one of them can obstruct the consensus building process.

There are two considerations that determine the relative influence of each participant. The first concerns the attributes of the actors they represent in the policy process. The exact nature of relevant attributes can vary based on the type of actor in question: for blocs of states acting together influence often comes through voting power; for large states influence usually depends on power (both military and economic) outside of the Assembly; for medium or small states influence often rests on their reputations as effective "go-betweens" on numerous contentious issues; for secretariat officials influence lies in their distribution of information as well as in their reputations for impartiality; and for NGO representatives influence stems from their willingness to act when states are unwilling or unable to do so.[43]

The second consideration concerns participant autonomy. This is relevant to consensus building because participants must often walk a fine line between pursuing the interests of the actors they represent and actually participating in the give and take of Assembly politics.[44] In other words, delegates must balance their instructions from home with their ultimate freedom to act. The exact mix of these tendencies in a delegate varies across actors, issues, time, and individuals;[45] however, there are two basic patterns. First, delegates from large states receive more detailed instructions than those from smaller states, and second, delegates from states interested in an issue receive more detailed instructions than those from less interested states.[46] As a result, certain participants might be able to pursue strategies other than those dictated by the attributes of the actors they represent.

The chances of reaching a consensus on an issue can be influenced by variation in attributes and autonomy, which leads to two additional propositions:

*Proposition 9:*   The more active the representatives of middle powers in the decision unit, the greater the likelihood of consensus.
*Proposition 10:*  The greater the degree of autonomy of the participants in the decision unit, the greater the likelihood of consensus.

A few brief comments on each of these are necessary. First, in regards to middle powers, examples of states that perform the role of "go-betweens" effectively include Canada and the Scandinavian countries.[47] Second, in regards to proposition ten, the basic logic is that increased autonomy allows for more flexibility in the negotiation process, thereby making compromise more possible.[48] Based on these propositions, participants can select from two types of strategies to support or oppose a particular policy option: manipulating the procedures[49] and more traditional means of leverage such as persuasion, bargaining, coalition-building, log-rolling, and package dealing.[50] This choice of strategy will structure the nature of participant interaction and influence the chance of reaching a consensus on a particular issue.


## NETWORKING

The fifth and final factor to be included in the framework relates to formal and informal networking between the participants in the decision-making process. UN scholars have argued that the public and private sides of UN processes are interrelated and must be considered together.[51] Furthermore, some scholars have completed detailed studies which conclude that, since networking allows heterogeneous interests to be narrowed down to a few crucial issues, it has an indispensable role to play in consensus building.[52] Likewise, new theoretical insights regarding international organizations have also highlighted the importance of boundary-role occupants and linking-pin organizations.[53] While these concepts are most relevant for the interorganizational level, they do provide insights into the dynamics involved at the decision unit level.

Networking can be divided into two types of activities: formal and informal. Formal networking refers to the ad hoc negotiating groups which are used extensively in the Assembly.[54] These "fire brigades" are created by the presiding officer in order to allow for intense negotiations between representatives of a variety of different actors. Informal networking, on the other hand, refers to gatherings in the back of meeting halls, "the fine art of corridor sitting," conversations in delegate lounges, and social functions at missions.[55] This yields four propositions:

*Proposition 11:* If formal ad hoc negotiating groups are established by the presiding officer, then there is a greater likelihood of consensus.

*Proposition 12:* If the members of negotiating groups look beyond their narrow interests with the support of those they represent, then there is a greater likelihood of consensus.

*Proposition 13:* If informal networking is present on an issue, then there is a greater likelihood of consensus.

*Proposition 14:* The better the working relationship between the members of the decision unit, the greater the likelihood of consensus.

A few additional comments about these propositions are necessary. First, proposition twelve is based on studies of the Assembly but is also consistent with the notion of boundary role occupants discussed above.[56] Second, the "working relationship" in proposition fourteen relates to personal attributes discussed under leadership such as experience and reputation. And finally, since these behind the scenes dynamics are important but hard to analyze, networking should be covered last in the analysis as more of a residual explanation for the success or failure of consensus building.


## THE CASE STUDY

Security Council reform has been on and off the General Assembly's agenda across the entire fifty-one year history of the United Nations. Debate has frequently centered on the size and composition of the Council's membership, and changes were made in 1965 when the size of the Council was increased from eleven to fifteen members. The issue appeared on the agenda again during 1979 and 1980, but debate effectively ended when votes were not taken on several draft resolutions.[57]

However, the end of the Cold War, the resurgence of Security Council activity in the early 1990s, and the impending fiftieth anniversary of the UN in 1995 all fostered an environment where organizational reform became a major topic of concern in 1991 and 1992.[58] This was manifested in regards to the Security Council on December 11, 1992 when the General Assembly passed resolution A/RES/47/62 which instructed the Secretary-General to gather written comments from member states on a possible review of Council membership and called for an item entitled "Question of equitable representation on and increase in the membership of the Security Council" to be placed on the agenda of the Assembly's 48th session. This issue has remained on the Assembly's agenda through the 51st session in 1997.


### Decision Unit

The first step in examining the five year consensus building process that resulted from the 1992 resolution is to identify the actors and arenas which comprise the decision unit relevant to Security Council reform. In terms of arenas, the picture is fairly clear. Some limited discussion has taken place in the Special Committee on the Charter of the United Nations and on the Strengthening of the Role of the Organization which reports to the Sixth (Legal) Committee.[59] Likewise, the Security Council itself has received numerous letters from members and even discussed this issue on several occasions.[60] In addition, the Plenary of the General Assembly has also taken up this issue during General Debate and when this specific agenda item has been discussed, usually during October or November of each year.[61]

However, the primary arena in which the issue of Security Council reform has been addressed is the Open-Ended Working Group on the Question of Equitable Representation on and Increase in the Membership of the Security Council and Other Matters Related to the Security Council.[62] The Working

Group was set up on December 3, 1993 by Assembly resolution A/RES/48/26 and it began meeting in January of 1994. Its scope of concern is organized around two clusters of issues. The first deals with the size and composition of the Council (including new membership categories and voting procedures) whereas the second deals with other working methods of the Council (such as transparency, consultation with interested parties, information analysis capabilities, and relations with other UN bodies). Also, the Working Group is chaired by the President of the General Assembly (aided by two Vice-Chairmen), open to all members of the UN, and guided by the goal of trying to reach a consensus on a proposal that could then be presented to the Assembly.

Due to the importance of Security Council reform, a variety of different types of actors have offered their own proposals or observations, both within and outside of the United Nations. For instance, a variety of NGOs have offered either comprehensive plans for UN reform or at least their own proposals for a new and improved Security Council.[63] However, the ability of NGOs to participate in the decision unit is limited because the Working Group has been conducting all of its deliberations behind closed doors.[64] The only avenues of influence which have been openly afforded to these actors are when the representatives of member states attend NGO sponsored conferences or working groups on Security Council reform.[65]

There are other types of actors in the Assembly who have enjoyed greater access to this Working Group. First, presiding officers elected each session have played an important role. They have been reluctant to advance specific proposals for reform,[66] but they have played a key role in structuring the deliberation process and exchanging information, something that will be addressed under leadership below. Second, both Secretaries-General during this period have voiced their support for Council reform, but they too have been reluctant to take a specific position on it.[67] Finally, groups of states acting as a bloc have also taken positions on this issue, but they have been hampered as actors by the fact that there are disagreements within each of these blocs regarding the specifics of Council reform.[68]

As a result, the most important participants in the Working Group are representatives of member states. Over the past four years, more than half of the member states have advanced a position on Council reform.[69] While some of these statements contain only vague language, others offer specific and concrete proposals for addressing current deficiencies. Some of these positions will be considered in the following section on interests; the important point in regard to this section is that member states remain the dominant actors in regard to this particular issue.

Now that the arenas and actors relevant to this particular issue have been identified, the three propositions regarding the decision unit should be considered. First, in regard to the number of participants in the decision unit, we would expect consensus to be less likely. This is true because the Working

Group is open to any and all members of the UN, thereby making the membership of that body almost as large and diffuse as the UN itself. Second, in regard to procedures, we would expect consensus to be more likely. This is true because the procedures used in that body are generally more open and flexible than the more structured processes found in the Plenary itself.[70] And finally, in regard to the involvement of nonstate actors in the decision unit, we would expect consensus to be less likely. This is true because nonstate actors like NGOs have been denied a seat at the table and have been forced to try and influence the Working Group through more indirect means.

### Interests

The second step in examining consensus building regarding Security Council reform focuses attention on the interests of the actors in the decision unit. As was discussed in the previous section, some actors (such as presiding officers and the Secretary-General) who play a potentially important role in this process are reluctant to take a public position, preferring instead to focus their efforts on facilitating negotiation. In addition, while some NGOs have offered suggestions in regard to the size and composition of the Council, much of their lobbying effort has centered specifically on trying to increase NGO access to Council deliberations.[71] And finally, while there have been some common group positions on broad issues regarding reform (such as the NAM proposal to increase nonpermanent seats by eleven), relatively cohesive bodies such as the European Union have been unable to reach agreement on specific proposals.[72] As a result, the interests which are most relevant for this particular case are those advanced by the member states themselves.

As of March, 1997, member states have focused much of their attention thus far on the first cluster of issues, those dealing with the composition of the Council and the use of the veto. The working methods are seen as a high priority item, but it is likely that they will receive serious attention only once cluster one has been addressed.[73] The first proposition relating to interests focuses on the degree of convergence among the preferences of the actors in the decision unit. In regard to Council size, there is widespread agreement that the membership must increase but little agreement on exactly what type of seats should be added (permanent versus nonpermanent) and which states should get these seats.[74] Furthermore, in regard to the veto, there is little agreement on even the need for change, let alone on any specific proposals. As a result, we would expect consensus to be less likely because of these differences.

The interests of countries which have taken a firm position on Council reform are summarized in table 2.2.[75] In most cases their comments refer to proposals that have already been tabled in regard to cluster one. On the issue of Council composition, they include: (1) additional permanent seats for two industrialized countries from the Northern hemisphere, (2) additional

**Table 2.2.  Selected Country Positions on Security Council Reform**

| Country | Position on Security Council Reform |
|---|---|
| Algeria | Separate veto and permanent membership; limit veto to Chapter VII concerns. |
| Angola | Two new permanent seats for Africa with veto or eliminate veto altogether; permanent seats for other regions. |
| Australia | New permanent seats for Japan, Germany, and under-represented regions; increase number of nonpermanent seats for balance; total size about 25. |
| Austria | Two to 5 new permanent seats for Japan, Germany, and developing world; increase nonpermanent seats for balance; total size about 25; discuss veto. |
| Bangladesh | Expand size into low or mid 20s; no specification on type or allocation of seats. |
| Belgium | Two to 5 new permanent seats for Japan, Germany, and developing world; increase nonpermanent seats for balance; total size about 25; discuss veto. |
| Belize | Five to 8 new permanent seats (at least 2 from each regional group); 10 new nonpermanent seats; eliminate veto or modify it to multiple veto. |
| Brazil | Five new permanent seats with veto; 3 or 4 new nonpermanent seats; no expansion for only industrial states and wary of rotating regional seats. |
| Bulgaria | Permanent seats for Japan, Germany, and other influential regional states; expand nonpermanent seats with one more allocated to Eastern Europe. |
| Chile | Permanent seats for Japan and Germany; increase nonpermanent seats to make council more representative and balanced; total size about 25. |
| China | Increase size to low 20s; increase representation of developing countries and small or medium states; no specification on type of seats. |
| Colombia | Increase nonpermanent seats (and allow reelection); phase out permanent seats; eliminate veto, limit it to Chapter VII, or move to multiple veto. |
| Comoros | Allow greater access to small and medium-sized states; no specifics on how. |
| Croatia | Expand both types of membership; total size about 25; review permanent members every 10–15 years; move to system of multiple vetoes. |
| Cuba | Increase size to 23; no new industrialized states; 3 from Asia, 2 from Africa, 2 from Latin America, 1 from Eastern Europe; eliminate or restrict veto. |
| Czech Republic | Add 2–5 permanent seats for Japan, Germany, and developing world; add nonpermanent seats for balance; total size 25; no new membership categories. |
| Ecuador | Increase nonpermanent seats; permanent seats for Japan, Germany, Brazil, and at least 1 each from Africa, Asia, and Latin America; eliminate veto. |

*continued*

**Table 2.2. Selected Country Positions on Security Council Reform** *(continued)*

| Country | Position on Security Council Reform |
|---------|-------------------------------------|
| Egypt | Add 2 permanent seats without veto; add 3 regional rotating seats (one each for Africa, Asia, and Latin America); restrict or eliminate veto. |
| Estonia | Two to 5 new permanent seats for Japan, Germany, and developing world; increase non-permanent seats for balance; total size about 25; discuss veto. |
| Fiji | Expand permanent seats; increase nonpermanent seats to 17 (9 from Africa/Asia, 2 from Eastern Europe, 3 from Latin America, 3 from Western Europe). |
| France | Add up to 5 permanent seats for Japan, Germany, and developing states; expand nonpermanent seats; total size at 20 or 21. |
| Germany | Add 5 permanent seats with veto for Japan, Germany, and 1 each from Asia, Africa, and Latin America; add 4 or 5 nonpermanent seats for developing states; skeptical of semi-permanent seats; total size about 25; restrict veto. |
| Ghana | Add at least 2 permanent seats and several nonpermanent seats for Africa; limit veto to Chapter VII concerns and allow assembly to override veto. |
| Guyana | Prefer to add only nonpermanent seats but rotation seats merit attention. |
| Hungary | Two to 5 new permanent seats for Japan, Germany, and developing world; increase non-permanent seats for balance; total size about 25; discuss veto. |
| India | Add at least 11 new seas including at least 5 permanent seats with veto. |
| Indonesia | Expand both types of seats for developing states; discuss revision of veto power; skeptical of regional rotating seats. |
| Iran | Eliminate or at least review veto power; expand nonpermanent seats first. |
| Iraq | Add seats (type unclear) for Asia, Africa, and Latin America; phase out veto. |
| Ireland | Add 2–5 permanent seats for Japan, Germany, Ireland, and states from Asia, Africa, and Latin America; add non-permanent seats for balance; total size about 25; veto should be curtailed. |
| Italy | No new permanent seats (opposed to Germany); add 8–10 non-permanent regional seats rotating among 3 states periodically elected by Assembly; keep ban on immediate reelection; total size 25–32; restrict or modify veto. |
| Japan | Five new permanent seats (1 for Japan) with veto; consider rotating seats for Asia, Africa, and Latin America; add nonpermanent seats for balance. |
| Kenya | Two permanent seats for Africa; add nonpermanent seats; total size at least 25; veto no longer justified. |
| Libya | No new permanent seats; add nonpermanent seats; eliminate veto power. |
| Malaysia | Add 8 permanent seats; favors "permanent regional representation"; add nonpermanent seats; total size of 26; eliminate veto or use multiple veto. |
| Mexico | No new permanent seats; add 5 nonpermanent seats (1 for each region); wary of regional rotation; limit veto to Chapter VII concerns or use multiple veto. |

| Country | Position on Security Council Reform |
| --- | --- |
| New Zealand | No new permanent seats; add nonpermanent seats; eliminate or restrict veto. |
| Nigeria | Add 5 permanent seats (2 for Africa, 2 for Asia, 1 for Latin America) with veto; add nonpermanent seats for developing states; skeptical of regional rotation; limit veto to Chapter VII concerns and move to eliminate it. |
| Nordic Countries | Add 5 permanent seats (Japan, Germany, Asia, Africa, and Latin America); add 3 nonpermanent seats; total size 23; discuss veto; keep immediate reelection ban. (This group includes Norway, Sweden, Finland, Denmark, and Iceland.) |
| Pakistan | No new permanent seats; add nonpermanent seats for developing states. |
| Poland | Permanent seats for Japan and Germany; enhanced representation for Asia, Africa, and Latin America; greater access for Eastern Europe; total size 21–25. |
| Romania | Permanent seats for Japan and Germany; proposals for rotating seats deserve consideration; maintain balance among regions; total size about 25. |
| Russia | Increase size to low 20s; no specification on type or allocation of seats; veto is vital and should not be modified or restricted in any way. |
| Singapore | Expand size including new permanent seats; but new nonpermanent seats must come first; regional rotation is good for Africa but not for any other region. |
| Slovenia | Two to five new permanent seats for Japan, Germany, and developing world; increase nonpermanent seats for balance; total size about 25; discuss veto. |
| South Africa | Add 11 new members including 6 permanent seats (2 each for Asia, Africa, and Latin America); let regions select who fills each of these seats. |
| South Korea | No new permanent seats; add 8 new nonpermanent seats that have 4 year terms; current permanent members subject to review; phase out veto. |
| Spain | Moderate increase in size, mainly in nonpermanent seats; consider rotation seats; modify all voting rules and limit veto to Chapter VII concerns. |
| Swaziland | Two permanent seats for Africa; minimum of 25 nonpermanent seats; ensure geographical balance in both types of membership; curtail veto. |
| Tanzania | Two permanent and additional nonpermanent seats for Africa; ensure geographical balance in both types of membership; veto is outdated. |
| Tunisia | Expand both types of seats; permanent seats for Japan and Germany only if Asia, Africa, and Latin America each get 1; permanent regional seats through rotation merits attention; limit or even eliminate veto. |
| Turkey | Increase size to 25; add 10 nonpermanent seats that rotate among 3 countries for each; allow list of rotating states to be reviewed every 12 to 16 years. |

*continued*

**Table 2.2. Selected Country Positions on Security Council Reform *(continued)***

| Country | Position on Security Council reform |
|---|---|
| Ukraine | Increase size to 25 or 26; permanent seats for Japan and Germany; give 8 seats to regional groups for rotation; at least 1 for Eastern Europe; modify veto. |
| United Kingdom | Permanent seats with veto for Japan and Germany; add representation for developing states; total size no more than 20 or 21; maintain the veto as is. |
| United States | Permanent seats for Japan and Germany are required; add other seats to bring in developing states (no specifics on type or allocation); total size about 20; discuss permanent regional rotation; no change in veto; end ban on reelection. |
| Venezuela | Expand both types of seats; ensure regional balance in both types; supports seat for Brazil; supports regional rotation seats; limit or eliminate veto. |
| Zimbabwe | Add at least 2 permanent seats each for Africa, Asia, and Latin America (with veto); add regional non-permanent seats as well; reconsider veto. |

*Note:* Table 2.2. contains fifty-six country positions and one group position.

permanent seats for three to five developing countries, (3) a 2+3 formula with additional permanent seats for two industrialized countries and three developing countries (from Asia, Africa, and Latin America), (4) adding regional rotating seats which several alternating countries would hold, and (5) an increase only in nonpermanent seats by as many as eleven and the possibility of periodic reelection of members.[76] On the veto, the options include: (1) giving the veto to new permanent members, (2) keeping the veto as is, (3) limiting it to only certain issues (such as Chapter VII concerns), (4) using a multiple veto system (where two or more negative votes are required), and (5) eliminating the veto altogether.

Since member state interests regarding Council reform are so divergent, the framework directs our attention toward the interests of those specific members of the decision unit which find these issues especially salient. However, it is possible to conclude that almost every UN member finds these issues salient due to the importance of the Council in recent crises around the globe. In addition, the level of participation on this issue in the form of oral and written comments has been extremely high, making it likely that members would be willing to commit their resources in support of their positions. As a result of this high level of salience, we would expect those in the minority position to do everything they can to obstruct agreement, thereby making consensus less likely.

## Leadership

The third step in examining decision making on Security Council reform is to consider the presence and role of leadership in the consensus building process. The framework addresses three aspects of this issue: is formal leadership present, is ad hoc leadership present, and is this leadership legitimate, credible, and respected? In answer to the first of these questions, formal leadership is present on this issue, most notably in the form of presiding officers elected each session. As was mentioned before, the Working Group on Security Council Reform is chaired by the President of the General Assembly and two delegates also serve as Vice Chairmen.[77] One might argue that the leadership provided by these Chairmen is hampered because each of them serves for only one year. However, this shortcoming is at least in part mitigated by the fact that one of the Vice Chairmen, Wilhelm Breitenstein, has served for three years. Therefore, based on the presence of formal leadership, we would expect consensus to be more likely on this issue.

In the case of the remaining propositions on the role of leadership, the picture is less clear since the final type of data, direct contact with participants, has yet to be gathered. However, a few preliminary observations are possible. First, there does appear to be some ad hoc leadership emerging from a variety of different places. For instance, based on its coordinating role in the NGO Working Group on Security Council Reform, it seems clear that Global Policy Forum has taken a leading role, at least within the NGO community. In addition, a select group of countries (including Italy, the Nordic states, Austria, New Zealand, Malaysia, Singapore, and Zimbabwe) have also assumed what appear to be leadership roles.[78]

Furthermore, there is at least some evidence that this formal and informal leadership has been perceived as credible, legitimate, and beneficial. This is reflected by the fact that many of the formal leaders have served in the Assembly for years, building up their experience and reputations such that they have the support of many members.[79] In addition, nearly every speech before the Working Group or the Plenary begins with praise for these individuals. And while it is possible to argue that this practice is just a formality, one can assume that it reflects at least some underlying support for the efforts of the leadership. As a result, consensus would appear to be more likely in this case, but only access to participant data will shed sufficient light on these dynamics to support more definite conclusions.

### Strategic Interactions

The fourth step in understanding consensus building on Security Council reform is to analyze the interaction between the different members of the decision unit. As was mentioned above, in the case of consensus decisions this interaction depends on the attributes and autonomy of all actors involved in the process. Without access to data from participants, it is impossible to make any firm conclusions regarding their autonomy. However, the general pattern identified by previous UN scholarship is that participant autonomy is decreased when the issue is especially salient, as it is to nearly every member in this particular case.[80] As a result, proposition ten would lead us to expect that consensus will be less likely.

The second concern when it comes to participant interaction in the decision unit relates to the resources or attributes each actor can use to try and influence other members of the group. For instance, the United States, the United Kingdom, Japan, and Germany, all of whom share a desire to include Japan and Germany as permanent members in the Council, have a tremendous amount of leverage over the other actors because they are the four top financial contributors who collectively provide nearly half of the annual UN budget (that is when they are paid up).[81] On the other hand, developing states usually find their leverage through collective action because their greater numbers can bloc any action or proposal in the Assembly, even if a formal vote is taken. And although they have been unable to agree on specific proposals, they do share a common concern that the number of nonpermanent seats must be increased in order to improve the geographical balance in the Council (this is the official NAM position).

Since these two sides find themselves in conflict regarding reform and each has potentially useful resources at their disposal, there is opportunity for middle powers to come in and help foster a compromise. Fortunately in this case, a group of middle powers has emerged to perform a "go-between" role across these different groups. These states include Italy, the Nordic countries, Australia, New Zealand, Malaysia, Singapore, and Zimbabwe.[82] These countries have been able to cross some traditional lines of conflict and offer unique and creative reform proposals (see table 2.2). As a result, we would expect consensus to become more likely as long as their role in the reform process continues.

## Networking

The fifth and final step in examining consensus building involves an exploration of the public and private, formal and informal networking that takes place within the Assembly. As was the case with leadership and strategic interaction, the lack of data from participants in the process limits the nature of the findings on this factor. However, available sources do provide some limited insights into the dynamics of networking regarding Security Council reform. First, it is notable that there has been no effort on the part of the Chairmen or Vice Chairmen to set up formal ad hoc negotiating groups on any specific subset of the Working Groups are of concern. Instead, all of the statements, proposals, and working papers have been handled within the entire Working Group. If we relate this realization to proposition eleven, we find that consensus should be less likely.

Furthermore, proposition twelve directs attention to the nature of the interests of those actors in the negotiating groups, with broader interests helping to facilitate consensus. Since no negotiating groups have been used, there has been little reason for many of the members to look beyond their own narrow interests (as is reflected by the great diversity of positions in table 2.2). This, in turn, further decreases the likelihood of reaching a consensus.

However, proposition thirteen focuses on the presence or absence of informal networking outside of the official meetings. The idea is that certain members may take it upon themselves to start working together towards a solution. There is considerable evidence that this process has begun. First, although group actors have been unable to agree on specifics, they have made an effort to forge common positions on the broad strokes of Council reform (such as support within NAM for 11 new members). Second, during this reform process some states have been willing to come together and offer joint statements or common working papers.[83] Furthermore, states have used their statements as a way to express agreement with the positions advanced by others.[84] And finally, there are reports that numerous bilateral meetings between states at UN Headquarters and in country capitals have been held in regards to Council reform as of March, 1997.[85]

As a result of these informal contacts, it is possible to conclude that the likelihood of consensus has increased. In addition, proposition fourteen examines the working relationship found in the decision unit. While some members have expressed frustration at the unwillingness of certain permanent members to be explicit regarding their preferences on reform (particularly regarding new nonpermanent seats for developing states), much of the give and take in the Working Group has remained quite amicable, even between states with divergent preferences such as Germany and Italy.[86] As a result, we would expect the likelihood of consensus to be greater as long as this atmosphere of mutual respect persists.

## CONCLUSIONS

The results of this case study regarding consensus building on Security Council reform are presented in table 2.3. The preliminary conclusions regarding each proposition in the decision-making framework are presented. The most striking result is that the seven independent variables that seem to inhibit consensus building are balanced by seven others that appear to facilitate it in this case. This would suggest that there is still a possibility that a consensus on Council reform can be reached, but also that the recent willingness of some participants (such as Germany and Japan) to push for a majority rule decision on a select set of key issues may end up being the most likely outcome of the reform process.

**Table 2.3.    Preliminary Case Study Results**

| Propositions | Variables | Likelihood of consensus |
|---|---|---|
| One | Size | Decrease |
| Two | Procedures | Increase |
| Three | Non-state actors | Decrease |
| Four | Convergence | Decrease |
| Five | Minority salience | Decrease |
| Six | Formal leadership | Increase |
| Seven | Ad hoc leadership | Increase |
| Eight | Legitimate leadership | Increase |
| Nine | Middle powers | Increase |
| Tenth | Autonomy | Decrease |
| Eleventh | Formal groups | Decrease |
| Twelve | Broad perspective | Decrease |
| Thirteen | Informal networking | Increase |
| Fourteen | Working relationship | Increase |

*Note:* These results are those for which the least amount of data is available.

Table 2.3 allows us to make even more detailed conclusions regarding the chance of reaching a consensus on this particular case. For instance, all variables considered under decision unit and interests (except one) are acting in a manner that inhibits consensus building. On the other hand, all three variables under leadership point to an increased likelihood of consensus. Finally, the strategic interaction and networking variables are more mixed in their apparent effect on the chance of consensus. Low participant autonomy and the absence of formal negotiating groups suggest that consensus will be difficult whereas the presence of effective middle powers and informal networking indicate that a consensus could in fact be reached. These results indicate that divergent interests and a large decision unit make consensus building difficult, but that legitimate leadership and effective networking can still set the stage for a successful outcome.

Furthermore, this preliminary case study has several beneficial implications for future research. First, it indicates that the variables contained in the framework do provide useful leverage in understanding global consensus building. Second, it highlights the importance of access to the participants in the policy process because only they can shed adequate light on some of the central factors that facilitate consensus building such as leadership and networking. Third, the fact that this case has mixed preliminary results and has yet to come to a final resolution in the Assembly highlights the need for comparative analysis. While this study may give an indication of the influence of each variable, the results would be more robust if they were consistent with the dynamics found in other decision cases. This would help to increase the generalizability of the findings and allow for the research to make a more direct contribution to theory building in the study of international organizations.

## NOTES

1. For a discussion of the effects of the end of the Cold War on the UN, see Rosenau 1992; for a discussion of this increased demand, see the introduction in Weiss, Forsythe, and Coate 1994, 10.

2. This observation is drawn from Kennedy and Russett 1995, 57.

3. See Baehr and Gordenker 1994, 158, and Kostakos 1995, 74–75.

4. This point is made quite persuasively in Menon 1996, 1.

5. These frustrations are highlighted in Russett, O'Neill, and Sutterlin 1996, 65.

6. See A/RES/47/62 (December 11, 1992) and A/RES/48/26 (December 3, 1993).

7. This is based on observations found in Kratochwil and Ruggie 1986 and Rochester 1995.

8. Marin-Bosch 1987 has completed a statistical analysis of this development in the Assembly over time. Kaufmann 1994, 27–28, and Peterson 1986, 82–90, have also offered the same observation.

9. See Cox and Jacobson 1973, 7, and Peterson 1986, 53–54.

10. In an interview with *Asahi Shimbun* newspaper on January 31, 1997, Ambassador Razali Ismail of Malaysia, President of the General Assembly during its 51st session, suggested that consensus on Security Council reform was "practically impossible" to achieve and that a two-thirds majority formula may be used instead (translated from Japanese by Hirofumi Goto and posted to the Global Policy Forum web page at www.globalpolicy.org). However, Ambassador Razali has indicated on several occasions that consensus would be the preferred procedure for drafting a proposal for Security Council reform. For instance, see his opening statement to the 51st session of the Assembly on September 17, 1996, which can be found in UN Press Release GA/9091.

11. For example, see Keohane 1967, 221–22; Kay 1969, 958; Alger 1970, 444; Rochester 1986, 812; Kratochwil and Ruggie 1986, 754; and Kaufmann 1994, 28.

12. For example see Claude 1971, which was first published in 1956.

13. The classic texts are Mitrany 1943 for functionalism, E. Haas 1958 and Nye 1970 for neo-functionalism, Nye and Keohane 1971 for transnational relations, Keohane and Nye 1977 for complex interdependence, and Krasner 1983 for regime analysis. These writings have been extensively reviewed in Archer 1983 and Gordenker and Saunders 1978.

14. See Rochester 1986, 800–02, and Kratochwil and Ruggie 1986, 753 and 774.

15. Examples of these efforts are Jonsson 1986 who brings interorganizational theory to the study of international organizations, Ness and Brechin 1988 who draw on organizational sociology for their key concepts, and E. Haas 1990 who focuses on the role of adaptation, learning, and knowledge in organizational change.

16. Even within the past few years, scholars have once again observed the need for systematic exploration of UN decision making, see Kaufmann 1994, 28, and Rochester 1995, 199.

17. Examples of these efforts include Alger 1966 and 1967, Keohane 1967, 1969a, and 1969b, and Cox and Jacobson 1973.

18. The best examples of this type of work are Kaufmann's 1962 (reprinted in 1980) study of UN decision making and his 1988 study of conference diplomacy. Kaufmann is a former Permanent Representative to the UN from the Netherlands. See also Narasimhan 1988.

19. Examples of this type of study are Peterson 1986 and Bailey 1964.

20. This approach is explained in detail in Hermann, Hermann, and Hagan 1987.

21. This definition is drawn from Kaufmann 1980, 127–29, and Peterson 1986, 84–88.

22. Scholars have highlighted the fact that the environment of an international organization can also influence its internal processes and performance, see Cox and Jacobson 1973 and Ness and Brechin 1988. These authors assume that the influence of the environment can be isolated from the other factors they consider; however, this study argues that the environment can only influence the consensus building process through one of the five factors included in the framework. Therefore, even though the environment is not explicitly mentioned, the framework is designed to take account of its influence.

23. This is true because some of the factors, such as ad hoc negotiating groups, are only going to be relevant when some of the earlier factors are not present.

24. See Hermann, Hermann, and Hagan 1987.

25. Authors who discuss the range of participants in the political processes of the UN include Kaufmann 1980 and 1988, Jacobson 1984, Cox and Jacobson 1973, Bailey 1964, and Peterson 1986.

26. Due to pressures on the Plenary, most draft resolutions are handled in these committees, see Nicholas 1975, 111 and Alger 1967, 51. And since each one has its own character and lines of conflict, their political dynamics vary, see Kaufmann 1980, 32–40, Peterson 1986, 272–76, and Bailey 1964, 104.

27. For an example of the public choice literature see Frey 1984, 214–22 and for the cartel literature see Spar 1994, 28–33 and 237–43.

28. Examples of flexible procedures include more abstract notions such as shared understandings that emerge over time and more concrete practices such as allowing time for informal consultations.

29. NGOs and the Secretariat have received the most attention in this respect. For NGOs see Alger 1995, Stanley Foundation 1994, Willetts 1996, and Weiss and Gordenker 1996. For the Secretariat see Alger 1965, 285, Kaufmann 1988, 78–99, and Peterson 1986, 214–17 and 279–83.

30. Interests can usually be identified from policy statements or inferred from the positions taken on certain issues. However, this can be problematic because actors may publicly assert that there interests are one thing when their true underlying motivation is something different and any one specific position on an issue has the potential to be consistent with more than one type of interest.

31. See Jacobson 1984, 103, Keohane 1967, 223, Alger 1967, 63, and Kaufmann 1980, 10–16.

32. This notion relates to the literature on consensual knowledge in organizations (E. Haas 1990) and in epistemic communities (P. Haas 1992). However, it has also been mentioned specifically in relation to the General Assembly, see Alger 1989, 3–4 and Kaufmann 1988, 57–67.

33. Arguments supporting this "common sense" in the case of the General Assembly can be found in Alger 1989, 3–4 and Kaufmann 1988, 57–67.

34. Discussions of this can be found in Alger 1989, 3–4 and Kaufmann 1988, 31–33, 52–54, and 69–73.

35. These roles are discussed in Kaufmann 1988, 100–13 and Cox and Jacobson 1973, 397–99.

36. Scholars who have addressed the importance of leadership by the presiding officer include Alger 1967, 52, Kaufmann 1980, 138–39, Peterson 1986, 279–83, Bailey 1964, 111, and Nicholas 1975, 114.

37. Discussions of the role of personal attributes can be found in Keohane 1969a, 883, Cox and Jacobson 1973, 20, Nicholas 1975, 106, Alger 1967, 75–77 and 1989, 3–4, and Kaufmann 1988, 133–46.

38. Bailey 1964, 111, Alger 1989, 3–4, and Kaufmann 1988, 69–73 discuss these dynamics.

39. For support of this see Keohane 1969a, 883, Alger 1967, 75–77, and Kaufmann 1988, 69–73.

40. This is true because the formal procedures help to determine how much influence each member will have on the decision, see Cox and Jacobson 1973, 7, Peterson 1986, 53–54, and Keohane 1967, 233.

41. Majority rule requires less support so decisions made in this manner can usually include unambiguous language. On the other hand, consensus requires the support, or at least acquiescence, of all members thereby encouraging compromise. This gives rise to the paradox that majority decisions appear strong but often remain inoperable whereas consensus decisions seem vague but may be more likely to appear in the policies of member states.

42. See the citations in footnote eight. In addition, evidence of this was also found in a cursory survey of voting records on all resolutions and decisions over the past seven years (data found in Annual Review of United Nations Affairs, published annually by Oceana Publications).

43. For information on the attributes of blocs see Moskowitz 1980, 12, Peterson 1986, 294–96, and Kaufmann 1980, 87–100 and 1988, 146–59; for large states see Keohane 1967, 222–23 and Riggs and Plano 1994, 65–68; for small states see Kaufmann 1980, 17–18; for secretariat officials see Kaufmann 1988, 100–13, Cox and Jacobson 1973, 397–99, and Peterson 1986, 214–17; and for NGOs see Peterson 1986, 227–38, Kaufmann 1980, 32, Stanley Foundation 1994, Alger 1995, and Willetts 1996.

44. An extensive discussion of this is Jacobson's notion of the representative and participant subsystems (1984, 100–03 and 110–14), but authors such as Nicholas 1975, 136–37, have also mentioned it.

45. See Kaufmann 1980, 111, and 1988, 170, and Peterson 1986, 285.

46. While this notion of autonomy has most often been applied to state delegates, it can be extended to other actors that participate in the Assembly. The rule of thumb would be that large or interested IGOs or NGOs would provide the most detailed instructions whereas those that are smaller or less interested would allow for a greater degree of autonomy.

47. See Kaufmann 1980, 17–18 for a discussion of why these actors fill this role effectively.

48. This is similar to Putnam's notion of a two-level game (1988); however, Putnam argues that the smaller the autonomy of a negotiator, the greater their leverage at the international level because it forces others to move toward their position. Proposition ten is based on a different logic, and is supported by the cartel literature, see Spar 1994, 16–17, 219–29, and 243–55.

49. Examples include deferring the issue to another body, selecting a different voting rule, introducing alternate proposals, and delaying a vote by adjourning the

meeting. See Kaufmann 1980, 120–23, 130–37 and 1988, 16–17 and Peterson 1986, 32–33, 60–61, and 71–79.

50. Many of these traditional means of leverage are related to procedures as well; however, the difference between the two is that the second type also depends on the actual substance of the specific proposals under consideration, see Keohane 1967, 222 and Kaufmann 1980, 112–13 and 1980, 160–70.

51. See Alger 1972, 462, Peterson 1986, 10 and 91–113, and Kaufmann 1988, 3.

52. This is discussed in Alger's 1989 article on the 1963 Special Session of the General Assembly.

53. See Jonsson 1986 for detailed discussions of both of these concepts.

54. While the work of these groups is complex and difficult, states are often eager to serve on them because it can give them the opportunity to have a significant influence on a decision, see Alger 1989, 3–4 and 21–29, Peterson 1986, 272, and Kaufmann 1980, 16–17.

55. In the short-term this allows participants to plan strategies and exchange ideas; in the long-term it allow them to form a network of friends with whom they have good working relationships, see Alger 1961, 135–36, and 1966, 147; Kaufmann 1980, 116–17, and 1988, 173–74; and Peterson 1986, 211–16.

56. See Alger 1989, 21–29, Kaufmann 1980, 16–17, and Jonsson 1986, 41–42.

57. The issue was placed on the agenda in November of 1979 in response to a member state letter, see A/34/246. Several draft resolutions were debated over the following thirteen months, see A/34/L.57, A/34/L.57/Add.1, A/34/L.63, A/34/L.63/Add.1, A/35/L.34, A/35/L.34/Rev.1, and A/35/L.34/Rev.2*.

58. Muller 1992 provides background information and UN documents regarding these reform efforts.

59. This is reflected in the annual reports of the Special Committee, see A/44/33, A/46/33, A/48/33, A/49/33, and A/RES/50/52.

60. For example, see S/PV.3611, S/1994/1313, S/PRST/1994/62, S/1994/1238, S/1994/1237, S/1994/1231, S/1994/1221, and S/PRST/1994/22.

61. For instance, see the following verbatim transcripts of Assembly meetings: A/51/PV.11, A/50/PV.60, A/50/PV.58, A/50/PV.57, A/49/PV.49, A/49/PV.31, A/49/PV.30, A/49/PV.29, A/47/PV.106, and A/47/PV.21. Also, see the following UN Press Releases: GA/8963, GA/8966, GA/8967, GA/8968, GA/8969, GA/9098, GA/ 9101, GA/9102, GA/9108, GA/9121, GA/9123, GA/9129, GA/9144, GA/9145, GA/9146, GA/9147, GA/9151, GA/9175, and GA/ 9207.

62. Basic information on this working group can be found in two background papers prepared for the 49th Annual DPI/NGO Conference held in New York from September 10 to 12, 1996. These can be found at the conference's web page at www.un.org/moreinfo/ngolink/conferen.htm.

63. Examples of reform proposals from NGOs include the Commission on Global Governance 1995, The Independent Working Group on the Future of the United Nations 1995, the Stanley Foundation 1996, and the Global Policy Forum (several reports on their web page at www.globalpolicy.org).

64. This frustration has been most clearly articulated by the Global Policy Forum, see the Information Statement on the NGO Working Group on the Security Council posted on their web page.

65. The Global Policy Forum web page offers two examples: a Conference on Security Council Reform cosponsored by GPF and the Network on Global Governance

held on May 23, 1994 and the NGO Working Group on the Security Council which was set up in early 1995 and includes over eighty NGOs. These meetings have provided NGOs with the opportunity to interact with more than fifteen state delegates.

66. See the following comments by three recent Assembly Presidents: Ambassador Samuel Insanally's speech to GPF's Conference on Security Council Reform on May 23, 1994, Ambassador Diogo Freitas do Amaral's press conference on December 21, 1995 (UN Press Release GA/9043), and Ambassador Razali Ismail's speech to the Assembly on September 17, 1996 (UN Press Release GA/9091).

67. See Boutros Boutros-Ghali's speech to the Mexican Foreign Ministry on March 4, 1996 (UN Press Release SG/SM/5906), his speech in Korea on April 1, 1996 (UN Press Release SG/SM/5944), Kofi Annan's speech to the National Press Club on January 24, 1997 (UN Press Release SG/SM/6149), and his press conference on February 13, 1997 (UN Press Release SG/SM/6156).

68. These blocs include the Non-Aligned Movement, the Group of 77, the British Commonwealth, the South Pacific Forum, the Organization for African Unity, the Rio Group, and the Ibero-American Group. The lack of agreement regarding specific proposals in these groups is represented by the fact that many of their statements contain vague language, see A/51/473, A/51/471, A/50/758, A/50/752, A/50/702, A/50/475, A/49/920, A/49/532, A/49/479, A/49/422, A/49/287, A/48/484, and A/48/291.

69. Over one hundred members responded to the Secretary-General's original call for written comments on this issue, see Russett, O'Neill, and Sutterlin 1996, 65 and A/48/264.

70. Since meetings of the Working Group are closed, there is little direct evidence in support of this conclusion. However, the basic description of the Working Group provided at the 49th Annual DPI/NGO Conference web page, the number of working papers circulated by members states in the Working Group, and the nature of member state proposals in the Working Group suggest that the procedures of that body are more open and flexible than those found elsewhere in the UN System.

71. These efforts have been centered in the NGO Working Group on Security Council Reform. Information on its meetings and policy papers can be found at the Global Policy Forum web page.

72. NAM's preference for eleven new nonpermanent seats was stated by Mr. S. Thanarajasingam, Deputy Permanent Representative of Malaysia, at a meeting of the NGO Working Group on Security Council Reform on September 20, 1995. The inability of the EU to agree on a common proposal was stated by Ambassador Francesco Paolo Fulci, Permanent Representative of Italy, at a press conference on February 1, 1996 (UN Press Release DH/2072). The only exception is the Nordic Group, see table 2.2.

73. This is based on the fact that most statements by state delegates have focused on cluster one issues and that the agenda of the Working Group has thus far been dominated by these issues.

74. See Menon 1996 and 1997 and Russett, O'Neill, and Sutterlin 1996, 65.

75. These interests were compiled in March, 1997 from UN documents, articles, statements, and working papers. See A/48/264, A/49/965, Menon 1996 and 1997, Russett, O'Neill, and Sutterlin 1996, postings to UN Mission home pages (listed at www.undp.org/missions), postings to the GPF web page, and the records and press releases listed in the footnote regarding Plenary discussions of Council reform.

76. These are outlined in background papers found on the 49th DPI/NGO Conference web site.

77. Chairmen have included Samuel Insanally (Guyana), Amara Essy (Cote d'Ivoire), Diogo Freitas do Amaral (Portugal), and Razali Ismail (Malaysia). Vice Chairmen have included Wilhelm Breitenstein (Finland), Chew Tai Soo (Singapore), Nitya Pibulsonggram (Thailand), and Asda Jayanama (Thailand).

78. Their role has been highlighted by Jim Paul in a policy paper on Security Council reform posted to the Global Policy Forum web page in February 1995.

79. For instance, Razali Ismail had served as Malaysia's Permanent Representative to the United Nations for eight years before being selected President of the General Assembly in 1996.

80. Both of these arguments have already been presented a greater length earlier in the paper so they will not be repeated here.

81. There is increased speculation that if the current series of meetings in the Working Group does not result in a consensus-based reform package, Japan and Germany may use their financial muscle to force a majority rule decision in the Assembly regarding new permanent seats for them on the Council. It should be mentioned that until recently this sort of tactic seemed highly unlikely, but frustration continues to grow as the reform process drags on (see Jim Paul's March 7, 1997 posting on Security Council reform on Global Policy Forum's web page).

82. See Jim Paul's February 1995 policy paper on Council reform posted to the GPF web page.

83. Two examples of this include a joint statement by Austria, Belgium, the Czech Republic, Estonia, Hungary, Ireland, and Slovenia in A/49/965 on September 18, 1995 and a joint working paper by New Zealand and Argentina dated May 17, 1996 and presented to the Working Group on June 7, 1996 (posted to the Global Policy Forum web page).

84. This observation is based on a careful reading of Plenary debate and statements to the Working Group, but evidence of it can also be found in table 2.2.

85. Reference to the meetings can be found in Menon. 1997, 1.

86. Again, this observation is based on a careful reading of Plenary debate and statements to the Working Group, but evidence of it can also be found in table 2.2.

## REFERENCES

Alger, Chadwick F. 1995. "Citizens and the UN System in a Changing World," in Yoshikazu Sakamoto, ed,. *Global Transformation: Challenges to the State System.* Tokyo, Japan: UN University Press, 301–29.

———. 1989. "Negotiating a Consensus on Peacekeeping Finance: The United Nations Special General Assembly Session of 1963," in Johan Kaufmann, ed. *Effective Negotiation : Case Studies in Conference Diplomacy.* Dordrecht, The Netherlands: Martinus Nijhoff Publishers, 1–44.

———. 1972. "Decision Making in the United Nations." *Transnational Associations* 10: 460–64.

———. 1970. "Research on Research: A Decade of Quantitative and Field Research on International Organizations." *International Organization* 24(3): 414–50.

———. 1967. "Interaction in a Committee of the United Nations General Assembly," in J. David Singer, ed., *Quantitative International Politics: Insights and Evidence.* New York: The Free Press, 51–84.

———. 1966. "Interaction and Negotiation in a Committee of the United Nations General Assembly." *Peace Research Society: Papers* 5: 141–59. The Philadelphia Conference.

———. 1965. "Decision-making Theory and Human Conflict," in Elton B. McNeil, ed. *The Nature of Human Conflict.* Englewood Cliffs, N.J.: Prentice Hall, 274–92.

———. 1961. "Non-Resolution Consequences of the United Nations and Their Effect on International Conflict." *Journal of Conflict Resolution* 15: 128–45.

Archer, Clive. 1983. *International Organizations.* London: George Allen and Unwin.

Baehr, Peter R. and Leon Gordenker. 1994. *The United Nations in the 1990s.* New York: St. Martins Press.

Bailey, Sidney D. 1964. *The General Assembly of the United Nations: A Study of Procedure and Practice.* Westport, Ct.: Greenwood Press.

Claude, Inis L. 1971. *Swords into Ploughshares: The Problems and Progress of International Organization.* New York: Random House.

Commission on Global Governance. 1995. *Our Global Neighborhood.* London: Oxford University Press.

Cox, Robert W. and Harold K. Jacobson. 1973. *The Anatomy of Influence: Decision Making in International Organization.* New Haven, Ct.: Yale University Press.

Frey, Bruno S. 1984. "The Public Choice View of International Political Economy." *International Organization* 38(1): 199–223.

Gordenker, Leon and Paul R. Saunders. 1978. "Organisation Theory and International Organization," in Paul Taylor and A.J.R. Groom, eds. *International Organization: A Conceptual Approach.* London: Francis Pinter, 84–107.

Haas, Ernst. 1990. *When Knowledge is Power.* Berkeley: University of California Press.

———. 1958. *The Uniting of Europe: Political, Social, and Economic Forces, 1950–1957.* Stanford: Stanford University Press.

Haas, Peter M. 1992. "Introduction: Epistemic Communities and International Policy Coordination." *International Organization* 46: 1–35.

Hermann, Margaret G., Charles F. Hermann and Joe D. Hagan. 1987. "How Decision Units Shape Foreign Policy Behavior," in Charles F. Hermann, Charles W. Kegley Jr. and James N. Rosenau, eds. *New Directions in the Study of Foreign Policy.* London: Allen and Unwin, 306–36.

Independent Working Group on the Future of the United Nations. 1995. *The United Nations in Its Second Half-Century.* New York: Ford Foundation.

Jacobson, Harold K. 1984. *Networks of Interdependence: International Organization and the Global Political System.* New York: Alfred A Knopf.

Jonsson, Christer. 1986. "Interorganizational Theory and International Organization." *International Studies Quarterly* 30: 39–57.

Kaufmann, Johan. 1994. "The Evolving United Nations: Principles and Realities." *ACUNS Reports and Papers* 4. The John W. Holmes Memorial Lecture.

———. 1988. *Conference Diplomacy: An Introductory Analysis.* Dordrecht, The Netherlands: Martinus Nijhoff Publishers.

——. 1980. *United Nations Decision Making*. Rockville, Md.: Sijthoff and Noordhoff.

Kay, David A. 1969. "A Note on Robert O. Keohane's 'Institutionalization in the United Nations General Assembly' and Keohane's response." *International Organization* 23(4): 951–59.

Kennedy, Paul and Bruce Russett. 1995. "Reforming the United Nations." *Foreign Affairs* 74(5): 56–71.

Keohane, Robert O. 1969a. "Institutionalization in the General Assembly." *International Organization* 23(4): 859–96.

——. 1969b. "Who Cares about the General Assembly?" *International Organization* 23(1): 141–49.

——. 1967. "The Study of Political Influence in the General Assembly." *International Organization* 21(2): 221–37.

Keohane, Robert O. and Joseph S. Nye Jr. 1977. *Power and Interdependence: World Politics in Transition*. Boston, Mass.: Little Brown.

Kostakos, Georgios. 1995. "UN Reform: The Post-Cold War World Organization," in Dimitris Bourantonis and Jarrod Weiner, eds. *The United Nations in the New World Order: The World Organization at Fifty*. New York: St. Martins Press, 64–80.

Krasner, Stephen D. 1983. *International Regimes*. Ithaca, N.Y.: Cornell University Press.

Kratochwil, Friedrich and John Gerald Ruggie. 1986. "International Organization: The State of the Art on the Art of the State." *International Organization* 40: 753–76.

Marin-Bosch, Miguel. 1987. "How Nations Vote in the General Assembly of the United Nations." *International Organization* 451: 705–24.

Menon, Bhaskar. 1997. "Kofi Annan Takes a Cautious Approach to UN Reform." *The Interdependent* 22(4): 1 and 6.

——. 1996. "UN Reform: A Work in Progress." *The Interdependent* 22(1): 1 and 8.

Mitrany, David. 1943. *A Working Peace System*. Printed in 1966 in Chicago by Quadrangle Books.

Moskowitz, Moses. 1980. *The Roots and Reaches of United Nations Actions and Decisions*. Rockville, Md: Sijthoff and Noordhoff.

Muller, Joachim W. 1992. *The Reform of the United Nations*. New York: Oceana Publications. Two volumes in the series "Annual Review of United Nations Affairs."

Narasimhan, C. V. 1988. *The United Nations: An Inside View*. New Delhi, India: Vikas Publishing House.

Ness, Gayl D. and Steven R. Brechin. 1988. "Bridging the Gap: International Organizations as Organizations." *International Organization* 42: 245–74.

Nicholas, H. G. 1975. *The United Nations as Political Institution*. London: Oxford University Press.

Nye, Joseph S., Jr. 1970. "Comparing Common Markets: A Revised Neo-Functionalist Model." *International Organization* 24(4): 796–835.

Nye, Joseph S., Jr. and Robert O. Keohane. 1971. "Transnational Relations and World Politics: An Introduction" and "A Conclusion." *International Organization* 25(3): 329–49 and 721–48.

Peterson, M. J. 1986. *The General Assembly in World Politics*. Boston, Mass.: Allen and Unwin.

Putnam, Robert D. 1988. "Diplomacy and Domestic Politics: The Logic of Two-Level Games." *International Organization* 42(3): 427–60.

Riggs, Robert E. and Jack C. Plano. 1994. *The United Nations: International Organization and World Politics*. Belmont, Calif.: Wadsworth Publishing Company.

Rochester, J. Martin. 1995. "The United Nations in a New World Order: Reviving the Theory and Practice of International Organization," in Charles W. Kegley, ed., *Controversies in International Relations Theory: Realism and the Neoliberal Challenge*. New York: St. Martins Press, 199–221.

———. 1986. "The Rise and Fall of International Organization as a Field of Study." *International Organization* 40: 777–814.

Rosenau, James N. 1992. *The United Nations in a Turbulent World*. Boulder, Colo.: Lynne Rienner.

Russett, Bruce, Barry O'Neill and James Sutterlin. 1996. "Breaking the Security Council Restructuring Logjam." *Global Governance* 2(1): 65–80.

Spar, Debora L. 1994. *The Cooperative Edge: The Internal Politics of International Cartels*. Ithaca, N.Y.: Cornell University Press.

Stanley Foundation. 1996. *The United Nations and the Twenty-First Century: The Imperative for Change*. Report of the 31st United Nations of the Next Decade Conference held in Gleneden Beach, Oregon.

———. 1994. *The UN System and NGOs: New Relationships for a New Era?* Report of the 25th United Nations Issues Conference held in Muscatine, Iowa.

Weiss, Thomas G., David P. Forsythe and Roger A. Coate. 1994. *The United Nations and Changing World Politics*. Boulder, Colo.: Westview Press.

Weiss, Thomas G. and Leon Gordenker. 1996. *NGOs, the UN, and Global Governance*. Boulder, Colo.: Lynne Rienner Publishers.

Willetts, Peter. 1996. *"The Conscience of the World:" The Influence of Non-Governmental Organizations in the UN System*. London: Hurst and Company.

# 3

# UN Rapid Deployment Capability: Exploring an Instrument of Conflict Prevention

*H. Peter Langille*

> The planning of peacekeeping operations is the ultimate challenge because you never know where you have to operate; you never know what they want you to do; you don't have the mandate in advance; you don't have forces; you don't have transport; and you don't have money. . . We always have to start from zero. Each and every operation that we start, we start with nothing.
>
> —Major-General Frank van Kappen,
> Military Advisor to the Secretary-General, March 1997[1]

Frequent delays, human suffering and death, diminished credibility, opportunities lost, escalating costs – just some of the tragic consequences of slow and inappropriate responses. Unprecedented demand for prompt UN assistance has highlighted the deficiencies of existing arrangements, challenging the Organization, as well as member states. While it is widely acknowledged that the UN has been denied sufficient resources, neither has it had the appropriate mechanisms with which to respond. Fortunately, modest progress is now evident on an array of complementary reforms. As to be expected, there are limitations and other potentially viable options, but few easy or immediate remedies.

International efforts to enhance UN rapid deployment capabilities have focused primarily on improving peacekeeping. The larger process involves measures to organize the contributions of member states, as well as the establishment of basic mechanisms within the UN's Department of Peacekeeping Operations (DPKO). Several initiatives are quite promising.

Approximately twenty-seven member states, designated "Friends of Rapid Deployment," are cooperating with the DPKO to develop a rapidly deployable mission headquarters (RDMHQ). As well, since 1994 a DPKO team has organized the UN Stand-by Arrangement System (UNSAS) to expand the quality and quantity of resources that member states might provide. To complement this arrangement, the Danish government, in cooperation with seven regular troop contributors, has pledged to organize a multinational Stand-by High Readiness brigade (SHIRBRIG).[2]

SHIRBRIG will likely improve the tactical foundation by promoting further cooperation in multilateral planning, establishing training and readiness standards, and furthering the pursuit of inter-operability. By year's end, the void at the operational level within the Secretariat should be partially filled by a permanent, albeit skeletal, UN rapid deployment mission headquarters. At the strategic level, the Security Council has agreed to provide further consultation with troop contributors.[3]

Thus, as the tactical, operational, and strategic foundation is strengthened, participants look for a corresponding response at the political level. Hopefully, these arrangements will combine to inspire a higher degree of confidence and commitment among member states. In short, these various "building blocks" are gradually forming the institutional foundation for future peacekeeping. Initially, they are likely to circumscribe activity to Chapter VI, albeit, within a flexible interpretation of 'wider' peacekeeping.[4]

The efforts of the UN Secretariat, the 'Friends' and member states such as Denmark, Canada, and the Netherlands have been laudable, and deserve support. There remain a number of issues, however, that warrant further effort and scrutiny. This paper is a preliminary exploration of several of the initiatives being developed for the creation of a UN rapid deployment capability. It provides an overview of recent proposals, considers the progress within DPKO and the related efforts of Friends of Rapid Deployment, and identifies the potential limitations of the new arrangements. Finally, a cumulative development process is proposed as a means to expand on this foundation.

How are we to assess such initiatives? Within the Secretariat, one focus is on reducing response times.[5] Other considerations must address whether these measures, when combined, contribute to:

1. Providing a widely valued service.
2. Increasing confidence in the UN's capacity to plan, manage, deploy, and support at short notice.
3. Alleviating the primary worries of potential troop contributors.
4. Generating a supportive political will and adequate financing.
5. Encouraging broad participation.
6. Ensuring sufficient multidimensional and multifunctional elements for modern conflict prevention and management.

7. Enhancing the training, preparation, and overall competence of potential participants.
8. Instilling a unity of purpose and effort among the various participants.[6]

We must also ask whether the measures under way are sufficient to build an effective and reliable UN capability. Viewed over the short, mid, and long term, the question also arises as to whether these initial efforts are likely to build a solid foundation with the capacity for modernization and expansion. Alternatively, is there a risk of being locked into another *ad hoc*, conditional system requiring last-minute political approval and improvisation prior to each mission?

If UN rapid deployment capabilities are to contribute to the shift from reactive conflict management to preventive action, further supportive measures are critical. Both member states and the UN Secretariat are likely to need powerful encouragement to engage in a long-term development process, but such a process may offer the best prospect of institutionalizing and consolidating a reliable and effective UN capability.


## BACKGROUND

Since the release in 1992 of former Secretary-General Boutros-Ghali's *Agenda for Peace*, there has been a wide-ranging discussion of the UN's options for responding to violent conflict.[7] Among the various catalysts for the debate were the Secretary-General's call for peace enforcement units and Article 43-type arrangements, as well as Sir Brian Urquhart's efforts to revive Trygvie Lie's proposal for a UN Legion.[8] As these ideas began to attract a constituency, they also generated apprehension and a search for less ambitious options in many national capitals.

Opinion on the subject of any UN capability is always mixed. The debate here tended to follow two perspectives: the "practitioners" who favored strengthening current arrangements, and the "visionaries" who desired a dedicated UN standing force or standing emergency capability.[9] With notable exceptions, the official preference focused on pragmatic, incremental reform that could be accomplished within the structure of the UN Secretariat and available resources.[10] The latter was also assumed to entail fewer risks, fewer obligations and more control.

In the early years of the decade there were promising indications of support for some form of UN rapid reaction force.[11] The need for a new instrument was widely recognized in the aftermath of Bosnia, Somalia and the failure to avert the Rwandan genocide. But few governments were willing to back their rhetoric with meaningful reform. Prior commitments tended to be followed by carefully nuanced retractions.[12] There were exceptions, notably among middle-power, regular UN troop contributors.

## NATIONAL STUDIES

Prior to the fiftieth anniversary of the United Nations, the Netherlands, Canada, and Denmark commenced studies and consultative processes to develop options for a UN rapid reaction capability. These studies were followed by concerted diplomatic efforts to organize a wider coalition of member states and secure the cooperation of the UN Secretariat. These initiatives were instrumental, first, in narrowing the range of short-term options—allaying fears of a potentially large and expensive supra-national intervention force—and second, in informing others as to how they might best contribute to the process.

### The Netherlands Study

In 1994, the Netherlands began to explore the possibility of creating a permanent, rapidly deployable brigade at the service of the United Nations Security Council. A team of experts conducted the study, and an international conference was convened to review their initial report. They then released The Netherlands Non-Paper, "A UN Rapid Deployment Brigade: A Preliminary Study," which identified a critical void in the UN peacekeeping system. If a crisis were not to escalate into widespread violence, they argued, it could only be met by dedicated units that were instantly deployable: "the sooner an international 'fire brigade' can turn out, the better the chance that the situation can be contained."[13]

The focus, the Dutch stressed, should not be on the further development of the UN Standby Arrangements System[14] so much as a military force along the lines advocated by Robert Johansen[15] and Brian Urquhart[16]—a permanent, rapidly deployable brigade that would guarantee the immediate availability of troops when they were urgently needed. The brigade would complement existing components in the field of peacekeeping and crisis management. Its chief value would be as a stopgap measure when a crisis was imminent,[17] and its deployments would be of strictly limited duration. The brigade's tasks would include preventive action, peacekeeping during the interval between a Security Council decision and the arrival of an international peacekeeping force, and deployment in emergency humanitarian situations.[18] The annual cost of a 5,000-person brigade was projected at approximately US $300 million, the initial procurement of its equipment at $500 to $550 million.[19] "Adoption" of the brigade by one or more member states or by an existing organization such as NATO was recommended as a means of reducing the expenses of basing, transportation, and equipment acquisition.[20]

The nonpaper succeeded in stimulating an international exchange of views. It was clear, however, that only a less binding, less ambitious arrangement would be acceptable, at least for the immediate future. A minority of member states were supportive of the Dutch initiative, but by far the majority were opposed to any standing UN force, and even the modest expenditures outlined.

## The Canadian Study

In September 1995, the Government of Canada presented the UN with a study entitled, *Towards a Rapid Reaction Capability for the United Nations*,[21] with twenty-one recommendations to close the UN's capability gap in the short to mid term.[22] The report also offered five recommendations to stimulate further research and development over the long term.[23]

After establishing the need for a rapid reaction capability,[24] the report examined a number of principles such as reliability, quality, and cost-effectiveness[25] before identifying the primary components of such forces in France, the United States, and NATO.[26] Among the elements deemed necessary were an early warning mechanism, an effective decision-making process, reliable transportation and infrastructure, logistical support, sufficient finances, and well-trained and equipped personnel. The UN system was then evaluated with respect to these requirements.[27]

A range of problems spanning the political,[28] strategic,[29] operational, and tactical levels were identified and addressed. The intent was to "create an integrated model for rapid reaction from decision making at the highest level to the deployment of tactical levels in the field."[30] The report made a case for building on existing arrangements to improve the broader range of peacekeeping activities.

At the operational level, however, the UN suffered a dearth of related capabilities. Several new mechanisms were imperative, including a permanent operational-level rapid reaction headquarters.[31] This multinational group of thirty to fifty personnel, augmented in times of crisis, would conduct contingency planning and rapid deployment as authorized by the Security Council. The headquarters would have a civil affairs branch and links to related agencies and nongovernmental and regional organizations.[32] Aside from liaison and planning, it was to be tasked to a wide variety of training objectives.

The vanguard concept was highlighted as "the most crucial innovation in the UN's peace support operations over the next few years."[33] It would "link the operational level headquarters with tactical elements provided by Member States to the Secretary-General through the standby arrangements system."[34] It entailed identifying national vanguard component groups that might be called upon as needed by the operational-level headquarters.[35] These forces would remain in their home countries under the command of national authorities until they were notified by the Secretary-General and authorized to deploy by their own national government.

The Canadian study reaffirmed "broad support for the general directions of the Secretary-General and the UN Secretariat in building its peace operations capability for the future."[36] Recommendations were also developed to appeal to a broad range of supportive member states. This would be an inclusive, cooperative building process with the objective of developing a unity of both purpose and effort. Charter reform would be unnecessary, nor would there be additional expenses for the organization. In many respects, it was a compelling case for pragmatic, realizable change within the short to medium term. "Clearly, " the report cautioned, "the first step is to implement these ideas before embarking upon more far-reaching schemes which may in the end prove unnecessary."[37]

## The Danish-Led Multinational Study

In January 1995, the Danish government announced that it would be approaching a number of nations for support in establishing a working group to develop a UN Stand-by Forces High Readiness Brigade (SHIRBRIG).[38] Thirteen member states with extensive experience in peacekeeping agreed to explore the option of a rapid deployment force within the framework of the UN's Stand-by Arrangement System.[39]

The guiding assumption of the study was that a number of countries could, "by forming an affiliation between appropriate contributions to the [UNSAS], make a pre-established, multinational UN Stand-by Forces High Readiness Brigade available to the United Nations, thus providing a rapid deployment capability for deployments of a limited duration."[40] It was noted that the brigade should be reserved solely for providing an effective presence at short notice, and solely for peacekeeping operations, including humanitarian tasks.[41] National units would be required on fifteen to thirty days' notice and be sustainable for 180 days.

Standardized training and operating procedures, familiar equipment, and joint exercises, it was felt, would speed up national decision-making processes in times of crisis, as would the fact that the operating conditions for troop contributors would be understood in advance. Moreover, with an agreed focus on being "first in" and "first out," participants would have some assurance of the limited duration of their deployment.

Agreement would still be required from individual participating nations. To address the concerns of countries that might have reservations over a particular operation, a relatively broad pool of participants would provide sufficient redundancy among units.[42] States could, therefore, abstain from an operation without jeopardizing the brigade's deployment.

As proposed, SHIRBRIG was to provide the United Nations with immediate access to a versatile force comprising a balance of peacekeeping capabilities, thus overcoming a primary impediment to rapid reaction. The proposal soon attracted a supportive constituency within the UN Secretariat and among regular troop contributors, including Canada and the Netherlands. The Canadian study, similarly, generated considerable enthusiasm among member states.[43] Owing to its comprehensive approach, the UN MILAD, Major-General Frank van Kappen, referred to the Canadian study as the "red wine that linked the other studies together."[44]

It is noteworthy that these three national studies were seen not as mutually exclusive but as compatible by their respective Foreign Ministers.[45] In 1995, UN Under Secretary-General for Peacekeeping, Ismail Kittani, categorized them under "(a) what the UN can do now, (b) what member states can do, and (c) what is still in the future."[46]

## CORRESPONDING DEVELOPMENTS

### Friends of Rapid Deployment

On the occasion of the United Nations' fiftieth anniversary, Canadian Foreign Minister André Ouellet and his counterpart from the Netherlands, Hans Van Mierlo, organized a ministerial meeting to generate political support for UN rapid deployment capabilities.[47] To promote the initiative, especially among the major powers, Canada and the Netherlands announced the creation of an informal group called the "Friends of Rapid Reaction," co-chaired by the Canadian and Dutch permanent representatives in New York. Although they used the Canadian study as a basis for discussions,[48] it was agreed that this would henceforth be a multinational effort. Indeed, by the fall of 1996, the group had expanded to include Argentina, Australia, Bangladesh, Brazil, Canada, Chile, Denmark, Egypt, Finland, Germany, Indonesia, Ireland, Jamaica, Japan, Jordan, Malaysia, The Netherlands, New Zealand, Nicaragua, Norway, Poland, Senegal, South Korea, Sweden, Ukraine, and Zambia. The Friends also succeeded in attracting the cooperation of the UN Secretariat, particularly officials in DPKO.

Initially, they concentrated on building support for an operational-level headquarters, expanding standby arrangements, and explaining the vanguard concept. As it became apparent that the Danish proposal included many of the objectives of the vanguard concept, and the technical details had already been researched and agreed upon through an extensive multinational study, interest in the vanguard concept was superseded by a wider interest in the SHIRBRIG model.

The Friends' efforts in 1996 continued to focus on improving the Stand-by Arrangements System, but they also began to assist DPKO in coordinating the implementation of a Rapidly Deployable Mission Headquarters. A number of technical working groups were established to refine plans and proposals to improve logistics, administration, financing, sustainability, and strategic lift. The emphasis for 1997 was initially to be on developing a mechanism to coordinate the activities of peacekeepers, UN police forces, NGOs, and other UN agencies, but the need to establish clear guidelines for logistics emerged as a more urgent priority.

Despite having secured a relatively broad base of support, it is apparent that the consultative process of the Friends could have been more thorough. Several representatives of the nonaligned movement, including a few of the larger troop-contributing member states, were annoyed at having been left 'out of the loop.' In October 1996, for example, Pakistani ambassador Ahmad Kamal said that he "supported the concept of a rapid deployment headquarters team but was concerned at the action of a self-appointed group of 'Friends of Rapid Reaction' operating without legitimacy, and having half-baked ideas developed without broad consultations with the countries most concerned."[49] In turn, the Friends' agenda would be temporarily delayed as some members of the nonaligned movement (NAM) challenged specific arrangements.

But efforts to develop a UN rapid deployment capability were not confined solely to the Friends. The United Nations Special Committee on Peacekeeping Operations meets each spring to consider the global situation and forwards recommendations to the General Assembly. In 1996 the committee was composed of thirty-six member states, with fifty-seven others attending as observers. Although the committee hardly represents a vanguard of new thinking on peacekeeping, it does provide an important consultative forum, and over the past two years rapid deployment has been featured prominently in their report, with strong endorsements of both the standby arrangements and the rapid deployment mission headquarters.[50] Concerns would subsequently arise over equitable regional representation in the RDMHQ and the wider use of gratis personnel within DPKO. Some were also reluctant to support the SHIRBRIG on the grounds that it appeared to be an exclusive coalition that had no authority to present its arrangement as a 'UN' brigade.[51]

### DPKO and the UN Secretariat

There have been numerous heartening changes within the UN Secretariat over the past six years.[52] In 1992, for example, the office responsible for peacekeeping was reorganized as the Department for Peace-Keeping Operations (DPKO) in order to locate and coordinate in one department the political, operational, logistics, civil police, de-mining, training, personnel, and administrative aspects of peacekeeping operations. A Situation Centre was established within the DPKO in May 1993, to maintain communications with the field and provide information to missions and troop contributors. At the same time, a Civilian Police Unit was developed in DPKO's Office of Planning and Support, assuming responsibility for all matters affecting civilian police in peacekeeping operations.

A Training Unit was established in DPKO in June 1993 to increase the availability of trained military and civilian personnel for timely deployment.[53] A Policy and Analysis Unit was formed to assist with coherent, long-term guidance. In 1994, the DPKO established the Mission Planning Service (MPS) for the detailed planning and coordination of complex operations.[54] To enhance analysis, evaluation, and institutional memory, the Lessons Learned Unit was instituted in early 1995. To improve logistics, especially at the beginning of an operation, the Field Administrative and Logistics Division was incorporated into DPKO. More recently, approval was given to utilize the Logistics Base at Brindisi, Italy, as a center for the management of peacekeeping assets. Despite very limited financial and personnel resources, DPKO is achieving a professional level of planning and coordination across a challenging spectrum of tasks.

The development of a rapid deployment mission headquarters and the expansion of the UN Standby Arrangement System are themselves part of a larger, ongoing process to improve the UN's capacity to manage increasingly complex operations. Rapid reaction was a prominent theme in the former Secretary-General's 1995 *Supplement to An Agenda for Peace.*[55] He cautioned that problems had become more serious with respect to the availability of troops and equipment. "In these circumstances," he wrote,

I have come to the conclusion that the United Nations does need to give serious thought to the idea of a rapid reaction force. Such a force would be the Security Council's strategic reserve for deployment when there was an emergency need for peacekeeping troops. It might comprise battalion-sized units from a number of member countries.[56]

In response, the President of the Security Council indicated that "all interested Member States were invited by the Council to present further reflections on United Nations peacekeeping operations, and in particular on ways and means to improve the capacity of the United Nations for rapid deployment."[57] The Security Council also narrowed the range of options, expressing its concern that the first priority in improving the capacity for rapid deployment should be the enhancement of existing standby arrangements.[58] In the near term, it appears that this will be the foundation on which much of the potential for rapid deployment will depend.

### United Nations Standby Arrangement System (UNSAS)

In 1993, Boutros Boutros-Ghali identified the need for a system of Standby Arrangements to secure the personnel and materials required for peacekeeping. This system was specifically intended to improve the capability for rapid deployment. The Standby Arrangements System (UNSAS) is based on conditional commitments from member states of resources that could be made available within agreed response times. The resources range from military units and individual civilian, military, and police personnel to specialized services and equipment.[59]

UNSAS serves several ends. First, it provides the United Nations with a precise understanding of the forces and capabilities a member state will have available at an agreed state of readiness. Second, it facilitates planning, training, and preparation for both participating member states and the UN. Third, it provides the UN not only with foreknowledge of a range of national assets but also a list of available options if a member or members refrain from participating in an operation.

In 1994, a Standby Arrangements Management Team was established within DPKO to identify UN requirements in peacekeeping operations, establish readiness standards, negotiate with potential participants, establish a database of resources, and assist in planning and procedures. Progress to date is encouraging.

By May of 1998, seventy-four member states had confirmed their willingness to provide standby resources, representing a total nearing 100,000 personnel (99,400) that could, in principle, be called on.[60] The majority of states also provided detailed information on their specific capabilities. Response times were registered according to declared national capabilities.[61] Resources were divided into four groups on the basis of their potential. The majority (58 percent) of the overall pool fall into the first two categories of (1) up to 30 days, and (2) between 30 and 60 days.[62] In other words, the UN has a conditional commitment of over 50,000 personnel on standby that are assumed to be capable of rapid deployment. While UNSAS cannot guarantee reliable response, UN planners now have the option of developing contingency and fallback strategies when they anticipate delays. In the words of one senior DPKO official, "this is now the maximum feasible option."

Some mission success has been partially attributed to UNSAS. As reported, the information available under the standby arrangements proved most helpful in the planning for and subsequent deployment to peacekeeping operations in Haiti, Angola, Guatemala, and the former Yugoslavia, in particular the successful United Nations Transitional Administration in Eastern Slavonia, Baranja, and Western Sirmium (UNTAES). More recently, the UNSAS helped officials coordinate the preventive deployment operation (MINURCA) for the Central African Republic. Favorable circumstances in this instance also facilitated a rapid deployment.[63]

The former Secretary-General wisely cautioned, however, that while national readiness is a necessary prerequisite, it does not in itself give the UN a capacity for rapid deployment.[64] Several problems remain to be resolved. Only half of those participating have a capacity to provide their own support functions. The Organization is still confronted with shortages in a number of critical areas, including headquarters support, logistics, communications, health services, engineering, civilian police and both air and sea transport.

## United Nations Rapidly Deployable Mission Headquarters (RDMHQ)

As a complement to the UN Standby Arrangement System, the Secretary-General decided to pursue the Canadian proposal to create a rapidly deployable mission headquarters (RDMHQ),[65] a multidimensional unit of military and civilian personnel tasked to assist deployment and manage the initial phases of a peacekeeping operation.[66] The RDMHQ is designed as an operational unit with a tactical planning function.

Owing to budgetary constraints, the RDMHQ is officially described as the "skeleton" of a mission headquarters. Once approved, eight individuals are to be assigned to the RDMHQ on a full-time basis, including its Chief of Staff and specialists in fields such as operations, logistics, engineering, and civilian police. They are to be based in New York. The UN has received approval for their deployment into a mission area without further authorization at the national level.

Aside from the eight full-time staff, twenty-four additional personnel will remain in their home countries until required for training or deployment. Twenty-nine personnel in the Secretariat are also to be double-tasked and assigned to the RDMHQ, but will continue with their regular assignments until needed.[67] This initial team of sixty-one personnel is to coordinate rapid deployment and manage an operational-level headquarters even in missions with the broadest mandates. Once deployed, the headquarters is to remain in a mission area for three to six months, pending the arrival of and transition to a normal headquarters. Major-General Frank Van Kappen has detailed the five primary tasks of the new RDMHQ:

1. Translating the concept of operations prepared by the mission planning service into tactical subplans.
2. Developing and implementing RDMHQ preparedness and training activities; providing advice to the Head of Mission for decision making and coordination purposes.
3. Establishing an administrative infrastructure for the mission.
4. Providing, during the early stages of the operation, essential liaison with the parties.
5. Working with incoming mission headquarters personnel to ensure that, as the operation grows to its full size and complexity, unity of effort to implement the Security Council mandate is maintained.[68]

The Friends group has stipulated that the RDMHQ will require the following capabilities:

1. It must be deployable at very short notice.
2. It should be able to deploy for up to six months.
3. It should provide initially the nucleus of a headquarters for a new PKO.

4. It must be integrated into DPKO as a core function in order to retain its inter-operability with UN headquarters in New York.
5. It must be capable of undertaking technical reconnaissance missions prior to deployment.
6. It must have undertaken operational deployment preparations prior to its commitment. This must include such things as the production of Standard Operating Procedures and the completion of pre-deployment training.[69]

Attempts to secure funding and wider political support for the RDMHQ's eight core positions were insufficient and repeatedly stymied. Several nations agreed to supply personnel, as well as a percentage of startup costs in a specific trust fund. However, gratis personnel raised concerns over equitable opportunity for personnel of developing nations and the trust funds did not attract sufficient money. Some officials remain confident the required resources will clear the committee approval process in the fall of 1998. While recruitment and staffing may be controversial, the RDMHQ should be operational by 1999.

## SHIRBRIG

The Standby Forces High Readiness Brigade should complement UNSAS with an integrated unit that has a projected response time of fifteen to thirty days. As proposed, SHIRBRIG is to consist of 4,000–5,000 troops, comprising a headquarters unit, infantry battalions, and reconnaissance units, as well as engineering and logistical support. The brigade is to be self-sustaining in deployments of up to six months' duration and capable of self-defense.[70]

On December 15, 1996, seven countries signed a letter of intent to cooperate in establishing and maintaining this high readiness brigade.[71] A steering committee and a permanent planning element is now in place.[72] SHIRBRIG is expected to be fully operational next year. The objective, and the basis for cooperation, is to provide the UN with a well-trained, cohesive multinational force to be deployed "in Chapter VI operations mandated by the Security Council and with the consent of the parties."[73] Participants would thus have a mutual understanding of their combined capabilities as well as their specific roles and requirements:

This would enhance the efficiency of a possible deployment and would enhance the safety of the troops when deployed. Common procedures and interoperability would be developed to allow for better operational planning, to insure common assessment of the operational requirements, optimize movement planning and reduce costs.[74]

SHIRBRIG offers a cost-efficient model that may be emulated elsewhere. As Danish officials informed the Friends Group, "the conceptual work done so far on the establishment of a multinational UN [SHIRBRIG] carries a relevance far beyond the group of nations participating in the present project. The concept could inspire other groups of nations to take a similar initiative."

Other nations have expressed support for the development of an African Crisis Response Initiative.[75] Among the first steps are to ensure an inclusive process that strengthens indigenous capabilities with training assistance, as well as Partnership agreements. Although the planned force is not ready to be listed as a resource within the UNSAS, further supportive coordination could eventually lead to its development as a SHIRBRIG.[76]

## SUCCESS IN THE SHORT TERM

In four years, efforts to develop a UN rapid deployment capability have initiated changes at the political, strategic, operational, and tactical levels. More countries are participating in UNSAS, a significant proportion at a high level of readiness. Within the year, the RDMHQ should provide the nucleus of an operational-level headquarters that can assist in the planning and establishment of operations worldwide. 'Partnership' agreements are being encouraged to help ensure wide regional representation and competence. Training is improving with the support of DPKO and national peacekeeping training centers. Participants have developed a better understanding of the various requirements, and many are increasingly confident of their ability to contribute. Improving the wider unity of effort and purpose is on the agenda of civilian and military elements, NGOs, agencies, the UN, and member states. Member states and their defense establishments have seen marked progress in the planning and execution of recent UN peace operations. DPKO is acquiring new respect for a high level of professionalism.

In hindsight, one could argue that there was a case to be made for developing this new UN capability in the context of prevailing practices, resources, and structures. Considering the impediments of limited political will, insufficient funding, and overworked personnel answerable to 185 bosses with divergent interests, the progress to date should not be underestimated. Moreover, it has been accomplished in the absence of powerful national champions, and most observers recognize that the larger UN system is not altogether amenable to rapid modernization. Some officials assume that the task is well under way, with 73 percent of the recommendations either accomplished or in the process of being implemented. As early as 1996 a Canadian briefing paper noted that, "between the Group of Friends and the initiative of the Secretariat, 19 of the 26 recommendations have been acted upon in the past nine months."[77] In the same year, Kofi Annan claimed that the lead-time of the UN's rapid deployment capabilities would be reduced by 50 percent during the next two years.[78]

Nevertheless, one might argue that these arrangements reflect the pursuit of agreement only slightly above the level of the lowest common denominator. The context placed a priority on modest short-to-mid term changes that could be promoted among diverse states without major controversy, major funding or major national contributions. Few can be heralded as visionary, courageous gestures that correspond to the wider human and global security challenges of the next millennium. Hans van Merlo, co-chair of the Friends of Rapid Deployment, acknowledged that progress has been modest; "that given the complexities, this is going to be an incremental process, but one where we cannot afford to let up."[79] Unfortunately, controversy and political opposition have now diminished the momentum of the 'Friends' and, to a lesser extent, the Secretariat. The 'Friends' have yet to decide whether they will reconvene. There are valid, shared concerns that ideas emanating from this group will be actively opposed. In response, some diplomats believe that the only remaining option is to leave rapid deployment to the UN Secretariat; that a restructuring from within may gradually occur on the basis of pragmatic evaluations and lessons learned. Clearly, the wider initiative has reached a political impasse. There is little indication that further initiatives, or even incremental steps, are being actively pursued. Yet the larger task is far from finished.

## POTENTIAL LIMITATIONS

If rapid reaction is a demanding concept, it is an even more difficult reality to achieve. The organization must be sure of each critical element in the process. Missing components and conditional agreements can only lead to delays. It may be wise, therefore, to temper our expectations by acknowledging some inherent problems.

Standby arrangements for nationally based units do not provide an assurance of their immediate availability. As the former Secretary-General acknowledged in 1995, "a considerable effort has been made to expand and refine standby arrangements, but these provide no guarantee that troops will be provided for a specific operation."[80] He noted further that "the value of the arrangement would of course depend on how far the Security Council could be sure that the force would actually be available in an emergency."[81] With respect to UNSAS, there are few, if any, certainties. The promptness with which national contingents are provided will depend on the discretion of participating member states, the risks perceived, and the level of interests at stake.[82]

Reliability will be a key determinant of rapid deployment. In the case of UNSAS, there is no assurance that the political will exists. Critics frequently point to the refusal of member states to provide adequate forces to avert the

1994 catastrophe in Rwanda. Not one of the nineteen governments that had undertaken to have troops on standby for UN peacekeeping agreed to contribute to the UNAMIR mission under these arrangements.[83] Proponents of UNSAS now have grounds to argue that the system has been expanded and improved, but commitment to the system will have to be far more comprehensive and binding if it is to succeed. The onus is now clearly on member states to demonstrate the viability of this system.

Once approved for deployment, standby units will have to stage independently and assemble in-theatre. For some, this will be their first experience working together, and it will likely occur under conditions of extreme stress. Some military establishments are reluctant to acknowledge the need for prior training of their personnel beyond a general combat capability. Thus, high standards of cohesiveness and interoperability will be difficult to assure in advance. Moreover, the UN will continue to be confronted with the complex task of coordinating lift capabilities for participating elements across the world. This, too, can only slow deployment. Logistics and sustainment arrangements are gradually improving, but the UN is still coming to grips with the challenge of supplying different national contingents with a wide range of equipment.

A UN RDMHQ of some sixty-one personnel could provide the necessary impetus for developing and coordinating headquarters arrangements, but there are legitimate doubts about its ability to fulfill its five primary tasks in any period of intense activity where it may face multiple operations. Even in its full composition, it is still only the shell of an operational mission headquarters. As presently constituted, it is best seen as a necessary improvisation, an arrangement that may need to be rapidly augmented.

Current plans entail a multidimensional RDMHQ of both civilian and military personnel. This is to be encouraged, as it has grown out of the requirement to address the diverse needs of people in desperate circumstances. SHIRBRIG, however, is a purely military force. While this may facilitate the brigade's initial organization, planners would be wise to expand its composition with civilians in both planning and deployable elements. For there are limitations to what military force alone can achieve. To secure respect, legitimacy, and consent (i.e., host nation approval) it is increasingly important, even in rapid deployment, to provide a broader range of incentives and services in the initial stages of a UN operation.

Another early concern was whether the Vanguard concept would lead to wider participation or to a two-tiered system of peacekeeping. All those participating in SHIRBRIG have been leading contributors to UN peacekeeping missions. They represent an élite capability. They are also predominantly Caucasian, wealthy, and from the North; the exception being Argentina which recently agreed to participate in the brigade. Wider representation may be necessary to achieve legitimacy.

In sum, while current efforts are definitely helpful, additional arrangements may be necessary to provide reliable and effective responses to increasingly complex conflicts.

## POSSIBLE ROLES

There are numerous potential tasks for a UN rapid deployment capability. Roles and responsibilities for specific missions will vary with Security Council mandates, of course, and much will depend on what is provided and on what terms. Expectations vary considerably over the priority of tasks that should be incorporated into planning.

Many officials propose that any rapid deployment capability should assume responsibility for the initial stages of a peacekeeping mission. Deployable elements will be the first in to establish security, headquarters, and services, and then the first out, to be replaced by regular peacekeeping contingents within four to six months. Such a capability is also seen as the preferred instrument for preventive deployment.[84] Moreover, as the effectiveness of any UN rapid deployment capability will diminish once a conflict has escalated to open warfare, there is a case to be made for restricting its early use to proactive and preventive measures. If it is to succeed in stemming imminent crises, an enduring emphasis will have to be accorded to flexibility and mobility. In 1995, Sir Brian Urquhart outlined the following range of potential roles:

1. To provide a UN presence in the crisis area immediately after the Security Council has decided it should be involved.
2. To prevent violence from escalating.
3. To assist, monitor, and otherwise facilitate a cease-fire.
4. To provide the emergency framework for UN efforts to resolve the conflict and commence negotiations.
5. To secure a base, communications, and airfield for a subsequent UN force.
6. To provide safe areas for persons and groups whose lives are threatened by the conflict;
7. To secure humanitarian relief operations.
8. To assess the situation and provide first-hand information for the Security Council so that an informed decision can be made on the utility and feasibility of further UN involvement.[85]

Urquhart expressed support for a new standing UN capability in which the "rules of engagement and for the use of force will be different from either peacekeeping or enforcement actions." Flexibility was a prerequisite: the force "will be trained in peacekeeping and problem-solving techniques but will also have the training, expertise and esprit de corps to pursue those tasks in difficult, and even violent circumstances."[86] Indeed, such a mechanism can be more easily justified if it can provide a cost-effective and timely response to an array of challenges.

The confusion emanating from discussions of what a rapid deployment capability is intended for stems partly from two distinct but complementary objectives.[87] Initial interest in developing a rapid-deployment capability was premised on the need to improve peacekeeping. But expectations were also raised at the prospect of a mechanism which would be capable of prompt, decisive responses to desperate situations; even those which necessitated humanitarian intervention and limited enforcement. In the near term, these latter hopes may not be fulfilled.

As we begin to understand the need for increasingly flexible options and a wider array of instruments, the range of choice appears to have narrowed. UNSAS stipulates that the resources will be used exclusively for peacekeeping.[88] Similarly, the RDMHQ and SHIRBRIG are also strictly for Chapter VI operations. While this may attract initial support, it may entail political and operational constraints. In cases involving extreme violations of human rights, including genocide, the UN may be unable to intervene rapidly if the situation demands a mandate beyond peacekeeping. Strict adherence to Chapter VI, could diminish the wider deterrent effect, as well as its capacity for dissuasion.

The prospects for preventive deployment in the critical early stages of a conflict may be impeded by delays in arranging the consent of various factions or agreement among contributors. The experience of the past decade suggests that even supportive member states are inclined to "wait and watch" as they assess the risks, the costs, and the conditions for participation. Incipient distant crises seldom present the images or the political pressure necessary to mobilize governments into preventive action.

This dilemma may be partially resolved with 'wider' peacekeeping. Over the past four years, it has become an increasingly sophisticated exercise combining positive incentives with coercive strategies. Kofi Annan has indicated that UN operations will continue to evolve and expand with two main tasks: first, suppressing violence with a credible coercive capacity, the purpose of which is to intimidate recalcitrants into cooperating; and second, assisting the parties toward reconciliation with the provision of rewards in the mission area, including what the military refers to as "civic action," as well as broader peace incentives.[89] Expanded multidimensional operations now entail some of the more robust tools associated with limited enforcement, as well as broader peace-building services. Security Council mandates for Chapter VI operations have acknowledged these wider requirements and DPKO has demonstrated its capacity to provide sound guidance and planning. An array of expanded tasks may be accommodated within Chapter VI, but these and others that require immediate preventive action will continue to challenge both the UN and its member states. Neither will be able to escape the need for more substantive resources, new mechanisms, and innovative practices.[90]

## A PROPOSAL TO EXPAND THE FOUNDATION[91]

The development of a reliable and effective UN capability will take time, vision, and a coherent, goal-oriented plan, one that is guided by a long-term sense of purpose and the prospect of contributing to a critical mechanism for conflict prevention and humanitarian assistance. As we look to the long term, it is evident that there will be a need for further measures that complement and build on the existing foundation. The prospect of immediately initiating some form of UN standing capability is remote, but an ongoing cumulative development process appears feasible. Several stages are envisaged in this development. As capabilities are consolidated at each stage, one can anticipate a parallel expansion in the scope and scale of potential activities. One assumes the UN will require a capability commensurate with the tasks it is likely to be assigned.

There are several cost-effective options that merit consideration by the United Nations, its member states, and interested parties. The following sequential proposals are intended to stimulate further discussion and analysis:

**Stage One**

Revitalize and expand the consultative process of all supportive parties with the following objectives:

1. SHIRBRIG.
2. Wider regional representation in initial brigade.
3. A concerted effort to promote establishment of similar arrangements in other regions.
4. Integration of civilian elements to ensure provision of necessary services.
5. Research into the financing, administration, basing, equipment, and lift arrangements necessary to ensure immediate responses from co-located, standing national SHIRBRIG units.

*UNSAS*

Given the promising foundation established, promote standby political commitments whether through a new and expanded Memoranda of Understanding or Article 43.

*UN Standing Capability*

Initiate a parallel inquiry into the option of dedicated UN volunteer elements with particular emphasis on administration, financing, recruitment, terms of service, remuneration, training, basing and command.

**Stage Two**

1. Establish a UN rapid deployment base, with consideration accorded to the use of redundant military bases to provide existing infrastructure for training and equipment stockpiling, as well as nearby access to air and sea lift for prompt staging.
2. Develop a permanent, operational-level headquarters at the UN base. Experienced officers, civilian experts, and qualified planners can be seconded to the base and co-assigned responsibility to expand the operational and tactical foundation for future efforts.
3. To manage a variety of complex tasks effectively, it is in the interests of all parties to shift from a skeletal RDMHQ within UNHQ, New York to a static, expanded operational-level headquarters at the UN base. It would also be prudent for cost-effectiveness, as well as for the obvious benefits from a military, doctrinal, and administrative perspective, to co-locate two field-deployable tactical (mission) headquarters at this base.

**Stage Three**

1. Assign the national elements of a SHIRBRIG group to the UN base for a one to two-year period of duty; the general reluctance to move quickly can be partially overcome by stationing these multinational elements in a sound operational and tactical structure. The response times of standing multinational elements should be considerably quicker than the projected fifteen- to thirty-day response from home-based national SHIRBRIG elements. Tactical units and civilians would still remain under national political control and operational command. Locating these elements under the operational control of the permanent headquarters would provide the opportunity to begin multinational training, exercises, lift, and logistics coordination. Standing co-located national units would enhance overall effectiveness, increase the prospect of timely national approval and faster responses.
2. Launch an ongoing process of doctrine development for the range of diverse elements likely to be required in future multidimensional operations. Emphasize the unity of purpose and effort necessary to coordinate and integrate the various elements into a cohesive team.
3. Identify five appropriately dispersed regional facilities to serve as UN bases for the preparation and deployment of other SHIRBRIG groups;

the potential of several multinational UN SHIRBRIG's would fill a void in the current system of conflict management. With forward-thinking leadership and success in initial trials, its capacity and mandate could be extended to conflict prevention of a more demanding nature.

**Stage Four**

1. Recruit and co-locate professional UN volunteers into distinct capability component groups of both the headquarters and field-deployable elements at the initial UN base. Gradually integrate volunteers into a dedicated UN Standing Emergency Capability of 5,000 personnel under one of the two field-deployable mission headquarters. Provide personnel with advance training and two complete, modern equipment kits (one for training and one pre-packed for immediate staging).
2. Ensure UN elements have a credible stand-alone strength for emergency deployments of approximately 3,250 civilian and military personnel. The integration of UN volunteers into this group should be viewed as a complementary and mutually reinforcing stage in the development of an increasingly effective UN rapid deployment capability. Its relatively small size would alleviate fears of a new supranational force. Moreover, the use of this relatively discrete UN emergency capability could only be authorized by the UN Security Council and directed by the UN Secretary-General or his special representative.

A standing emergency capability with dedicated UN volunteers might respond to a crisis within eighteen hours of a decision by the Security Council. Expanding the operational and tactical structure of this capability to include dedicated UN personnel would also expand the range of options at the political and strategic levels. As the Commission on Global Governance reported in 1995, "the very existence of an immediately available and effective UN Volunteer Force could be a deterrent in itself. It could also give important support for negotiation and the peaceful settlement of disputes."[92] The Report of the Independent Working Group on the Future of the United Nations expressed its preference for a standing UN Volunteer Force to enhance the UN's performance in both time and function.[93] The Carnegie Commission report acknowledged that "a standing force may well be necessary for effective prevention."[94] A Canadian discussion paper on the issue acknowledges that:

It would provide the UN with a small but totally reliable, well-trained and cohesive group for deployment by the Security Council in urgent situations. It would break one of the key log-jams in the current UN system, namely the insistence by troop contributing nations that they authorize the use of their national forces prior to each deployment. It would also simplify command and control arrangements in UN peace support operations, and put an end to conflicts between UN commanders and contingent commanders reporting to national authorities.[95]

The case for rapid deployment, early preventive action, and a dedicated UN standing capability is premised on the need not only to avert human suffering, but also to reduce the high costs of major peacekeeping and enforcement operations, not to mention the reconstruction of war-torn societies.[96] "A rapid response group," according to Sir Brian Urquhart, "should be seen as a vital investment for the future, and one which by its very nature, is designed to act at the point where action can be most effective, thus eliminating or reducing the necessity for later, larger, less effective, more costly options."[97]

Recurring costs of this composite capability proposal have been estimated at US \$253 million per annum. The startup costs might be reduced by acquiring a redundant military base capable of hosting 10,000 personnel. Ultimately, the UN will also require its own equipment if the deployable elements of a standing capability are to be interoperable. Standardization of equipment and vehicles would greatly reduce overall costs in terms of manpower and overhead. To acquire such equipment anticipates an expenditure of approximately US \$500 to \$600 million. Clearly, this new UN capability would not entail a significant financial burden if shared proportionally among 185 member states.[98]

A host of related issues will have to be addressed before any standing capability becomes a reality. Financing is one concern. Developing the organizational and operational capacity of the United Nations to the point where it has the confidence of member states is another. But these issues hardly preclude the need to design a compelling sequence of steps that will facilitate the transition to a viable, permanent UN capability. Making the case for a more robust force, Carl Kaysen and George Rathjens write:

> There could be great benefit in getting on with dealing with these other problems—regardless of the creation of a standing military force—but we do not believe that progress in the analysis of the case for a standing force, and possibly its recruitment and training should be delayed pending its resolution. We do concede the case for such a force will be much stronger to the extent one can assume substantial progress in these other areas.[99]

The Netherlands study demonstrated that many of the technical obstacles are surmountable. The Danish study did not rule out permanently assigning military units to the UN, but acknowledged that it was a long-term option.[100] And the Canadian study noted that, "no matter how difficult this goal now seems, it deserves continued study with a clear process for assessing its feasibility over the long term."[101]

One of the initial statements of the Canadian study also pointed to the process: "any plan to operate a standing force presupposes adjustments at the political, strategic and tactical levels, which in many cases must be put in place on an incremental basis, starting as soon as possible."[102] Many of these adjustments are now in place. Although no time frames were established, evidence suggests we are now in the mid-term of the process.

## CONCLUSION

As we enter the new millennium the UN will have a rudimentary rapid deployment capability for wider peacekeeping. The UN Secretariat and the Friends of Rapid Deployment have played a pivotal role in both prompting and implementing supportive changes. The majority of their short-to mid-term objectives have either been achieved or are being implemented: there are substantive increases in the quantity and quality of resources listed in the UN Standby Arrangement System; a UN rapid deployment mission headquarters will soon be available to assist in the critical start-up phase of new operations; and a multinational Standby High-Readiness brigade should be operational next year.

As Kofi Annan wrote, "the initiatives taken by these countries have been valuable both for what they have achieved in themselves and for the way in which they have refocused the debate among peacekeeping contributors at large." He went on to note: "in the context of that wider group, however, a number of further actions will need to be taken if we are to intervene more effectively in either a preventive or curative capacity."[103] Fortunately, both the UN and member states now have a base foundation on which to take further action.

There are cost-effective and more reliable options that merit serious consideration and action. Over the past four years, there have been noteworthy attempts to model the composition of viable UN standing forces.[104] Several of these studies have demonstrated that there are few, if any, insurmountable operational or tactical impediments. To date, however, little attention has been accorded to the question of how such a mechanism might be established.

Both pragmatists and visionaries recognize that the current political and financial context is not conducive to the immediate establishment of a UN standing force. Nor, in the recent period of unprecedented activity, has the Organization been prepared to manage additional, controversial capabilities. Yet rapid changes, and the wider challenges of interdependence, will gradually alter the prevailing context. The debate over UN standing capabilities may have temporarily subsided, but the idea and the vision are unlikely to fade—they are intimately twinned to the UN and hopes for global human security. In the words of Stephen Kinloch, "driven back, the idea will, as in the past, ineluctably re-emerge, Phoenix-like, at the most favourable opportunity."[105]

Rather than await the next favorable opportunity, or the next catastrophe, we can begin to consider how such models or dedicated UN standing elements might be gradually introduced as a complementary expansion on current arrangements.[106] In this respect, independent analysis will be necessary to generate the ideas that can move events.[107] Among the challenges that warrant consideration by the academic community are:

1. Generating a broader public and professional understanding of current UN rapid deployment initiatives and the various options available for enhancing these efforts.
2. Planning a coherent, evolutionary process for the further development of UN and multilateral efforts (i.e., developing a logical and supportive sequence of stages or "building blocks" to ensure a cumulative development process).
3. Identifying transition strategies to help foster and integrate professional volunteers into a dedicated UN standing capability.
4. Building the unity of effort and purpose necessary to coordinate national units, as well as standing UN volunteer civilian and military elements into a composite UN emergency capability that can respond to diverse challenges.

Modest progress has been made since William R. Frye made the case for a planned evolution in his seminal 1957 study, *A United Nations Peace Force*. We have yet to achieve Frye's objective, but it is worth recalling his words:

Establishment of a small, permanent peace force, or the machinery for one, could be the first step on the long road toward order and stability. Progress cannot be forced, but it can be helped to evolve. That which is radical one year can become conservative and accepted the next.[108]

## NOTES

This chapter is the revised update on a paper initially presented to the Annual Meeting of the International Studies Association, Toronto, March 1997. It expands on research undertaken while the author was a member of the Core Working Group of the Canadian Study to Enhance a United Nations Rapid Reaction Capability. I am indebted to this group, particularly to Major James Hammond (CF) and Carlton Hughes. A number of individuals in the UN Secretariat provided additional insight and information. Special thanks are extended to: Chris Coleman, First Officer, Policy Analysis, DPKO; Andrew Greene, Policy Analysis; Col. Cees van Egmond, Chief Mission Planning Service; Col. Kulikov, Deputy Director, Mission Planning; Col. Peter Leentjes, Chief Training Unit; Peter Dew, Office of Operations; Comm. Marik Jamke, Head

Standby Arrangements Management Unit; Col. Carlos Daniel Ravazzola, Standby arrangements Management Unit; LTC Bernard Saunders, RDMHQ Implementation Team; Frederick Schottler, Information Officer, DPI; Ambassador David Karsgaard, Permanent Representative of Canada to the United Nations; Ambassador Michel Duval, Permanent Representative of Canada to the United Nations; Gabriel Dueschner, First Officer, Mission of Canada to the United Nations; Paul Meyer, Director, IDC, DFAAIT, Canada; Col. Ernie Reumiller, Head Peacekeeping Section, IDC, DFAIT, Canada; Line Poulin, Desk Officer, IDC, DFAIT, Canada; LTC. In Sorenson, Military Advisor, Danish Mission to the United Nations; Major Claus Laws, Asst. MILAD, Danish Mission to the United Nations; LTC. Steve Moffat, Director Peacekeeping Policy, DND, Canada; Prof. Andy Knight, Bishops University; and Sir Brian Urquhart, former UN Under-Secretary-General. Unless otherwise indicated, the views expressed in this article, as well as any errors or omissions, are the author's.

1. Major General Franklin van Kappen, Military Advisor to the Secretary-General quoted in "Standby Arrangement System: Enhancing Rapid Deployment," *UN Chronicle* 1, 1997: 2 (www.un.org/Pubs/chronicle/1997/pl3ily97.htm)

2. On 15 December 1996, Austria, Canada, Denmark, The Netherlands, Norway, Poland, and Sweden signed a "letter of intent" concerning Cooperation of the Multinational United Nations Stand-by Forces High Readiness Brigade in Denmark. The Czech Republic, Finland, and Ireland were observers. Danish Ministry of Defence, "Status in the establishment of the Multinational UN Stand-by Forces High Readiness brigade (SHIRBRIG)", 19 December 1996, see www.undp.org/missions/denmark/policy/standby.htm.

3. As noted in a Canadian briefing paper, "the Security Council adopted a Presidential Statement that strengthens the consultations between the Council and troop contributor nations. The two key changes that enhance this process are: that consultations will be chaired by the Security Council Presidency alone rather than jointly with the UN Secretariat. This advance should allow for future meetings to focus on policy issues and political aspects of new or existing Security Council mandates. The UN Secretariat will continue to chair separate troop contributor meetings to discuss operational issues. The second change is that the Security Council, when considering peacekeeping operations, will now hold meetings with prospective troop contributors that have already been approached by the Secretariat." See Canada, DFAIT, "An Update on the Canadian Study, *Towards a Rapid Reaction Capability for the United Nations*," prepared by Daniel Livermore, Director of Regional Security and Peacekeeping, Summer 1996, 5.

4. The term 'wider peacekeeping' involves tasks beyond those associated with traditional peacekeeping. The term's origins stem from the [British] Directorate of Land Warfare, *Wider Peacekeeping*, Field Manual. It has come to be used synonymously with 'expanded' peacekeeping, 'next generation' peacekeeping and 'future' peacekeeping.

5. United Nations Security Council, "Progress Report of the Secretary-General on Standby Arrangements for Peacekeeping," S/1996/1067, 24 December 1996, 3.

6. A number of these criteria are drawn from the Government of Canada's report, *Towards a Rapid Reaction Capability*, Ottawa, September 1995. See, for example, chapter 2, "Principles of the Study," 8–16.

7. Boutros Boutros-Ghali, *An Agenda for Peace: Preventive Diplomacy, Peacemaking and Peace-keeping*, Report of the Secretary-General Pursuant to the State-

ment Adopted by the Summit Meeting of the Security Council on 31 January 1992, New York, 17 June 1992 (A/47/277-S/2411), paras. 42–44.

8. See Brian Urquhart, "For A U. N. Volunteer Military Force," *The New York Review of Books* XL(11) 10 June 1993: 3–4. For an early response to the Urquhart proposal, see Lord Richard Carver, "A UN Volunteer Military Force: Four Views," *The New York Review of Books* XL(12) 24 June 1993: 59.

9. For a more thorough overview of these diverse perspectives see, Stephen P. Kinloch, "Utopian or Pragmatic? A UN Permanent Military Volunteer Force," *International Peacekeeping* 3(4) Winter 1996: 166–90.

10. See, for example, the Canadian Department of National Defence, "Report on Consultations UN Rapid Reaction Capability Study," May 1995, Prepared by LTC Joe Culligan, DIPOL 3.

11. This was evident as early as Aug. 1992, when U.S. presidential candidate Bill Clinton expressed support for a voluntary UN rapid deployment force. In February 1993 U.S. Secretary of State Warren Christopher informed the UN Secretary-General that the United States would back proposals for a UN rapid deployment force. On various occasions, Russian statesmen endorsed UN standby forces, negotiation of Article 43 agreements, and even their readiness to commit forces to a UN army. In 1992 French President François Mitterand called for revitalizing the UN Military Staff Committee and offered to commit 1,000 French soldiers at its disposal on forty-eight hours' notice with another 1,000 ready for UN service within a week. See the section on "Presidential Support" and "International Support" in Capt. Edward I. Dennehy, LTC William J. Droll, Capt. Gregory P. Harker, LTC Stephen M. Speakes, and LTC Fred A. Treyz, III, "A Blue Helmet Combat Force," Policy Analysis Paper 93-01, National Security Program, Harvard University, 1993, 9–10.

12. A number of the early commitments of member states such as the United States and France were overlooked in their subsequent responses to the UN General Assembly and to the Secretary-General's *An Agenda for Peace*. See "Statement of France," 28 July 1993 in response to *An Agenda for Peace*, in "Improving the Capacity of the United Nations for Peacekeeping: Report of the Secretary-General— Addendum," UN doc. A/48/403/Add. l/Corr. l, November 2, 1993; and U.S. Presidential Decision Directive 25, or *The Clinton Administration's Policy on Reforming Multilateral Peace Operations* (Washington, D.C.: U.S. Department of State Publication 10161, May 1994); cited in Adam Roberts, "Proposals for UN Standing Forces: History, Tasks and Obstacles," in David Cox and Albert Legault, eds., *UN Rapid Reaction Capabilities: Requirements and Prospects*, (Cornwallis: The Canadian Peacekeeping Press, 1995), 1–15.

13. See The Netherlands Non-Paper, "A UN Rapid Deployment Brigade: A Preliminary Study," revised version, April 1995, 3.

14. The Netherlands Non-Paper, 4.

15. See Robert C. Johansen, "UN Peacekeeping: The Changing Utility of Military Force," *Third World Quarterly* 12 April 1990: 53–70.

16. Brian Urquhart, "For a UN Volunteer Military Force."

17. The Netherlands Non-Paper, 5.

18. The Netherlands Non-Paper, 8.

19. The Netherlands Non-Paper, 18.

20. The Netherlands Non-Paper, 14–15.

21. *Towards a Rapid Reaction Capability for the United Nations,* September 1995. The report was formally tabled on September 26, during the UN's fiftieth anniversary. The rationale for the study was outlined by Canada's Minister of Foreign Affairs, André Ouellet: "the experience of the last few years leads us to believe that we need to explore even more innovative options than those considered to date. Recent peace-keeping missions have shown that the traditional approach no longer applies. As we have seen in Rwanda, rapid deployment of intervention forces is essential. In light of the situation, the Government of Canada has decided to conduct an in-depth review of the short-, medium- and long-term options available to us to strengthen the UN's rapid response capability in times of crisis. Among these options, we feel the time has come to study the possibility, over the long term of creating a permanent UN military force. We will ask the world's leading experts for their input and will inform all member states of the results of the study." Notes for An Address by André Ouellet, Minister of Foreign Affairs, to the 49th General Assembly of the United Nations, New York, 29 September 1994, 7.

22. See chapter 5, "A Practical Agenda for Reform: The Short to Medium Term," 36–54.

23. See chapter 6, "A Vision of the Future: The Long-Term Prospects for Rapid Reaction," 55–65.

24. See chapter 1, "Why Rapid Reaction," 1-7.

25. See chapter 2, "Principles of the Study," 8–16.

26. See chapter 3, "The Record of Rapid Reaction: Recent Experience," 17–23.

27. See chapter 4, "Elements of Rapid Reaction: How the UN Shapes up," 25–35.

28. Among the proposals for reform at the political level were the establishment of a troop contributors' committee for each operation, a troop contributors' forum to consider general issues of an operational nature, and convening informal groups of "friends" to deal with related issues. Five recommendations pertained to improving various financial procedures. Notes for An Address by André Ouellet, 37–42.

29. At the strategic level, there were calls for refining the early-warning capabilities of the Secretariat and advancing cooperation with member states toward the development of an "early-warning alert" system. The report advised strengthening the Department of Peacekeeping Operations with additional staff, strengthening the office of the Military Advisor, initiating rosters of senior military commanders, developing standing contractual arrangements with suppliers, particularly with respect to the provision of strategic movement, and producing packages of equipment for generic missions. Both the Secretary-General and member states were urged to continue refining and strengthening the Standby Arrangements System established in 1993. The Secretary-General was encouraged to use new techniques such as the "peacekeeping services agreement" to facilitate more rapid deployment and efficient support services. Member states were asked to explore the advanced identification of personnel with expertise in relevant areas to assist the UN in responding to urgent situations. Notes for An Address by André Ouellet, 43–46.

30. Notes for An Address by André Ouellet, 54.

31. Notes for An Address by André Ouellet, 51.

32. As indicated in the report's title, a concern arose that the approach should be on enhancing a UN capability rather than simply a force. The increasing complexity of UN operations, as well as the requirement for a coordinated unity of effort also pointed to the need for both a multidimensional and a multifunctional capability.

33. The report noted that the Vanguard concept "is based on the principle of linking all of the levels of the UN system, especially an operational headquarters and mission groups provided by member states at the tactical level, for the purpose of deploying a force as rapidly as possible for a brief period, either to meet an immediate crisis or to anticipate the arrival of follow-on forces or a more traditionally organized peacekeeping operation,"52.

34. Notes for An Address by André Ouellet, 52.

35. Notes for An Address by André Ouellet, 52. "Both member states and the Secretary-General were encouraged to organize UN standby units into multinational-capability components," corresponding to function, with appropriate training and exercising to enhance readiness. "These capability components might include some of the newer tasks of multidimensional operations (natural disaster relief, humanitarian emergencies), working in close conjunction with other sectors of the UN and other nongovernmental organizations."

36. Notes for An Address by André Ouellet, 52.

37. Notes for An Address by André Ouellet, 55.

38. Chief of Defence, Denmark, "United Nations Stand-by Arrangements for Peacekeeping: A Multinational UN Stand-by Forces High Readiness Brigade," 25 January 1995. Denmark conducted four international seminars between May and August 1995. Participating nations were Argentina, Belgium, Canada, Czech Republic, Denmark, Finland, Ireland, Netherlands, New Zealand, Norway, Poland, and Sweden. The DPKO was also represented.

39. See Chief of Defence Denmark, "Report by the Working Group on a Multinational UN Stand-by Forces High Readiness Brigade," 15 August 1995.

40. Chief of Defence Denmark, "Report by the Working Group on a Multinational UN Stand-by Forces High Readiness Brigade," 9. It was noted that Allied nations with a tradition of peacekeeping were a natural choice when forming the core and setting the standards for a future brigade. Others would have to be encouraged to participate to secure impartiality.

41. "Report by the Working Group on a Multinational UN Stand-by Forces High Readiness Brigade," 10–11.

42. A nation's right to decide whether or not to participate on a case-by-case basis would thus be protected. It was assumed "this would be accomplished through the maintenance of a brigade pool of 'extra' units which would 'back up' those units which might not be made available due to national decision."

43. Canada, DND, "Report on Consultations UN Rapid Reaction Capability Study," May 1995, Prepared by LTC Joe Culligan, DIPOL 3.

44. Cited in the briefing summary of WKGR8708 — Friends of Rapid Reaction Meeting, 4 Dec. 1995 by Canadian MILAD, Col. Michael Snell.

45. See Lloyd Axworthy, Hans van Mierlo, and Niels Helveg Petersen, "Let's Team Up to Make UN Peacekeeping Work," *International Herald Tribune* 22 October 1996, at www.undp. org/missions/denmarktpolicy/article. htm.

46. Cited in the briefing summary of WKGR8708—Friends of Rapid Reaction Meeting, 4 December 1995, by Canadian MILAD, Col. Michael Snell.

47. Among the other participants at this meeting were ministers of Australia, Denmark, New Zealand, Senegal, Nicaragua, Ukraine, and Jamaica.

48. See Canada, DFAIT, "An Update on the Canadian Study, *Towards a Rapid Reaction Capability for the United Nations*," prepared by Daniel Livermore, Director of Regional Security and Peacekeeping, Summer 1996, 4.

49. Cited in "Daily Highlights," 25 October 1996, Central News Section, Department of Public Information, United Nations.

50. See United Nations General Assembly, Report of the Special Committee on Peacekeeping Operations, "Comprehensive Review of the Whole Question of Peace-Keeping Operations in all their Aspects," A/50/230, 22 June 1995, Section 3, 12, and A/51/130, 7 May 1996, Section 5, 13.

51. See, for example "Concern over High Readiness Brigade Expressed at Special Committee on Peacekeeping Operations," GA/PK/152, March 31, 1998.

52. For a brief review of the related changes in DPKO, see Kofi Annan, "The Peace-keeping Prescription," in Kevin M. Cahill, ed., *Preventive Diplomacy: Stopping Wars Before They Start* (New York: Basic Books, 1996), 185–86. For a more critical perspective, see Trevor Findley, "Armed Conflict Prevention, Management and Resolution," *SIPRI Yearbook, 1996: Armaments, Disarmament and International Security* (London: Oxford University Press, 1996), 53–60.

53. DPKO's Training Unit has guidelines, manuals, and other materials to assist member states in preparing military, civilian, and police personnel for UN assignments. The Training Unit has also helped improve and standardize peacekeeping training through seminars, workshops, and assistance teams.

54. The Mission Planning Service is the focal point for all peacekeeping planning. Its activities include guidelines and procedures to streamline mission planning, generic guidelines for troop-contributing countries (from which mission-specific guidelines are formulated), the preparation of standard operating procedures for essential functions, and in-house studies pertaining to issues such as command and control, rules of engagement, and structure of mission headquarters. See "General Framework, United Nations Peacekeeping," (www.un. org:80/depts/dpko/mp.htm)

55. Boutros Boutros-Ghali, *Supplement to An Agenda for Peace: Position Paper of the Secretary-General on the Occasion of the Fiftieth Anniversary of the United Nations*, A/50/60, S/1995/1, 3 Jan. 1995.

56. As the Secretary-General noted, "these units would be trained to the same standards, use the same operating procedures, be equipped with integrated communications equipment and take part in joint exercises at regular intervals. They would be stationed in their home countries but maintained at a high state of readiness." *Supplement to An Agenda for Peace*, 11, § 44.

57. See Statement by the President of the Security Council on 22 February 1995 (S/PRST/1995/9).

58. Statement by the President of the Security Council.

59. See United Nations, DPKO, "United Nations Standby Arrangements System Description." See also United Nations, Security Council, "Progress Report of the Secretary-General on Standby Arrangements for Peacekeeping" (S/1996/1067) 24 December 1996.

60. See "United Nations, Department of Peacekeeping Operations," "Monthly Status Report: United Nations Standby Arrangements," May 1, 1998, at www.un.org/ depts/dpko/rapid/str.htm.

61. As noted, response time is defined by the UN as the period between the time the formal request to provide resources is made and the time these resources are ready for airlift/sealift to the mission area.

62. "Annual Update Briefing to Member States on Standby Arrangements," May 29, 1997, 2.

63. These favorable circumstances with MINURCA were partially the result of early warning, sound planning, institutional familiarity, the smooth transition phase from the former Chapter VII operation, national support and French assistance with air lift.

64. Other determining factors include "political approval and support at the national level, availability of airlift/sealift, a capacity for mission management and logistic sustainment in the field, as well as the conclusion of the necessary administrative procedures."

65. Notably, the Special Committee on Peacekeeping Operations also urged the Secretary-General to develop a rapidly deployable headquarters team in their spring 1995 report. This request was subsequently endorsed by the General Assembly in Resolution 50/30 (1995). The proposal for such a headquarters was also at the forefront of the priorities of the Friends of Rapid Deployment. See "Rapid-Reaction Headquarters Possible by Fall: Canadian Led Proposal Calls for Small Group to Assess World Crises," *Ottawa Citizen*, 23 July 1996.

66. Major-General Frank Van Kappen, Military Advisor to the Secretary-General, "Presentation on the Rapidly Deployable Mission Headquarters (RDMHQ)" to the Special Committee on Peacekeeping Operations, 24 Oct. 1996. Also cited in "Peacekeeping Operations Committee –5," Press Release PK/144 140th Meeting, 24 Oct. 1996.

67. Van Kappen, "Presentation on the RDMHQ," 5–7.

68. Van Kappen, "Presentation on the RDMHQ," 4–5.

69. Friends of Rapid Deployment, Technical Working Group Paper, "A Rapidly Deployable Headquarters: Roles, Functions and Implementation," 26 Mar. 1996. As this paper noted, "this headquarters would be multinational, drawing its personnel widely from contributing member states of all regions. It would also be multidimensional, reflecting the requirements of the more complex operations of the 1990s, with a substantive civilian staff of diverse experience in the areas of civilian police, humanitarian assistance, human rights, and legal affairs. This headquarters would be a 'first-in, first-out' operation, moving into an area rapidly but capable of being removed equally quickly. It should be capable of directing at least 5,000 personnel, possibly more if it is augmented at the time of deployment. This staff, seconded or loaned by Member States to the UN Secretariat, could be deployed into a theatre of operations under the authority of the Security Council and at the direction of the Secretary-General but without further authorization at the national level."

70. Ministry of Foreign Affairs, Denmark, "Background Paper about Establishing a Multinational UN Standby Forces Brigade at High Readiness (SHIRBRIG)," Meeting of Foreign Affairs Ministers in the "Friends of Rapid Deployment" Group, New York, 26 September 1996, at www.undp.org/missions/denmark/policy/shirbrig. htm.

71. Austria, Canada, the Netherlands, Norway, Poland, Sweden, and Denmark signed the "Letter of Intent." The Czech Republic, Finland, and Ireland participated as observers. See "Status in the Establishment of the Multinational UN Standby Forces High Readiness Brigade," Danish Ministry of Defence, 19 December 1996. (www.undp.org/missions/denmark/policy/standby.htm)

72. An implementation group has been working on further details since March 1996. It has been agreed that a permanent planning element of approximately twenty

officers will be established in Denmark, at Hoevelte Barracks north of Copenhagen. The costs of establishing and running this group will be shared among participating nations.

73. Moreover, Danish officials write that when SHIRBRIG is deployed it will be "subject to UN command and control arrangements and operate exclusively under the direction of the Secretary-General or his Special Representative and under the operational control of the Force Commander for the operation." Ministry of Foreign Affairs, Denmark, "Background Paper about Establishing a Multinational UN Stand-by Forces Brigade at High Readiness (SHIRBRIG)," 1–2.

74. Ministry of Foreign Affairs, Denmark, "Background Paper about Establishing a Multinational UN SHIRBRIG," 2.

75. At present, this is a nascent regional arrangement based upon several sub-regional groups. Supportive financial and training assistance for diverse groups has been provided by France, the United States and Britain. As projected, the ACRI is to assume primary responsibility for conflicts on the continent. Arrangements have yet to be finalized between participating states, the Organisation of African Unity (OAU) and the United Nations.

76. It is noteworthy that in the Secretary-General's recent report on Africa, he urged "the establishment of an international mechanism to assist host Governments in maintaining the security and neutrality of refugee camps and settlements." As noted, "such a mechanism might encompass training, logistics, financial support, the provision of security personnel and the monitoring of national security arrange-ments." Report of the Secretary-General, "The causes of conflict and the promotion of durable peace and sustainable development in Africa," at www.un.org/ecosocdev/geninc/sgreport/report.htm#peacekeeping.

77. Canada, DFAIT, "An Update on the Canadian Study: Towards a Rapid Reaction Capability for the United Nations," Briefing Paper prepared by Daniel Livermore, Di-rector, IDC, Summer 1996, 4.

78. Cited in "Daily Highlights," 25 October 1996, Central News Section, Depart-ment of Public Information, United Nations.

79. Statement by Hans van Merlo, Deputy Prime Minister and Minister of Foreign Af-fairs of the Kingdom of the Netherlands, "The United Nations: Joining Forces," Septem-ber 23, 1997, 3, at www.undp.org/missions/netherlands/speeches/52ndga.htm#rapid.

80. Boutros Boutros-Ghali, *Supplement to an Agenda for Peace*, A/50/60, 3 Jan. 1995, 11, § 43.

81. Boutros-Ghali, *Supplement to an Agenda for Peace*, 11, § 44.

82. The former Secretary-General previously cautioned, "the system of standby arrangements does not so far ensure the reliability and speed of response which is re-quired in such emergencies. It is essential that the necessary capabilities are reliably available when they are needed and can be deployed with the speed dictated by the situations. It is evident that member states possess such capabilities; what is needed is the will to make them available for the execution of Security Council mandates." Cited in "Peace-keeping in a Changing Context"; see www.un.org.

83. Boutros Boutros-Ghali, *Supplement to An Agenda for Peace*, A/50/60, S/1995/1, 3 Jan. 1995, 18, § 43.

84. As Kofi Annan writes, "rapid response is vital particularly from a preventive perspective, because in cases like Rwanda, the conflict's worst effects are often felt in

its earliest stages. A rapid response is thus essential if we are effectively to limit the range, extent and momentum of a conflict." Kofi Annan, "The Peacekeeping Prescription," in Cahill, *Preventive Diplomacy*, 184.

85. Sir Brian Urquhart, "Prospects for a UN Rapid Response Capability," Address to the Twenty-Fifth Vienna Seminar on Peacemaking and Peace-keeping for the Next Century, Government of Austria and the International Peace Academy, Vienna, 3 Mar. 1995, 6.

86. Urquhart, "Prospects for a UN Rapid Response Capability," 7.

87. Confusion was compounded by the announcement that the Government of Canada would be conducting an in-depth study into the option of a UN Standing Force.

88. See "United Nations Standby Arrangements: System Description," 2.

89. Kofi A. Annan, "P. K. and Crisis Management: Where Are We Going?" Tokyo, 23 September 1996, 3–8.

90. Fortunately, the arrangements now being implemented are not a "done deal." They represent a promising start, yet they need not, and should not, be viewed as having achieved sufficient reliability or sophisticated capability.

91. This section draws on the previous work of Peter Langille, Maxime Faille, Carlton Hughes, and Major James Hammond, "A Preliminary Blueprint of Long-Term Options for Enhancing a UN Rapid Reaction Capability," in Cox and Legault, *UN Rapid Reaction Capabilities*, 179–200.

92. Report of the Commission on Global Governance, *Our Global Neighbourhood*, (New York: Oxford University Press, 1995), 112.

93. The Report of the Independent Working Group on the Future of the United Nations, *The United Nations In Its Second Half-Century*, a project supported by Yale University and the Ford Foundation, 1995, 21–23.

94. Carnegie Commission on Preventing Deadly Conflict, *Preventing Deadly Conflict: Final Report*, (Washington, D.C.: Carnegie Commission on Preventing Deadly Conflict, 1997), 66. It should be noted that this report did not endorse UN volunteers but proposed the establishment of rapid reaction force of 5,000–10,000 troops to be drawn from sitting members of the Security Council.

95. Canada, DFAIT, "Improving the UN's Rapid Reaction Capability: Discussion Paper," 29 April 1995, 3.

96. For a recent variation of this argument see, Lionell Rosenblatt and Larry Thompson, "The Door Of Opportunity: Creating a Permanent Peacekeeping Force," *World Policy Journal* Spring 1998: 36–42.

97. Brian Urquhart elaborates on this point: "experience of recent UN operations shows that even a small, highly-trained group, with high morale and dedication, arriving at the scene of action immediately after a Security Council decision, would in most cases have far greater effect than a larger and less well prepared force arriving weeks or even months later. The failure to come to grips with a situation before it gets completely out of hand usually necessitates a far larger, more expensive and less effective operation later on." See Urquhart, "Prospects for a UN Rapid Response Capability," in Cox and Legault, *UN Rapid Reaction Capabilities,* 3–35.

98. Urquhart, "Prospects for a UN Rapid Response Capability," 196. For further detailed analysis of similar projected expenses see, Jean Krasno, "A United Nation's Rapid–Deployment Permanent Force: Cost Analysis," paper prepared for the Yale University United Nations Study Program, 1994.

99. Carl Kaysen and George Rathjens, *Peace Operation by the United Nations: The Need for a Volunteer Military Force* (Cambridge, Mass.: Committee on International Security Studies, 1996), 13.

100. "Report by the Working Group on a Multinational UN Stand-by Forces High Readiness Brigade," 7.

101. *Towards a Rapid Reaction Capability*, 62.

102. Canada, DFAIT, "Canada Announces a Study to Improve the UN's Rapid Reaction Capability," Press Release No. 1, 4 July 1995, 4.

103. Kofi Annan, "The Peacekeeping Prescription," in Cahill, *Preventive Diplomacy*, 186.

104. Aside from the Netherlands "Non-Paper" and a section of the Canadian study, see Carl Kaysen and George Rathjens, *Peace Operations by the United Nations: The Case for a Volunteer UN Military Force* (Cambridge, Mass.: Committee on International Security Studies, 1996); Carl Conetta and Charles Knight, *Vital Force: A Proposal for the Overhaul of the UN Peace Operations System and for the Creation of a UN Legion* (Cambridge, Mass.: Commonwealth Institute, 1995); and Sir Brian Urquhart, "Prospects for a UN Rapid Response Capability," in Cox and Legault, *UN Rapid Reaction Capabilities*, 30–35. A particularly ambitious proposal is included in Joseph E. Schwartzberg, "A New perspective on Peacekeeping: Lessons from Bosnia and Elsewhere," *Global Governances* 3(1) January–April 1997: 1–15.

105. Stephen P. Kinloch, "Utopian or Pragmatic? A UN Permanent Military Volunteer Force," *International Peacekeeping* 3(4) Winter 1996: 185.

106. For an earlier attempt at outlining this stage-by stage process, see Langille, Faille, Hughes, and Hammond, "A Preliminary Blueprint of Long-Term Options for Enhancing a UN Rapid Reaction Capability," 179–200.

107. Unfortunately, at least in the near term, there is unlikely to be further research of this evolution within government, and there is little evidence of government assistance for related research. Neither is a research program of this nature on the agenda of the UN Secretariat or DPKO. Major-General Frank van Kappen, suggested that a study of a UN Standing Emergency Group would have to be conducted in co-operation with other UN Departments. But one should not be overly optimistic about the prospects of these departments engaging in a cooperative inquiry that many member states do not support. van Kappen acknowledged, however, that "further studies could be done by establishing within UNHQ and/or Member States could sponsor a Working Group. Studies could be conducted in a sponsor county with participants from Member States well as from UNHQ." See, Major-General Frank van Kappen, MILAD, DPKO, "Implementations of the Canadian Recommendation on Rapid Reaction Capability," Summary of Presentation on 4 Dec. 1995, 1–4.

108. William R. Frye, *A United Nations Peace Force* (New York: Oceana Publications, 1957), 106–107.

# III

## ARMS CONTROL AND COLLECTIVE SECURITY

# 4

# Chinese Perspectives on Multilateralism: Implications for Cooperative Security in Asia Pacific

*Jing-dong Yuan*

The last few years have witnessed the emergence of what may be called Asia-Pacific multilateralism—the multiplication of channels of dialogues on regional security issues at both governmental and nongovernmental (track two) levels. It has been acknowledged and increasingly accepted among both policymakers and the academic community that a multilateral approach to Asia-Pacific security issues, with its emphasis on confidence building, preventive diplomacy, and conflict resolution, can make important contributions to the maintenance of regional stability and the promotion of the region's continuing economic development and prosperity. This security-building effort reflects a genuine belief that through regularized dialogues and consultation, existing regional conflicts can be more effectively managed (if not resolved) within the parameters of agreed-upon norms and established procedures, without recourse to threats, coercion, and/or the use of force.

The extent to which this emerging Asia-Pacific multilateralism can succeed as an effective mechanism in promoting Asia-Pacific cooperative security depends on a host of factors. Realist cautions against the "false promises" of neoliberal institutionalism aside, the perspectives and attitudes of major powers toward regional multilateral security dialogues can be an important factor in determining their chance of success as viable supplements to traditional bilateral security arrangements and the regional balance of power. That the very catalyst of Asia-Pacific multilateralism can be said to have arisen from uncertainty about the region's future security outlook in anticipation of U.S. military drawdown and hence a potential "power vacuum" inviting aspiring regional powers such as China and Japan further underlines the importance of getting the latter actively and positively involved in the security-building endeavor.

Chinese perspectives on, and involvement in, Asia-Pacific multilateral security dialogues have to date been characterized as being cautious and passive at best, and skeptical and dismissive at worst. The prevailing view is that China's approach to regional security issues remains decidedly realist: that it prefers bilateralism to multilateralism; and that it continues to hold that big-power relationships and the regional balance of power, rather than multilateral dialogues among regional states, remain the key to stability and the resolution of existing issues. The underlying factors that discourage China from embracing multilateralism have been identified as Beijing's concern that regional multilateral forums may be used to single out and criticize China for its military buildup and its increasing assertiveness with territorial disputes in the South China Sea, as well as its unwillingness to see matters it considers domestic (e.g., the Taiwan issue) internationalized.

Underlying these analyses are a number of assumptions that have yet to be carefully examined. A prominent one is that multilateralism, and in particular one that is modeled after the Conference on Security and Cooperation in Europe (CSCE/OSCE), presents a much better mechanism in dealing with regional security issues without taking into consideration the fact that Asia Pacific is vastly different in terms of history, culture, economic development, and security concerns/priorities. Another assumption suggests that other Asia-Pacific countries are much more receptive than China is to multilateralism and in institutionalizing regional security arrangements without, however, clearly delineating the criteria for comparison. The conclusion, if these assumptions stand, is obvious: that China is increasingly being depicted as a major obstacle to the success of regional security building efforts because of its unwillingness to fully embrace the principles of multilateralism. And Beijing's policies seem to be reinforcing such a pessimistic view: the continuing military buildup, the growing assertiveness in the South China Sea, and the recent saber-rattling in the Taiwan Strait.

Clearly, these are all legitimate concerns, and need to be addressed. However, of greater significance is the need to understand the principles and operational codes of Chinese foreign policy guiding its external relations. This paper represents a preliminary effort at sketching an outline of describing Chinese approaches to regional security issues and multilateralism, and at drawing attention to some of the questions important for future research. In the following sections, I first review Chinese views on the post–Cold War international order and discuss some of the security threats China must face under the new environment. Next I discuss some of the major features of what I call "conditional multilateralism" that captures the tension between China's globalist principles regarding regional security cooperation and its distinctly realist approaches toward regional security issues. Finally, I try to place Chinese policies within the contexts of both the debates in international relations theory and the evolving Asia-Pacific multilateral security framework. Several conclusions are drawn from this study. First, Chinese attitudes toward multilateralism should be seen in evolutionary, rather than comparative, terms. In this regard, although the record presents a mixed picture, the general impression is that China has gradually become more receptive to multilateralism. Second, conditional multilateralism represents Beijing's effort to bridge the gap between the globalist principles it advocates and its realist approaches to regional security issues. Selective involvement demonstrates its willingness to cooperate while preconditions for participation allow it to retain freedom of maneuver. Finally, China's approaches to multilateralism must be understood in the broader contexts of history, specific policy objectives, and the dynamics of domestic politics.

## CHINESE VIEWS ON POST-COLD WAR INTERNATIONAL ORDER

The end of the Cold War has deprived one luxury that China had been enjoying all along: a global power status within the framework of the strategic triangle "without first having acquired the reach or the requisite normative and the material resources of a global power."[1] The decline and demise of the Soviet Union, the collapse of communism in Eastern Europe, the U.S.-led victory in the Gulf War, and the appearance if not the reality of a "unipolar moment" have presented China with both opportunities and challenges. What the post–Cold War international political and economic order (the Chinese never use the phrase "world order") would and should be like, and what role China should and can play in its creation have important implications. The principles that Beijing has postulated in the past few years are characteristic of Chinese approaches: proposing for the establishment of an equal and just international order (*jianli gongzheng heli de guoji xinchixu*) and warning against hegemony and power politics (*baquan zhuyi he qiangquan zhengzhi*).[2]

China has suggested that a new international political order should be based on the United Nations Charter and the Five Principles of Peaceful Coexistence (mutual respect for territorial integrity and sovereignty, mutual nonaggression, noninterference in each other's internal affairs, equality and mutual benefit, and peaceful coexistence). This has been a continuous theme throughout both government policy pronouncements and academic writings. The Five Principles have been extolled as widely accepted, time-tested, and universally applicable norms guiding interstate relations.[3] At the same time, Chinese analysts have commented with notable reservations on President Bush's call for a "new world order," with its four underlying principles (the peaceful settlement of disputes, solidarity against aggression, reduced and controlled arsenals, and the just treatment of all peoples). While the Chinese raise no objection to the first principle on Bush's list, and may endorse the third with some preconditions, they are wary of the second, fearing the United States may use such as a justification and abuse the power under UN auspices to serve U.S. and Western interests. And they certainly object to the last point of Bush's proposal lest it be turned into a pretext for interfering with other countries' (read China's) internal affairs, in particular with regard to such issues as human rights. Indeed, Beijing is highly suspicious of Washington's advocacy of a "new world order," which is viewed as nothing less than a system dominated by U.S.-led Western capitalist countries, which can undermine China's national interests.[4] One Chinese analyst bluntly points out that "the new world order advocated by the United States and other Western powers is nothing more than a revised expression of power politics made to fit the new situation. In fact, what's behind it is the leadership of the United States, and the power sharing between the United States, European powers and Japan; . . . the ultimate goal is a world completely dominated by capitalist countries."[5] Understandably, China has time and again emphasized the importance of incorporating the principles of territorial integrity and sovereignty, and noninterference of each other's internal affairs into any consideration of the establishment of a new international order. Indeed, Chinese scholars suggest that they form the basis of any new international order.[6]

While Chinese perspectives on a new international order may be regarded as idealistic in rhetoric (i.e., presenting universal principles without committing China to any specific obligations and responsibilities), to a certain extent, they reflect Beijing's inability, rather than its unwillingness, to see such ideals being implemented. Under such constraints, the least Beijing can and must do, is to separate itself from other major powers and demonstrate a moral high ground.[7] However, the advocacy of international egalitarianism is no substitute for sound policy to promote national interests. Whenever tension arises, it is the latter rather than the former that must dictate Beijing's external behaviors.

This probably explains why China's policies remain distinctly realist in substance. While advocating and promoting the principles of equality and justice in international affairs and in the construction of a new international order, Chinese experts recognize that great powers remain an important factor and contend that any international order is based on the existing structure of international power distribution and serves its purposes.[8] One Chinese analyst argues: "It is a reality that countries in the world differ in size. The proposition that all countries, large or small, enjoy sovereign equality and have the right to participate in the settlement of international issues through consultation does not negate the important role big countries play in international affairs. Big countries assume special responsibilities in world affairs."[9]

Indeed, balance of power features prominently in Chinese thinking about the post–Cold War order not by choice but out of necessity. What has emerged in recent Chinese discussions on Asia-Pacific security are such concepts as the "new trilateral relationship" (Japan, China, and the United States) replacing the Cold War strategic triangle (the United States, China, and the Soviet Union);[10] the quadrangular-power relationships (China, Japan, Russia, and the United States), and the five-force interactions (the four powers plus ASEAN). Chinese scholars contend that

> the future security of the region will depend primarily on maintaining a balance of power in which no one country plays a dominant role. The prospects for such a stable power balance, they say, have been substantially enhanced by the emergence of a pluralistic regional strategic environment in the post–Cold War era in which the major powers—including the United States, Japan, China, Russia and the Association of Southeast Asian Nations (ASEAN)—constrain each other. Stability of the post–Cold War regional environment is strengthened not only by this increasing diffusion of power, but also by the improvement in relations among the major powers in the region.[11]

Another perspective views post–Cold War Asia Pacific as being affected by the coordination and changes of relationships among the five centers of force in the region—the United States, China, Japan, Russia, and ASEAN.[12] The dynamics of such relationships, we are told, can play a significant role in ensuring regional security and stability.[13] One Chinese scholar elaborates:

> the international relationship in Asia-Pacific is moving towards a new, relatively balanced pattern membered by quadrangular and multilateral forces. . . . By 'quadrangular' we mean a quadrangular relationship among China, Japan, the United States and Russia, which has emerged out of the faded U.S.–USSR–China triangle and resulted from the disintegration of the former Soviet Union and the rise of Japan. Either judging from the power equation or from the intra-regional relationship among East Asian countries, the new quadrangular relationship is unprecedented in the history of East Asian international relations. . . . The foresaid 'multilateral' structure has dual meanings. First, it refers to the multilateral relations among the members of the above-mentioned quadrangle. Then it refers to the various rising forces in Asia-Pacific other than the four countries as well as the multilateral relations between these forces and the four countries.[14]

Chinese perspectives on the new international order also reflect an increasing emphasis on state sovereignty and noninterference in domestic affairs. While recognizing growing interdependence, China has remained steadfast with regard to these principles. According to one Chinese scholar:

> The principle of state sovereignty is a fundamental one in international law. Sovereignty is one of the vital factors for the existence of states and an indispensable feature of the subject of international law. Any theory claiming sovereignty to be outdated is groundless.[15]

Indeed, China appears more receptive to multilateralism where sovereignty issue is not immediately on the line (e.g., participation in international economic institutions such as the IMF and World Bank); at the same time, China has been less than forthcoming with regard to the institutionalization of a security arrangement that would require partial ceding of state sovereignty (e.g., transparency, onsite inspection, human rights).

The above discussion clearly demonstrates that the defining feature of China's understanding of the post–Cold War international security environment is its realist approach. Not surprisingly, its response to perceived future security threats is one of *realpolitik*. States remain the key players in international relations and state sovereignty an ultimate goal. To achieve security and preserve sovereignty in an anarchical international system of constant change and flux requires that one keep and enhance its capabilities. Security is absolute and a strong and prosperous state and a powerful military (*fuguo qiangbing*) remain the only guarantor of national security. Whatever stratagems the country may adopt under different circumstances, the ultimate goal has always been to protect national interests. During the Cold War, a minimum yet credible deterrence was crucial to China's security; in the post–Cold War era, the ability to preserve state sovereignty and territorial integrity broadly defined requires a military capability that can ensure victory in local conflicts. Interdependence and therefore an appreciation of cooperative security to enhance one's own security and the necessary change in foreign policy have not been accepted as the basic approach.[16]

## CHANGING SECURITY ENVIRONMENT AND CHINESE THREAT PERCEPTIONS

The end of the Cold War, the transformation of Eastern Europe, and the disintegration of the Soviet Union have affected China's security environment and threat perceptions in important ways. On the one hand, Sino-Soviet normalization and the continuing improvement of the Sino-Russian relationship have removed a major source of threat to China's security; on the other hand, precisely because of the demise of the Soviet Union, the ability of China to exploit its position in the strategic triangle has been greatly reduced. During the Cold War, China compensated for its weakness through its alignment and realignment with either of the two superpowers. Chinese foreign policy concentrated on securing a favorable position within the constraints of superpower competition. With the end of the Cold War, China finds itself increasingly on the receiving end within the emerging international strategic environment.[17] The difficulties China faced during the Gulf crisis of 1990–1991 and afterwards are a clear manifestation of the kind of constraints it now must encounter in formulating and implementing foreign policy at both the global and regional levels.[18] Beijing increasingly views post–Cold War uncertainties and security threats as multifaceted, less well-defined, and coming from a number of sources.[19]

## The United States

Obviously, the United States remains a major factor in Beijing's threat perception and affects its formulation of security policies. The continued presence of U.S. military forces in the region, and in particular a resilient U.S.-Japan security alliance would keep Tokyo from seeking remilitarization. In this regard, the role of the United States can be a stabilizing one. At the same time, the U.S. military presence not only is an antithesis to what China does not stand for, namely, the proclaimed objection to the stationing of troops on foreign soils, the recent U.S. military movement (the dispatching of two carrier battle groups to the region) during the Taiwan crisis may demonstrate to the Beijing leadership that the United States can pose a major obstacle to what China wants to achieve, namely, the recovery of Taiwan and the disputed territories in the South China Sea. There are also concerns about U.S. attempts to subvert China's socialist system through "peaceful evolution." The policies of "enlargement" and "comprehensive engagement" are viewed in Beijing with unconcealed suspicion. The former has been characterized as a manifestation of U.S. hegemony and power politics on the rise while the latter has been described as an attempt to "participate in and influence" the direction of development of China's domestic and foreign policies.[20] Particularly worrisome is Washington's advocacy for "liberty, democracy, and human rights," which is interpreted as nothing but a pretext for interference in the internal affairs of other countries, with China as a major target.[21]

## Japan

The rise of Japan and its aspiration for becoming a normal power commensurate with its economic and technological prowess also present a major challenge to China. In recent years, Beijing watches with increasing concern some of the worrisome developments: recurring trade disputes between Tokyo and Washington and potential consequences for the future of the U.S.-Japan security arrangement; the growing demands in Japan calling for fundamental change of its role in international affairs from that of a "junior partner" to one of equal partnership among the United States, Japan, and Western Europe; and Tokyo's attempt to build a defense capability commensurate with its national power.[22] The last development has already manifested itself in several areas: a rising military expenditure consistently exceeding the one percent of GNP limit, with the 1995 defense budgets amounting to US $47 billion, the second largest in the world; a notable change in defense doctrine from the principle of "self-defense" to a military strategy of "offensive defense," and the concomitant expansion of its maritime defense line to 1,000 nautical miles to the south in fulfillment of its new-found missions of shipping escorts and the protection of vital sea lanes of communications; and Japan's involvement in the development of the next generation of FSX attack fighter and its plutonium programs.[23] Finally, there is the unresolved but recently resurfacing territorial dispute over the Diaoyu (Senkaku) Islands. Although the Chinese have demonstrated considerable restraint regarding the issue, Beijing nevertheless has taken every conceivable public opportunity to reiterate China's indisputable sovereignty over the islands. The PLA's patience may already be wearing thin, as the army newspaper declared in a recent article that "even though China needs some foreign investment, anyone who thinks we will give in on the Diaoyu Islands issue is making a monstrous mistake."[24]

## India

India presents another source of potential threat to China's security. The last few years have seen the normalization and improvement of bilateral relations between Beijing and New Delhi.[25] However, the change from antagonism to dialogue, and from tension to relaxation, has not resolved the decade-long territorial disputes in the border areas—one of the fundamental issues that had strained bilateral relationship in the past. The current Sino-Indian détente can be regarded as at best an exercise of conflict management rather than conflict resolution. Added to the difficulties of constructing long-term stability in both bilateral relationship and in the South Asian subcontinent are India's nuclear weapons programs, the continued distrust and animosity between Pakistan and India, and the emerging rivalry and potential conflicts between India and China over influence and control in Myanmar. Until these issues are properly managed, and eventually resolved, India will remain an important factor in China's threat and security calculations.[26]

## Korea

Beijing is also concerned with the stability in the Korean peninsula, another potential flash point that can seriously threaten China's security.[27] North Korea's nuclear programs and Washington's penchant for brinkmanship and sanctions to pressure Pyongyang into submission are seen in Beijing as highly destabilizing and deeply deplored. An improper handling of the situation, Beijing fears, could lead to serious consequences ranging from the undesirable, namely, the potential for nuclearization of the sub-region, to the unthinkable.[28] Clearly, China has high economic and security stakes in managing the crisis and peacefully resolving the issues of both North Korea's nuclear programs and unification of the two Koreas.[29] And there are broader national interests to be served through effective management of the Korean issue. China increasingly looks to South Korea for expanded opportunities in trade, investment and technology transfers. This requires subtle balancing acts that address Seoul's security concerns (i.e., North Korea's nuclear program) without unduly alienating Pyongyang. Yet another consideration is that Beijing also recognizes the utility of using the Korean issue to advance its fundamental national interests across the board, including its dealing with the United States. These multiple, and indeed competing, interests to a large extent explain the equivocal nature of Beijing's Korea policy.

## Taiwan

For some time to come, the Taiwan issue will remain a key element of Chinese security consideration. Despite the growing cross-Strait economic interaction in recent years, Beijing's ultimate goal—the unification of the mainland and Taiwan—remains a rather distant prospect. Chinese leaders on various occasions have proposed that the formula of "one county, two systems" should be the basis of negotiations towards eventual unification. While Beijing maintains that it seeks a peaceful unification, it has never ruled out the use of force. The military exercises of 1995–1996 reflect equal frustration with the slow pace of cross-Strait political interchanges and alarm at Taiwan's increasingly open bid for international recognition, and the dynamics of domestic politics at a crucial moment of post–Deng power transition. The lack of any substantive progress in negotiation and hence the indefinite delay in unification have serious consequences for Beijing. It is expected that Taiwan's politics will increasingly be indigenized, with a new generation of leadership feeling no particular attachment to the mainland; at the same time, continued U.S. weapons sales, in particular the delivery of F-16s and possibly a theater anti-missile defense system, will further enhance Taiwan's defense capabilities. These developments in all likelihood will encourage the independence movement on the island.[30]

## Territorial Disputes

Beijing also sees potential threats to its sovereignty and territorial integrity. China's ability to enforce its claims over disputed territories in the South China Sea, its ability to successfully manage the return of Hong Kong and Macau to the mainland, and the eventual unification of mainland and Taiwan will serve to demonstrate how its security interests can be protected. The recent military exercises demonstrate as much Beijing's frustration with the slow pace of across-Strait interchanges, alarm with the island leadership's ever open bid for international recognition, and the dynamics of domestic politics at a crucial moment of power transition. Indeed, the Taiwan issue may become the test of how China's security is defined and protected.

### Nuclear Proliferation

A fifth source of uncertainty and potentially a serious security concern for Beijing is the spread of nuclear weapons in the region. China today faces a number of declared and de facto nuclear states on its periphery: Russia, Kazakhstan, India, Pakistan, North Korea, and Japan. This certainly complicates China's defense planning and its nuclear strategies and serves as an important factor in Beijing's arms control and disarmament calculation.[31]

### Economic Security

Finally, a long-term security concern is the fear that unless a stable international environment is maintained, disruption of peace will hamper China's efforts in its modernization drives and therefore will widen the gap between China and the advanced industrialized countries and the newly industrialized economies (NIEs).[32] Chinese experts perceive economic and scientific challenges in the coming decades as constituting the major security threat to the country.[33] Indeed, while constantly extolling the regional stability and economic prosperity in Asia Pacific as compared to other regions, Beijing remains concerned that regional and local conflicts could seriously affect its modernization programs which, using the terminology of "comprehensive national strength," is regarded as the basis for national security.

It is against these changing threat perceptions and the reassessment of the security environment that China's post–Cold War security policy was formulated. It consists of three major tasks: (1) Modernization. Efforts are expanded to ensure the current favorable international environment for economic development; (2) Sovereignty. This includes eventual reunification with Taiwan as well as implementation of "one country, two systems" in Hong Kong and Macau, and the protection of the country's territorial integrity; and (3) Anti-hegemony. Any manifestation of hegemony and power politics is considered threatening to peace and stability and therefore must be opposed.

That economic development is in command derives from the recognition that international competition is shifting from military confrontation to one that tests a country's overall economic, scientific and technological capabilities. Security is no longer affected by the military power of other countries alone; it is contingent on a host of factors. The building of the country's comprehensive national strength (*zonghe guoli*) is the only way to ensure China's long-term security. The emphasis on national reunification and sovereignty both reflects an eagerness to eradicate the legacy and remains of "the hundred years humiliation" and demonstrates the continued sensitivity to perceived and real encroachment on China's territorial integrity. The growing attention to maritime interests and the cultivation of a "conception of sea as territory" (*Haiyang guotuguan*) reflects both a recognition of the potential of maritime resources for national economic development and a realization that China must enhance its ability to protect its claimed maritime territories. Anti-hegemonism is as much directed towards the United States as it is to serve as a warning to Japan, which is increasingly being viewed as harboring political and military ambitions, hence constituting a long-term potential threat to China's security.

## CONDITIONAL MULTILATERALISM: CHINESE APPROACHES TO REGIONAL SECURITY

China's basic assessment of the security situation in Asia Pacific is a dialectic one. On the one hand, the security environment in the region is characterized as stable and peaceful, with economic development the priority for most countries; on the other hand, there remain factors of uncertainty and sources of instability.[34] Within such contexts, the establishment of a new political order in the region, according to Chinese analysts, requires the following: (1) resolving existing conflicts and preventing new ones; (2) promoting regional arms control and disarmament; (3) establishing state-to-state relations based on the Five Principles of Peaceful Coexistence; (4) respecting each country's right to decide its own course of democratization conducive to political stability; (5) promoting regional economic cooperation and prosperity; and (6) setting up regional security dialogues based on regional specificities.[35]

Chinese positions on the multilateral approach to Asia-Pacific security have undergone noticeable changes. China seems to have gradually moved toward acknowledging the utility of multilateralism, while still hesitant about adopting institutionalized mechanisms right away. In March 1992, Chinese Vice Foreign Minister Liu Huaqiu proposed "to establish gradually a bilateral, sub-regional, and regional multi-channel and multi-layered security dialogue mechanism so as to hold consultations on the issues concerned and to strengthen interchange and confidence."[36] Qian Jiadon, the deputy secretary general of the State Council's Center for International Studies, said that a unified regional security mechanism like the Conference on Security and Cooperation in Europe (CSCE) was not appropriate to the diversity of the Asia-Pacific region; rather, multi-channeled, multi-tiered dialogues that were both bilateral and multilateral, intergovernmental and nongovernmental, were the most feasible answer for the region.[37]

During the 1994 ASEAN Regional Forum (ARF) in Bangkok, Chinese Vice-Premier and Foreign Minister Qian Qichen proposed the following principles and measures for Asia-Pacific security cooperation:

1. Establishing new types of state-to-state relations characterized by mutual respect and amicable coexistence should be established on the basis of the UN Charter and the Five Principles of Peaceful Coexistence;
2. Establishing economic ties on the basis of equality and mutual benefit and mutual assistance with a view to promoting common economic development;
3. Having consultations on an equal footing and peaceful settlements as norms in handling disputes between countries in the Asia-Pacific region in order to gradually remove the destabilizing factors;
4. With the purpose of promoting peace and security in the region, adhering to the principle that armament should only be used for defensive purposes, and avoiding an arms race of any form. Avoiding nuclear proliferation. Nuclear states should not be the first to use nuclear weapons and should not use or threaten to use them against non-nuclear states or nuclear-free zones. Proposals on establishing nuclear-free zones and zones of peace should be supported;
5. And promoting bilateral and multilateral security dialogues and consultations in various forms in order to enhance understanding and confidence.[38]

China's evolving positions on Asia-Pacific security can be characterized as what I call "conditional multilateralism." Its essence is to present China as a supporter of the emerging regional security dialogue while at the same time avoid committing itself to a more institutionalized arrangement whose norms and rules may constrain Beijing's freedom of action. Conditional multilateralism allows China to be part of the process of building regional security, influence its agenda, and have a voice in its pace and direction; selective involvement accrues experience in dealing with issues cooperatively while preconditions for its participation would allow Beijing to retain the ability to maneuver. Such posturing has as much to do with Beijing's inherent suspicion about the effectiveness of multilateral approaches in handling regional security, as with its concern that multilateral forums may be used for "China bashing."

There are a number of distinct features about China's conditional multilateralism: (1) The multi-channel approach. Regional security issues should be dealt with by a variety of channels, including bilateral, multilateral, and sometimes unilateral approaches at governmental and nongovernmental levels. Indeed, China's approach to regional security issues can be seen as distinctly bilateral, arguing that under certain circumstances bilateral approaches can be more appropriate in resolving security issues (e.g., Sino-Russian agreement on reducing military forces in the border areas); (2) The minilateral approach. Beijing continues to emphasize the importance of major powers in managing regional security issues; (3) A gradualist approach. The regional security building process should begin with bilateral dialogues, moving to sub-regional, and then region-wide ones. Issues should be dealt with from an order of ascendance, i.e., from the relatively easy to the more difficult; and (4) An Asia-Pacific approach. The region, because of its special characteristics—history, culture, economic development, political systems, religion, etc., should not blindly copy the CSCE model; substance is more important than form. Dialogues, confidence-building measures should serve to enhance political trust, which is the basis of stable security relationships.

## Multi-Channel Approach

China continues to view bilateral approaches as an effective way of dealing with not only security issues but also inter-state relations in general. Chinese experts maintain that bilateral relations among the region's major powers, rather than a multilateral security structure, is the primary factor affecting security and stability in Asia Pacific, with the U.S.–China–Japan relationships as the key.[39] Indeed, post–Tiananmen Square Chinese diplomacy has been characterized by its almost single-minded objective of improving bilateral relations with all neighboring countries.[40] Bilateral security dialogues have been regarded by China as the basis of multilateral approaches. One Chinese analyst points out, "bilateral problems can only be solved within the bilateral framework of the countries concerned. Attempts to solve bilateral problems within a multilateral framework often complicate these problems and make them even more difficult to solve. Therefore, the security framework of the Asia-Pacific region should be based on bilateral security relations."[41] The large number of local disputes and conflicts may not easily be susceptible to settlement through negotiation mechanisms modeled on CSCE. "A more realistic approach," suggests another Chinese analyst, "would be U.S.-Soviet talks on [the] reduction of military confrontation in the region. And parallel with this, talks among indigenous Asia-Pacific countries concerned on disputes over territorial claims, marine rights and the like through a certain dialogue mechanism. Thus, a unique form of security mechanism geared to the peculiarities of the Asia-Pacific region will gradually take shape in the course of settling these disputes."[42]

## Minilateral Approach

What China has shown more interest in regarding Asia-Pacific security is what can be termed as a "minilateral" approach, i.e., how regional security issues can be managed through cooperation between major powers. Indeed, notwithstanding their customary calls for the equitable participation of states large and small in international affairs, recent Chinese writings on regional security are replete with role prescriptions for major powers. One Chinese scholar holds that the current international order can be characterized as composing of one superpower (the United States) and four subordinate powers— the European Union, Japan, Russia and China. The so-called "four triangles," with the United States at the core of each spoke, would have much impact on global and regional security orders.[43] Another Chinese analyst suggests that

> what merits special attention is that the changes in the relations among the four big powers, the United States, the Soviet Union, China and Japan, are of great importance to the political, economic and security relations in the Asia-Pacific region. ..the maintenance of a balanced development of relations in the Asia-Pacific region by the four big powers, . . . is of great significance to peace and stability in this region.[44]

## Gradualist Approach

Big power relations are not just necessary, but indeed imperative, for regional security. One Chinese analyst goes even further in arguing that "any structure can not go without balance of power or equilibrium in some form and to some extent, not to speak of the fact that balance of power has been an important security mechanism dating back to ancient times, and has also been an important constituent part of the present-day international security mechanism."[45] Henry Kissinger would certainly appreciate that *A World Restored* can still find an accepting audience in China three decades after its first publication.

Chinese scholars have suggested that the process of building regional security should follow the principles of moving from bilateral to regional/ multilateral arrangements; from confidence building measures (CBMs) to security arrangements to regional disarmament; from informal/nonofficial to formal/governmental discussions, and a gradual process that requires time and patience. Overnight establishment of a security arrangement modeled after others may not be helpful.[46] One Chinese analyst argues that given the region's complexity in terms of the different political systems, the variety of issues, and different priorities countries face, a gradualist approach is more appropriate. The logical steps should be to resolve regional hot spots and other bilateral disputes first; enhance economic cooperation, and then build upon improved bilateral relations the foundation for a region-wide, multilateral framework.[47] The emphasis is put on a gradual, step-by-step approach, "dealing with issues in ascending order of difficulty," and through preliminary informal consultations and discussions.[48]

Qian Qichen, Chinese Foreign Minister, again emphasized the importance of a gradualist approach during the 1995 ARF. Reminding his audience of the special characteristics of the Asia-Pacific, Qian suggested that the region's security building efforts were a completely new enterprise and that required patience. Some of Qian's recommendations included moving from the relatively easy to the more difficult issues; seeking common grounds and reserving differences; and beginning with preliminary informal discussions and consultations on the principles, content, scope, and method of cooperation in security matters. CBMs should be broader in scope and not confined to the military sphere only and should encompass political, economic, and social fields as well. "Developing multilateral cooperation in security matters in the Asia-Pacific region is a long-term, complex, and completely new project," pronounced Qian, and ARF "should take account of the reality of the Asia-Pacific region's diversity, and proceed from the distinctive features of the post–Cold War new international situation. It should not blindly and indiscriminately copy the models of other regions or past models. . . . Political will is of primary importance in building interstate trust."[49]

*Asia-Pacific Approach*

Finally, Asia Pacific's specific characteristics and diversity in history, culture, religion, and economic development requires a distinctly Asia-Pacific approach, in particular at a time when countries in the region are still in the process of adjusting their foreign policy objectives and priorities in view of the post–Cold War realities. The essence of that approach is to recognize that substance is more important than form, that informal relations may be preferred over formal institutions, that dialogue is valuable in and of itself, and that a set of overlapping informal dialogues at the bilateral, sub-regional, and region-wide levels may be more appropriate at this moment than an overly institutionalized European model.[50] Under such circumstances, the European experience can be drawn on—but not copied after—in Asia Pacific.[51]

Nor is there an urgency to establish a transparency mechanism. Rather, efforts should be made to narrow differences and reach common consensus with regard to the principles and forms of regional security arrangements.[52] The important point is to establish confidence rather than hastily seek institutional forms. CBMs should not be confined to the military sphere only. Instead, a more useful way of conducting CBMs is to begin with nonmilitary issues. Once confidence and trust have been established in political, diplomatic, and economic spheres, it then can be voluntary for countries concerned to set up CBMs in military areas (exchange of military information, observing military exercises, transparency in defense doctrines and weapons acquisitions, etc.).[53]

The purpose of transparency is to enhance confidence and trust, not to obtain unavailable information. In other words, the aim of increasing transparency should be to enhance security rather than undermine it. There must be a differentiation between strong and weak states. Rather than carry out transparency across the board in the whole region, it might be more helpful if such measures could be first carried within border areas between countries where traditionally there have been confrontations or too close military contacts.[54] There is also the consideration that through transparency China's weakness will be revealed, which would undermine its deterrence. Certainly, a universally applied transparency is not acceptable while it can be considered only in bilateral or trilateral contexts.[55]

## THE LOGIC OF CHINA'S CONDITIONAL MULTILATERALISM

To suggest that China is less than forthcoming toward a multilateral approach to regional security issues only raises one of several important questions concerning the broader debates about international cooperation and the behavior of rising/aspiring powers. The more appropriate questions are if, and how, China is different from other major powers with regard to multilateralism; what are the conditions for the creation of security regimes; how China's history, strategic culture, and domestic politics affect its perspectives on multilateralism; how and to what extent past experiences in multilateral settings influence and shape China's attitudes and behaviors; and finally, if there are more than one "script," or version of Chinese multilateralism.

International relations scholars have long debated the range of options states can adopt in conducting their relations and the possibility of international cooperation under anarchy. Realists are normally pessimistic and argue that relative-gain considerations make international cooperation elusive, if not altogether impossible. Liberal institutionalists, on the other hand, point out that international cooperation is not only possible but also highly desirable because it reduces transaction costs and makes interstate relations more predicable. At the same time, both have come to recognize that absolute/relative-gains considerations can be situation-contingent and depend on specific conditions; so must be the prospect of international cooperation.[56]

The realist understanding of international relations would suggest that international cooperation will be difficult but possible to some degree under certain circumstances. In this regard, realism would explain states' willingness to behave cooperatively and their participation in multilateral arrangements, be they international organizations and acceptance of certain norms and principles concerning behavior, as largely utility-oriented. In other words, states choose cooperation out of rational choice. Two points immediately come to mind: One, that states, and in particular great powers, may be less than forthcoming if they see multilateral arrangements as potentially constraining; and two, they may be prepared to endorse multilateral arrangements if the latter do not impose significant constraints or if nonparticipation per se accrue no absolute gains but relative losses (in terms of opportunities created through collective actions or simply the tarnishing of image).

The above discussion indicates that whether a state is more receptive to multilateralism or more cooperative in security issues can be highly situation-specific and may never be consistent. Brian Job has identified what he calls "deep" multilateralist arrangements with relatively narrow and exclusionary membership, and "shallower" forms of multilateralist commitments with broader and more inclusive membership. There is always a tension, or tradeoff between the two; more so in the context of regional perspectives and practices. Regional powers tend to eschew multilateral arrangements that may entail domination or restrictions imposed on them by major powers. They are also likely to avoid such multilateral forums that may constrain their autonomy and freedom of action.[57] Clearly, the two present different scenarios for policymakers. In China's case, a "deep" form entails commitments that it may not be willing to make; on the other hand, a "shallower" form, as ARF currently stands, may be more appealing simply because the principles, norms, and rules are still in the process of being suggested, discussed, rather adopted, and that China can, by virtue of its participation, influence that process. At the same time, Beijing's nonparticipation probably will accrue more discernable benefits but quite significant loss in image.

Whether or not, and in what form, will security arrangements be established may to a large extent depend on the "interrelationship of structural, cognitive and (resulting) behavioral factors." While structural variables such as the distribution of power, geography, state resources, etc. may offer opportunities for or constrain players, it is the cognitive features of the environment that would determine the particular form of security arrangements.[58] In other words, the "non–like-minded" must convert to the "like-minded" within a defined group of states or in a specified geographic region before a particular security arrangement can take shape and be adopted. China has yet to become the "like-minded" vis-à-vis its neighbors with regard to a broad range of issues. For this to happen, significant "learning" must take place within China's current or/and future leadership.[59] This refers to two concepts: learning in the sense that growing experience in various multilateral forums will make the Chinese both aware of the many benefits resultant from active participation and better multilateralists; and learning to the extent that there is a fundamental change in their perceptions of the nature of threat and the appreciation that there are alternative, and hopefully more cost-effective ways of dealing with security dilemmas other than the traditional, realist self-help approaches. While one may suggest that learning has certainly occurred in the first instance, that in the second, namely, the recognition of security interdependence and relevant policy changes, has yet to take place.

There are additional variables we must also consider, which set the broader contexts of Chinese approaches toward multilateralism. They are the regional characteristics, and China's past experience and the dynamics of domestic politics. Unlike the case in Europe, where multilateral institutions such as NATO and WTO dominated the security architecture during the Cold War, in Asia Pacific, approaches to security had been either unilateral (self-reliance) or bilateral; indeed, most defense arrangements have involved the United States at one end and one of the Asia-Pacific countries at the other. The few exceptions to this general rule, such as the Southeast Asia Treaty Organization (SEATO), or the Five Power Defense Arrangement (FPDA), have not played a predominant role in regional security. On the contrary,[60] this probably explains the initial U.S. response, which was lukewarm at best, to initiatives aimed at setting up a multilateral, region-wide security framework.[61]

Asia-Pacific multilateralism will have to take into consideration the particular features of its strategic culture. This includes "longer time horizons and policy perspectives than those which characterize Western thinking and planning; reliance on bilateral rather than multilateral approaches to conflict resolution and security planning; . . . commitment to the principle of noninterference in the international affairs of other countries; styles of policy making which feature informality of structures and modalities, form and process as much as substance and outcome, consensus rather than majority rule, and pragmatism rather than idealism; multidimensional or comprehensive approaches to security; and roles for the military that go beyond national defense to include politics, economic development and social affairs."[62] Indeed, it was with such recognition that the North Pacific Cooperative Security Dialogue (NPCSD), when it was proposed in 1990, deliberately "envisioned a more gradual approach to developing multilateral institutions, recognized the value of existing bilateral arrangements, and encouraged ad hoc, informal dialogues (habits of dialogues), and inclusive participation until conditions mature for more formal institution-building."[63]

Another point that should be kept in mind is that not until the early 1990s have there emerged numerous proposals for the regional multilateral security frameworks and only since then has there been a general trend toward discussing new mechanisms for regional cooperation on security matters. Today, there are a multitude of security dialogues at various levels, or what may be called "multiplex," "multilayered," or multifaceted" structure.[64] Some of the principles of cooperative security have only recently taken roots: assurance rather than deterrence; multilateral process to replace or at least co-exist with bilateral military alliance; and promotion of both military and nonmilitary security. If progress in Asia-Pacific multilateralism must be judged against its own past, considering, for instance, the fact that the CSCE/OSCE has been more than twenty years in the making, while one of the earlier, more serious efforts—the North Pacific Cooperative Security Dialogue (NPCSD) initiative—had its origin merely six years ago, and the Asia-Pacific version approximate to CSCE/OSCE—the ARF—only began less than two years ago, we may begin to assess China's progress in quite a different light.

The differences between China and its neighbors regarding their attitudes toward multilateralism may simply reflect a matter of degree. Indeed, it is understood that ASEAN members have rejected the adoption of a CSCE-type institution but are more receptive to informal, looser dialogues and consultations for exchanging views within the sub-region or across Asia-Pacific over security issues.[65] At the same time, within ASEAN, conflicts are normally resolved through ad hoc, bilateral consultations rather than resort to the more legal, multilateral mechanism within the organization.[66] And there are some compatibilities between China and ASEAN countries: economic development as first priority, resistance to Western pressure on human rights issues, and political stability.[67]

Chinese approaches toward multilateralism should be judged within the broader contexts of its past experiences, its current concerns, and the dynamics of its domestic politics. China has been cautious about adopting multilateral approaches out of a number of reasons: the limited and negative experience; the fear of small states ganging up against China (China bashing); and the concern that multilateral security forums may give Taiwan legitimacy. China's limited experiences in the past with multilateralism were far from positive. A few examples will suffice: The League of Nations and its acquiesce in Japanese invasion of China in 1931; the Soviet attempt to control China through both the 3rd Communist International and later the COMECON. China also suspects, (and has tried to stop), that the territorial disputes in the South China Sea and China's military buildup may be turned into *the* issues at regional security forums.[68] Finally, Beijing is highly sensitive about de facto recognition of Taiwan's legitimacy through participation in some of the regional security dialogues. The stalemate concerning membership of both China and Taiwan in the Council for Security Cooperation in Asia Pacific (CSCAP) to a large extent is due to Beijing's objection to Taiwan's participation.[69]

Domestic politics has always featured prominently in China's foreign policy making; indeed, there are discernable linkages between domestic politics and foreign policy behavior.[70] Such linkages become all the more pronounced during periods of uncertainty due to leadership succession and power transition, which makes flexibility difficult. The current leadership does not wield the kind of power held by the old generation of revolutionaries and consequently initiatives on their part are less of a possibility than negotiated compromises. Within such a framework, important foreign policy decisions that touch upon important and sensitive issues such as state sovereignty and territorial integrity will normally not be subject to multilateral considerations. Another factor that must be considered is that external environment exerts less of a direct impact on Chinese policy making. While the international system acts to encourage certain behaviors and discourage others, the defining variable remains domestic.[71]

Another way of understanding Chinese approaches to multilateralism is what Samuel Kim regards as the tension between rhetoric and practice, theory and praxis. China tends to propose principles well beyond its capabilities; at the same time, there is the practical side of Chinese foreign policy that seeks to realize maximum security benefits while minimizing moral and normative costs. This would explain the meshing of principled stand (*jiben luxian*) with practical adaptations under certain circumstances.[72] Yet a third way to understand Chinese multilateralism is what can be called the rhetorical and substantive of Chinese foreign policy. This leads to a combination of rigidity and flexibility in Chinese international behaviors. As long as fundamental national interests can be secured, Beijing has been willing to be more flexible with regard to how certain issues should be handled.[73]


## CONCLUSION

How do we assess Chinese perspectives on and approaches to multilateralism? One can examine this aspect along two different dimensions. One is the presence of China in the various multilateral processes/institutions. The other is the acceptance of multilateralism as a norm of dealing with regional security issues. On the surface, China has been a rather consistent, if only passive, participant in various multilateral forums as practiced in the Asia-Pacific context: (1) ad hoc cooperation on specific disputes and conflict resolution (e.g. Cambodian peace process, the South China Sea workshop); (2) "sub-regional" cooperation (ASEAN); (3) formal governmental efforts at the regional level, such as the ARF; (4) track-two programs (CSCAP); and (5) UN-sponsored and multilateral institutions and processes having a bearing on regional security issues.[74] On the other hand, Beijing has demonstrated a clearly variegated approach toward multilateralism; in other words, there are different "scripts" or versions of Chinese multilateralism in different environments (e.g., UN as opposed regional forums), and for different issues (e.g., economic as opposed to security). Conditional multilateralism represents but one version of what may be a whole repertoire of Chinese strategies of presenting its foreign policy.

To say that China has consistently held a dubious, if not hostile, attitude toward multilateral institutions and regime-generated rules may be simplistic and even misleading. What is clear, though, is that China's approach to multilateralism betrays a degree of varigatedness and selectiveness. While Chinese policy declarations have tended to be all things to all, Chinese behaviors in various international organizations have demonstrated a gradual movement toward accepting the norms and principles of existing regimes rather than challenging them head on. Samuel Kim's studies of Chinese behaviors in international organizations show that the degree of Chinese acceptance of and compliance with norm, principles, and rules may be a function of the extent to which the so-called "global learning," which induces "global thinking," is actually taking place. Positive learning can be facilitated through positive participatory experiences. However, there is a strong utilitarian element in the Chinese acceptance of the rules, norms, and principles.

To the extent that existing international order facilitates China's goals of modernization (e.g., aid, investment, and technology transfer from the capitalist world), there is no need to challenge it. The learning process is important in that both the domestic and international variables interact in shaping the leadership's cognitive maps of what China's interests, role, and policy should be.[75]

## NOTES

1. Samuel S. Kim, "China's Pacific Policy: Reconciling the Irreconcilable," *International Journal* 50(3) Summer 1995: 466.

2. Samuel Kim has characterized Chinese foreign policy pronouncements as "multi-principled posturing—and multiple role playing," that is, the postulating of different principles under different circumstances, and addressing different issues. This tendency derives from an inability to resolve the imbalance between principle and power. "China and the World in Theory and Practice," in Samuel S. Kim, ed., *China and the World: Chinese Foreign Relations in the Post-Cold War Era* (Boulder, Colo.: Westview Press, 1994), 9.

3. See, for example, Xu Yimin, "The Five Principles of Peaceful Coexistence Are the Basic Principles in Handling Inter-State Relationships," *International Strategic Studies* (Beijing) 3, September 1994: 1–4.

4. Sun Kun, "International Repercussions of the Gulf War," *Contemporary International Relations* (Beijing) 10, 1991: 1; Chen Qimao, *"Guanyu zai yatai diqu jianli zhengzhi xinchixu de tansuo,"* *Guoji Wenti Yanju* ["Seeking for a New Political Order in the Asia-Pacific Region," *International Studies* (Beijing) 1, January 1992: 2.

5. Du Gong, "Some Perceptions of a Changing Pattern of International Relations," *International Studies* (Beijing) 4, October 1991: 5.

6. Xu Xin, "Changing Chinese Security Perceptions." *NPCSD Working Paper* No.27 (Toronto: North Pacific Cooperative Security Dialogue: Research Programme, York University, April 1992), 8–9.

7. For a lucid analysis, see Samuel S. Kim, "China and the Third World in the Changing World Order," in Kim, ed., *China and the World: Chinese Foreign Relations in the Post-Cold War Era* (Boulder, Colo.: Westview Press, 1994), 128–68.

8. Chen, "Seeking for a New Political Order in the Asia-Pacific Region," 1.

124                                    *Chapter 4*

9. Wan Guang, "Challenges Facing the World Today and the Establishment of the New International Order," paper presented at the Beijing Symposium on a New International Order, September 2–4, 1991, 7; quoted in David Armstrong, "Chinese Perspectives on the New World Order," *The Journal of East Asian Affairs* 8(2) Summer/Fall 1994: 471–72.

10. Xu, "Changing Chinese Security Perceptions," 12–13.

11. Banning Garrett and Bonnie Glaser, "Beijing's View on Multilateral Security in the Asia-Pacific Region," *Contemporary Southeast Asia* 15(1) June 1993: 16.

12. Guo Zhenyuan, "Prospects for Security Cooperation in the Asia-Pacific Region," *Beijing Review* 37(38) July 11–17, 1994: 21.

13. Chen Qimao, "Asia-Pacific Awaits Great Geo-Strategic Changes," *Contemporary International Relations* (Beijing) April 1991: 5.

14. Liu Jiangyong, "On the Current Changes in the Asia-Pacific Political Scene," *Contemporary International Relations* (Beijing) 2(3) March 1992: 11–13.

15. Wang Jiafu, "International Law and a New International Order," paper presented at the Beijing Symposium on a New International Order, September 2–4, 1991, 3; quoted in Armstrong, "Chinese Perspectives on the New World Order," 471.

16. David Shambaugh, "Growing Strong: China's Challenge to Asian Security," *Survival* 36(2) Summer 1994: 43–59.

17. William T. Tow, "China and the International Strategic System," in Thomas W. Robinson and David Shambaugh, eds., *Chinese Foreign Policy: Theory and Practice* (Oxford: Clarendon Press, 1994), 115–57.

18. Yitzhak Shichor, "China and the Gulf Crisis: Escape from Predicaments," *Problems of Communism* XL(6) November–December 1991: 80–90.

19. Wang Jisi, "Comparing Chinese and American Conceptions of Security," *NPCSD Working Paper* No.17 (Toronto: North Pacific Cooperative Security Dialogue: Research Programme, York University, September 1992), 16.

20. Sa Benwan, "A Review of the U.S. Concept of 'Enlargement Strategy,'" *International Strategic Studies* (Beijing) 4, December 1993: 12–16, and "Shi `quanmian jiecu' haishi `quanmian canyu,'" *Liaowang* ["The Two Faces of the Policy of `Comprehensive Engagement,'" *Outlook Weekly*] 44, October 30, 1995: 56.

21. Huang Tingwei and Wang Yulin, "*Jisu bianhua zhong de guoji xingshi*," *Xiandai Guoji Guanxi* ["International Situation under Rapid Change," *Contemporary International Relations*] 3, August 1990: 7.

22. Huang and Wang, "International Situation under Rapid Change," 5; Chen Zhuang, "Japan: A Bumpy Road to 'Big Power Diplomacy,'" *Contemporary International Relations* 9, May 1991.

23. Pan Junfeng, "The Trend of Development of Japan's Military Strategy," *International Strategic Studies* (Beijing), 3, 1988: 15–20; *Renmin Ribao (People's Daily)*, overseas edition, November 1, 1995, 1.

24. Quoted in "Rocks of Contention," *Far Eastern Economic Review*, September 19, 1996, 14–15.

25. Wang Hongyu, "Sino-Indian Relations: Present and Future," *Asian Survey* XXXV(6) June 1995: 546–54.

26. J. Mohan Malik, "China-India Relations in the Post-Soviet Era: The Continuing Rivalry," *The China Quarterly* 142, June 1995: 317–53; and idem, "Sino-Indian Rivalry in Myanmar: Implications for Regional Security," *Contemporary Southeast Asia* 16(2) September 1994: 137–56.

27. Weixing Hu, "Beijing's Defense Strategy and the Korean Peninsula," *Journal of Northeast Asian Studies* 14(3) Fall 1995: 50–67.

28. One Chinese diplomat told this author that the United States doesn't seem to have the slightest clue that the North Koreans are capable of not only bluffing but also acting in a most irrational manner if cornered, and not caring much about the consequences.

29. Banning Garrett and Bonnie Glaser, "Looking Across the Yalu: Chinese Assessment of North Korea," *Asian Survey* XXXV(6) June 1995: 528–45; Robert E. Bedeski, "Sino-Korean Relations: Triangle of Tension, or Balancing a Divided Peninsula?" *International Journal* L(3) Summer 1995: 516–38.

30. Yan Xuetong, "*Zhongguo anquan zhanlue de fazhan qushi*" ["The Evolving Trends of Chinese Security Strategy"], *Liaowang Weekly* 8/9, February 19, 1996, 50–52.

31. On China's arms control and disarmament policies, see, Banning N. Garrett and Bonnie S. Glaser, "Chinese Perspectives on Nuclear Arms Control," *International Security* 20(3) Winter 1995–1996: 43–78; Lisbeth Gronlund, David Wright and Yong Liu, "China and a Fissile Material Production Cut-off," *Survival* 37(4) Winter 1995–1996: 147–67; Alistair Iain Johnston, "China's New 'Old Thinking,'" *International Security* 20(3) Winter 1995–1996: 5–42; J. Mohan Malik, "China's Policy towards Nuclear Arms Control in the Post-Cold War Era," *Contemporary Security Policy* 16(2) August 1995: 1–43.

32. Bonnie S, Glaser, "China's Security Perceptions: Interests and Ambitions," *Asian Survey* 33(3) March 1993: 253.

33. Qimao Chen, "New Approaches in China's Foreign Policy: The Post-Cold War Era," *Asian Survey* 33(3) March 1993: 240–41.

34. Lu Zhongwei, "*Yatai anquan xingshi xiangdui wending*," *Liaowang* ("A Relatively Stable Asia-Pacific Security Environment," *Outlook Weekly*) 27, July 4, 1995: 41–43.

35. Chen Qimao, "Seeking for a New Political Order in the Asia-Pacific Region," 5–8.

36. "Disarmament and Security Are the Necessary Conditions for Peace and Security," *People's Daily*, March 24, 1992, 4; cited in Susan L. Shirk, *Chinese Views on Asia-Pacific Regional Security Cooperation*, NBR Analysis, December 1994, 7.

37. Shirk, *Chinese Views on Asia-Pacific Regional Security Cooperation*, 7.

38. "China's Position on Asia-Pacific Security," *Beijing Review* 37(32) August 8–14, 1994: 21–22.

39. Garrett and Glaser, "Views from Beijing," 18.

40. James C. Hsiung, "China's Omni-Directional Diplomacy: Realignment to Cope with Monopolar U.S. Power," *Asian Survey* XXXV(6) June 1995: 573–86.

41. Guo Zhenyuan, "The Main Problems Affecting the Security in Asian-Pacific and The Principles Governing the Establishment of a Security Mechanism in the Region," *CCIS International Review* 1, August 1994: 53–54.

42. Chen Qimao, "Asia-Pacific Awaits Great Geo-Strategic Changes," 6–7.

43. Xue Mouhong, "The New World Order: Four Powers and One Superpower?" *Beijing Review* 38(39): September 25–October 1, 1995: 19–20.

44. Zhu Chun, "A Probe Into the Question of Security and New Order in the Asia-Pacific Region," *International Strategic Studies* (Beijing) 1, March 1991: 13–14.

45. Shen Qurong, "Security Environment in Northeast Asia: Its Characteristics and Sensitivities," *Contemporary International Relations* (Beijing) 2(12) December 1992: 11.

46. Si Chu, "Confidence-Building in Asia-Pacific," *Beijing Review* 34(9) March 4–10, 1991: 15–16.

47. Zhu Chun, "A Probe Into the Question of Security and New Order in the Asia-Pacific Region," *International Strategic Studies* (Beijing) 1, March 1991: 15.

48. "Qian on Security Cooperation," *Foreign Broadcast Information Service— China Daily Report –95-148* (hereafter *FBIS-CHI*), 2 August 1995, 1.

49. "Qian on Security Cooperation," *FBIS-CHI-95-148*, 2 August 1995, 1.

50. Shirk, *Chinese Views on Asia-Pacific Regional Security Cooperation*, 10.

51. Guo Zhenyuan, "Asian-Pacific Region Remains Peaceful," *Beijing Review* 39(6) February 5–11, 1996: 9–10.

52. Guo Zhenyuan, "Prospects for Security Cooperation in the Asia-Pacific Region," *Beijing Review* 37(38) July 11–17, 1995: 22.

53. Si Chu, "Confidence-Building in Asia-Pacific," *Beijing Review* 34(9) March 4–10, 1991: 15–16.

54. Luo Renshi, "On the Ways of and China's Efforts in Increasing Transparency in the Asia-Pacific Region," *International Strategic Studies* 4, 1995: 11–12.

55. Shirk, *Chinese Views on Asia-Pacific Regional Security*, 11.

56. Robert O. Keohane, ed., *Neorealism and Its Critics* (New York: Columbia University Press, 1986); David A. Baldwin, ed., *Neorealism and Neoliberalism: The Contemporary Debate* (New York: Columbia University Press, 1993).

57. Brian Job, *Multilateralism: The Relevance of the Concept to Regional Conflict Management*. Working Paper No.5 (Vancouver, BC: Institute of International Relations, University of British Columbia, 1994), 2, 23–24.

58. Job, *Multilateralism*, 7.

59. Jack S. Levy, "Learning and Foreign Policy: Sweeping a Conceptual Minefield," *International Organization* 48(2) Spring 1994: 279–312.

60. William T. Tow, "Contending Security Approaches in the Asia-Pacific Region," *Security Studies* 3(1) Autumn 1993: 75–116.

61. James A. Baker, III, "America in Asia: Emerging Architecture for a Pacific Community," *Foreign Affairs* 70(5) Winter 1991–1992: 1–18.

62. Desmond Ball, "Strategic Culture in the Asia-Pacific Region," *Security Studies* 3(1) Autumn 1993: 46–47.

63. David Dewitt, "Common, Comprehensive, and Cooperative Security," *The Pacific Review* 7(1) 1994: 7–8.

64. Paul M. Evans, "Building Security: The Council for Security Cooperation in the Asia Pacific (CSCAP)," *The Pacific Review* 7(2) 1994: 125–39.

65. Dewitt, "Common, Comprehensive, and Cooperative Security," 6.

66. Sheldon W. Simon, "Realism and Neoliberalism: International Relations theory and Southeast Asian Security," *The Pacific Review* 8(1) 1995: 18.

67. Simon, "Realism and Neoliberalism," 16.

68. Shirk, *Chinese Views on Asia-Pacific Regional Security*, 11.

69. Paul M. Evans, "The New Multilateralism in the Asia-Pacific and the Conditional Engagement of China," in James Shinn, ed., *Weaving the Net: Conditional Engagement with China* (New York: Council on Foreign Relations Press, 1996), 261.

70. Wang, "Comparing Chinese and American Conceptions of Security," 5.

71. David Bachman, "Domestic Sources of Chinese Foreign Policy," in Samuel S. Kim, ed., *China and the World: Chinese Foreign Relations in the Post-Cold War Era* (Boulder, Colo.: Westview Press, 1994), 42–59.

72. Samuel S. Kim, "China and the Third World in the Changing World Order," in Kim, ed., *China and the World*, 128–68.

73. Quansheng Zhao, "Patterns and Choices of Chinese Foreign Policy," *Asian Affairs* 20(1) Spring 1993: 3–15.

74. Evans, "The New Multilateralism in Asia Pacific," 256–58.

75. Samuel S. Kim, "Thinking Globally in Post-Mao China," *Journal of Peace Research* 27(2) May 1990: 191–209.

# 5

# Participatory Management of the Commons

*A. W. Harris*

In the class of natural resources or "spaces" which help to define the global expanse, the Antarctic region has at times become a contentious topic. The 1959 Antarctic Treaty[1] was designed in part to create a management regime for the region, and has substantially succeeded in that endeavor, as can be clearly illustrated by reference to the Antarctic Treaty System (ATS) a group of actors (predominately states) and a set of norms, rules, and policies, which have done much to create an administration for the Antarctic.[2] Despite the recognized accomplishments of the ATS, an argument can be made suggesting that the present composition of the ATS is not optimal, either in terms of providing adequate environmental protection to the region, or in terms of the sovereign equality of states.

In this paper I will propose two major changes in the ATS, and I will provide substantive grounds for holding the belief these changes should be made. First, I will advance the case that an enlargement of the Antarctic Treaty Consultative Party (ATCP) membership (a key decision-making subgroup of ATS states, distinct from Contracting Parties, a second subgroup of ATS states, sometimes referred to as Non-Consultative Parties, that have acceded to the Antarctic Treaty, but have not gained ATCP status) is a reasonable step. It is a reasonable step given the fact that many countries not now members of this subgroup of the ATS, are expected to abide by the latter's declared practice, policies and rules. ATS practice, and its policies and rules are derived from the operation and activities of Antarctic Treaty Consultative Meetings (ATCMs), and only ATCPs may vote or have meaningful participation in ATCMs. States not part of the ATCP subgroup (whether or not they are Contracting Parties) had little or no part in the construction of such policies and rules. Secondly, I will suggest that ATCP member states, that have heretofore not been receptive to calls for a widening of ATCP membership (except under strict, exclusionary criteria), may become more open to a wider membership if certain conditions are met. Those conditions include an explicit recognition of both the breadth of scientific and administrative knowledge attained by the ATCP states, and of the laudable benefits brought to the Antarctic region, through the past "stewardship" of the ATCP member countries. Certain amendments to ATS operating procedures would enable long-standing ATCPs to maintain their investment in the ATS by preserving their policy making preeminence in a larger, more representative body.

Thirdly, I will argue that the protection of the Antarctic region's environment itself, would be promoted through the creation of a more inclusive membership. This would be so because of a greater ability to prevent "logrolling" relationships from being struck between fellow ATCPs (having expended large investments in science and exploration in the region), possibly seeking to limit the rigor of inspection of their respective Antarctic sites. Such logrolling relationships might be constructed in order to avoid potentially costly consequences from a detection of violations of ATS environmental safety standards. The ATCPs are interested in limiting the costs, in money and time, attached to complying with ATS environmental standards. On a revolving basis, different ATCPs have been given responsibility for conducting the observation and inspection of Antarctic scientific and exploratory sites, so that environmental standards will more likely be met.

The ATCPs have agreed that observation and inspection of Antarctic sites is a necessary component to their stewardship of the region. But to date, the individuals serving as observers on inspection teams must be nationals of an ATCP. I will provide an argument suggesting that such a condition poses an unnecessary risk to the Antarctic region. This risk could be lessened if nationals from states not conducting substantial scientific activity in the region could be assigned as observers on Antarctic site inspection teams. A brief presentation of ATS structural components provides an appropriate starting point for my general discussion.

## ATS INSTRUMENTS

Both the Antarctic Treaty Consultative Parties (ATCPs),[3] which have the right to participate in decisions by casting votes in Antarctic Treaty Consultative Meetings (ATCMs), and ATS member states (Contracting Parties)[4] which are not Consultative Parties (in this paper I will refer to Consultative Parties and Contracting Parties together as simply Antarctic Treaty Parties or ATPs), and therefore do not cast votes in ATCMs, strongly believe in the viability of the existing ATS. Particular ATCPs hold this view so strongly, they even assert that the Antarctic Treaty itself, the foundation of the ATS system,[5] has become binding over nonparties to, as well as parties to the treaty.[6] Whether the original Antarctic Treaty, or the set of subsequent instruments that have been promulgated which have come to comprise the ATS, truly are binding on nonparties is an arguable point. In addition to the 1959 Antarctic Treaty, that set of instruments is generally thought to include the following: the Agreed Measures for the Conservation of Antarctic Fauna and Flora;[7] the Convention for the Conservation of Antarctic Seals;[8] the Convention for the Conservation of Antarctic Living Marine Resources (CCAMLR);[9]10, 240, *reprinted in* 19 I.L.M. 937 (1980). the Convention for the Regulation of Antarctic Mineral Resource Activities (CRAMRA);[10] the Protocol on Environmental Protection to the Antarctic Treaty (the Madrid Protocol);[11] and another organ of the ATS, the Scientific Committee on Antarctic Research (SCAR).[12] There is some argument as to whether CRAMRA should be considered a viable component of the ATS because it has not entered into force, and to some extent has been "superseded" by the Madrid Protocol. However, many commentators continue to view the document as an ATS component because it speaks to issues not adequately addressed in any other instrument.[13]

Certain countries have articulated strong objections to the ATS regime, although in recent years these voices have admittedly been somewhat muted. The diminished level of complaint seems to have occurred partially due to the advent of the Madrid Protocol,[14] and partially because several large developing states have acceded to the Antarctic Treaty in recent years.[15] In the years preceding the signing of CRAMRA there was a good deal of concern on the part of developing countries that the notion of Antarctica mineral exploitation was gaining in technical feasibility and becoming more politically tolerable. If this were true (as the June, 1988, signing of CRAMRA seemed to indicate) then in a vein similar to the position voiced by developing countries in the Third United Nations Law of the Sea Treaty ( UNCLOS III)[16] negotiations toward deep seabed exploitation, those countries expressed the belief that potential benefits from Antarctica mineral exploitation should be shared equitably by all the world's peoples, not just by those technologically capable countries able to execute the exploitation. Because CRAMRA has been placed "in abeyance," and supplanted by the Madrid Protocol, which instituted a moratorium on Antarctic mineral exploitation, a portion of the developing countries' expressed concern has been dampened. But this waning level of concern has not been pervasive. Non-ATPs (Non-Antarctic Treaty Party states that are neither Consultative nor Contracting Parties to the Antarctic Treaty) have continued to ask difficult (in their view) questions, and point to perceived ATS shortcomings. A central issue in this regard is one of equity.

## THE BINDING THESIS

A number of observers have argued that the ATS has gained the status of customary international law. If this is so, then the obligations provided by the treaty components of the ATS, as well as those obligations posed by the *measures*,[17] *decisions*,[18] and *resolutions*[19] of the ATCMs bind non-ATPs as well as ATPs. The action taken by the ATCPs in the Seoul ATCM to disaggregate its decision-making process was itself a "decision." Prior to Seoul the ATCPs had simply issued "Recommendations," at the conclusion of the ATCMs, pertaining to a wide range of topics, from waste disposal to tourism.[20] One commentator has surmised that the entire ATS has been elevated to customary law because there has been insufficient challenge from states outside the ATS, and because the ATS was a reflection of customary law even when it was negotiated.[21] An alternative but related view is that "the treaty itself would not bind the third state, but the existence of the treaty may lead to the development of a rule of customary law that would be binding on a third party."[22]

A third observer, Dagmar Butte, states that it is quite possible to mount an "insufficient challenge," or an Art. 36 of the Vienna Convention argument (i.e., non-ATPs have not adequately voiced objections in a concerted fashion, and therefore assent is implied), despite the fact that at least one original signatory state (Great Britain) has publicly stated it does not believe the Antarctic Treaty was meant to become binding on nonsignatories.[23] Butte goes on to posit that because a number of the Contracting Parties have indicated they believe the Antarctic Treaty, and by implication, the ATS it has engendered, "represents a codification of state practice,"[24] there are grounds for holding to the view that the ATS has achieved customary law status.

An interesting corollary argument rests on the idea that the success of the ATS in achieving the laudable goals of environmental protection and resource conservation, in and of itself lends to the ATS a measure of validity such that the ATS should be granted customary law status, in the sense that states outside the system should not undertake any actions that run contrary to ATS practice.[25] By extension, the argument would label action by non-ATP states, taken in opposition to ATS practice, as distinctly threatening to the protection of the region's fragile condition. Thus, the weight of this successful ATS practice "binds" non-ATP states to act in accordance with such practice.

This position of the ATS as binding on nonsignatories to the Antarctic Treaty, although not uniformly held in the literature, certainly is easily ascertained. But at the same time there is a second posture put forward by some analysts, which holds that the same non-ATP states which are regarded as bound by the Antarctic Treaty, should not be granted access to the decision-making procedures of the ATS, without first meeting rather exacting stipulations. Any country may accede to the Antarctic Treaty, and initially be granted Contracting Party, or non-Consultative Party status.[26] Upon accession a country may gain Consultative Party status by demonstrating an "interest in Antarctica by conducting substantial scientific research activity there."[27] But the cost of conducting "substantial" activity in the Antarctic is prohibitive for most developing countries.[28]

Because only Consultative Parties may vote in the deliberations occurring during ATCMs, ATCP status is what many non-ATPs desire, seeing accession alone as less than a meaningful step, and this is a contributing factor in explaining why still relatively few (in terms of the larger global community) countries have signed the treaty. Of course, if the ATCPs modified their procedures and allowed non-Consultative parties to participate in the ATCMs in a material fashion, the latter circumstance could change.

I would argue that modifying the ATS in the direction of greater participation by current non-ATPs, would not make the administration of the ATS (particularly its ability to make policy decisions) unduly complex, as long as weighted voting and special majorities were introduced into ATS decision making for suitable issues. Moreover, current ATCP states would have their investments in the form of financial expenditures supporting exploration and scientific expeditions to the region explicitly recognized and protected by the judicious application of appropriate special majority decision rules and weighted voting ratios. I contend that the ATCP group of countries should be expanded (by modifying the entry standard of "substantial scientific activity") to include more current non-ATPs as well as current Contracting Parties in decision making. But if such an expansion occurred, the current consensus decision rule would likely have to be altered so that the current ATCPs would not be impeded by a single state or group of states adamantly opposed to a proposed course of action. If sustained, resolute opposition could conceivably result in the departure of certain current ATCPs from the ATS. The likelihood of this outcome is lessened, it seems to me, if there is a reduced dependence on consensus within the ATS.[29]

## ADAPTATION ARGUMENT

The ATCPs have not been averse to the insertion of at least limited voting mechanisms into particular instruments of the ATS, even though they have not taken this step insofar as ATCM rules of procedure are concerned. To be sure, consensus decision making has been incorporated as an integral component of specific instruments.[30] Language in the Antarctic Living Resources Convention (CCAMLR) calls for consensus voting in the Convention's Commission[31] on matters of substance. The question of whether an issue is a matter of substance is itself treated as a matter of substance and is therefore decided by consensus.[32] It should of course not be an unanticipated development that a belief in the proficiency of consensus decision making to produce widely countenanced decisions has been reproduced in ATS instruments. The preference for consensus is clearly posited in the 1959 Treaty.[33] This preference for consensus has been extended to ATS instruments by the ATCPs in the interest of gaining a large number of accessions to the Treaty. This was the case, for example, with the CCAMLR, when the initial U.S. preference for a two-thirds majority voting rule in the Commission[34] (established under that instrument) pertaining to conservation matters, was withdrawn in favor of a consensus rule.[35] In order to gain the support of all participating parties in the negotiations for a U.S. Draft Convention, some of whom had doubts as to the wisdom of injecting a two-thirds voting rule into Commission procedures, the U.S. relented, and agreed to the consensus method.[36] This withdrawn U.S. proposal suggests that certain ATCPs foresaw the possible need within the CCAMLR framework for a decision-making process apart from a reliance solely on consensus.

This recognition was explicitly inserted into the decision-making machinery for CRAMRA. Although the Antarctic Mineral Resource Commission[37] has a consensus decision-rule for matters pertaining to the identification of areas for possible exploitation,[38] it has a three-quarters majority decision-rule for most other substantive matters,[39] and a simple majority for procedural matters.[40]

The Commission shall "identify" an area for possible exploitation only after it receives reports of the Scientific, Technical, and Environmental Advisory Committee[41] and Special Meeting of the Parties,[42] that taking such action is consistent with the Convention. Whether to identify such an area is a Commission decision taken by consensus.[43]

But it is worth noting that when crafting CRAMRA language, even on an issue as central as the control of exploration and development activities, the ATCPs included voting mechanisms. An Antarctic Mineral Resource Regulatory Committee must be established for any area the Commission identifies for possible exploration and development.[44] Each Committee has the responsibility to insure that any proposed exploratory activity is consistent with the Convention. In their deliberations the Regulatory Committees' decision-rule for most substantive decisions is a two-thirds majority.[45] Thus, although one might expect the general decision-rule to be that the greater the magnitude of the decision to be made, the greater a reliance on consensus or even unanimity, this appears not to be so in the case of certain important CRAMRA functions.

Although I am arguing for less of a dependence on consensus decision making by the ATCPs, some observers have suggested that a move to append voting rules to the ATCM decision making procedures would increase the likelihood of "defection" (exit from the ATS) by ATCPs not apprehensive about conducting activity in the Antarctic region outside the ATS.[46] But a contrary argument has been offered by Tenenbaum, where she holds the position that the veto power given to any ATCP-member at the ATCMs because of the consensus decision-rule, would itself foment conflict and possible defection under certain conditions.[47]

Any long-term impasse between states concerned with providing access for exploitation to their nationals and those states opposing such access may result in the breakdown of the entire system. Oil or gas shortages or political turbulence in oil-producing nations might exacerbate any continuing impasse. The end result may be that major developed consuming states will simply withdraw from the Convention and independently pursue development activities.[48]

Certainly, the Madrid Protocol has abrogated the concern in this quotation with mineral exploitation of Antarctica.[49] But the general argument is that a particular state or bloc of states may become highly dissatisfied with the ability of one other opposing state to block initiatives of the former. If this dissatisfaction is sufficiently severe, the impeded state or states may elect to defect from the organization.[50]

## TRANSPARENCY

"Transparency in the polar regions has come to mean nothing more or less than having reliable sources of information about developments in those regions."[51] Proceeding from the language of the Antarctic Treaty, it is clear the framers understood the necessity for good information pertaining to operations in the Antarctic. Art. 7 states that the parties shall have the right to designate observers to carry out any inspections,[52] and that "each observer designated in accordance with the provisions of paragraph 1 of this Article shall have complete freedom of access at any time to any or all areas of Antarctica." [53] In addition, "all areas of Antarctica, including all stations, installations and equipment within those areas, and all ships and aircraft at points of discharging or embarking cargoes or personnel in Antarctica, shall be open at all times to inspection by any observers designated in accordance with paragraph 1 of this article."[54]

But the obligation that operations in Antarctica remain "open to inspection" did not prevent the construction of an airstrip by the French at the Dumont d'Urville station on Point Geologie which began in 1983,[55] and which proved to be highly destructive to penguin rookeries in the local area. By 1985 evidence had accumulated leaving little doubt that the dynamiting necessary to clear land for the airstrip had killed apparently roosting penguins, as well as rendered damage to rookeries.[56]

It is disturbing that the ATCPs apparently knew the French activity was having an adverse effect on indigenous Antarctic fauna, and yet the ATCPs did not take steps to persuade the French to cease the construction work altogether, or to find alternative construction methods. There is no chronicle of diplomatic efforts by any of the ATCPs of record at the time, to approach the French with these concerns.[57] The French action was seemingly a violation of Arts. VI and VII of the 1964 Agreed Measures on the Conservation of Antarctic Fauna,[58] but the ATCPs did not take the French to task for such an apparent breach. One observer has made the following comment:

> The attitude of the ATCPs apparently was that this situation was better left to the French to handle than to be stirred up in public controversy by other governments. French compliance with the Agreed Measures failed, enforcement by the other ATCPs was set aside, and maintenance of a conflict-free Antarctic Treaty Consultative process was given priority over punishing violations of international law affecting the Antarctic continent.[59]

## AUTONOMOUS INSPECTION

Article VII of the Antarctic Treaty establishes that all areas of Antarctica, and essentially all activities within the region, are perpetually subject to inspection by observers so designated by the ATCPs.[60] But only the Consultative Parties may conduct inspections, which means there is a lack of an "independent" inspection organ, i.e., an administrative body which would include designated inspectors originating from non-ATCP states.[61] This may not be an inherent deficiency in the ATS general framework, but questions have been raised about the adequacy of the improved inspection procedures found even in the Protocol.[62] The Protocol does make the stipulation that a report be propagated after any inspection which might occur.[63] This is no doubt an improvement over the inspection procedures in the Antarctic Treaty, but the value of these reports will be contingent upon the rigor and thoroughness with which they are conducted, and that will in turn be partly dependent on the identity of the inspectors. Art. 14(2)(b) of the Protocol appears to raise the possibility, at least, that inspectors may be drawn from a pool of individuals that were not nationals of an ATCP.[64] But even if this were to occur, the inspection process would be administered by the ATCP state which had made a designation of inspectors from individuals that were not nationals of an ATCP. The point being that this administrative structure would dilute the "independent" character of the inspection process. Ridgewell is right to refer to this process as essentially a "national inspection scheme."[65] It is the latter attribute to which Ridgewell apparently refers when she states "it is unlikely that these provisions will be used to establish any institutional inspection system in the near future."[66]

The matter of independent review, while it may be "contrary to Antarctic traditions,"[67] is more than minor, and is not moot. Although he was addressing the issue of an ATCP's discretion regarding whether an activity is environmentally harmless or is one which should be subject to an impact assessment, and not inspection procedures themselves, one observer has noted that in general, independent review adds an important safeguard element to any environmental regime.[68] The absence of independent review is an issue which would appear to diminish the efforts of the ATCPs (in at least some instances) to effectively protect the Antarctic environment.

It might be inferred that provision for critical review of proposed Antarctic activity was introduced through Arts. 3(5) and 3(6) of Annex I to the Protocol.[69] But Ridgewell makes an astute observation concerning this possible inference. "Much will depend upon the attitude of the parties in practice. It has always been open to other ATCPs to raise possible breaches of obligations within the ATS at ATCMs under existing procedures. However, the closed shop or club system of the ATS has rendered this form of 'peer pressure' ineffective and, on occasion, politically unattractive."[70] In making this statement Ridgewell appears to be alluding to the possibility that the ATCP states have failed to be, or have been tempted to show a less than stringent vigilance toward each other's Antarctica activities. One manner in which this circumstance could occur would be when particular ATCP states had made sufficiently large investments supporting certain activities on the continent, such that an inspection and call by other ATCPs, for a halt to the activity would be quite costly.[71]

This circumstance would then pose at least the possibility of a "logrolling" relationship, with two or more ATCPs, each "averting their gaze" from the activities of the other, thereby introducing unwarranted environmental risk into the region. It could be argued that interested nongovernmental organizations (NGOs) which have been allowed to participate in the ATCMs, have helped to provide a greater "transparency," which has heretofore been absent, into the Antarctic environmental regime and have produced benefit for the region. That is, the diligent attentiveness exercised by NGOs attending ATCMs might be able to prevent logrolling agreements amongst the present ATCPs from being struck.[72] But, however diligent particular NGOs may be in placing questionable ATCP policies or positions on the table during ATCMs, this activity, although commendable, does not seem to me to serve as well as a check against logrolling, as would actual participation on inspection teams. Presently, of course, it remains the case that only ATCPs may conduct actual physical inspections, and surely this is so not just by happenstance.[73]

During the 1998/99 Antarctic "season" (with adequate daylight and reasonable ambient temperatures), a major joint inspection was conducted by ATCPs Germany and the UK. The latter country reported on its inspection efforts during ATCM XXIII in WP23.[74] The inspection process included a close examination of twenty-one land based sites, as well as two tourist vessels.[75] Although the general tone of the report is commendatory, there are some specific criticisms, along with recommendations for improvements in certain practices. Probably the two most prominent criticisms were: first, lax procedures in fuel handling and storage; and second, the less than keen attention given to the disposal of waste and sewage.[76] One must presume that these are two continuing functions of any ongoing scientific endeavor, and the UK and Germany made recommendations which would attempt to meet what appear to be, in the words of an NGO that has been one of the most persistent critics of ATCM policies, "chronic deficiencies" in Protocol implementation.[77] Most of these recommendations were in response to the range of criticisms mentioned above; in response to the two specific criticisms articulated earlier, the report called for an improved set of "fuel handling and storage practices, and "more consistency on waste and storage disposal practices."[78]

An earlier inspection carried out by Norway in December, 1996, may be more illustrative of my point in this discussion.[79] The sites inspected by Norway were Neumayer (Germany), SANAE IV (South Africa), Maitri (India) and Novolazarevskaya (Russia). The information report submitted by Norway to the twenty-first ATCM in Christchurch, noted that even though the Madrid Protocol had not at that time entered into force, "all the stations visited were managed as if most of the Protocol's provisions were already binding."[80]

This 1996 inspection report, following what had become accepted practice, issued a number of recommendations following the conclusion of the Norwegian team's work at the multiple sites. Two of the more prominent of those recommendations included in the report were to construct "(i) an inventory of locations of former activities, including fuel depots and waste sites, should be made, to avoid such information being lost; [and pursue] (iv) development of contingency plans for possible fuel spills and innovative means to further reduce risks of such spills should be given priority."[81] Clearly, the safe handling and storage of fuel, and the disposal of wastes, have received repeated attention through the inspection methods implemented by the ATCPs.

Whether such attention indicates a concern by particular inspection teams that procedures followed by certain ATCPs exhibited a disturbing laxity pertaining to the issues of fuel storage, and waste disposal, may be an unwarranted inference. But the question is whether, even if its inspection teams did find evidence suggesting a lack of due diligence on the part of fellow ATCPs, during the latter's activities at their respective stations relative to the fuel storage and waste disposal safety issues, Norway would place that information in its report. I suggest it is not inconceivable that Norway would "avert its gaze" from such evidence, if Norway believed it was itself not without culpability on the same or related environmental issues.

For a number of years certain NGOs have been granted either "observer" or "expert" status by the ATCPs.[82] But such status applies to participation at the ATCMs themselves (which in and of itself is helpful), and as mentioned above, does not extend to a physical presence on actual inspection teams. Although the "watchdog" work ethic of NGOs[83], such as the Antarctic and Southern Ocean Coalition (ASOC), in "pushing" the ATCPs has been commendable, this pressure has for the most part taken place within the ATCMs. There has been no discernible movement to insert an NGO presence into inspection teams. I will return below to the issue concerning the possible identity of external or autonomous inspection teams. But it should not go unmentioned that the concerns about less than vigorous prosecution of inspection responsibilities extends to the conservation arena. "In many cases the scientists working in protected areas[84] are also empowered to act as site inspectors. While this arrangement appeals because it is convenient operationally, and practical, it may not be the most appropriate way to guarantee the achievement of conservation goals."[85] The 1959 Treaty itself provides little guidance as to what steps might be taken if an inspection was undertaken which disclosed that violations of the Treaty had taken place.[86]

However, it could be argued that the "logrolling" issue was addressed in Art. VII of the 1959 Treaty. Art. VII grants to each Contracting Party "the right to designate observers to carry out any inspection provided for in the present Article."[87] But since observers "shall be nationals of the Contracting parties which designate them,"[88] and since all current Contracting Parties have, by definition, a "vested interest" in Antarctica by virtue of their having "conducted substantial scientific activity" there, the logrolling problem seemingly was not fully addressed by the 1959 Treaty. This oversight may have helped prompt Art. 14(2)(b) of the Protocol, which, as has been pointed out elsewhere, and remarked on above, seems to allow for the designation of observers that were not nationals of an ATCP.[89] But this is not the "international inspection" called for by some observers,[90] and the present inspection procedures, still appear to have a certain "inadequacy," [91] and have been characterized as "ineffective" or even "politically unattractive."[92]

The Protocol specifies that a function of the Committee for Environmental Protection (CEP) is to provide advice "on inspection procedures, including formats for inspection reports and checklist for the conduct of operations."[93] A copy of all inspection reports is to be received by the CEP.[94] It has been noted that a full evaluation of the CEP has to await developments now that the Protocol has entered into force,[95] which in part at least, means waiting to see what procedures emerge from future ATCMs which would set parameters for inspections carried out by ATCP designated observers.[96] But it must be kept in mind that the CEP is an advisory body; it does not itself devise policy.[97] The CEP is thus inherently limited, and the inspection reports that are to be submitted to it (as well as to all ATCPs, including the inspected party) can not produce anything more than recommendations for revised procedures, including "institutional inspections," if it is concluded from the reports that the inspection process has been less than vigorous.

## AN ANALOGOUS ILLUSTRATION

There can be no assurances that a greater clarity in transparency would be achieved through the extension of Contracting Party (ATCP) status to states heretofore not eligible for that status. Candidate states would be those that have an "interest" in Antarctica, but are not presently "conducting substantial scientific research activity there."[98] In order to best serve the purpose of avoiding the formation of logrolling relationships among the ATCPs, one possible path would be to enlarge ATCP membership to those states who claim an interest in the stewardship of the global commons, but who may not have committed significant scientific resources to study specific components of that commons.

With the incorporation into the ATS of states without significant resources committed for the purposes of exploration or scientific activity, it would then be possible to implement the kind of "autonomous" inspection outlined above. That is, representatives from these "disinterested" (only from the standpoint of lacking any motivation to protect a *material* investment in the region) states could provide at least part of the membership for inspection teams now intermittently deployed by the ATCPs. This step would not provide a guarantee of greater protection for the Antarctic, but in my judgment would increase the likelihood of such an outcome.

It may occur to certain readers that my emphasis on autonomous inspection for the ATS is unwarranted, but I do not believe so. If the experience of the International Whaling Commission (IWC)[99] pertaining to the issue of autonomous or independent inspection can serve as a caution for the ATS, then I would hold to the position which suggests the ATS would be well served to move toward a more inclusive membership. Reiterating this admonition is appropriate at this point in the discussion because the authority and effectiveness of the IWC has recently been called into question, partly as a consequence of the latter's inability to implement a genuinely independent inspection and observer regime. Such a regime has come to be seen as a necessary component of the Whaling Commission's regulatory responsibilities, as specified in the International Convention for the Regulation of Whaling (ICRW).[100]

A prime stimulus leading to the recent questioning of IWC effectiveness has been the discovery of a major deception by the former Soviet Union, which was an IWC member (the successor Russian Federation remains a member) and at one time a state possessing one of the world's leading whaling industries. Documentation provided by staffers working within the former Soviet Fisheries Ministry now indicates that the magnitude of the Soviet under reporting of annual whale catches was egregious. "For example, from 1948 to 1973, the Soviet Union killed 48,477 humpback whales rather than the 2,710 it officially reported to the IWC."[101] The blatantly excessive Soviet violations of IWC quota allotments extended beyond a single species. [One] Soviet ship reported killing 152 humpbacks and 156 blue whales during the 1960s. Revised figures from Russia's whaling commissioner indicate that the actual figures were 7,207 humpbacks, 1,433 blue whales and 717 right whales, the latter being a species protected from harvesting by the IWC since the 1930s.[102]

If the current Russian government could attribute these violations of IWC quotas to inadvertent statistical error, or administrative mismanagement, then the recent revelations would seem less malevolent in terms of the evident disregard for the conservation of several whale species. But this appears to not have been the case whatsoever. As Ray Gambell, the former Secretary of the IWC, has put it, "[w]e knew there was a black hole in our calculations which did not make sense. Now we know that thousands of whales we thought were protected have been systematically slaughtered. The enormity of the deception is staggering."[103] In addition to the clear disregard for the health of protected whale species, it is immensely discomforting that the Soviet Union could execute this deception with such apparent ease, over such a long period, and with such deliberation.

On the last point, the deliberation underpinning the Soviet acts, there is little question.

Data have recently been presented correcting the catch estimates submitted from Soviet whaling operations in the Southern hemisphere from 1949/50. The earlier official figures submitted by the USSR *were substantially falsified* to conceal large scale violations of the international regulations. Such evidence has reinforced the need for the establishment of totally credible inspection and international observer schemes for any future whaling activities (emphasis added).[104]

The IWC has traditionally relied upon the whaling industry for data on the annual catch by national industries of different whale species.[105] As indicated by the "black hole" reference above, the IWC now realizes there was a substantial under reporting of catches, and not only by the Soviet Union. It has now been concluded by Norwegian scientists that Norway's whaling industry has significantly under reported its catch of minke whales.[106] What made this under reporting possible was principally due to the IWC's reliance on an observer and inspection system which, although well intentioned, was less than rigorous. Individuals were placed with the purpose of inspecting shore stations, as well as factory ships, in order to enforce IWC quota limits. But "[b]ecause the inspector is from the same nation that he is policing, inspection is often lackadaisical. The nationals are too sympathetic to their country's commercial and economic interests to make the voluntary program effective."[107]

Apparently recognizing there were certain inconsistencies in the data being provided to it by member states, in 1972 the IWC implemented an Independent

Observer Scheme, providing a bilateral mechanism whereby two states volun-tarily agree to exchange observers.[108] In this mechanism the observers of one state are to take up duties on the ships of the second country, and report any discerned violations to the IWC. But even this mechanism's attempt at "au-tonomous" inspection has proven insufficient, because many of the violations referred to above regarding Norwegian takes of minke whales, occurred after the implementation of the Independent Observer Scheme.[109]

Thus, for the period 1947–1972, the period covered by the data Russian scientists provided to the IWC in the mid-1990s,[110] the Soviet Union deliber-ately undercut a primary mission of the IWC, that is, "to provide for the proper conservation of whale stocks." [111] From at least 1977, Norwegian sci-entists now report that the Norwegian industry has purposely under reported to the IWC its catch of North Atlantic minke whales and thus "undermined the Scientific Committee's [of the IWC] assessment of the species."[112] The IWC's mission had thus again been impeded. Since the 1982 imposition of a "moratorium" (a reduction to zero of catch limits for commercial purposes of all whale species)[113] the IWC has sought to substantially revamp its regula-tory procedures in order to more effectively carry out the "conservation of whale stocks" mission.

This revamping of the IWC's regulatory procedures is referred to by the IWC as a "revision" of its management policies, the Revised Management Procedure.[114] But before this procedure is implemented the IWC believes it must have confidence the new procedure will be more effective than the procedure previously in place. To date, the IWC has not been able to achieve a sufficient level of confidence in the revised procedure, for the most part because of an inability of the members to agree on an effective inspection and observation regime. The issue has been put in the following terms by a long-term observer of the IWC:

The present impasse in the IWC has arisen because the majority of the IWC members consider that, in light of the devastating history of overex-ploitation by vessels whose activities were supervised *only by national in-spectors*, international inspection is indispensable if whaling is ever to be re-sumed. The IWC has therefore decided that the Revised Management Procedures now agreed to in principle, under which whaling could be re-sumed on stocks deemed to have recovered, should not be made opera-tional until a Revised Management Scheme, establishing international super-vision and control and humane killing methods, has been instituted (emphasis added).[115]

It is clear then, that the IWC itself considers the 1972 Independent Ob-server Scheme, in which the national inspectors from *two member whaling states* would be exchanged between the vessels of each country, to have been largely ineffectual. But agreement on a new inspection regime as part of the Revised Management Scheme has proven to be elusive. "The IWC has met several times to discuss implementation of an observer program. The most difficult issues are who should bear responsibility for the cost of implementation, and whether the IWC observers should take precedence over national inspectors if there is room for one extra person on a boat."[116] The latter suggestion, assigning specifically to the international institution a cadre of inspectors, thereby eliminating altogether any "national" character of individuals identified as an "IWC observer," is one of two proposals to gain an "independent" inspection function for the IWC which has been put forward. The other submission has been to assign observers from non-whaling states to the boats of whaling states. Because there are IWC members that have no whaling fleets whatsoever, this idea would have the observers drown out non-whaling IWC member states. Referring to the now somewhat dated Independent Observer Scheme, one commentator has suggested: "One way to strengthen the voluntary program would be for the IWC to assign the observers, matching a whaling nation with a non-whaling partner; for example, Japan and the United Kingdom."[117]

The basic intent of the IWC seems reasonably evident. One observer has noted that alone, the "catch limit algorithm" or CLA, a new statistical estimation procedure for whale populations abundance,[118] may not be sufficient to address the concerns of many countries. These states, members and non-members of the IWC, want assurances that adequate statistical, as well as observation and inspection, procedures are incorporated into the Revised Management Procedure.

Many countries are concerned that given the past history of whaling, even [the CLA] procedure may not be sufficient. These countries are anxious to have a further shell of detail around the CLA incorporating data requirements needed to monitor the efficacy of the RMP, and a fully agreed international observer scheme designed to allow *transparent* operations in whaling nations to the international community (emphasis added).[119]

Provision for allowing the international community to view transparent operations on the part of ATCP states, which will prove beneficial for the Arctic region, is the basic thesis of this final part of my paper. Similar to the criticism lodged against the 1972 IWC Independent Observer Scheme, instituting an observer and inspection mechanism which provides that the inspecting teams for Arctic scientific and exploration sites to be drawn only from ATCP states, that is, states which have carried out substantial scientific activity in the Arctic, brings unnecessary risk to the region.

Recall that even in the event the ATS inspectors were to be drawn from a pool of individuals that were not nationals of an ATCP, and this is not a certainty, the inspection process would still be *administered* by the ATCP state which had made the designation of inspectors from non-ATCP nationals in the first place.[120] Thus, the exchange of observers between ATCPs in the ATS system would not vitiate the likelihood of a logrolling relationship between

ATCPs, potentially harmful to the Arctic region. Avoiding the possibility of logrolling relationships between ATCP countries involved in an inspection of each other's Arctic sites, was a central topic in my earlier discussion.[121]

Currently, because it is still the case that observers "shall be nationals of the contracting parties which designate them,"[122] and because all ATCPs have "conducted substantial scientific activity"[123] in the Arctic, the designated nationals of one ATCP could well be "too sympathetic"[124] to the interests of those private groups or government agencies from a second ATCP conducting scientific activity, to make the ATP exchange program operate effectively. Thus, logrolling relationships between ATCPs might go undetected due to insufficiently rigorous inspections.

Given that misreporting or under reporting to the IWC of catch data continued even after the IWC's 1972 Independent Observer Scheme was introduced, there would appear to be some likelihood of logrolling relationships having been struck between IWC member whaling states. This at least appears to be a fair inference to make. If such relationships were arrived at within the ATS, it would not be because "the inspector was from the same nation that he is policing."[125] As we have seen, this is not the practice of the ATS, that is, within the ATS there is a designation of national observers by fellow ATCPs, and these observers are assigned duties of inspecting Arctic sites other than those of their own country. Rather it was due to the recruitment of observers by the ATS only from states with substantial scientific activity in the Arctic, i.e., ATCPs. "Because the whaling nations were the only ones, in general, who were prepared to finance these schemes, it was necessary for the observers to be nominated and exchanged on a bilateral basis *among the active parties* (emphasis added)."[126]

The latter circumstance appears to be analogous to conditions in the IWRC whaling regime pertaining to the question of an "effective inspection and observation scheme,"[127] which has been recognized by the IWC as inadequate to the task of protecting whale populations.[128] A bilateral exchange of nationals to serve as observers of each other's whaling activities demonstrably did not work within the regime created by IWRC. The analogy here is that the bilateral observation scheme within the IWRC regime, has strong similarities to the scheme (although not strictly an exchange) instituted in the ATS. If the analogy holds, then one of the proposals mentioned above as a remedy to the apparent failure (to prevent logrolling and consequent harm to marine mammal natural resources) of the IWC inspection scheme, might pertain to preventing potential failure (logrolling and consequent harm to the Arctic region natural resource) in the ATS scheme.

The first of the earlier mentioned proposals was to have independent observers designated by the IWC, obviating any national character attached to them.[129] In effect, the independent observers would be employed by, and serve at the pleasure of, the IWC. But the ATS has no working Secretariat, thus making administration of such a scheme quite difficult. A second proposal was for the IWC to match "a whaling nation with a non-whaling partner,"[130] that is, have individuals from non-whaling states serve as observers on whaling state vessels (this second proposal seems to have had the presumption that the non-whaling states would be IWC members, but that need not be the case). Such a proposal would have the goal of strengthening the voluntary Independent Observer Scheme, currently scheduled to be replaced with a revamped mechanism by the IWC.

A workable facsimile of such a mechanism, applied to the ATS inspection scheme, would seem feasible and desirable for the same reason articulated in the discussion on the IWC. Within the IWC the goal of a revised observation and inspection scheme is to prevent a continuation of "the devastating history of overexploitation"[131] of numerous whale species. The ATS observation and inspection design has the goal of protecting "the Antarctic environment and dependent and associated ecosystems."[132] Observation and inspection would lessen the likelihood that environmental damage extending from Antarctic activities, and more than "minor or transitory,"[133] would go undetected. But if the observation and inspection was left to be implemented only by nationals of ATCP states, the possibility of introducing "unwelcome subjectivity and diversity" into the inspection process would become more significant.

## CONCLUSIONS

The ATS could move more forthrightly toward a replication of the direction the IWC is currently moving. That is, nationals from states *not* currently conducting substantial activity in the region, could serve as observers conducting inspections of Antarctic sites operated by ATCPs (states which are conducting substantial activity in the region). These "inactive" (in the Antarctic), but not "disinterested" states which would provide observers, could be drawn from the large group of countries outside of the ATS altogether, that is, countries that have not signed, nor have acceded to the Antarctic Treaty (non-ATPs). The inactive, or "dormant" states providing observers could also be selected from the Contracting Parties to the Antarctic Treaty (ATPs), which have not achieved Consultative Party status (ATCPs).

But in my judgment a third option seems preferable. That would be to grant ATCP status, either to certain ATP states or to non-ATP states, which have voiced an interest in greater participation in the ATS, as I proposed much earlier in this paper.[134] The administrative details of arranging the recruitment and training of observers from "dormant states," and assigning to those observers duties of inspecting Antarctic sites operated by ATCPs, would become more manageable, it would seem, if these details could be worked out within the context of an ATCM. Since only ATCPs have a major voice at ATCMs, the process becomes more direct, and thus more manageable once particular states, inactive in terms of conducting scientific activity in the region, have been designated ATCPs.

In sum, I have tried to present an argument favoring a more inclusive ATCP membership because there is an expectation that states currently not part of that membership remain bound by its rules and norms. My contention has also been that a more comprehensive ATCP membership is feasible if the rules of institutional governance are properly configured. Most importantly, the goal of reducing the risks of environmental damage to the world's most pristine ecological system, I have claimed can be more effectively promoted through the adoption of a more stringent monitoring and inspection scheme. This scheme can achieve greater proficiency by incorporating the assistance of states not engaged in substantial activities in the region, into the scheme's operation.

If the goal of Antarctic preservation is to be made more achievable, I have tried to show why a more inclusive ATCP membership must be created. I have tried to demonstrate that this more inclusive membership can be instituted without prejudice to the interests of the present ATCP states. Finally, I have argued that issues of fairness and equity should not be excluded from discussions of Antarctic governance, if the stewards of the region are to maintain reasonable expectations of compliance by all states, with the rules, norms, and policies promulgated by the Antarctic region's governing institution.

## NOTES

1. Signed at Washington December 1, 1959. *Entered into force* June 23, 1961. 12 U.S.T. 794; T.I.A.S. 4780; 402 U.N.T.S. 71.

2. The term "system" has wide acceptance and usage. The original impetus for the creation of the ATS was to put into place a "framework for cooperation in scientific research." See Waller, *Death of a Treaty: The Decline and Fall of the Antarctic Minerals Convention, Vanderbilt Journal of Transnational Literature* 22, 1989: 631, 659. See also Keyuan, "The Common Heritage of Mankind and the Antarctic Treaty System," *Netherlands International Law Review* 38, 1991: 173, 183, 195.

3. ATS members that were ATCPs at the conclusion of the 1999 23rd Consultative meeting in Lima, Peru, were Argentina, Australia, Belgium, Brazil, Bulgaria, Chile, China, Ecuador, Finland, France, Germany, India, Italy, Japan, Republic of Korea, the Netherlands, New Zealand, Norway, Peru, Poland, the Russian Federation, South Africa, Spain, Sweden, UK, United States, and Uruguay.

4. Members of the ATS that were Contracting Parties, not ATCPs, at the conclusion of the 1999 23rd Consultative Meeting in Lima, Peru, were: Austria, Canada, Columbia, Cuba, the Czech Republic, Denmark, Greece, Guatemala, Hungary, the Democratic Republic of Korea, Papua New Guinea, Romania, Slovak Republic, Switzerland,

Turkey, Ukraine, and Venezuela. To better understand what it means for states to be Contracting Parties and not an ATCP see Money, "The Protocol on Environmental Protection to the Antarctic Treaty: Maintaining A Legal Regime," *Emory International Law Review* 7, 1993: 163, 174–76.

5. A definition of the Antarctic Treaty System in the sense of enumerating the elements that comprise it is found in Art. 1(3) of the 1991 Madrid Protocol (formally known as the Protocol on Environmental Protection to the Antarctic Treaty). They are: the Antarctic Treaty itself, measures taken by the ATCPs under or pursuant to the Treaty, discrete international legal instruments in force which are associated with the Treaty, and measures taken by the ATCPs under those instruments. See Redgewell, "Environmental Protection in Antarctica: the 1991 Protocol," *International and Comparative Law* 43, 1994: 599, note 5 and accompanying text.

6. *See* UN Document A/C.1/43/PV. 45.

7. These measures were a special subset of policy recommendations of the ATCPs produced during the 1964 Third Antarctic Treaty Consultative Meeting in Brussels. A number of the issues addressed in these measures have been revisited by the Madrid Protocol. *Done* June 2–13, 1964, *entered into force* January 14, 1998. 17 U.S.T. 991, 996, T.I.A.S. No. 6058, modified in 24 U.S.T. 1802, T.I.A.S. No. 7693 (1973).

8. *Done* June 1, 1972, *entered into force* March 11, 1978. 27 U.S.T. 441, T.I.A.S. No. 8826, reprinted in 11 I.L.M. 251 (1972).

9. Done May 20, 1980, entered into force April 7, 1982. 33 U.S.T. 3476, T.I.A.S. No.

10. Done June 2, 1988, opened for signature November 25, 1988, reprinted in 27 I.L.M. 859 (1988). Because of political opposition from certain ATCPs and since the Madrid Protocol has since come into being, CRAMRA has not entered into force and very well may never be, and consequently may arguably not be considered part of the ATS proper.

11. Done June 21, 1991, adopted October 4, 1991, entered into force January 17, 1998, reprinted in 30 I.L.M. 1455 (1991).

12. SCAR makes recommendations to the ATCPs concerning candidate research projects and also receives commissions from the ATCPs to initiate certain projects which could lead to ATCP recommendations See Joyner, "Antarctica and the Indian Ocean States: The Interplay of Law, Interests, and Geopolitics," *Ocean Development and International Law* 21, 1990: 41, 45.

13. See Green, "Antarctic Baselines: An Alternative Formulation," *International Journal of Marine and Coastal Law* 11, 1996: 333, 338, n. 15. For a good discussion of the difficult path the CRAMRA has taken within the ATS see Waller, *supra* n. 2, *passim*. The opposition to CRAMRA's entry into force was led most forcefully by two ATCP states, France and Australia. See McColloch, "Protocol on Environmental Protection to the Antarctic Treaty—The Antarctic Treaty—Antarctic Minerals Convention—Wellington Convention–Convention on the Regulation of Antarctic Minerals Resource Activities," *Georgia Journal International and Comparative Law* 22, 1992: 211, 213–19. See also Joyner, "CRAMRA's Legacy of Legitimacy: Progenitor to the Madrid Environmental Protection Protocol," *Antarctica and Southern Ocean Law and Occasional Paper Series* 7, *passim* (1995), where Joyner contends that CRAMRA remains relevant to any general discussion of the ATS.

14. Referring to the drafting negotiations one observer has commented that the intent of CRAMRA was to create a "management regime for the regulation of Antarctic

minerals activities," as stated by Joyner and Lipperman, in "Conflicting Jurisdictions in the Southern Ocean: The Case of an Antarctic Minerals Regime," *Virginia Journal of International Law* 27, 1986: 1, 5–6. But the Madrid Protocol has imposed, in the opinion of a number of observers, a fifty-year moratorium on mining, at a minimum, and has made any effort to supersede that moratorium, or to begin a mining effort at the end of the fifty year period, quite difficult. This difficulty resides in the fact that a number of Consultative Parties have become so strongly opposed to any mining initiation on the continent. As long as they remain so opposed, the language of the Protocol will continue to be quite stringent. See Blay, "New Trends in the Protection of the Antarctic Environment," *American Journal of International Law* 86: 377, 394.

15. Three large developing countries, China, India, and Brazil, have acceded to the Antarctic Treaty in recent years. China has now gained Consultative Party status (1985) after acceding to the Antarctic Treaty in 1983; India and Brazil are also Consultative Parties, both having been granted that status in 1983. There does not appear to be much evidence of a concerted "movement from within" by these and other developing country ATPs (Consultative and nonconsultative parties), to speak on behalf of non-ATPs during the ATCMs. China looks positively on the "merits of the ATS," and has generally not supported UN General Assembly resolutions castigating the ATS. At the same time China has expressed concerns that the ATS enable "more countries, especially developing countries, to participate fully in Antarctic activities." See Keyuan, *supra* note 2, at 188. India seems to hold the view that the ATS is not in need of replacement or radical overhaul, although further "evolution" might be desirable. See Joyner, *supra*, n. 12, at 41, 58–59. At least one commentator believes that Brazil upholds "current requirements" for membership in the ATS as appropriate because that country believes this is the surest way to bring about responsible action on the part of states operating in the region. See Butte, "International Norms in the Antarctic Treaty," *International Legal Perspective* 3, 1990: 1, 33.

16. Done, December 10, 1982, entered into force November 16, 1994, reprinted in 21 I.L.M. 1261, hereinafter (UNCLOS III).

17. "A text which contains provisions intended to be legally binding once it has been approved by all the Antarctic Treaty Consultative Parties will be expressed as a Measure recommended for approval in accordance with paragraph 4 of Article IX of the Antarctic Treaty, and referred to as a 'Measure.'" Antarctic Treaty Consultative Parties, *Decision I (1995) on Measures, Decisions and Resolutions*, Final Report of the Nineteenth Antarctic Treaty Consultative Meeting (Seoul), May 8–19, at 89–91 (1995) 35 I.L.M. 1188 (1996).

18. "A decision taken at an Antarctic Treaty Consultative Meeting on an internal organizational matter will be operative at adoption or at such other time as may be specified, and will be referred to as a "Decision." *Id*. at 1188.

19. "A hortatory text adopted at an Antarctic Treaty Consultative Meeting will be contained in a 'Resolution.'" *Id*. at 1189.

20. See Schatz, "Antarctic Treaty Consultative Parties: Measures Relating to the Furtherance of the Principles and Objectives of the Antarctic Treaty," 35 I.L.M. 1165, 1167, 1174. In accordance with Article IX, paragraph 1 of the 1959 Antarctic Treaty, representatives of the contracting parties are to meet on a regular basis (currently on an annual schedule) to recommend measures to their respective governments. These measures convey policy proposals that adhere to the principles and promote the ob-

jectives of the 1959 Treaty. These proposals are put forward for ATCP governments to approve only after they have been adopted through consensus by ATCP delegates during an ATCM. Paragraph 4 of Article IX in the Treaty states that upon unanimous approval by ATCP Contracting Parties, measures "become effective." But it is not clear whether the latter phrase should be construed to mean ATCM recommendations are legally binding on all Consultative Parties or on non-Consultative Parties, or both. There is some debate about this question, a debate which has been cast as an issue centered on whether ATCM recommendations are to be regarded as "soft law," or "hard law." Joyner, "Recommended Measures Under the Antarctic Treaty: Hardening Compliance with Soft International Law," *Michigan Journal of International Law* 19, 1998: 401, 402. Prof. Joyner writes that soft law can bring compliance only on a voluntary basis, while hard law creates unambiguous rights and duties for sovereign states. Joyner is clear in characterizing ATCM recommendations are soft law; but at the same time he also makes a forceful case that these recommendations "carry a certain measure of legal authority." He states: "On the other hand, when a measure is composed in language that clearly aims to convey legal obligations—and that measure receives the necessary approvals and 'becomes effective'—the effect of that approval is to activate the legal obligations explicitly contained in that measure. It is thus both the content of the measure and its successful approval by all ATCP governments that confer legally-binding status on the measure's effect." *Id.* at 410. For further discussion *see infra* n. 118.

21. See Kindt, "Ice Covered Areas and the Law of the Sea: Issues Involving Resource Exploitation and the Antarctic Environment," *Brooklyn Journal of International Law* 24, 1998: 27, 45.

22. See Madsen, "A Certain False Security: The Madrid Protocol to the Antarctic Treaty," *Colorado Journal of International Environmental Law and Policy* 4: 458, 471.

23. Vienna Convention on the Law of Treaties, done May 23, 1969, entered into force January 27, 1980, reprinted at 8 I.L.M. 679 (UN Document A/CONF. 39/27) (1969). On the position of Great Britain regarding the binding nature of the Antarctic Treaty *see* Butte, *supra* n. 15, at 1, 17.

24. Butte, *supra* n. 15, at 18. Butte cites the statement of the Chilean representative in a UN Secretary-General Rep., UN Doc A/39/583, pt. 1, at 33. For an extended discussion of the position Chile has taken regarding the ATS and the Antarctic region see Joyner, "Antarctica and the Latin American States: The Interplay of Law, Geopolitics, and Environmental Priorities," *Geo Environmental Law Review* 4, 1991: 1, 17–23.

25. See McCulloch, *supra* n.13, at 227; Kindt, *supra* n.21 at 47.

26. Antarctic Treaty, *supra* n. 1, Art. XIII (1), 12 U.S.T. at 796.

27. *Id.* art. IX (2), 12 U.S.T. at 798.

28. There is wide agreement on the difficulties faced by developing states in mounting any sustained research effort in the Antarctic. See F. M. Auburn, *Antartica Law and Politics* 1982: 147–53; Money, *supra* n. 4, at 178.

29. Within the UNCLOS framework, the Council (the foremost executive organ of the Authority) was given a "balanced" structure so that countries with differing concerns and interests would better be able to protect those interests, and the motivation for leaving the negotiations or failing to comply with the Treaty would be diminished. Thus, countries were assigned to the Council based on whether they were exporters

or importers of seabed minerals, the size of their investment in preparation for mining, and the like. Such balance was believed necessary since issues pertaining to the equitable sharing of economic benefits derived from activities on the seabed must be decided by consensus. See UNCLOS III, *supra* n. 16, art. 161(1)(a)(b)(c)(d)(e), 21 ILM. at 1300. Although the ATCMs have a consensual decision-rule, such a balance drawn from the community of states is lacking.

30. Consensus decision making has been defined in several different ways. A definition that seems unclouded and useful was provided by the 1974 UN World Population Conference. That Conference defined consensus as "a general agreement obtained without a vote but without there necessarily being unanimity." 56 UN ECOSOC, Supp. 3A (UN Doc. E/5462), at 18 (1974). Although Angelini and Mansfield appear to interpret consensus as requiring all parties to register approval of a proposal, rather than there simply being an absence of any party's rejection of said proposal, the authors make specific note of the consensus decision-making process within the ATCMs. *See* Angelini and Mansfield, "A Call for U.S. Ratification of the Protocol on Antarctic Environmental Protection," *Ecology Law Quarterly* 21, 1994: 163, 184.

31. CCAMLR, Art. XVIII, *supra* n. 9, 27 I.L.M. at 876. This article created the Commission, the most important decision making body under this instrument.

32. *Id.* Art. XXII (1), 27 I.L.M. at 879.

33. Antarctic Treaty, *supra* n. 1, Art. XII (1)(a) specifies that amendments to the Treaty can only occur by virtue of a consensual decision. The same condition holds for "measures in furtherance of the principles and objectives of the Treaty," Antarctic Treaty, *supra* n. 1, Art. IX(4).

34. See Frank, "The Convention on the Conservation of Marine Living Resources," *Ocean Development and International Law Journal* 13, 1983: 291, 301.

35. Frank, "The Convention on the Conservation of Marine Living Resources," 309.

36. Frank, "The Convention on the Conservation of Marine Living Resources," 310.

37. CRAMRA, *supra* n. 10, art 18(1), 27 I.L.M. at 876. Membership in this body is open to those states which held ATCP status at the time the CRAMRA was opened for signature, to any acceding state while it is engaged in substantial scientific, technical, or environmental research relevant to decisions made under the Convention, or to a state sponsoring exploration or development activities under a required Management Scheme, *Id.* article 8(2)), at 876.

38. *Id.* art. 22(2), at 879. If an "operator" engaged in prospecting activities finds that further exploration is warranted, it may ask the Commission to "identify an area for possible exploration and development of a particular mineral resource or resources." *Id.* art. 39(1), at 887.

39. *Id.* n. 10, art. 22(1), at 879.

40. *Id.* art. 22(3), at 879.

41. *Id.* art. 23(1), at 879.

42. *Id.* art. 28(2), at 882.

43. *Id.* art. 41(2), at 888.

44. *Id.* art. 29(1), at 883.

45. *Id.* art. 32(3), at 884.

46. See R. L. Friedheim, *Negotiating the New Ocean Regime*, 357 (1993). Friedheim's position is that pushing to incorporate voting rules in complex multilateral ne-

gotiations, in the interests of gaining concrete results more quickly, only fosters "defection" by those parties able to avoid or absorb the costs of not being signatories. He suggests that in such conferences "participants must be willing to accept consensus as maximum consultation, as the decision rule." *Id.* at 357. This is a viable argument, but in the case of the ATS the risk of ATCp defection due to the incorporation of voting rules, seems minimal in my judgment, precisely because of their prior investment in the regime.

47. See Tenenbaum, "A World Park in Antarctic: The Common Heritage of Mankind," *Virginia Environmental Law Journal* 10 (1990): 109, 125.

48. Tenenbaum, "A World Park in Antarctic: The Common Heritage of Mankind," 125.

49. See Blay, *supra* n. 14, at 394.

50. Tenenbaum, "A World Park in Antarctic: The Common Heritage of Mankind," 125.

51. Bederman, "Theory on Ice: Antarctica in International Law and Relations," 39 *Virginia Environmental Law Journal,* 467 (1999).

52. Antarctic Treaty, *supra* n. 1, Art. 7 (1), 12 U.S.T. at 797.

53. *Id.* Art. 7(2), 12 U.S.T. at 797.

54. *Id.* Art. 7(3), 12 U.S.T. at 797.

55. See Antarctica and Southern Ocean Coalition, *The French Airstrip—A Breach of Antarctic Treaty Rules?* Antarctica Briefing, NO. 9, July 30, 1986.

56. See Joyner, "Protection of the Antarctic Environment: Rethinking the Problems and Prospects," *Cornell International Law Journal* 19, 1986: 259, 268–70.

57. Joyner, "Protection of the Antarctic Environment: Rethinking the Problems and Prospects," 269.

58. Agreed Measures for the Conservation of Antarctic Fauna and Flora, *supra* n. 7, 17 U.S.T. at 998..

59. See Joyner, *supra* n.20, at 417.

60. Antarctic Treaty, *supra* n. 1, Art. VII(3), 12 U.S.T. at 798.

61. See Joyner, *supra* n. 20, at 416.

62. As noted by Angelini and Mansfield, the Protocol "appears to create a new class of observers," selected by the ATCPs to execute inspections as mandated by a specific ATCM. See Madrid Protocol, *supra* n. 11, art. 14 (2), 30 I.L.M. at 1467.. But there is no language calling for a formal institution with the authority to require compliance with inspection procedures which may be drawn during an ATCM. See Angelini and Mansfield, *supra* n. 30, at 199.

63. Madrid Protocol, *supra* n. 11, art. 14(4), 30 I.L.M. at 1467. The reports are to be circulated amongst all ATCPs ( including the inspected party), the CEP, and the public.

64. Madrid Protocol, art. 14(2)(b), at 1467.

65. See Ridgewell, *supra* n. 5, at 612.

66. Ridgewell, 612.

67. Vicuna, "The Protocol on Environmental Protection to the Antarctic Treaty: Questions of Effectiveness," *Georgetown International Environmental Law Review* 7, 1994: 1,5.

68. Vicuna, "The Protocol on Environmental Protection to the Antarctic Treaty," 5.

69. Ridgewell, *supra* n. 5 at 620. Art. 3(5) states that unless there has been an opportunity for consideration of the draft CEE by an ATCM, advised by the CEP, "no final

decision shall be taken to proceed with the proposed activity." Madrid Protocol, *supra* n. 11, Annex 1, art. 3(5), 30 I.L.M. at 1474. In addition, Madrid Protocol, art. 3(6), at 1474, of Annex I, stipulates that if comments are received on the draft CEE, then 'a final Comprehensive Environmental Evaluation shall address and shall included or summarize comments received on the draft Comprehensive Environmental Evaluation.

70. Madrid Protocol, 621.

71. See Money, *supra* n. 4, at 194.

72. See McColloch, *supra* n. 13, at 65.

73. See Joyner, "Antarctica and the Law of the Sea," *San Diego Law Review* 18: 415, 416.

74. See Antarctic and Southern Ocean Coalition, *ASOC Report on the XXIII Antarctic Treaty Consultative Meeting* (1999), at www.asoc.org/currentpress/currentpress/limarpt.htm, in which reference is made to XXII ATCM/WP23, where the UK made extensive comments on the joint inspection it carried out with Germany.

75. Antarctic and Southern Ocean Coalition, *ASOC Report on the XXIII Antarctic Treaty Consultative Meeting*, para. 81.

76. Antarctic and Southern Ocean Coalition, *ASOC Report on the XXIII Antarctic Treaty Consultative Meeting*, para. 81.

77. Antarctic and Southern Ocean Coalition, *ASOC Report on the XXIII Antarctic Treaty Consultative Meeting*, para. 82. The ASOC has been indefatigable in its scrutiny of the environmental and conservation regime constructed during the ATCMs.

78. Antarctic and Southern Ocean Coalition, *ASOC Report on the XXIII Antarctic Treaty Consultative Meeting*, para. 81.

79. See ATCPs, Final Report of the Twenty First Antarctic Treaty Consultative Meeting, Item 10: para. 98, reprinted at www.icair.org.nz/treaty/meetings/xxi-nz/part1.html. The reference is made there to an information paper (XXI ATCM/INF 37) produced by Norway, which conveyed the findings of the Norwegian inspection team. This inspection was undertaken pursuant to Article VII of the Antarctic Treaty.

80. ATCPs, Final Report of the Twenty First Antarctic Treaty Consultative Meeting, para 99.

81. ATCPs, Final Report of the Twenty First Antarctic Treaty Consultative Meeting, para 100.

82. *See* Antarctic and Southern Ocean Coalition, *supra* n. 74, at para. 1. The ASOC states that it was invited to participate in the Lima meeting as an expert, which grant access to materials related to meeting agenda items.

83. ncluded among those organizations, aside from the ASOC, having been given expert status at the ATCMs were the World Trade Organization (WTO), the United Nations Environmental Program (UNEP), the International Association of Antarctic Tourism Operators (IAATO), and the International Union for the Conservation of Nature (IUCN). See Final Report Of The XX Antarctic Treaty Consultative Meeting, Agenda Item 167, reprinted at www.icair.iac.org.nz/twenty/treaty/meetings/xx-utrecht/p1final.html.

84. A Specially Protected Area (SPA) is designated under the Agreed Measures of 1964 as an area afforded singular protection by virtue of containing ecosystems of unique or outstanding scientific interest. *See* Agreed Measures for the Conservation of Antarctic Fauna and Flora, *supra* n. 7, art. VIII, 17 U.S.T. at 999.

85. Keage, Hay, and Russell, "Improving Antarctic Management Plans," *Polar Record* 25, 1989: 309, 310.

86. See generally, Pietro Guiliani, "Inspections under the Antarctic Treaty," in 459 *International Law for Antarctica* (Francisco Francioni and Tullio Scovazzi, eds. 1996).

87. Antarctic Treaty, *supra* n.. 1, art. VIII (1), 12 U.S.T. at 798..

88. Antarctic Treaty, art. VIII(1), at 798.

89. See *supra* text accompanying notes 62–65.

90. Angelini and Mansfield, *supra* n. 30, at 199.

91. See D. Rothwell, *The Polar Regions and the Development of International Law*, 83 (1996);

92. See Ridgewell, *supra* n. 5, at 621.

93. Madrid Protocol, *supra* n. 11, art. 12, para. 1(h), 30 I.L.M. at 1466.

94. Angelini and Mansfield, *supra* n. 30, at 199.

95. See Bederman, *supra* n. 51, at 484.

96. See Ridgewell, *supra* n. 5, at 612.

97. "The functions of the Committee shall be to provide advice and formulate recommendations to the parties in connection with the implementation of this Protocol, including the operation of its Annexes, for consideration at Antarctic Treaty Consultative Meetings, and to perform other such functions as may be referred to it by the Antarctic Treaty Consultative Meetings." Madrid Protocol, *supra* n. 11, art. 12(1), 30 I.L.M. at 1466.

98. On this point of inspections executed for the purpose of environmental protection see Francioni, "The Madrid Protocol on the Protection of the Antarctic Environment," *Texas International Law Journal* 28, 1963: 48, 64. Prior to the Madrid Protocol a major, although not the only, emphasis for inspection was to verify compliance with the 1959 Treaty provisions concerned with the ban on any activities having a military aspect. See Angelini and Mansfield, *supra* n. 30, at 185.

99. The International Whaling Commission (IWC) is the regulatory body created by the International Convention for the Regulation of Whaling , December 2, 1946, 62 Stat. 1716, T.I.A.S. No. 1849, 62 Stat 1716, 161 U.N.T.S. 72 [hereinafter ICRW] with Schedule of Whaling Regulation, entered into force Nov. 10, 1948, amended by Protocol of Nov. 19, 1956, U.S.T. 952, T.I.A.S. No. 4228, 338 U.N.T.S. 366. Implementing legislation for the Convention in the United States is the Whaling Convention Act of 1949, 16 U.S.C. §916 (1988). The Preamble to the ICRW sets out the mission of the convention to be, in part, "to provide for the proper conservation of whale stocks and thus make possible the orderly development of the whaling industry." Preamble to the ICRW, *Id.* 161 U.N.T.S. at 72. Article IV of the Convention sets out, in part, the mission of the IWC, which is to:

> (a) encourage, recommend, or if necessary, organize studies and investigations relating to whales and whaling; (b) collect and analyze statistical information concerning the current condition and trend of the whale stocks and the effects of whaling activities thereon; (c) study, appraise, and disseminate information concerning methods of maintaining and increasing the population of whale stocks. *Id.* 161 U.N.T.S. at 79.

100. Article V of the ICRW states that the IWC is to adopt "regulations with respect to the conservation and utilization of whale resources." *Id.* art V(1), 62 Stat. at 1719, 161 U.N.T.S. at 80.

101. Caron, "Current Development: The International Whaling Commission and the North Atlantic Marine Mammal Commission: The Institutional Risks of Coercion in Consensual Structures," *American Journal of International Law* 89, 1995: 154, 171 [citing] Angier, "Tests Find Meat of Endangered Whales for Sale in Japan," *New York Times*, September 13, 1994, at D9.

102. Burns, "The International Whaling Commission and the Future of Cetaceans: Problems and Prospects," *Colorado Journal of Environmental Law and Policy* 8, 1997: 34, 63 [citing] "Russia Admits Whale Slaughter Rate Twice What it Reported," *Chicago Tribune*, February 21, 1994, 4.

103. Caron, *supra* n. 101 [citing] Hearst, "Soviet Files Hid Systematic Slaughter of World Whale Herds," *Gazette* (Montreal), February 12, 1994, at D9.

104. Gambell, "The International Whaling Commission Today," in *Whaling in the North Atlantic—Economic And Political Perspectives*, Gudrun Petursdottir, ed. Proceedings of a conference held in Reykjavik, Iceland, March 1, 1997, reprinted at www.highnorth.no/Iceland/th-in-to.htm [citing] Zemsky, Berzin, Mikhalyev, and Tormosov, *Materials on Whaling by Soviet Whaling Fleets (1947–1972)* 4 (1995).

105. See Burns, *supra* n. 102, at 62.

106. Burns, 62 [citing] Holt, "Leaks and Loopholes," *Whalewatcher* Summer 1986: 13.

107. Spencer, "Domestic Enforcement of International Law: The International Convention for the Regulation of Whaling," Colorado Journal of International Environmental Law and Policy 2, 1991: 109 115.

108. Spencer, "Domestic Enforcement of International Law," 115.

109. See Burns, *supra* n. 102, and accompanying text.

110. See Gambell, *supra* n. 104. The reference is to the data provided by scientists working for the Russian government as cited by Gambell, see Zemsky et. al., *Materials On Whaling By Soviet Whaling Fleets (1947–1972)* (1995).

111. *See infra* n. 99, and accompanying text.

112. Burns, *supra* n. 102, at 62.

113. For the full text of the moratorium see Leich, "Contemporary Practice of the United States Relating to International Law: Environmental Affairs," *American Journal of International Law* 19, 1985: 431, 435.

114. See Gambell, "International Management of Whales and Whaling: An Historical Overview of the Regulation of Commercial and Aboriginal Subsistence Whaling," *Arctic* 46, 1993: 97, 101.

115. Birnie, "Review: The International Politics of Whaling," *Arctic* 51, 1998: 67, 68.

116. Walters and Dugger, "The Hunt for Grey Whales: The Dilemma of Native American Treaty Rights and the International Moratorium on Whales," *Columbia Journal of International Law* 22, 1997: 319, 350, n. 173.

117. Spencer, *supra* n. 107, at 116.

118. Bridgewater and Anderson, "Whales or Whalers?" *Search* 24, 1993: 190, 192.

119. Bridgewater and Anderson, "Whales or Whalers?" 192.

120. *See infra* n. 62, and accompanying text.

121. *See infra* notes 71 and 72, and accompanying text.

122. Antarctic Treaty, *supra* n. 1, art, VIII (1), U.S.T. at 798.

123. Antarctic Treaty, art. VIII (1), at 798.

124. See Spencer, *supra* n. 107, and accompanying text.

125. Spencer, n. 211, and accompanying text.

126. Gambell, *supra* n. 114, at 100. To put forward financial considerations as an explanation for having observers only from ATCP states may have some legitimacy, but creates some irony. It is financial considerations which prevent many current non-ATCPs from being admitted into that circle, because they do not have the resources to carry out substantial scientific activity in the Arctic region. In addition, because of those same financial considerations, the ATS is claiming that non-ATCPs are not able to provide observers to the ATS inspection regime. But it would seem to me, for the sake of region protection, the current ATCPs might be willing to bear the brunt of the cost attached to recruiting nationals from current non-ATCP, or non-Antarctic Treaty Party (ATP), countries to serve as ATS observers. The latter step would only occur if the ATCPs held the belief that the occurrence of logrolling within the ATS is conceivable, and that it is worth taking steps to prevent it.

127. Gambell, *supra* n. 104, at 4.

128. Gambell, 4, [citing] International Whaling Commission, "Chairman's Report of the Forty-Sixth Annual Meeting," *Report of the International Whaling Commission* 45, 1995: 15, 26, 43–44.

129. See *infra*, n. 116, and accompanying text.

130. See *infra* n. 117, and accompanying text.

131. Birnie, *supra* n. 115, at 69.

132. Madrid Protocol, *supra* n. 11, Art. 8, 30 I.L.M. at 1464.

133. Madrid Protocol, Annex I, Arts. 2–4, at 1474.

134. See *infra* notes 28–29, and accompanying text.

# IV

## DISPUTE RESOLUTION

# 6

# Contemporary Diplomacy and Conflict Resolution: The Intertwining

*John D. Stempel*

## ABSTRACT

Post–Cold War international affairs have moved the international arena away from bloc politics toward a multipolar, multicivilizational world with different zones, issues, and politics. Diplomacy is evolving away from purely national (and bloc) advocacy of the Cold War period, toward an older configuration of concern with overall security and system management on one hand, and fixation with more local and subnational problems on the other. This shift lends greater importance to diplomacy as an intellectual framework and an active, practical process for understanding and carrying out conflict resolution, political reconciliation, and community-building across a much wider range of issues and in more venues than the traditional, relatively narrow post-Westphalian conception of diplomacy permitted. Because of this shift, diplomatic conflict resolution/negotiation skills deserve more study and application at both theoretical and practical levels among a far wider range of people. However, as an area of middle range theory, diplomacy is often dismissed by practitioners, while as a professional activity it is often downplayed by "scientific" scholars. The significant blending of international and domestic affairs into an "intermestic" mix means an overwhelming majority of people, like the nineteenth-century bourgeois gentlemen speaking prose, are practicing diplomacy without knowing it. The comfort, if not the safety, of the planet requires that we all get better at it.

# DIPLOMACY IS[1]

"The art of letting someone else have your way."

—Lester Pearson

"The art of saying 'nice doggie' while you find a bigger rock."

—Wynn Catlin

"The Art and Profession of conducting negotiations between nations."

—Ernest Satow

Diplomacy has been around since the dawn of human organizations expressed as some or all of the following concepts: As a philosophical approach to international relations; a set of behaviors; and a process of conducting relations between sovereign units. For the past five hundred years, the post-Westphalian period, it has been the primary mode of official representational communication between sovereign states. Emissaries representing rulers were dispatched well before the birth of Christ, and differing traditions of diplomacy have existed in most of the world's cultures from the earliest times.[2]

With the end of the Cold War, the parameters of the international political environment have shifted, producing an altered spectrum of issues, rapid communication and faster transportation, a blurring of the distinctions of sovereignty as transnational and subnational challenge the monopoly of a geometrically expanded number of nation-states, and a breakdown of the intellectual categories by which diplomacy has heretofore been understood. One result of this breakdown has been the so-called post-modernist or late modern assault on previous ways of viewing the diplomatic undertaking.[3] Some scholars suggest that speed and perception have essentially produced an "antidiplomacy" in which power is more "real" in time than in space, and that a new approach is required to understand the power of new technologies as well as, in Der Derian's words, the "technostrategic forces" in diplomacy and the ethical considerations they call forth.

The goal of this paper is to take as broad a look as possible at the changing international political environment—the new structure, new conditions and new issues, and to see how these affect the theory and practice of diplomacy. The principal thesis here is that issues of conflict resolution and the skills this calls forth—persuasion, negotiation, problem-solving, and ethical management of force—remain the core of diplomacy in a political era which has burst the narrow bounds of post-Westphalian Western experience and need to be broadened considerably in both theory and practice.

## THE SHIFTING ENVIRONMENT

In his most recent book, Sam Huntington asserts that the international politics of the future can best be viewed as a clash of civilizations, that the contemporary world is a "multipolar, multicivilizational" world, and that civilizations are now interacting in ways they have never done before. Some assumptions of the past forty years—that modernization was producing a universalist civilization or the Westernization of non-Western Societies—are false. A civilization-based world order is emerging, with countries grouping themselves around the "lead" states of their civilization. Nation states remain the principal actors, and conflict takes place primarily along the "fault lines" between civilizations—at the moment largely between Muslims and non-Muslims.

The survival of the West as a civilization depends on Americans and Europeans affirming their Western identity and rallying to protect it against challengers from non-Western societies. Avoidance of global war "depends upon world leaders accepting and cooperating to maintain the multicivilizational character of global politics."[4] In Huntington's view, diplomacy's most important aspects are traditional national security concerns, the classical "high politics." In this somewhat pessimistic, conflict-oriented view of the future, Huntington has been accused of overplaying civilization at the expense of the state and maintaining the traditional categories of realist politics and a focus on security when the real contemporary action is elsewhere.[5]

Max Singer and Aaron Wildavsky, in *The Real World Order: Zones of Peace, Zones of Turmoil,* offer a more upbeat, somewhat different view of a world that is new in many important respects. They divide the world into the zone of peace (the developed, industrialized, democratic countries which do not war on each other—and comprise 15 percent of the world) and the zone of turmoil, the other 85 percent of the world, where poverty, war, tyranny and anarchy will continue. The good news is that along with the turbulence will come the "difficult processes of economic and political development which will cause wealth, democracy, and peace gradually to spread through these zones."[6]

Singer and Wildavsky do speak of supranational units and subnational units, but see the world gradually improving, as long as the principal units remain democratic. They attack the pessimism about poverty and chaos which claims to derive from the feeling of being cast adrift without a current strategic imperative, and suggest that if America acts in concert with other major democracies (and the UN, if it can be brought along), most issues can be managed. They conclude that the future looks so much better than it has, and that "while we do not have in hand the means to solve problems that have never been solved before, processes are under way that have a fair prospect of removing these historic evils, if we have the patience to wait another century or so."[7]

These are the two broadest-brush pictures of contemporary international relations. There are others, of course. James Rosenau was an early exponent of turbulence, suggesting that the world is passing through a turbulent time of change in which two tendencies contend: (1) A centralizing trend pulling economies together (hence the creation of supranational institutions, groups, and nongovernmental organizations); (2) which is counterbalanced by a decentralizing trend: in the absence of strategic bipolarism, local, national, ethnic and group issues which were submerged are surfacing as important sources of conflict, eroding traditional sovereignty.[8]

Rosenau is not entirely incompatible with Huntington and Singer/ Wildavsky, but more micro-oriented. Somewhat more draconian are the chaos theories, articulated by Robert Kaplan. In a thoughtful article and subsequent book, Kaplan suggests that chaos is enveloping parts of the developing world (Singer and Wildavsky's "zone of turmoil") which may lead to a greater breakdown of order and heightened conflict unless something is done.[9]

Like the savants feeling the elephant, each of these hypotheses has sufficient truth to be taken seriously. All, whether optimistic or pessimistic, see a role for the diplomat and the international political system to deal with conflict. Seldom do they explore in depth the implications of the geometric progression of nations from the 50 which founded the United Nations in 1945 to the 184 members of today, and hardly ever do they note the issues this raises for "diplomacy" as an institution—the relative lack of training and socialization for diplomats from emerging countries and even the lack of respect for diplomatic techniques and institutions.

One feature that clearly emerges from each of these studies is the expanded nature of cross-cultural contacts. If there is anything that distinguishes the nature of diplomacy from other political activity, it is the preponderantly cross-cultural nature of diplomatic communications and exchanges. While a number of writers speak of the "diplomatic culture," as a separate entity, the expanded number of players and growth in influence of non-Western players requires significantly greater cross cultural competence for effective diplomatic and foreign policy activity than the international system has required for the past 500 years.[10]

In the future-projection category, world order scholars speak of the necessity to resolve issues of governance and survival. One of the most eloquent of these, Richard Falk, stresses the need to tame and abolish war, and for America to see her own interests in global terms and exert the necessary leadership to create a holistic vision of international politics which will transcend the destructiveness of modern science and create "a new unity of science, aesthetics, and religious institutions."[11]

Writers on political economy stress the importance of multinational corporations and other economic groups, nongovernmental organizations and international bodies. "Economic diplomacy" is emerging as a principal form of statecraft, and economic issues often become the key political questions of the day, more relevant to more citizens' concerns than most other issues. As Lester Thurrow notes,

> Shifts in technology, transportation, and communications are creating a world where anything can be made anywhere on the face of the earth and sold everywhere else on the face of the earth. National economies fade away. A substantial disconnect arises between global business firms with a worldview and national governments that focus on the welfare of "their" voters. Countries splinter, regional trading blocs grow, the global economy becomes ever more interconnected.[12]

Although political economy writings have maintained a national focus, it is now beginning to look in other directions.[13] It is in precisely this area that an interesting and important development with a high potential impact on diplomacy has gone almost unnoticed.

The rapid rise of state/provincial and local involvement in international affairs over the past 10 to 15 years has opened up a whole new area of "diplomacy" involving state and city trade missions (Atlanta has run its own foreign policy for years,) and economic activity had grown dramatically. The American Council of State Governments notes that 39 U.S. states and Puerto Rico operate an average of four overseas offices each, and that more American states have offices in Tokyo (45) than in Washington D.C. (42). The Council comments in its 1996 annual report that "the basic driving force in the world today is metropolitan regions with populations of at least 50 million and high tech communications and transportation infrastructure.[14] Lest one think this is merely an American phenomenon, the Council adds that the European Community has created a Council of Regions which now has 230 members. Local government authorities in Europe and elsewhere have international dealings as well.

While the primary focus for state activity is economic development, involvement in foreign affairs does not stop there. Tourism campaigns send state officials abroad regularly; sister cities exchanges increase communication. Even in the political arena, states recognize potential conflict, but proceed ahead anyway. In the 1980's and early 1990's, states withheld investment in South Africa to pressure the apartheid government to reform. While the American government sports a one-China policy, legislatures in 42 states have passed resolutions supporting Taiwan's bid to join the UN Constitutional prohibitions against state agreements with foreign entities are being eroded by recent Supreme Court decisions which have greatly expanded state options through "implied consent" findings.

In March 1989, Kentucky floated a one million-yen bond issue in Japan— without even informing the U.S. Embassy until it was concluded. The Kentucky

Economic Cabinet today operates one of the more sophisticated currency exchanges in the world to balance its currency risk. About the same time, Illinois loaned Poland $100 million. States have even taken over federal functions. Under a special exemption from the Logan Act, which prohibits private citizens not representing the national government from "conducting foreign affairs," a binational commission now regulates cross-border immigration and runs a development fund. The state of Washington and the Canadian Province of British Columbia run national immigration posts along their borders, presumably but not necessarily obeying federal guidance.[15]

Much is going on which looks an awfully lot like diplomacy, but isn't called that by name. If there is an understudied area in contemporary diplomatic studies, subnational diplomatic activity surely qualifies. There may be more than 2,000 individuals working at this kind of diplomacy across the United States—state and local activity may well exceed that at the federal level in terms of tasks done, if not scope of issues. Thus it may be useful to speak of "macro" diplomacy at the national level, and "micro" diplomacy of subnational units or groups, perhaps with different sets of parameters from the more traditional state representatives.

The final environmental shift to be identified is the increasing involvement of domestic political and mass opinion with foreign policy issues. If foreign policy was an "intermestic" problem twenty-five years ago, it is even more so today. This was first noticed in trade policy, and led to the organizational creation of the President's Special Trade Representative in an effort to get diplomacy and touchy domestic trade issues better integrated.[16]

Harold Saunders, former U.S. Assistant Secretary of State, first and most clearly identified the impact of interdependence and the growing importance of foreign policy issues to previously uninvolved or marginally affected citizenry. In a 1991 essay, he suggested that this deepening involvement would even affect how nations relate, opening up the way for citizen diplomacy, Track II diplomatic efforts, and a broader conception of diplomacy that transcends elite transactions.[17]

Despite current conventional wisdom about American disinterest in foreign affairs and a turn inward, systemic factors are pressing toward greater involvement of attentive elites and special interest groups in foreign policy issues. This is especially true when the "elites," i.e. the political leadership of a country, turn their focus toward domestic issues. Excellent descriptions of such "double-edged" diplomacy or multi-track diplomacy are now available, but neither academics nor practitioners have fully integrated this into their thinking.[18] Recent public opinion studies show that Americans retain an interest in, and concern for, foreign policy issues even if the saliency of most issues has gone down with the ending of the Cold War. Two 1994 studies of American Foreign Policy, deal explicitly with the role of public opinion, and one offers comparative material on the linkages between elite, attentive action and mass involvement. Both also infer that contemporary opinion may be even more issue-specific than it has in the past.[19]

Despite these apparently contradictory trends of involvement, the diplomatic establishment has been under steady fire and budget shrinkage for over a decade. In her first major speech, incoming U.S. Secretary of State Madeline Albright noted that in the past four years, the Department of State has cut 2,000 employees, closed more than 30 overseas posts, and slashed foreign assistance by nearly one third, and that she had lobbied hard with her predecessor late in 1996 to have the Department's budget increased.[20] For the past two years, various groups from the New York Council on Foreign Relations, the Chicago Council on Foreign Relations, several foundations, and the American Foreign Service Association have been waging a campaign to preserve the diplomatic component of federal leadership.

From the standpoint of the intertwining of diplomacy and conflict resolution, their arguments had one important common theme: It is dangerous and impolitic to shrink the diplomatic corner of the national security triad—defense, intelligence and diplomacy. By a circumstance peculiar to the United States, the defense and intelligence budgets are behind a national security "firewall," and not subject to the usual political horse-trading on domestic issues. The diplomatic/foreign aid/information affairs budgets, on the other hand, are subject to shrinkage and have been reduced significantly (and perhaps dangerously)—almost 50 percent over the past ten years. If the diplomatic options are not to be preserved and funded, then the country's best chance to avoid conflict through diplomacy will slowly atrophy, and in that case, the other legs of the triad—defense and intelligence—will almost certainly have to be used at much greater cost.

Other nations' foreign affairs functions have undergone similar budgetary stress, although perhaps none quite as severe as the United States. At this point, none seem to have placed themselves in the intellectually peculiar position of cutting their own funding while simultaneously refusing to pay their United Nations assessment. In the American instance, this is driven by three elements: budgetary pressure, serious interest in withholding funds to produce reform, and finally, the anti-UN ideological views of American conservatives, one of whom, Sen. Jesse Helms, is chairman of the crucial U.S. Senate Foreign Relations Committee. The arguments made to support a more forthcoming posture toward the United Nations also stress maintaining a conflict resolution/conflict management capability which is asserted to be far less expensive in the longer run than maintaining the necessary national capability to meet emergent international crises.

In the international and political environment, it is thus apparent that there are more cross-cultural interactions than previously, no overarching international vision or widely agreed-upon intellectual paradigm, greater involvement of subnational units and groups in international affairs coupled with simultaneously less directly expressed interest by the general public at large. The democracies do not want to fight, there is only one military superpower, the United States, and countries and groups tend to focus on local problems which were given less priority in the bipolar period.

## TOUGH ISSUES

Arising from the environment outlined above, over the seven to ten years a series of issues have come to the fore, many of which have intractable sides to them. Absent the demands of bloc ideology powering either side of a bipolar split or a "third force," religious, ethnic, and classical nationalistic (or self-determination) problems have arisen. Despite George Bush's announcement of a "New World Order," none was forthcoming (nor is likely to be anytime soon). In the Western democracies and Japan, people and governments turned to issues and problems whose resolution had been postponed by the demands of the Cold War. A general belief that the "End of History," in Francis Fukuyama's famous term, had arrived and that liberal democracy and market capitalism reigned triumphant, conveniently ignored religious antagonisms in the Middle East and elsewhere.

However, before the snows of winter 1991 had set in, the world was treated to the beginning of what William Pfaff described as "the modernity of ancient hatreds" with the emergence of serious ethnic conflict in the Balkans.[21] This was followed by the ethnic strife that tore the Sudan and Somalia apart, accompanied by ill-fated attempts by the nations to work first through the United States and then through the UN.[22] The United States went into Haiti, and the UN and the Europeans tried to mute ethnic strife in Rwanda. The collapse of the Soviet Union and the creation of 15 new states in that region led to "ethnonationalism," and the growth of new states in Eastern Europe and elsewhere based on an expression of ethnic identity through nation-building.[23]

Dealing with ethnic conflict has become a growth industry over the past few years. Some excellent descriptive studies have been produced, and suggestions advanced for dealing with these issues—always involving a heavy emphasis on conflict resolution of both a formal and informal nature.[24] This has not yet been fully reflected in government organizational and bureaucratic arrangements; in fact, the increasing privatization of this kind of activity—logistics for the UN forces in Somalia and Yugoslavia, security forces of the new governments of the ex-Soviet Union, relief management in parts of Africa and Yugoslavia, for example—add yet another possible new dimension to foreign policy management.

Another other major emergent element on the international scene is the reintroduction of religion into a more active relationship with diplomacy.

Viewed with a long lens, that began with the creation of the state of Israel and the subsequent Muslim reaction to it, and the concurrent Hindu-Muslim clash over the partition of British India. In the near term, the theocratic, anti-Western basis of the Iranian revolution made explicit the connection between religion and politics and foreshadowed the emergence of significant radical fundamentalist movements in Egypt and Algeria. The best general summation of this development is found in the volume *Religion, the Missing Dimension of Statecraft*, which features several cases of involvement by religiously motivated actors in all regions of the world. That book, which includes Barry Rubin's thoughtful earlier article, outlines the collapse of the modernizing supposition that religion will be a declining force as nations develop.[25] In the opening chapter, Douglas Johnson sounds a prophetic and exhortative note that outlines the impact of religious, ethnic and nationalistic hostilities on international relations, and the growing importance of conflict resolution:

> As one looks to the end of the century and beyond, the challenges of preventing or resolving conflict are likely to prove even more formidable than they have in the past. The problems posed by today's ethnic and nationalistic hostilities, whether inter- or intrastate, have shown themselves to be peculiarly resistant to diplomatic compromise ... Far greater insight into the human dimensions of conflict and its resolution will be required on the part of foreign policy and religious practitioners than has been demonstrated to date.[26]

The implication is that if policy makers and diplomats are to deal effectively with this set of contemporary problems, they will need both greater cultural (religious, ethnic, national) understanding and greater conflict prevention/resolution skills. The number of writings and diplomatic memoirs dealing with such issues in this way began to increase in the 1980s, and a number of scholars have begun to analyze religious issues in deeper terms. Significant efforts are being made to increase Western understanding of Islamic thought and diplomacy,[27] and there are signs that increasing efforts are going to be made to relate Chinese traditions to contemporary Chinese diplomacy.[28] There is even growing understanding that religion plays a critical role in the development process—are Islam and Democracy compatible, can Hindu nationalism coexist with Indian democracy, and within the Christian community itself, what is the impact of Eastern orthodoxy on building democracy in the Balkans?[29]

The more intractable "clashes" between civilizations or religions become, the more the question of the relationship between diplomacy and the use of force is brought into question as well. The strategic deadlock of the Cold War has receded into the background, but the issue of war and violence remains, exacerbated by the lack of structure in the international system previously supplied by the two blocs during the Cold War. The emergence of open conflict in the states of the former Yugoslavia, between Azerbaijanis and Armenians and within states such as Haiti, Somalia, and Liberia raise the question of whether and how such conflicts shall be "managed." The era of the "not-quite wars" or the "teacup wars" is upon us.[30]

The doctrines of war, the nature of war, and the management of war are undergoing reanalysis. Part of this involves rethinking more traditional issues of European security and how international institutions relate to them, as well as national security issues.[31] However, a significant component of this review involves exploring anew problems involving the relationship between force and diplomacy in conflict resolution. From linkages between force and statecraft through studies of coercive diplomacy to assessments of peacekeeping, peacemaking, and nontraditional diplomacy, all are undergoing review and adaptation in the light of contemporary conditions.[32]

A related problem arising as the Cold War recedes is the relationship to and the importance of intelligence in the diplomatic process. The last decade has seen the beginning of a literature on intelligence and its place in both defense and foreign policy making.[33] The need for intelligence in order to understand other nations and cultures is widely accepted; some Western societies have some difficulty with the covert action feature of intelligence as opposed to the standard collections–analysis–dissemination aspects, and this does pose an ethical issue for many.[34]

With the reemergence of value issues in diplomacy and foreign policy, often as a result of the loosening up of the international structure following the Cold War, questions of "Just War" and "Just Peace" are again the subject of serious discussion. The Gulf War brought forth a vigorous argument on Just War and how morality should be viewed in international relations and American foreign policy in particular.[35] Over the past four years, a group of 23 scholars and theologians have studied questions of Just Peace theory, an outgrowth of the much older Just War theory. Their current efforts are embodied in a paper, *New Paradigm: Just Peacemaking Theory* by Glen Stassen of Fuller Theological Seminary.[36] Noteworthy in all these efforts is the emphasis placed on "partnership conflict resolution," negotiation, and creative problem solving. Certainly here is one strong ethical imperative for diplomacy-as-conflict resolution.

As an important part of the issue of using force and/or peacemaking is both the psychological and religious conception of the "other," and the "other-as-enemy." Interestingly enough, both psychology and religion seem to be on compatible tracks. Historical enmity, the indispensable enemy, negotiation with an enemy, and pacifism are all being examined in relationship to diplomatic/military activity.[37]

At a deeper level, religious scholars are starting to explore the question of "demonizing" the enemy, and getting at the roots of human hatred from that direction. One would not normally expect to find thoughtful information on this subject in a treatise on Satan, but Professor Elaine Pagels of Princeton provides just that as she sketches the Christian origins of demonization from the continuing struggle of men and women between God's spirit and demons belonging to Satan, which serves to "confirm for Christians their own identification with God and to demonize their opponents."[38] Getting to the heart of the human condition, she identifies the Christian struggle between the "profoundly human view that 'otherness' is evil, and the words of Jesus that reconciliation is divine."

Coping with and reversing demonization are issues that diplomacy in conflict resolution must deal with—and it needs all the help it can get. In every religious tradition there are great scholars who urge reaching out to "the other." Given the deeper enmities that fuel religious, ethnic and nationalist conflict in the world today, it may be wise, if not necessary, to delve into religious roots as well as psychological reality. It may be particularly important for the dominant Western tradition to do so, as an exercise in necessary humility, if nothing else. A superb and provocative place to begin is a thoughtful book which deals with the Christian, Hindu and Muslim traditions, *A New Vision of Reality: Western Science, Eastern Mysticism and Christian Faith*, by Father Bede Griffiths. He was a Benedictine monk who had C. S. Lewis as a university tutor and later ran an ashram in India for the last thirty years of his life. An intellectual soul-mate of American writer Thomas Merton, Griffiths stresses the common elements in Christian, Islamic, and Hindu theology, and shows they are all integral parts of a divine unity inclusive of diversity, which he calls the "perennial philosophy." In a video interview two weeks before he died in 1993, Fr. Bede said "The deeper you go into each religion fully, the more they have in common, and the closer they converge." The important difference between his concept of religious similarity and many religious views (especially radical fundamentalisms of all faiths) is Griffiths' strong support for contemporary science, which actually bolsters the diversity-in-unity view.[39]

The resulting implications for diplomacy and conflict resolution are easy to derive and to spell out: given a more accurate, organic and holistic conception of the universe, it is much easier, perhaps even imperative, to bring other problems into line to reduce conflict. Griffiths offers theological, intellectual and practical reinforcement for a view of the unity of mankind entirely compatible with the broadest views of liberal democracy, contemporary psychology, and science. Such a conception could aid in tempering the excess of egoism, unbridled sovereignty, and dehumanization of peoples now present in the international arena. It would emphasize communication, creative problem solving, and conflict resolution rather than brute force, religious conversion, or nationalism. As a philosophical basis for diplomacy, it may also help to bring more organic and less mechanistic models to the study of politics and diplomacy. This would reflect the current coming

together of science and religion in the work of eminent contemporary secular scholars as well,[40] and ease the transition of diplomacy from a narrow to
a broader paradigm.

## DIPLOMACY AND CONFLICT RESOLUTION

The above review of the international environment and emergent issues
should be enough to tell us that conflict resolution—a significant part of philosophy, behavior, and process—will be a key aspect of diplomacy as it approaches the millennium. Add to this the expanding range of activities which
could easily bear the label "diplomatic," if definitional parameters are ad-
justed, and one is forced to conclude that those who pass over slight "diplomacy" as conflict resolution activity do so at their peril. In the broadest sense,
while the potential for mass destruction is not as great as it was a decade ago,
it is also true that there is less control over those weapons and activities
which remain. Coping with nuclear or biological terrorism may
in time require more tactical and forceful measures in the immediate term. In
the long term, these threats can only be eased through conflict resolution,
political reconciliation, and community building (which are likely to involve
everything from religion to psychology and citizen diplomacy), as well as the
traditional skills of state-to-state interaction. "A modern diplomat may, however, find it as advantageous to be as familiar with the ways of the servants
of Mammon and mullahs as with the manner of negotiating with Princes."[41]

From an intellectual and conceptual standpoint, even those of the realist
persuasion, now "post-realists," recognize that:

> Post-realism refocuses on the manifestly political practices of international re-
> lations. To this end, it emphasizes diplomacy and discourse, communication
> and persuasion, [and includes concern with] superordinate, collective
> processes and structures, recognizing the role of organization generally and of
> institutions in particular for motivating and constraining action.[42]

The tasks of diplomacy thus stress the qualities and skills required for
communication, negotiation, problem solving, and bargaining, and the
exercise of those across cultural divides. Indeed, the literature and tools of
conflict resolution that have surfaced over the past decade or so reinforce
this. From Roger Fisher's *Getting To Yes*, which lays out the tactical approach to "negotiating agreement without giving in," at the individual and
small group level, to the recent significant (in both size and content) volume on *Managing Global Chaos: Sources and Response to International
Conflict*, which deals specifically with contemporary political and policy
issues, and illustrates how the values and virtues of conflict resolution are
apparent across the board.[43] At least two other major cross disciplinary

works in recent years also stress conflict resolution as the key element of diplomatic solutions.[44] Focus on preventive diplomacy, informal diplomacy, and other nontraditional alternatives are another important way that current studies have attempted to broaden the scope of diplomatic efforts, sometimes in spite of governments' unwillingness to take a broader look at issues.

In addition to the problem-focused studies above, there are those which focus on cross cultural issues and influences listed in footnote 10, especially Raymond Cohen's *Negotiating Across Cultures*. There is resistance in some academic quarters to focusing on cultural studies as "mushy," but there is no doubt that they are important for any study of the diplomatic process, whether theoretically pure or not.[45] Indeed, as the organic model of science noted earlier commands more attention, this sort of rigid behaviorist criticism may ebb considerably.

Of course, the same elements are critical for individual diplomacy, and also within the same culture—understanding the people involved, communicating interests, exploring new initiatives, engaging in joint problem-solving behavior, developing objective criteria, establishing a "best alternative" to negotiation. Hence, while problems may differ from "macro" diplomacy involving refugee flows, forceful incursions across borders, and ethnic and religious conflict over large areas, to "micro" diplomacy involving international trade deals between subnational units and an international company or the Red Cross and a beleaguered municipality, many of the substantive techniques are similar.

Mediation by definition involves conflict resolution, and many of the same skills apply in a trilateral setting involving two disputants and a mediator. In ongoing multilateral diplomacy, conflict management and preventive diplomacy play an even more important role. There have been many, and will be even more, disputes to which former U.S. Assistant Secretary of State Richard Murphy's wry 1991 observation on the Arab-Israeli dispute might apply: "It is our job to keep them from killing themselves off for 30 to 40 years until conditions are such that solutions become possible."

One area where micro and macro diplomacy differ is in the relationship of force to the conflict resolution process, and indeed toward policy making in these areas. In most situations involving micro diplomacy, the context or structure is fixed—international trade rules apply, internal or national rules set the context, or the situation is well circumscribed. Purely large-scale international affairs are more likely to involve a wider range of freedom to use and less restriction upon applied force, but politicians don't always recognize the difference. Options are greater than they were during the Cold War, and issues have opened up ranges of violence and force—low level conflict—that were less available or more proscribed in the earlier international environment.

## ORGANIZATIONAL AND EDUCATIONAL PROBLEMS

As applicability of diplomacy and conflict resolution skills intensify, both deserve more theoretical study and practical application among a wider range of individuals and organizations. Unfortunately, with the end of the Cold War, diplomatic establishments are being cut back in many countries— none so much as the United States over the past four years. That may be changing, as the current U.S. foreign affairs budget has been increased—but hardly enough to cover the costs of maintaining and training for the expanded American diplomatic role. When the new states of the former Soviet Union were created, the American Foreign Service staffed them with NO additional positions—taking officers from other areas. In the past four years, the Foreign Service Institute budget has been reduced (many would say gutted). The gap has been taken up in part at the research level by the U.S. Institute of Peace's expanded research program and greater commitments by the New York and Chicago Councils on Foreign Relations and new efforts by Committees on Foreign Affairs around the country. These will slowly improve public levels of understanding, even while professional training deteriorates.

Within the academic environment, "diplomacy" often gets short shrift on the one hand from practitioners (who believe diplomats are born, not made) and on the other from academics (who see "diplomacy" as rutted in the mushy middle range of theory and therefore not sufficiently rigorous to deserve serious attention). Alexander George has dealt with this problem superbly in his book *Bridging the Gap: Theory and Practice in Foreign Policy*,[46] describing both academic and practitioner attitudes and urging that a little understanding by each side would go a long way toward easing the posturing and attitude which disrupts understanding. Particularly useful for the study of diplomacy and conflict resolution are his three types of knowledge:

(1) An abstract conceptual model (or quasi-deductive theory) of each strategy.
(2) General (or "generic") knowledge of the conditions that favor the success of a strategy and, conversely, the conditions that make its success unlikely.
(3) An actor-specific behavioral model of the adversary.[47]

As noted earlier, conflict resolution and cross-cultural studies are subjected to the same academic/practitioner push-and-pull. There are sixteen to seventeen recognized graduate schools of international affairs, plus some twenty other programs operating in conjunction with other academic departments. While most of these are not expanding at the moment, they should rightly be the locus of effective practitioner/academic interchanges. It is not unreasonable to suggest, and may be a professional necessity, that these schools and their faculties become the dynamic middlemen for making middle range theory more productive along the academic/theoretical—practitioner/professional—citizen/ participant spectrum.

Training in mediation is given in many law schools, and more practical experience in mediations and counseling centers as well as labor-management seminars. Though such training may not always have an international component, it at least familiarizes people with the skills involved. The Department of Commerce does give trade-related courses and conferences, and some universities do provide special programs for training local officials. (One such example is the University of Kentucky's Patterson School, which organized a training program in export promotion for Appalachian Regional Development Officers). In the American context, however, these are a drop in the bucket—as the country becomes more involved with NAFTA, special emphases on Canada and Mexico have grown slowly. Undergraduate multi-disciplinary efforts to broaden horizons are falling prey either wholly or in part to academic budget tightening. In sum, at least in the United States, the problem is getting worse just when it should be getting better.

Developing greater individual capabilities and proper organizational arrangements across several levels of activity are necessary to move both awareness and capability to a higher plane. Both involve pulling together the kinds of material floating around in diverse places to develop a persuasive rationale and structure for action. To return to our opening description of diplomacy, a broader and more holistic approach must be taken to diplomatic philosophy, diplomatic behaviors and skills, and the process of conducting relations between units (principally states, but others as well).

The roots of a philosophy are already there in the works of diplomats-turned-scholars, those revising theories (such as the post-realists and world order writers), the religious traditions that speak to the unity of mankind, and even classical political thought.[48] As far as behaviors are concerned, one could do worse than begin with Harold Nicholson's characteristics of an ideal diplomat, and include the personal order principles offered by Stephen Covey in *Seven Habits of Highly Effective People*. His fourth principle is the admonition "Think win-win," an approach certainly familiar to students of negotiating strategy.[49]

Skills are taught mostly on the job, if taught at all. Along with the expansion of diplomacy in the post–World War II period, came internal discussion of the need for training in accounting and management as well as traditional instruction in protocol and technical skills for reporting and consular work. The argument here is negotiating, bargaining and problem-solving techniques and skills must be a key element of any diplomatic skill development. One might assume that this is already the case, but appallingly enough, the U.S. Foreign Service Institute over the past several years has not averaged more than one such course per quarter, and that a basic one-week review of the subject. Most diplomats do not even get that, particularly those from newly emerging nations.

Finally with respect to processes of diplomacy, a good deal more analysis and explanation is necessary for those newly arriving individuals and groups who are caught up in "diplomatic" activities, but who are not members of traditional diplomatic establishments, and citizens and "players" from other areas.

But it will not be enough simply to sharpen and articulate philosophy, add some skill training and tuck in some exposure to low-intensity conflict and chaos theory. These activities will need to be reflected organizationally in the way governments and transnational and subnational organizations deal with the growing "intermestic" mix of foreign affairs/domestic issues and growing transnational problems. The U.S. State Department made one stab at this in the early 1990s with its "Diplomacy for the Year 2000" reorganization, but this was soon overwhelmed by the budgetary hatchet of the mid-1990s. UN reform clearly fits into this category but the organizational and political problems faced by the new Secretary-General coupled with the complexities of U.S. efforts to clear up its substantial arrears will make immediate movement difficult. Although some interesting work has begun to emerge in this area, there needs to be more.[50]

Problem-solving conflict resolution is a key function of diplomacy that has substantial general usefulness. It appeals to people at every level of society and applies to every style of organization in one way or another. It could easily be the basis for demystifying diplomacy and spreading it to those who increasingly need it, as well as an integrating feature common to individuals, small groups, and bureaucratic organizations of all sizes.

Historically, diplomats have guarded the sacred jewels of their profession to keep the club small. The world simply won't let that happen today. The spillover of negotiations from government-to-government contacts to relationships between other entities, both supra- and sub-national, mandates use of diplomatic skills to make the planet run as smoothly. The division of specialization in academia does not generally reward those who seek to move beyond narrow specialization and take up the burden of integrating knowledge. Resource reallocation may ease this problem, but organizational constraints are likely to remain unless deliberate efforts are made to remove them.

In the final section of a paper produced for the 1995 ISA convention, this author suggested a wider emphasis on education in the concepts and skills of diplomacy—to cover high schools, churches, businesses, and journalists. On a more institutional basis, courses and training sessions were proposed for elective officials at state, local and national levels that were assuming responsibilities in the "intermestic" area.[51] The need remains. Efforts by the Councils of Foreign Relations and the Committees of Foreign Affairs mentioned earlier are helpful; work done by the Sister Cities Commission and World Trade Centers (particularly in cross-cultural education) have been valuable, but more needs to be done. The creation of a Diplomatic Studies Section in the ISA is an excellent opportunity if we insist that it exercise a broadening function, not simply remain a repository of individual disciplinarians, and if it expands to actively welcome thoughtful practitioners as well as academics. Lip service is not enough; energetic recruiting would pay significant dividends.

Finally, from a normative standpoint the spread of problem solving and conflict resolution skills and techniques in and of themselves will smooth the flow of human relations, ease tensions, and develop coping mechanisms for those involved. If, at the same time, the skills and habits of understanding, cross cultural awareness, and personal behavior that make a good diplomat are more widely spread, these will serve as a useful counter to in-your-face confrontation, religious intolerance and ideological zealotry, which promote more violent solutions to public issues. All—academic, religious leader, politician, and citizen alike—stand to benefit from that.

## NOTES

1. Quotations taken from Charles Freeman Jr., *The Diplomat's Dictionary*, (Washington, D.C.: National Defense University Press, 1994). A revised version is to be published by the U.S. Institute of Peace in May 1997.

2. An outstanding and quick historical review can be found in Jose Calvet de Magalhaes, *The Pure Concept of Diplomacy*, trans. Bernardo Futscher Pereira (Westport, Conn.: Greenwood Press, 1988). A more extensive history is available in the excellent recent work, Keith Hamilton and Richard Langhorne, *The Practice of Diplomacy: Its Evolution, Theory, and Administration* (New York: Routledge, 1995). James Der Derian, *On Diplomacy* (Malden, Mass.: Blackwell, 1987) also offers lucid discussion of the evolution of diplomacy.

3. James Der Derian, *Antidiplomacy* (Malden, Mass.: Blackwell, 1992), and R. B. J. Walker, ed., *Discourses of Global Politics: A Critical (Re)introduction to International Relations* (Boulder, Colo.: Lynne Reinner Press, 1994) outline this trend.

4. Samuel P. Huntington, *Clash of Civilizations and the Remaking of World Order* (New York: Simon and Schuster, 1996), 21; rest of paragraph extrapolated from chapters 1 and 12.

5. The most pointed challenges to Huntington are Richard E. Rubenstein and Jarle Crocker, "Challenging Huntington," *Foreign Policy* 46, Fall 1994: 113–28, and Stephen Walt, "Review Essay: Stephen Walt Analyses Samuel Huntington's 'Clash of Civilizations,'" *Foreign Policy* 106, Spring 1997: 177–89. Related commentary can be found in the September/October and November/December 1993 *Foreign Affairs* magazine.

6. Max Singer and Aaron Wildavsky, *The Real World Order: Zones of Peace, Zones of Turmoil* (Chatham House Publishers, 1993), 7.

7. Singer and Wildavsky, *The Real World Order,* 191 and chapters 6–8.

8. James N. Rosenau, *Turbulence in World Politics: A Theory of Change and Continuity* (Princeton, NJ: Princeton University Press, 1990), especially chapters 1, 7, 11, and 16.

9. Robert Kaplan, "The Coming Anarchy," *Atlantic Monthly* February 1994: 44–76; and Robert D. Kaplan, *The Ends of the Earth: A Journey to the Frontiers of Anarchy* (New York: Vintage Books/Random House, 1996).

10. Classical writers—de Callieres, Satow, Nicholson—all speak of a "diplomatic culture," but it is really the Western version they speak of. In addition to diplomatic culture, a number of contemporary students of diplomacy see cultural influence going much deeper into the diplomatic process. See for example, Raymond Cohen, *Negotiating across Cultures* (Washington, D.C.: U.S. Institute of Peace, 1991), especially pages 16–18; Glen Fisher, *International Negotiation: A Cross-Cultural Perspective* (Yarmouth, Me.: Intercultural Press, 1980); Howard J. Wiarda, *Ethnocentrism in Foreign Policy: Can We Understand the Third World?* (Washington, D.C.: American Enterprise Institute, 1985); and Jacob Bercovitch, ed., *Resolving International Conflicts* (Boulder, Colo.: Lynne Rienner, 1996), especially chapters 1 and 5.

11. Richard A. Falk, *Postmodern Politics for a Planet in Crisis: Policy, Process, and Presidential Vision* (New York: SUNY Press, 1993), xii and following. See also Richard A. Falk, *On Humane Governance: Toward a New Global Politics* (New York: Cambridge University Press, 1995), for a more extended discussion of taming war, individual accountability, and human rights. *Our Common Future,* Report of the UN Bruntland Commission, (New York: Oxford University Press, 1987), is a more detailed but less sweeping study of contemporary problems.

12. Lester Thurow, *The Future of Capitalism: How Today's Economic Forces Shape Tomorrow's World* (New York: Morrow Publishers, 1996), 9. A basic foundation is Robert Gilpin, *The Political Economy of the International System* (Princeton, N.J.: Princeton University Press, 1987).

13. For a highly lucid argument on the links between the political and economic, see Susan Strange, *The Retreat of the State: The Diffusion of Power in the World Economy* (New York: Cambridge University Press, 1996).

14. Dag Ryen, "State Action in a Global Framework," Council of State Governments, March 1996. Additional material in these paragraphs is taken from a more recent paper, Dag Ryen, "American States and Global Action," Council of State Governments, February 1997.

15. A 1991 article of mine, John D. Stempel, "Loosing it: The Decentralization of American Foreign Policy," *The Journal of State Government* (October–December 1991): 122–24, describes these and other instances of state-run foreign relations. The situation has gotten much more complex in the intervening six years. Earl Fry, et al., eds., *The New International Cities Era,* (Provo, Utah: David M. Kennedy Center for International Studies, Brigham Young University, 1989), describes city activities along the same lines. The recent Paul L. Knox and Peter J. Taylor, eds., *World Cities in a World-System* (New York: Cambridge University Press, 1995), while somewhat more academic, suggests that key cities have as much of a role in the international economy as most nations.

16. Stephen D. Cohen, *The Making of United States International Economic Policy: Principles, Problems, and Proposals for Reform,* 3d edition (New York: Praeger, 1988).

17. Harold Saunders, "An Historic Challenge to Rethink How Nations Relate," in *The Psychodynamics of International Relations, Vol. 1: Concepts and Theories,* ed.

Vamik D. Volkan, Demerious A. Julius, and Joseph V. Montville (Lanham, Md.: Lexington Books, 1990).

18. Peter B. Evans, Harold K. Jacobson, and Robert D. Putnam, eds., *Double-edged Diplomacy: International Bargaining and Domestic Politics* (Berkeley, Calif.: University of California Press, 1993); and Louise Diamond and John McDonald, *Multi-Track Diplomacy* (Washington, D.C.: U.S. Institute of Peace, 1996).

19. David A. Deese, ed., *The New Politics of American Foreign Policy*, (New York: St. Martin's Press, 1994), especially Thomas Risse-Kappen's chapter 11, "Masses and Leaders; Public Opinion Structure and Foreign Policy." Also exploring the engagement of Americans is Daniel Yankelovich and I. M. Destler, eds., *Beyond the Beltway*, (New York: The American Assembly and W. W. Norton, 1994).

20. Madeline Albright, "Building a Bipartisan Foreign Policy," Address at Rice Memorial Center, Rice University, Houston Texas, Feb. 7, 1997. For a perceptive early analysis of the new secretary, see George Gedda, "Albright Welcomed Abroad," *Foreign Service Journal* 74(2) February 1997: 20–27.

21. William Pfaff, "Invitation to War," in *The New Shape of World Politics,* a reader published by Foreign Affairs magazine, 242–52.

22. Robert Oakley and John Hirsh, *Somalia and Operation Restore Hope: Reflections on Peacemaking and Peacekeeping* (Washington, D.C.: U.S. Institute of Peace, 1995); Walter Clarke and Jeffrey Herbst, "Somalia and the Future of Humanitarian Intervention," *Foreign Affairs* 75(2) March/April 1996: 70–85.

23. Walker Connor, *Ethnonationalism* (Princeton, N.J.: Princeton University Press, 1994).

24. K. M. de Silva and R. J. May, eds., *Internationalization of Ethnic Conflict* (London: Pinter Publishers, 1991); Joseph V. Montville, ed., *Conflict and Peacemaking in Multiethnic Societies* (Lanham, Md.: Lexington Books, 1990). On dealing with ethnic and religious conflict: Michael S. Lund, *Preventing Violent Conflicts: a Strategy for Preventive Diplomacy* (Washington, D.C.: U.S. Institute of Peace, 1996); David R. Smock and Chester A. Crocker, *African Conflict Resolution* (Washington, D.C.: U.S. Institute of Peace, 1995); Jeffrey Herbst, "Responding to State Failure in Africa," *International Security* 21(3) Winter 1996/1997; and Kevin M. Cahill, M.D., ed., *Preventive Diplomacy: Stopping Wars Before They Start* (New York: Basic Books, 1996), which argues that social detection and early intervention should be as much honored in international relations as crisis management and negotiation.

25. Douglas Johnson and Cynthia Sampson, eds., *Religion, the Missing Dimension of Statecraft* (New York: Oxford University Press, 1994); and Barry Rubin, "Religion and International Affairs," *Washington Quarterly* 13(2) Spring 1990: 51–63 (also reprinted as chapter 3 in *Religion the Missing, Dimension of Statecraft*).

26. Johnson and Sampson, *Religion,* 7.

27. Regarding Islam, John Esposito's *The Islamic Threat: Myth or Reality*, 2nd edition (New York: Oxford University Press, 1995) and his *Islam and Democracy,* coauthored with John O. Voll, (New York: Oxford University Press, 1996), are good current examples. Carl Brown's classic *International Politics and the Middle East* (Princeton, NJ: Princeton University Press, 1984); an earlier effort by Pakistani diplomat Afzal Iqbal, *Diplomacy in Islam: An essay on the art of negotiation as conceived and developed by the Prophet of Islam* (Lahore: Institute of Islamic Culture, 1965); James Turner Johnson and John Kelsay's *Cross, Crescent and Sword: The Justification of*

*War in Western and Islamic Tradition* (Westport, Conn.: Greenwood Press, 1990); and John Kelsay's *Islam and War: The Gulf War and Beyond* (Westminster/John Kox Press, 1993), make an excellent combination. All are geared to practice as well as intellectual discussion.

28. The current issue of *Foreign Affairs,* March/April 1997, devotes several articles to this; Michael Mandelbaum, ed., *The Strategic Quadrangle: Russia China, Japan and the United States in East Asia* (New York: Council on Foreign Relations, 1995), deals with contemporary Chinese strategic diplomatic relationships.

29. Elizabeth H. Prodromou, "Toward an Understanding of Eastern Orthodoxy and Democracy Building in the Post–Cold War Balkans," *Mediterranean Quarterly* 5(2) Spring 1994: 115–38. For Islam, see Esposito and Voll, *Islam and Democracy*; on India, see Dennis Austin, *Democracy and Violence in Indian and Sri Lanka* (The Royal Institute of International Affairs, 1995).

30. "Not-quite wars" was first used by Dr. Vince Davis at a 1995 University of Kentucky conference dealing with the area between humanitarian relief operations and military operations other than war (OOTW), see Vincent Davis, ed., *Civil-Military Relations and the Not-Quite Wars of the Present and Future* (Washington, D.C.: U.S. Army War College Strategic Studies Institute, 1996). The phrase "teacup wars" belongs to Council on Foreign Relations President Leslie Gelb, "Quelling the Teacup Wars," *Foreign Affairs* 73(6) November/December 1975: 2–6.

31. Robert O. Keohane, Joseph Nye, and Stanley Hoffman, eds., *After the Cold War: International Institutions and State Strategies in Europe, 1989–1991* (Cambridge, Mass.: Harvard University Press, 1993); and Graham Allison and Gregory F. Treverton, eds., *Rethinking American Security: Beyond Cold War to New World Order* (New York: W. W. Norton and Co., 1992).

32. Among the best of these are: Paul Seabury and Angelo Codevilla, *War: Ends and Means* (New York: Basic Books, 1989); Gordon A. Craig and Alexander L. George, *Force and Statecraft: Diplomatic Problems of Our Time* (New York: Oxford University Press, 1983); Alexander L. George and William E. Simons, eds., *The Limits of Coercive Diplomacy,* 2d edition (Boulder, Colo.: Westview Press, 1994); Alex Morrison, ed., *Peacekeeping, Peacemaking or War: International Security Enforcement* (Ottawa: Canadian Institute of Strategic Studies, 1991). Concentrating on the United States, but still of some general use, is Peter J. Schrader, ed., *Intervention into the 1990s: U.S. Foreign Policy in the Third World,* (Boulder, Colo.: Lynne Reinner Publishers, 1992).

33. Michael Herman has just produced an exceptionally thoughtful study, *Intelligence in Peace and War* (New York: Cambridge University Press, 1996). Chung-in Moon's edited compendium outlines the problems of democratizing states with intelligence, Chung-in Moon and Jin-hyun Kim, eds., *Post–Cold War, Democratization, and National Intelligence* (Korea: Yonsei University Press, 1996). Also a classic: Adda B. Bozeman, *Strategic Intelligence and Statecraft* (Dulles, Va.: Brassey's, Inc., 1992).

34. W. Michael Reisman and James E. Baker, *Regulating Covert Action* (Yale University Press, 1992). Pat. M. Holt, *Secret Intelligence and Public Policy: A Dilemma of Democracy* (Washington, D.C.: Congressional Quarterly Press, 1995). Loch Johnson, *Secret Agencies: U.S. Intelligence in a Hostile World* (Yale University Press, 1996).

35. James Turner Johnson, *Just War Tradition and the Restraint of War: A Moral and Historical Inquiry* (Princeton, N.J.: Princeton University Press, 1981); James

Turner Johnson and George Weigel, *Just War and the Gulf War* (Washington, D.C.: Ethics and Public Policy Center, 1991).

36. Glen Stassen, "New Paradigm: Just Peacemaking Theory," unpublished draft paper by Glen Stassen, Fuller Theological Seminary, Pasadena, California.

37. Vamik Volkan, Joseph Montville, and Demetrios Julius, eds., *The Psychodynamics of International Relations, Vols. I and II,* (Lanham, Md.: Lexington Books, 1990 and 1991); Sam Keen, *Faces of the Enemy: Reflections of the Hostile Imagination* (New York: Harper and Row, 1986); Joseph McMillan, "Talking to the Enemy: Negotiations in Wartime," in *Essays on Strategy,* no. X, ed. Mary A. Sommerville (Washington, D.C.: National Defense University Press, 1993); and David R. Smock, *Perspectives on Pacifism, Christian, Jewish and Muslim Views on Nonviolence and International Conflict* (U.S. Institute for Peace, 1995).

38. Elaine Pagels, *The Origin of Satan* (New York: Random House, 1995), xvii and her conclusion, quoted in the next line, on 184.

39. Fr. Bede Griffiths, *A New Vision of Reality: Western Science, Eastern Mysticism and Christian Faith* (Springfield, Ill.: Templegate Press, 1989).

40. See for example, the work of Charles Birch, *On Purpose* (Sydney: New South Wales Press, 1990); and David Bohm, *Wholeness and the Implicate Order,* (New York: Routledge and Kegan Paul, 1980).

41. Hamilton and Langhorne, *The Practice of Diplomacy,* 245.

42. Francis A. Beer and Robert Hariman, eds., *Post-Realism: the Rhetorical Turn in International Relations* (East Lansing, Mich.: Michigan State University Press, 1996), 408.

43. Roger Fisher and William Ury, *Getting to Yes: Negotiating Agreement Without Giving In,* 2d edition (New York: Penguin Books, 1991); Chester A. Crocker and Fen Osler Hampson with Pamela Aall, eds., *Managing Global Chaos: Sources of and Responses to International Conflict* (Washington, D.C.: U.S. Institute of Peace, 1996).

44. Dennis Sandole, ed., *Conflict Resolution in Theory and Practice: Integration and Application* (Manchester, England: Manchester University Press, 1993); and Victor A. Kremenyuk, ed., *International Negotiation: Analysis, Approaches, Issues* (San Francisco: Jossey-Bass Publishers, 1991).

45. See for example, Christopher Shea, "Political Scientists Clash Over Value of Area Studies," *Chronicle of Higher Education,* January 10, 1997, A13.

46. Alexander George, *Bridging the Gap: Theory and Practice in Foreign Affairs,* (Washington, D.C.: U.S. Institute of Peace, 1993).

47. George, *Bridging the Gap,* 117 and chapters 2 and 10.

48. This paper's notes 2, 10, 11, 17, 32, 35, and 39 provide a starting point. Lewis Thomas, *The Fragile Species* (New York: Collier Books, 1992), makes a powerful case for need-conscious politics and foreign policy in chapters 7 and 8, for example; as does Bede Griffiths's *New Vision of Reality,* chapter 12.

49. Stephen Covey, *Seven Habits of Highly Effective People* (New York: Simon and Schuster, 1989), 204–34. Scott Peck, *The Different Drum: Community Making and Peace* (New York: Simon and Schuster, 1987), outlines conflict resolution and negotiation behavior appropriate for individuals and small groups.

50. Jerel A. Rosati, Joe D. Hagan, and Martin W. Sampson, III, eds., *Foreign Policy Restructuring: How Governments Respond to Global Change.* Kevin Cahill's *Preventive Diplomacy,* has a few ideas. Richard Falk's *On Humane Governance* makes

some thoughtful but not immediately practical proposals. Edward Luttwak, in chapter 2, "The Missing Dimension," in *Religion, the Missing Dimension of Statecraft,* offers the interesting suggestion that embassies might have "religious attaches." While this seems a poor substitute for a general increase in awareness of the importance of religion among all hands, it is at least an effort to deal with the organizational implications of the issue.

51. John D. Stempel, "Recasting Diplomacy," paper prepared for the 1995 ISA convention, revised and issued as a Patterson School Occasional Paper, November, 1995, 17–24.

# 7

# Yugo-Nostalgia, Pragmatism, and Reality: Prospects for Inter-Republic Cooperation

*James H. Seroka*

In 1991, the reality of Yugoslavia came to an abrupt end. In quick succession the republics of Slovenia, Croatia, Bosnia-Herzegovina and Macedonia broke off from the Yugoslav federal state and ended a seventy-five-year experiment in statehood. Four years after the declarations of independence, the successor states remain far apart, resentful of one another and convinced that each has been victimized by the other. Since 1991, there have been few serious attempts at reconciliation, and even the erstwhile alliance of Croatia and Slovenia has deteriorated and disappeared over time. Today, virtually no political party with any mainstream support advocates reconciliation, and all shun any identification with "Yugo-nostalgia" in any of its forms. In the near future, internal politics and other forces serve to work against any meaningful level of association or cooperation among the former Yugoslav republics. More significantly, the lack of progress towards regional cooperation endangers the movement towards pluralist democracy in each of these new states.

Social and economic pressures, in contrast to the political trends, would suggest that there would be strong counteracting pressures in favor of renewed cooperation. Significant percentages of the populations of the new republics are from mixed marriages and many considered themselves as "Yugoslavs" in earlier censuses and other legal documents. In addition, prior to 1991, the economies of each of the republics relied on the Yugoslav market to provide the economies of scale and purchasing power for economic survival. Now, the economies of each of the republics are shattered and none have been able to compete successfully in the European environment or find an alternative market to the former Yugoslav federation.

Even though the new borders and political systems have shattered many lives, few in any of the successor republics dare to call for a return to "normal" relationships. Just as in 1991, there is only silence now from those who hope to prevent the emergence of new barriers and more destruction of lives and property. The silence serves to strengthen the hands of authoritarian rulers and protects each republic from internal criticism. It also serves to isolate each republic from the European Union and the world community.

This paper reviews the current levels and trends of inter-republic cooperation and identifies those factors mitigating against cooperation and those in support of it. Third, the paper specifies what must be done politically to break the impasse and then gives an appraisal of the likelihood that such a breakthrough would occur without an external stimulus.

## PROSPECTS FOR COOPERATION AMONG THE REPUBLICS OF THE FORMER SOCIALIST YUGOSLAVIA[1]

### Current Appraisal

For all practical purposes the level of association and cooperation among the successor states to the Socialist Federation of Yugoslavia are primitive and shrinking over time. Visas between the Federal Republic of Yugoslavia and Croatia are very difficult to obtain and there is no direct telephone or other communication between these two core states of the former Yugoslavia. The border between Yugoslavia and Macedonia is closed for almost all legal purposes. Croatia and Slovenia are engaged in a war of nerves regarding the sea borders and unpaid financial claims between the two states.

In each of the new republics, property claims, financial obligations, contracts, professional certifications, etc. are unrecognized and unresolved. Citizens of the other republics or national minorities find themselves in difficult circumstances and often experience economic, social, judicial and other discrimination. While relations between some of the republics are worse than others, none of the new pairs can point to a high and growing feeling of cooperation and association.

The most extreme example of unresolved hostility is between the republics of Yugoslavia and Croatia. Here, three years after the war between the Croatian independence movement and elements of the Yugoslav National Army the level of hostility remains high. The borders between the two states are closed and unrecognized by the other. The governments of the two states do not recognize each other. The media in each portrays the other in unrelenting hostile ways. Communications are limited to family and humanitarian concerns, and each is engaged in a proxy war against the other in Bosnia.

What is most challenging is that neither side has tried to move towards reducing the level of hostility and tension regarding even simple humanitarian issues. For example, both republics maintain "offices" in the capitol of the other, but neither has used the "office" to resolve any major or even minor issues between them. These offices, rather than leading to a peaceful solution of thorny problems, have been heavily involved in propaganda wars with the other. The directors and staff of both of the offices feel powerless to do much to alleviate the situation, and both expressed a strong feeling of frustration in trying to solve particular individual problems.[2]

The Director and staff of the Yugoslav and Croatian "Offices" have diplomatic protection but no diplomatic rank or privileges. Each is empowered to communicate with its home government on issues such as certifying birth, marriage, education and property ownership. Neither is empowered to speak for its government, grant asylum, notarize records, issue passports, identification papers or visas or engage in any normal consular activities.

"Citizens" or claimants before both "offices" appeal to the "office" for resolution of numerous personal, family and humanitarian issues, but the obstacles are so high that relatively few of these issues get resolved. Statistics are meticulously kept, but seem to serve only as propaganda for one side against the other. In order to insure that the "offices" do not take upon ambassadorial or consular duties, both the Croatian and Yugoslav staff and directors have little diplomatic experience and do not report to the Yugoslav ministry of foreign affairs. The Yugoslav director in Zagreb, for example, is the former head of Radio-TV Zagreb and the Croatian director is a former University Professor from Zagreb.

Surprisingly, the foreign ministries of both countries have not centralized or given high organizational profiles to relations with the former Yugoslav states. Within the Croatian foreign ministry, Yugoslav affairs are handled by several disparate offices and generally considered a province of the Ministry of Defense. Within the Yugoslav Federal foreign ministry authority over Croatian issues are diffused across a number of divisions, including the unit for relations with neighboring countries.[3] No one within these units is authorized to undertake movement towards resolution of difficulties, and there is little hope that reconciliation will occur without substantial pressure from the outside.

The war in Bosnia, general embargo and UN sanctions against the Federal Republic of Yugoslavia are extremely powerful and significant factors in reducing the likelihood of further association and cooperation between these two states. Nevertheless, the paucity of close relationships between other potential pairs of former Yugoslav states suggests that the problem is much more substantial. Croatian-Slovenian relations are somewhat less than warm and cordial. While Croatian and Slovenian citizens can cross each other's borders without visas, they are not allowed to use the social services (e.g. hospitals, educational institutions, etc.) within the other republic. In addition Croatian or Slovenian citizens are not granted access for long-term domicile, economic preferences, or any other form of recognition or allowances in the other republics.

There has been no concerted effort to recognize the substantial degree to which the Croatian and Slovenian economies had been integrated and services between them coordinated. After an initial period of virtual duty free trade, Croatian and Slovenian goods are now taxed at the same customs level as for other states. On occasion, long term contracts, including energy transmission agreements, have been ignored or abrogated. Inter-enterprise contracts have been annulled and relatively trivial but emotionally explosive disputes over the borders and navigational waters have aggravated the relationship between Croatia and Slovenia. In fact, relations between Croatia—Slovenia are weaker than relations between any other non-former Yugoslav state. Rather than rein-tegrating and developing a more mature relationship following independence, these two previously complementary and highly integrated economies have continued to fragment and diverge.

## Association Incentives and Disincentives

From rational economic and social perspectives there are considerably more incentives for enhanced cooperation among the former Yugoslav re-publics than there are disincentives. From the perspective of the current po-litical elites, however, the balance of incentives/disincentives is in favor of discouraging political cooperation among the republics.

A glance at an economic perspective suggests that there are many benefits to enhanced cooperation among the former Yugoslav republics. The Social-ist Yugoslav economy, although highly decentralized, was also highly inter-dependent. Components of major heavy industries were diffused throughout the republics. Automobiles, transport machinery, electronics, etc. had com-ponents manufactured in several of the republics; energy sources, raw ma-terials, marketing, design and distribution often originated in republics other than that which assembled the product. Favorable economic treatment for domestic producers, and quotas or taxes on foreign imports gave Yugoslav producers a strong advantage in the home market. In addition, the increas-ing clout of the major trading blocks reduced profitable and favorable export possibilities for Yugoslav manufacturers.

Following the breakup of Yugoslavia, virtually every complex and major domestic manufacturer found its domestic market seriously reduced. It also found that its goods were not competitively priced and qualitative for suc-cessful entry into the Western European and North American markets, and that its fall-back market in Eastern Europe no longer existed. Manufacturers, in short, could not survive without heavy state subsidies and major compro-mises with the concept of a free market economy.

The service sector has also been seriously eroded and potentially de-stroyed by the politics of the breakup and the continuing tensions and threats of bloody conflict. Croatia, for example, earned as much as US $8 billion per year from tourism, an industry severely impacted by the potential for violence and instability. Each of the republics saw its revenues from international transit evaporate as hostilities and closed borders stretched on for several years. Foreign investments, use of licenses and other service fees also collapsed and could not be resurrected without a major change in the inter-republic climate. At best the continuance of inter-Balkan isolation has doomed each of the newly emerging economies to stagnation or steady deterioration.

Socially, there are virtually no advantages from continuance of boycotts, discrimination and closed borders among the former Yugoslav republics. The isolation of non-majority populations severely limits the strength of the society, increases the costs of control, alienates large proportions of the population, and weakens the legitimacy of most social institutions. Prior to the break-up of the Socialist Federation and the advent of "ethnic cleansing," over 5 percent of the population claimed "Yugoslav" as their nationality and over one third of the population in the typical republic did not belong to the majority nationality in that republic (see table 7.1).

As indicated by table 7.1, all the republics, save Slovenia, possessed large Yugoslav and nonindigenous populations. All the republics, save Slovenia, also have governments moving towards the authoritarian end of the political culture spectrum. Finally, all the republics, save Slovenia, have reported substantial human rights abuses and threats to individuals and minority groups.

From the perspective of the political leadership of the various successor republics there are substantive incentives towards maintaining the status quo and not moving towards inter-republic conciliation. Each of these regimes was founded on strong nationalist principles and owes its legitimacy to the defense of the primary nationality within the republic. The rapidly deteriorating economy has put substantive pressures upon each of the regimes beyond their capacity to cope, and the playing of the nationalist card buys time and support from its primary political base. Third, the redistribution of power and discrimination of national/ethnic minorities rewards the primary political base and commits that group to support of the nationalist agenda.

**Table 7.1. Percent of Population Claiming Yugoslav Nationality and Non-Majority Nationality by Republic, 1980 Census**

| Republic | Yugoslav Nationality | Non-majority Population |
|---|---|---|
| Bosnia-Herzegovina | 8% | 61% |
| Montenegro | 5% | 31% |
| Croatia | 8% | 25% |
| Macedonia | 1% | 33% |
| Slovenia | 1% | 9% |
| Serbia | 5% | 34% |

Movement towards pluralism would endanger the newly found wealth of the new nationalist elite. Fourth, the authoritarian controls of the nationalist regimes and erosion of individual rights can best by justified as a "temporary" expediency from the nationalist threat. Fifth, maintenance of a war footing and war economy can be justified through appeals to national survival against the "enemy nation" with a fifth column within the republic. Sixth, the incompetence of government policy or the leadership can be masked by the rhetoric of the struggle for the nation; thereby permitting opposition political parties to be marginalized.

The behavior of both the Serbian and Croatian opposition and governments illustrates these principles in action. For Serbia, effective criticism of the Serbian Socialist Party under Milosevic is limited to even more extreme threats from the ultra-nationalist right. Seselj's Radical Party gains attention by advocating programs such as the liquidation of 100 non-Serbs for every Serb killed in the struggle. The patriotism of more pluralist parties such as the Democratic Party or the United Left is questioned whenever government policy is criticized. The ability of the opposition to compete for political support is compromised by its inability to articulate a serious non-nationalist agenda.

In Croatia, the opposition parties have greater freedom to maneuver, but their ability to influence the national agenda is limited as long as the national issue remains unsolved. Economics, unemployment, social issues, education and other policy issues must take a back seat to the primary political issues of the Serbian rebel movement and the occupied territories. Like Serbia, Croatia's political development is paralyzed by nationalist issues. Like Serbia, Croatia's political leadership owes its position to nationalist fervor, not political, social or economic competence. Like Serbia, Croatia's moderate opposition cannot mount an effective campaign for political support until the nationalist issue is resolved. Thus, from the perspective of the political leaders in successor republics such as Yugoslavia and Croatia, there is no incentive for political accommodation and considerable cause for concern for involuntary retirement.[4]

## Breaking the Impasse

Appeals to economic rationality or humanitarian concerns are unlikely to be sufficient to compel substantive change in the policies of the Yugoslav successor states towards one another and to encourage a higher level of cooperation or association. One must recognize that the breakup of Yugoslavia occurred primarily because of nationalist concerns, and that any attempts at restoring a normal environment must accommodate itself to this reality. Without coming to terms with the nationalist reality, economic and humanitarian arguments for association or cooperation could be dismissed as "Yugo-nostalgia" by disgruntled ex-communist functionaries.[5]

An interesting commonality among the strong nationalist regimes is the resistance to change by the leadership, and the branding of potential change agents as national threats. For example, those who call for greater democratization and the devolution of authority from the capitol have been labeled as "separatists," and the unwillingness of the central governments in both Belgrade and Zagreb have actually increased these separatist feelings. The demands for Albanian autonomy in Kosovo, Hungarian limited self-rule in the Vojvodina, and Muslim autonomy in the Sandzak have been roundly condemned and resisted. Similar questioning, albeit on a more restrained level, by Istrian and Almatian regionalists in Croatia, or more forcefully by rebel Serbs in the Krajina have been resisted and condemned by Croatian authorities as threats to the integrity of the state. Today, the greatest impediment to general democratization and eventual inter-republic cooperation is the resolution of the minority self-rule issues and regional autonomy in Yugoslavia and in Croatia.

Pragmatic arguments for association carry little weight with the political leaderships in the former Yugoslav republics. Yugoslav, Croatian, Macedonian and even Slovenian leaders feel quite insecure about the permanence of their newly won independence and argue that any form of enhanced regional cooperation on a bilateral, but especially multilateral, basis rings of revanchism and a return to the old Yugoslavism. In every republic, "Yugo-nostalgia" has strong negative connotations. From a Croatian perspective, "Yugo-nostalgists" advocate a return to a system of Serb minority rule, repression of Croatian culture, and economic exploitation by Belgrade banks and economic enterprises. For Slovenians, "Yugo-nostalgia" is perceived as a barrier to prosperity and inclusion in Europe. For Macedonian leaders, Macedonia's poverty is attributed to the exploitation of their resources by Slovenians, Croats and Serbs. Among Serbs, "Yugo-nostalgia" implies the surrender of regional leadership and economic autonomy to the smaller and "less heroic" nationalities as well as the abandonment of "fellow Serbs" to cultural assimilation by the other republics' nationalities.

These strong but reinforcing negative images of regional association strongly suggest that any attempt at "normalization" take into account the nationalist and political issues. The negative images also demand that trust cannot be restored without some form of international institutionalization and guarantee of minority rights to supplement individual human rights guaranteed by the Helsinki agreement. Failure to guarantee minority protections with an international reference point would be a critical error and prohibit the lessening of tensions throughout the territory of the former Yugoslavia.

From Yugoslavia's perspective (i.e. Serbia) the "Greater Serbia" idea is linked inseparably to the fear of cultural assimilation and marginalization of Serbian minorities in Kosovo, the Krajina, Bosnia and Macedonia. From Croatia's perspective, Serb minorities are deadset upon sabotaging the Croatian state. From the perspective of Serb minorities, their identity is threatened with extinction by Croatian homogenization in the Krajina, or Albanian population growth in Kosovo. From the perspective of Hungarian and particularly Albanian minorities, they are treated as an alien nation with links to hostile outside powers and permanent outsiders in their own lands.

In brief, none of the minorities within the former Yugoslavia can accept the status quo. None of the minorities can accept a constitutional or other legal guarantee that is not backed up or enforced by some international body. Conversely, none of the new states is willing to accept an international guarantee unless such a guarantee is imposed upon all. In brief, if peace and resolution of the nationalist issue is to occur in the former Yugoslavia, there is a responsibility for the international community to recognize the legitimacy of minority concerns and to work to guarantee these rights and obligations in some concrete form.

The most dangerous course is that which is currently pursued by the international community; namely, to treat every nationality issue as a separate case, amenable to rational discourse, but not an international responsibility or obligation that is placed upon all. The link between democracy and individual human rights is now well recognized and supported. The link between democracy and group rights and responsibilities deserves equal attention and support. As is now obvious throughout the former Yugoslav federation, one cannot exist without the other and the only alternative is war and continued ethnic cleansing.

## NOTES

1. The author is grateful for the support of the International Research and Exchange Board, 1994.

2. Based upon interviews with the Director and staff of the Croatian Office in Belgrade and the Yugoslav Office in Zagreb in October 1984.

3. Based upon interviews with the competent authorities in the Foreign Ministries in Croatia and the FRY.

4. Source: Savezni Zavod za Statistiku, *Statisticki Godisnjak SFRJ 1989*, Belgrade: Savezni Zavod za Statistiku, 1990.

5. The threat to international peace potentially affects more than relationships between the constituent republics of the former Yugoslavia. Potentially, Italian-Slovenian, Italian-Croatian, Hungarian-Yugoslav, Albanian-Yugoslav, and Greek-Macedonian relationships can be strained.

## REFERENCES

Goldstein, Slavko. "Gradanski dijalog Srbi I Hrvati." *Erasmus* 5, 1995.

Kasapovic, Mirjana. *Izborni I stranacki sustav Republike Hrvatske,* Zagreb: Alinea, 1993.

Lovric, Jelena. "Jugo-tigar od papira?" *Nova List,* 18 June 1995: 2.

Mileta, Vlatko. "Hrvatsku je Jugoslavija stajala 102 milijarde dolaral!" *Vjesnik,* 24 June 1995: 5.

Pribicevic, Ognjen. "Politicka kultura I demokratskastabilnost," in *Izbonre Borbe u Jugoslaviji, 1990–1992,* edited by Vladimir Goati. Belgrade: Radnicka Stampa, 1993.

Savezni Zavod za Statistiku. *Statisticki Godisnjak Jugoslavijie, 1989.* Belgrade: Savezni Zavod za Statistiku, 1990.

Siber, Ivan. "Images of Croatian Political Parties." *Politicka Misao* 31(1) 1994: 188–201.

Stanovcic, Vojislav. "Civilno drustvo i vladavina prava u visenacionalnim zajednicama," in *Potisnuto Civilno Drustvo,* Vukasin Pavlovic, ed. Belgrade: Eko centar Beograd, 1995, 107–130.

Vasovic, Vucina and Vladimir Goati. *Izbori I izborni sistemi.* Belgrade: Radnicka Stampa, 1993.

# V

## INTERNATIONAL CRIME

# 8

# Dunblane and the International Politics of Gun Control

*Aaron Karp*

To anyone in the United States it was nothing short of amazing when Britain's House of Commons voted on June 11th of this year to end virtually all public ownership of hand guns. Aroused by the massacre of school children in Scotland a year before, public opinion throughout Britain immediately had focused on banning hand guns as the most appropriate and necessary response. Even so, passage of the measure was not easy, complicated by the priorities of electoral politics, repeatedly delayed and endangered. Compared to America's mature and well-financed lobbies the groups on both sides of the British debate seem amateurish in the extreme. Yet the results of their debate have been infinitely more substantive.

Since John F. Kennedy was assassinated with a mail-order rifle thirty-four years ago, gun control has been at the top of America's domestic policy agenda. Today violent crime in he United States is down from the worst of a few years ago, but over 240 million guns remain in public hands and Americans use them with exceptional frequency. In 1994—the latest year for comprehensive statistics—38,505 Americans were killed with firearms.[1] Numbed by such numbers, the United States has become a country where the word massacre no longer horrifies. Perhaps only could an event like the botched Los Angeles bank robbery on February 28th 1997—which saw the culprits holding off police with a fusillade of automatic rifle fire—not lead to a sweeping public investigation.

Despite this hesitation, the debate in the United States over public ownership of firearms has been the world's most advanced, punctuated by highly original research and incisive probing of fundamental issues. This is no longer the case. The new legislation puts the United Kingdom at the forefront of a global trend toward forthright action on firearms, a trend leaving the United States increasingly behind and isolated. Canada established a much stronger handgun regime in 1989. Australia long ago imposed stringent controls on handgun ownership and banned semi-automatic rifles and shotguns from public hands in 1996. New Zealand currently is doing the same. Several European countries are debating new restrictions on public gun ownership as well. In the United Nations, Japan is leading a unique coalition of countries that either are feeling the effects of wider gun ownership for the first time or have been affected by ethnic warfare, investigating illegal gun sales with an eye toward global recommendations.

It will be several years before the impact of Britain's handgun ban is fully understood. But already there is much to be learned from the process that led to the prohibition. Britain's new place at the vanguard of societies debating firearms policy also makes it a test case for other governments debating public firearms ownership. Whether or not other countries are willing seriously to consider equally restrictive measures may depend in no small part on the implementation of Britain's prohibition and its effectiveness keeping hand guns out of public hands.

## THE DUNBLANE MASSACRE

Thomas Hamilton, a troubled 43-year old former youth-leader and suspected pedophile, calmly walked into a primary school in Dunblane, Scotland, on 13 March 1996, carrying four legally owned hand guns and 743 rounds of ammunition. There he killed 16 four- and five-year-olds and their teacher before killing himself.[2] The attack aroused intense public concern and released a long-simmering debate over gun control. Britain's news media were obsessed with the case; even the broadsheet press kept it on page one for almost two months without interruption. Although gun ownership had never been a prominent element in British culture, Dunblane confirmed a general sense that the UK had drifted far from the public ideal of a nonviolent society where the police did not need to be armed. The cry for action had never been so intense.

There had been a similar outcry in 1987 when 14 people were killed in the Thames Valley town of Hungerford, 100 km West of London. Armed with a fully licensed AK-47 and three pistols, Michael Ryan walked along methodically shooting 14 people dead and wounding 14 more, ending the rampage with his own suicide. But no young children were killed then and the public anger was more easily assuaged. Margaret Thatcher's government, moreover, was considerably stronger and found it easier to respond rapidly. The resulting ban on assault guns, semi-automatic rifles and shotguns sailed through the House of Commons within weeks. The measure was popular and easily enforced since the numbers of such weapons were only begin-

ning to grow. Only 3,600 weapons were eliminated—compared to an estimated 2 million similar weapons owned by the American public—but the
speedy action was enough to quell public concern.[3] Although public senti-
ment ran strongly against handgun ownership too, the issue was not a salient
one and no anti-gun movement developed in Britain.

That the Hungerford murders could occur was largely the result of a sea
change in the international firearms market. Automatic weapons have been
available to the public in many countries for decades, but this traditionally
was a tiny part of the gun trade of interest only to collectors. That changed
in the early 1980s, when Chinese, Soviet and Eastern European makers of automatic rifles began to flood the market for sporting guns, pushing prices
down sharply and increasing exponentially the firepower available to the
public. Western manufacturers soon joined as well, focusing sales efforts for
assault weapons in the United States but soon finding buyers elsewhere. The
rising cocaine trade did much to inflate demand as well. In other regions ethnic warfare and social collapse have left hundreds of thousands or even mil-
lions of unregistered weapons, weapons which do not disappear just because war ends.[4]

The results can be seen in the new wave of violent attacks around the
world of which Hungerford was one of the first. Where assailants previously
were limited to slower manually operated guns, all too often they now use
automatic rifles and pistols. The effects of this increase in firepower are all
too obvious; in country after country, incidents that previously would have
led to injury now end in murder, and where they might have ended in murder they now can lead to outright massacres.

Also at work in Britain was a more general public concern with reversing
the decline of the civility long assumed to lay at he heart of British society
and culture. By superficial comparisons Britain remains a peaceful place; in
the last decade it averaged about 60 murders with firearms annually, compared to roughly 20,000 firearms murders (plus 18,500 suicides) in the
United States each year. Handgun related crimes have averaged about 3,500
annually compared to one million in the United States every year.[5] However
dramatic the comparison, statistics like these have the effect of making the
United States appear to be the norm, when in fact it is the unique example
of a pathologically violent industrial nation.

The rise of gun ownership and gun crimes in Britain is profoundly alarm-
ing to a society which places a much higher value on its sense of community
based on trust and predictability. Highly publicized and widely debated
crimes like the beating-death of two-year old James Bulger by two ten-year
old boys in 1992 and the racially motivated murder of Stephen Lawrence in
1993 did not involve firearms. Nor did the fatal stabbing of London head-
master Philip Lawrence in 1995. But these infamous deeds alerted the public to the growing violence of British society and aroused a growing sense

that steps must be taken to arrest the rise of a Clockwork Orange atmosphere in the streets.

While the debate over the decline of civility is not something restricted to the United Kingdom, it was there that pressure has been strongest to translate vague social anxiety into tangible public policy.[6] Even after these events mobilized public determination, however, there are limits on any government's ability to legislate solutions to public ills; prohibiting handguns stood out on a growing agenda of social problems as one field where action was possible and the effects clear.

## THE GOVERNMENT REACTS

Despite the vocal emotional reaction, none of the three parliamentary parties seemed interested in capitalizing on the issue. Like political parties in the United States when facing similar issues, they initially focused more on the dangers to their existing coalitions rather than the opportunities to build new support. The Commons, after all, must be one of the few legislatures in the world with its own shooting range. Within the ruling Conservative Party there was no consensus for action. The Tories respect their classical liberal roots, a tradition greatly reinvigorated during the eleven-year rule of Margaret Thatcher, who pioneered the path of privatization and rolling back the welfare state. Initially then-Home Secretary Michael Howard offered only a voluntary weapons turn-in. Liberal-Democrat leader Paddy Ashdown also opposed a ban, although he favored tighter licensing. Labor's shadow Home Minister Jack Straw was an impenetrable cipher at first, apparently waiting to see how the winds would blow.

Although he avoided commenting on specific options after Dunblane, John Major showed no compelling reason to reverse his party's established approach to national policy by leading a crusade against guns. He also had a worried faction to reassure, dominated by the country gentry. These were mostly men who had grown up in the rural Britain, a world where firearms—albeit rifles and shotguns, not hand guns—are considered a normal part of an economically well-to-do household. In the House of Commons they formed a backbench block of some 60 votes. They were much stronger in the House of Lords. Although Lords lost its ability to veto legislation long ago, it still has the power to slow it down, a potentially potent factor on an issue as dependant on the vicissitudes of public conviction as this one. With his party already divided over issues like the European Union and Northern Ireland, Major had no incentive to chase more controversy.

The Government's most substantive reaction was to appoint a commission. The assignment was given to Lord William Douglas Cullen. Although hardly a public figure, he was perhaps Scotland's most prominent jurist since the late 1980s when he presided over the inquiry into the Piper Alpha oil platform disaster. This was more than a sop to the press; in Britain the recommendations of official commissions are not ignored, they usually become policy. But Cullen's deliberate pace did little to reassure those demanding serious action in response to Dunblane. Reflecting the Government's consensus for careful deliberation, he was gradual and thorough, listening to 171 witnesses in 26 days of testimony, showing a balanced ear to both gun control advocates and Britain's shooting lobby. Few were surprised when his investigations tended to de-emphasize the general question of gun ownership and focused more on gun licensing procedures and school security. The approach won a sanguine reaction from shooting interests, who felt safe with Cullen.

Not surprisingly this methodical approach alarmed gun ban advocates. Although some recognized that his approach was pretty conventional, others feared that public momentum was in danger of running out of steam and that action must be taken before public attention drifted to other concerns. In fact Cullen's inquiry was highly efficient and in no sense slow. He had been commissioned, after all, within days of the massacre and he began hearing witnesses barely two months later. Nor was his approach any more satisfying to groups like the British Field Sports Society or the Shooters' Rights Association, who saw ineluctable momentum for gun law reform. None of this was satisfying, though, to those pressing for a sweeping prohibition and saw likely recommendations being diluted and the pace of action slipping.

## THE SNOWDROP APPEAL

The real catalyst for action came not from Whitehall but from the public itself. Begun two months after the massacre, the Snowdrop appeal started as a modest effort by friends and relatives of the Dunblane families to raise pressure for action to ban public ownership of handguns. Led by those most immediately affected, it received enormous public sympathy.

Even so, Snowdrop was a kitchen-table campaign, which its leaders admit was poorly organized and largely serendipitous. Unlike American counterparts like Mothers Against Drunk Drivers, there were no offices, no systematic plan, no budget and no advertising. After making their hopes known to the press, its leaders were surprised at the outpouring of national sympathy, as people wrote to request petitions. Media coverage played an important role, keeping the Dunblane killings on the front pages and maintaining high public concern over gun ownership. Even so, amateurism dogged the process; many of the lists were mislaid after being received or were found to be legally invalid.

In late July, the organizers of the Snowdrop appeal were under pressure to submit their petition to parliament before its summer recess. With 705,000 verified signatures at the time of its submission, it was formally presented through the normal procedures. Although Britain's unwritten constitution requires parliament to receive signed petitions there is no requirement that they be acted upon. Usually these are modest affairs that achieve little. Snowdrop might have ended as most such submissions usually do, but it captured the public mood demanding action after Dunblane.

The Government was waiting for the Cullen Commission to present its findings before acting and refused to be rushed. Meanwhile other groups began to speak out, most notably the majority of the nation's police organizations who also supported a total ban on public ownership of hand guns, but they counted for little politically. There was widespread suspicion that the Government, hoping to avoid antagonizing its rural constituents and traditional supporters, would wait until public pressure had subsided and offer only minimal reforms. Labor opposition leaders were very sympathetic to prohibiting handguns, but they too were not inclined to act. With a lead in the polls over 20 percent and the possibility that an election could be called anytime, Labor as well had no interest in acting divisively.

Already in August momentum for action was dissipating. The straight-forward good intentions of the Snowdrop appeal were sufficient to bring the issue before parliament, but the effort easily could have died there; greater tactical insight was necessary to insure action. It was at this point that one of the leading gun-ban advocates moved to center stage. A prominent social activist with an insider's knowledge of the Commons, Gill Marshall-Andrews, assembled a group of parliamentarians to cosponsor a bill to ban handgun ownership through an early-day motion. This obscure and seldom-used procedure permits back-bench members of Parliament to force the house to consider a proposal that otherwise would be overlooked in the rush of business. Based on consensus, it requires only the sponsorship of two MPs from each of the three parliamentary parties. Presented as an amendment to the 1988 Firearms Act, this bill would have banned public ownership of all hand guns.

## THE GOVERNMENT'S REVERSAL

Although John Major's cabinet lacked enthusiasm for the plan, his government was too weak to fight it. With the Conservative majority in the Commons down to an extremely thin margin—four seats at that point—it could not risk any loss of support and needed to suppress any proposal which risked a break in its own ranks. Labor saw the bill, which clearly had majority support across the house, as a chance to embarrass or even undermine the Government and began to support it more actively. If a coalition of Labor, Liberal Democrats and renegade Tories passed the bill over Government opposition it might have forced an election, which the conservatives were almost certain to lose. Consideration of the bill was now unavoidable. Caught in a damned-if-you-do-or-don't situation, the Government's natural response was to urge further caution, appealing for patience while Cullen completed his report.

The pressure to move on firearms may have been virtually irresistible, but skilled tactics might yet have rescued the situation for the Government had a way been found to avoid strong action. How John Major's Government chose instead to reverse its approach is unclear. One account centers on the role of the Scottish Secretary, Michael Forsyth. Deeply affected by the killings at Dunblane—the town lies in his own Stirling constituency—he was personally committed to a strong response. Due to redistricting, moreover, he also was almost certain to lose his seat in the next election (which is what happened), liberating him from his party's preoccupation with political survival. Already in early August he was speaking publicly on the need for a ban.

Regional tensions also were beginning to make themselves felt. Not only Forsyth, but other spokesmen for Scotland were pressing for a ban. Labor's then-shadow Scottish Secretary, George Robertson (after the May 1st election he became Britain's Defence Minister), went in front of his party to press for a ban from the outset. The leader of the Scottish National Party, the MP Alex Salmon, was at the forefront as well. Even the actor Sean Connery contributed to the sense that the handgun ban was an implacable regional interest.

This new insistence was registered at a cabinet meeting, no later than early September, where a member of the high-level Tory—Forsyth is the most likely possibility—rose to demand vigorous action on firearms. This was the first time a member of the government broke ranks with the consensus in favor of the least disruptive course of action. Michael Howard, the Home Minister who previously had been one of the strongest voices for moderation, was persuaded that prevarication no longer was tenable; intended to avoid confrontation, it was becoming a greater source of conflict itself.

The findings of the Cullen Commission, presented to the cabinet on October 14th and made public two days later, seem to have been crafted with an eye to the growing public consensus and the delicate needs of the Government.[7] The report concentrated not on public gun ownership but on the lax licensing procedures that allowed Thomas Hamilton to own his guns. The report concluded that no system of licensing could provide sufficient security against future massacres; that could come only by banning the most dangerous weapons themselves. But the report accepted the logic of firearms supporters that an absolute ban was not needed. Instead it stressed

the need to give police greater powers to evaluate applicants for firearms licenses and to revoke licenses, to improve school security and oversee
youth group leaders.

Despite the thrust of his analysis, Cullen surprised many observers by accepting the basic argument that hand guns were neither a necessary part of
society nor essential to the maintenance of civil liberties. Although he agreed
that banning them was readily feasible, he did not recommend a complete
ban. In a concession to shooting interests, he accepted the argument that
small caliber hand guns should be permitted in recognition of their role in
Olympic sports since 1896. This led Cullen to recommend banning only
hand guns over .22 caliber, although even the latter would have to be stored
exclusively in gun-club armories.

Much to the surprise of shooting interests, which were generally pleased
with Cullen's findings, the Government bill submitted to Parliament the next
day actually went beyond its recommendations. Presented as an amendment
to the 1988 Firearms Act, it presented a much stronger emphasis on the importance of restricting access to hand guns. The Government's decision to
support a partial handgun ban was met with angry protests within the Conservative party. Led by traditional spokesmen for rural areas in the House of
Lords, they argued that traditional rights were being sacrificed to score political points. None were more outspoken than the Earl of Shrewsbury who
went so far as to criticize the bill as a "monstrous injustice." The respected
MP Nicholas Budgen described the bill as "bad and ill considered government, a panic reaction."[8]

The conservative opponents' preferred response was to tighten licensing
and review procedures alone.[9] Their protests failed to win public support,
apparently because the larger issue of the right to gun ownership was not in
question; throughout the debate gun control advocates focused exclusively
on handguns, avoiding any attack on the right to own rifles and shotguns.
The spokesmen for shooting interests came off as shrill or, as in the case of
Prince Philip, completely out of touch with public opinion and common
sense.

The biggest difference between the Government and Snowdrop positions
was the concession to Tory opponents offered by Michael Howard, who
agreed to continued public ownership of .22 caliber target pistols to be kept
in secured facilities at Britain's 2,100 designated shooting clubs. Like any in-
decisive compromise, this move backfired politically, antagonizing virtually
everyone. It went too far to satisfy Conservative rebels who rejected not the
extent of the handgun ban, but its principle. By not going far enough it lost
the goodwill the government originally sought from gun control advocates.
When presented to parliament for its first vote on December 4, 63 Tories
voted against their party's amendment bill, which passed only because of the
support of Labor and Liberal-Democrat MPs.[10]

## POLITICS AGAIN

In December it appeared that the most serious challenge would come from Conservatives in the House of Lords, where agitation had been great and talk of lawsuits and demands for generous financial compensation were well received. As supporters of the bill recognized, the Lords could not kill the bill, but by slowing down action they potentially had the power to starve it to death. Although opponents' rhetoric received extensive media attention, however, there was not vigorous action to bloc the bill on the floor of the House of Lords, proof perhaps of its dilettantish role on this issue.

A much more serious challenge to the gun ban came a few weeks later from the bill's most natural supporters, the Labor opposition. The party which, after overcoming its own initial hesitation, had strongly advocated a complete ban on handguns and stood to gain the most from the passage of any new legislation suddenly showed that, as always, the process was not driven by principle alone. If greater political advantage could be found elsewhere, the handguns ban would be abandoned without hesitation. Labor had not abandoned its support, but it had become badly sidetracked. This raised the perverse spectacle of the most natural supporters of the legislation deliberately contributing to its death.

One week before the amendment to the Firearms Act was scheduled for its final vote in Commons, Labor was distracted by the distant possibility of undermining the Government and accelerating elections. This came in the form of an unrelated motion to penalize the Government for its weak handling of the bovine spongiform encephalopathy (mad cow disease) affair by docking the salary of then-Agriculture Minister Douglas Hogg. This was not as sophomoric as it appeared, given the extreme narrowness of the Government's majority. Here was an illustration of the secondary importance of the handguns legislation. Perhaps Labor would return to act on handguns immediately after coming to power, but there was no guarantee. Only after the defeat of this opposition motion—one day before the handgun vote—was the amendment assured passage.

Strenuous last minute efforts by renegade Tories to derail the measure by demanding greater financial compensation for owners and merchants were defeated (by a vote of 140 to 319) as were amendments permitting target pistols to be kept at home (115 to 394) but only with support from Labor opposition and the Liberal-Democrats. The final bill banning most public handgun ownership was passed by the assent of the Commons on 19 February 1997 and by the House of Lords the next day, with the Conservative Party still badly divided and essential support coming from opposition members.

As a result of this action a total of 160,000 legally registered handguns would be banned, their owners being offered L100 to L150 ($160 to $240) in compensation for each gun.[11] Except for museum pieces, the guns will be melted down. Only small caliber target pistols are permitted, and those only if kept in shooting club vaults—they cannot be stored at home—and their owners too are encouraged to turn them in and also will be compensated when they do. Despite spirited debate over the consequences for gun manufacturers and retailers, they will not receive financial help. In any event the loss to most firearms businesses probably will not be insufferable in a country where rifles and shotguns still outnumber handguns by roughly ten-to-one.

## BUT WILL IT WORK?

Five weeks after winning the 1 May 1997 parliamentary elections by a landslide, Tony Blair's new Labor government fulfilled a campaign promise by making the handguns ban comprehensive, eliminating the exemption for .22 caliber pistols. Inviting consensus, leaders of all three major parties allowed their members to vote their consciences, resulting in a lopsided vote on 11 June of 384 to 181.[12]

The ban, which already went further than any other Western country to eliminate one of society's most obvious sources of deadly violence, had become uncatagorical. This leadership makes Britain an emerging test case for other governments debating firearms policy. Whether or not other countries are willing to seriously consider equally restrictive measures may depend in no small part on the ease with which Britain's prohibition is implemented and its subsequent effectiveness at the job of keeping handguns out of public hands.

In the ritual of firearms policy debates, opponents of gun control typically site two basic reasons why strict measures will be ineffective. First, it is routinely stated that firearms cannot be taken out of public hands without broader attacks on civil liberties including the creation of a Gestapo-type secret police. Second, there is the belief that the desire for firearms is so strong that any effort to prohibit ownership will be undermined by the rise of black markets. Both arguments deserve serious consideration.

When it comes time to implement a firearms ban, the United Kingdom, other European and the Pacific rim countries may have real advantages over nations like the United States. Greater respect for the rule of law, a narrower sense of individualism and more willingness to sacrifice for the collective good seem to insure large-scale acceptance of a ban. Already voluntary weapons amnesties have shown that the British public are willing to comply. During the brief amnesty held immediately after the Dunblane shooting some 50,000 weapons were turned in.[13] With the ban now legally in place, there is little doubt that the vast majority of prohibited weapons will be offered voluntarily in short order.

Registered weapons will be gathered through public appeals, temporary amnesties and police notification to license holders. Financial compensation is not necessary when dealing with registered weapons—they are easily tracked down—although it obviously makes things go smoother. The promise of money is more important to address the problem of unregistered weapons. Incentives are one way to overcome the hesitation or procrastination that will keep too many weapons buried in drawers and wardrobes, even in the most civil of societies. These weapons pose two dangers. First, in violent societies like the United States, these are the weapons most likely to be fired accidentally, by children, or in crimes of passion. Secondly, they are most likely to be stolen, and become the most important source of guns for the truly violent.

The greatest problem standing before complete success is not compliance with the law by owners of registered weapons, but Britain's unregistered guns that also must be removed from circulation. The massacres at Hungerford and Dunblane, like the worst shooting sprees in the United States, Australia and Canada, were committed with legally held weapons by licensed owners. Opponents of gun control, however, have traditionally made unregistered guns the core of their objections to restrictions, which initially are certain to place a greater responsibility on law abiding gun owners, not criminals. The issue of illegally held weapons is less important in Britain than it would be in a country with lax registration laws like the United States, but even in the UK unregistered weapons play a growing role in gang violence and street crime. Some of these are in the possession of otherwise licensed gun owners, others are clearly held illegally. Their numbers have been estimated in the press at up to a million, but police officials have no firm idea.[14]

The key to eliminating unregistered weapons will be persistence and flexibility. It will require appeals to the public sense of legal responsibility, amnesty for those turning in unlicensed weapons, and in the end even financial rewards. A cycle of public appeals, amnesty and incentives will have to be repeated many times, but within three to five years the results will be clear in significantly reduced gun crimes and incidents.

Some prominent gun control advocates oppose financial compensation even for registered handguns, maintaining that respect for the public consensus and the law should be sufficient to insure compliance. Some have reacted with disbelief at the suggestion that owners be allowed to trade in illegal guns for cash as well. Cash incentives are important, though, to promote compliance and reduce the risk that stolen handguns will fall into criminal hands. Compensation is not needed to deal with habitual criminals. The most dangerous unregistered handguns will be recovered by the police in relatively short order. "Time-to-crime" studies, as they are known, have repeatedly confirmed that weapons in the hands of established criminals are used and apprehended within two to three years; repeat offenders are not the kind of people who plan their lives years into the future, saving their guns for the right moment; they tend to live spontaneously and their weapons are used and caught the same way.[15]

The problem with cash incentives is largely one of getting the sums right. If the compensation is too low, few people will comply; if the amount is too high a new black market will be created by people illegally importing weapons in order to sell them to the police. One of the most successful buy-back operations was in Haiti after the United Nations intervened there in 1994. Although it was widely feared that the operation would fail because of the extreme public insecurity and vulnerability, it turned into an astounding success, recovering over 13,000 out of an estimated 20,000 weapons in private hands.[16] More recently the drug-ravaged Colombian city of Cali has used amnesties alone to help cleanse its streets of firearms and reduce its phenomenal murder rate by one-fifth.[17]

Black markets are almost certain to arise from efforts to prohibit anything for which people are sufficiently willing to pay. Banning whole classes of small arms will create new opportunities for quick profits and undoubtedly will attract smuggling. This problem is important, but it should not be exaggerated; weapons smuggling cannot be stopped completely, but its worst effects are readily countered. Black markets will complicate enforcement of a ban, but they do not have the potential to undermine its credibility.

Black markets can prosper only under specific circumstances, where highly valuable and easily concealed goods can be sold readily and with minimal risk of getting caught.[18] Narcotics, gem stones and strategic technologies are ideal for illegal shipment and sale; the penalties may be great, but the actual risks can be manageable. Cigarettes are ideal as well; because of their bulk the risks of getting caught are high, but the penalties are acceptably low. Firearms, by comparison, are bulky and hard to conceal, they are not worth very much and they can be surprisingly difficult to sell. And to top it off the penalties for apprehension are severe. Five kilos of pure cocaine, for example, is worth a lot more than five kilos of firearms. Thus the risk of drug smuggling is much more manageable and the crime is more appealing.

A private smuggler dealing in guns undertakes exceptional risk for relatively small profit. To make enough money to offset the risks, a sale must involve hundreds of weapons and it must be repeated several times. But such large sales are extremely difficult to conceal and far too risky to repeat. It is not surprising that black markets never have been a major source of firearms except for peculiar situations, like across the open Canadian-U.S. border. For countries like the UK the problems are far less.

By historical accident, the first Western country to ban most handguns also happens to have the most experience of all in dealing with weapons smuggling. In the years since 1969, when the Irish Republican Army initiated its current campaign of violence, British customs, police and military authorities have done more than any nation to cultivate the skills of intercepting illegal shipments and confiscating illegally held firearms. Beginning with modest abilities and little success, British authorities gradually developed unique expertise identifying and controlling illegal arms shipments to the IRA. Their experience suggests that there will be little difficulty dealing with the most serious black market activities emerging in reaction to the hand gun ban.[19]

Through the 1970s the IRA relied extensively on weapons smuggled chiefly from the United States, where sympathizers elaborately packaged Armalite rifles (civilian M-16s) and other weapons in freight shipments (coffins were a favorite), shipped vehicles and small vessels, usually for delivery through the Irish Republic. Close cooperation between customs authorities and other law enforcement officials in North America, Ireland and the UK eventually ended this flow in the early 1980s. In the place of sympathetic individuals emerged a much more dangerous source in sympathetic governments like Czechoslovakia, East Germany and Libya. Closing these supply routes was much more difficult; only the end of the Cold War made it possible to end them altogether.

Since then the IRA has been starved of weapons and forced to moderate its attacks, a factor that contributed in no small way to the cease fire begun in August 1994. Even after the cease fire collapsed seventeen months later in February 1996, incidents have been limited, apparently not by preference so much as due to lack of weapons. The IRA retains a very serious arsenal, sufficient for years of carefully managed terrorist attacks. But the lack of new supplies has forced it to change tactics. Unable to smuggle nearly as much as it could use, the IRA has had no choice but to limit its attacks and rely more than ever on bombs rather than bullets, as it did in the London and Manchester bombings.

While the IRA is better known, even more can be learned from the experiences of the Irish National Liberation Army.[20] This IRA-splinter group traditionally relied on tiny shipments of arms, operating less like a major insurgency and more like the small-time smugglers likely to be faced as a result of Britain's handguns legislation. Through twenty-five years and numerous schemes and conspiracies, the INLA has been able to accumulate a politically significant but militarily modest arsenal, currently estimated by experts to include some 100 handguns and roughly two-dozen automatic weapons. Even this would not have been possible, however, by a terrorist band working alone. It required continual assistance from then-communist East European governments and the PLO. When forced to work through private channels, the INLA could bring guns in by ones and twos through the channel ports or Ireland in the 1970s and mid-1980s. But tactics had to be changed constantly; if the same smuggling procedure was repeated it usually was intercepted.

By the late-1980s it was becoming impossible for the INLA to replenish its arsenal. Weapons used typically had to be abandoned as part of hit-and-run tactics and could not be replaced. The growing expertise of British Customs and Excise authorities—currently numbering over 28,000—as well as renewed cooperation with the Republic of Ireland and the loss of support from other governments left the group unable to mount violent attacks except at enormous, and basically unacceptable, risk to its followers.[21] The loss of a reliable source of weapons helped provoke savage internecine fighting over goals and means, leading to the near-disappearance of the INLA in the early 1990s.

The IRA and INLA have proven that hermetic border controls are impossible—small numbers of firearms must be expected to make it through—but experience also shows that large quantities are readily excluded. Another lesson of the terrorist experience is that illegal weapons can not be stockpiled for long, since any use leads to heightened British Army and RUC searches. The only way to hold on to an illegal weapon is to keep its existence secret. This means above all not using it, which is tantamount to not having it. If used, its existence is revealed and it usually will be found and confiscated. Groups like the IRA and INLA do not own weapons in the conventional sense, rather they hold them temporarily, during a deadly interval between smuggling them into the United Kingdom and seeing them confiscated by British authorities. An obvious implication is that anyone with a standing need for firearms in the UK—be they the IRA, INLA, or criminal conspiracies—cannot expect to keep their weapons very long.

Two kinds of illegal arms markets will have to be addressed by British authorities. Initially the most important source of firearms probably will be private individuals working from the United States, where virtually anyone can buy a gun, limited only by the one-gun-a-month laws in many states and a new Federal regulation prohibiting sales to newly arrived residents and tourists. Disassembled and submerged in freight or luggage, weapons from the United States will start showing up across Britain just as they appeared in Northern Ireland twenty-five-years ago. Traditional police methods, though, should be sufficient to identify smuggling routes and trace individual suppliers. If law enforcement officials on both sides of the Atlantic are energetic, the problem will be contained readily enough, although it cannot be eliminated unless American gun laws change.

Of greater long-run concern are legally exported shipments from Eastern Europe, former Soviet states and China. Major export firms, often with criminal links but almost always possessing legal documentation, can be expected to take advantage of the porousness of Britain's channel ports to supply illegal clients. This gray market activity—gray because of the semblance of legality in the exporting country—will be much more difficult to control. Here customs authorities are almost always on their own; they cannot expect much help from the exporting country governments. Their most important ally will be Britain's Foreign and Commonwealth Office, which must raise the issue to the top of the nation's bilateral agenda with suspect countries.[22]

## A GROWING INTERNATIONAL ISSUE

Many British gun control advocates are content with the new legislation. Others already are calling for stronger restrictions on ownership of shotguns as well, although this is more controversial.[23] Even in its current form, Britain's path breaking legislation puts it at the forefront of international efforts to deal with gun violence, but it has growing company. Provoked by similar massacres, other countries are acting more forthrightly, legislating against firearms. Usually they too responded to a particularly egregious misuse of gun rights, but this was possible only because of a less permissive gun culture than the United States and a more easily motivated public.

Australian gun culture long ago branded the handgun an instrument of criminality. It is possible to own a handgun there, but the laws make it extremely difficult. Instead there are 4 million legally owned long guns, including a rising number of automatic weapons. After 35 people were killed during a madman's assault with automatic weapons on a tourist spot in Port Arthur, Tasmania in April 1996, there was immense pressure for swift action. Newly elected premier John Howard responded immediately. Two weeks after the Port Arthur incident the Federal government in Canberra directed the states to ban automatic rifles and multi-round shotguns.[24]

New Zealand has the most permissive gun laws and the widest public gun ownership of any OECD country after the United States. But it seems certain to raise licensing requirements and prohibit the most deadly firearms after a similar incident in February of this year in which a 22-year-old man killed six and wounded five with a rifle.[25] Canadians, who also tend to view handguns exclusively as criminal instruments, already had much stricter laws than the United States. After an assailant killed 14 women students and wounded 12 at the University of Montreal in December 1989, Canada established its own tight restrictions on semi-automatic weapons.

Despite innumerable similar incidents, America's restrictions on firearms are only modestly tighter than when Kennedy died some 35 years ago. Federal legislation is a skeletal system dealing only with the most extreme excesses of firearms. The 1934 National Firearms Act—passed after the worst of depression era gangsterism—prohibits most public ownership of really large weapons systems, especially fully automatic weapons like machine guns. The Gun Control Act of 1968—a reaction to the assassinations of Martin Luther King and Robert Kennedy—made it impossible to sell most kinds of firearms by mail, although this has been eroded in recent years by mail-order merchants offering older or ostensibly collectable weapons.

The 1993 Brady Act requires gun buyers to submit to checks for a criminal or other suspect past and also requires a five day waiting period between buying a gun and taking it out of the shop. Other regulations prohibit sales of imported semi-automatic rifles (but allow sales of second-hand or domestically manufactured models), prohibit sales of especially deadly ammunition, restrict purchases by foreign visitors and encourage use of safety locks.[26] Several states now limit purchasers to one firearm per month. Otherwise most American residents are guaranteed Constitutional rights to own and operate firearms.

It has become cliché to attribute America's remarkable gun culture to the unintended consequences of a Constitutional provision and the contemporary power of the National Rifle Association. But there is more at work here. The American debate long ago became hopelessly polarized and ritualized, preventing any real development of public opinion. Groups on both sides of the spectrum refuse to state their long-term goals, recognizing that greater clarity will stir-up reflexive opposition a lot faster than it inspires dispassionate thought. Thus the issue is totally dominated by routine repetition of ritual slogans; the partisans keep their real goals to themselves. A visit to the NRA website leaves one with the impression that the most serious needs of American society are to get rid of the Brady Law's five-day waiting requirement for gun buyers, restore imports of semi-automatic rifles and permit all citizens to carry concealed guns. The opposite side is led by Hand Gun Control, whose agenda is topped by a campaign for mandatory safety locks and a ban on Saturday night specials.[27]

The real debate for America, of course, is about whether hand guns and semi-automatic weapons should be in public hands at all, but no one with any political savvy will touch that with a barge pole. The public has grown accustomed to violence and refuses to be drawn into serious debate, while gun advocates have been able to assume a position of moral authority. This has been possible only because of the NRA's highly successful tactic of turning any question of misuse into a judgment on the individual, not the principle of gun ownership itself. Whether changing international attitudes toward firearms ownership or the problems posed by black market weapons from the United States can alter that situation remains to be seen.

## LEARNING FROM DUNBLANE

It is no coincidence that so many countries are suddenly taking action; no country is immune to the effects of the expanding market for automatic and other advanced firearms. The same transformation of the global arms market that fuels ethnic conflict in collapsing societies exacerbates violence in more stable regions as well. Mass murders—previously something that civil society could reliably prevent—are becoming fearsomely frequent as handguns and semi-automatic weapons become more available to private individuals.

Although the problems of firearms proliferation differ immensely from country-to-country, the worsening trends and growing public sensitivity are more uniform. Countries where public gun ownership has traditionally been accepted now are affected by extraordinary levels of violence. Where guns were present but restricted they are becoming increasingly visible and more likely to be used. And societies previously free of gun violence are beginning to feel its effects for the first time. Thus countries with gun cultures as diverse as Canada, Britain and Japan find themselves acting more or less simultaneously on their gun problems and even the UN has begun to consider the issue, however delicately.[28] It is a measure of the strength of this trend that the NRA has become increasingly alarmed and outspoken in its criticism of the new international politics of gun control.[29]

Each nation must chart its own course of action, but the pattern illustrated by Dunblane suggests that aggressive action typically will come only after further massacres. Public concern may be sincere and widespread, but it usually is not articulated or organized. Polling reveals the breadth of such feelings, as well as their lack of day-to-day priority. The exception is among outspoken opponents of controls who dominate the issue by default. The lack of public pressure usually leaves consideration of the issue up to public officials who must show strong leadership if more firearms violence is to be avoided. In lieu of such leadership, action tends to come only in response to catalyzing events. While firearms controls are essential if tragic violence is to be prevented, all too often such controls can be enacted only in reaction to tragedy. Rising public concern in Britain created the background for action. But without the Dunblane massacre or a comparable horror nothing would have happened. To see lives exchanged for any mere political principle is, at a minimum, wickedly unfair. Yet every country that has restricted the availability of firearms in recent years acted in response to the catalyzing effect of especially appalling incidents of gun violence.

Britain typically is regarded as a restrained and peaceful society, but there was nothing inevitable about its ban on handguns. To the contrary, the British experience demonstrates that even where the public consensus is strong, the firearms issue is highly vulnerable to political expediency. The gun ban was possible only because of unique political circumstances and the exceptional parliamentary skill of its supporters; even after the massacre, orthodox political processes could not generate the same response. Seeking to avoid controversy, neither the Conservative nor Labor parties initially were inclined to take a strong stand. Later both acted, but not with great conviction.

To the last, either party would gladly have abandoned the whole effort if doing so would have advanced their fortunes farther. The reform of Britain's gun laws illustrates the adage that general concerns can ignite debate, but tangible legislation comes only through the pressure of specific circumstances, and its final passage usually relies on a heavy dose of luck.

## NOTES

This essay is based primarily on interviews in the United Kingdom including members of parliament, Snowdrop, and the Gun Control Network, conducted in February 1997. The author also would like the numerous individuals with whom he spoke in preparing this essay, including Philip Alpers, John Frasure, Adam Garfinkle, Natalie S. Goldring, James McD. Hayes, Michael T. Klare, Tom Mason, Michael Mazaar, Geraldine O'Callaghan, Swadesh Rana, and Ian R. Taylor for their comments and encouragement.

1. National Center for Health Statistics, 1996.

2. The most thorough account is the official investigation of The Honorable Lord W. Douglas Cullen, *The Public Inquiry into the Shooting at Dunblane Primary School on 13 March 1996* (London: Her Majesty's Stationary Office, 16 October 1996), generally known as the Cullen Commission inquiry.

3. Liam Halligan, "Gun Law to Be Even Tougher," *Financial Times*, 10 January 1997.

4. Michael Klare and David Andersen, *A Scourge of Guns* (Washington, D.C.: Federation of American Scientists, 1996); Jasjit Singh, ed., *Light Weapons and International Security* (New Delhi: Indian Pugwash Society, 1995).

5. Ian Taylor, "Firearms Crime—After the Cullen Enquiry," paper presented to the Scottish Association for the Study of Delinquency, Edinburgh, 7 November 1996; Fred Barbash, "Britain Votes to Ban Handguns," *Washington Post*, 12 June 1997, A1.

6. The literature on politics of civility is growing rapidly, but useful summary is Michael Walzer, ed., *Toward a Global Civil Society* (Providence, R.I.: Bergahn Books, 1995).

7. "Lord Cullen's Main Proposals," *The Manchester Guardian*, 17 October 1996.

8. For example, see James Landale, "Howard's Advisor Says Gun Bill is Monstrous Injustice," *The Times*, 17 December 1996.

9. Lord Ivan Lawrence, "Why I Said 'No' to a Ban on Handguns," *The Telegraph*, 17 August 1996.

10. This all other House of Commons votes listed in this article were supplied by the Westminster Public Information Office to Ian R. Taylor.

11. Halligna, "Gun Law to Be Even Tougher," *op. cit.*; Alen Travis, "Howard Ups Gun Payouts But Fails to Quell Revolt," *The Manchester Guardian*, 5 December 1996.

12. George Jones, "Blair Vows to Push through Handgun Ban," *The Telegraph*, 14 May 1996; Joy Copely, "MPs Votes to Ban All Handguns," *ibid.*, 12 June 1997; Fred Barbash, "Britain Votes to Ban Handguns," *The Washington Post*, 12 June 1997, A1.

13. Philip Johnson, "Gun Amnesty Begins with a Plea by Howard," *The Telegraph*, 24 April 1996.

14. British sources are highly circumspect about the number of unregistered firearms; since Britons rarely use their guns there is no basis for even a vague estimate. Published figures, unsurprisingly, tend to come from American sources. The

one million figure is repeated in Fred Barbash, "Tough British Gun Control Bill Survives Attack—by Gun Opponents," *The Washington Post*, 19 November 1996, A16. Barbash later used an estimate of one to two million in "Britain Votes to Ban Handguns," *op. cit.*

15. Robert J. Spitzer, *The Politics of Gun Control* (Chatham, N.J.: Chatham House, 1995), 79; Erik Larson, *Lethal Passage* (New York: Crown, 1994); Franklin E. Zimring, *Gun Control* (Washington, D.C.: National Institute of Justice, U.S. Department of Justice, 1988).

16. Marcos Mendiburu and Sarah Meek, *Managing Arms in Peace Processes: Haiti* (Geneva, Switzerland: United Nations Institute for Disarmament Research, 1996).

17. "Take Out Life Insurance before You Enter," *The Economist*, 8 March 1997, 44.

18. Aaron Karp, "The Rise of Black and Gray Markets," *Annals of the American Academy of Political and Social Science* 535 (September 1994) 175–89; Karp, "The Arms Trade Revolution: the Major Impact of Small Arms," *The Washington Quarterly* 17(4) Autumn 1994: 65–78.

19. Accounts of the war in Northern Ireland tend to concentrate on the religious, ethnic, political and social aspects of the conflict, giving short-shrift to material aspects like arms transfers. A brief but important exception is Sean Boyne, "Uncovering the Irish Republican Army," *Jane's Intelligence Review*, August 1996: 343–46.

20. Sean Boyne, "INLA: the Deadly Hand of Irish Republicanism—part 2," *Jane's Intelligence Review*, February 1997: 55–57.

21. Jim Kelly, "Customs to Step up Assault on Fraud," *Financial Times*, 7 March 1997, 9.

22. The EU has begun to act more aggressively on smuggling in general. Editorial, "Brussels to Reform Smuggling Controls," *Financial Times*, 13 March 1997, 3; "Fraud across EU Borders," *ibid.,* 15.

23. Matthew Paris, "A Long Shot at Gunmen," *The Times*, 14 February 1997.

24. Geoffrey Martin Lee, "Killings Lead to Sweeping Gun Ban in Australia," *The Telegraph*, 13 May 1996.

25. Simon Louisson, "Shotgun Rampage Shocks N. Zealand," *The Washington Times*, 10 February 1997, A11.

26. "Remarks by the President at Signing of Directive on Handgun Safety Locks," *USIA Wireless File*, 3 May 1997, file no: 97030504.TXT; Paul Bedard, "Clinton, with NRA Support, Sets Stricter Gun-buying Laws," *The Washington Times*, 16 May 1997, A11; John F. Harris, "U.S. Warning Buyers: Guns Not for Minors," *Washington Post*, 12 June 1997, A16.

27. An exceptionally balanced assessment of the stereotypes of the gun control debate is William Weir, *A Well Regulated Militia: the Battle Over Gun Control* (North Haven, Conn.: Archon Books, 1997).

28. United Nations Commission on Crime Prevention and Criminal Justice, *Criminal Justice Reform and Strengthening of Legal Institutions, Measures to Regulate Firearms*, resolution E/CN.15/1997/L.19.Rev.1 (Vienna, Austria: United Nations, 7 May 1997)

29. Katharine Q. Seelye, "National Rifle Association Is Turning to World Stage to Fight Gun Control," *New York Times*, 2 April 1997, A12. Tom Mason, *Statement of the National Rifle Association of America/Institute for Legislative Action Before the United Nations Panel of Government Experts on Small Arms*, New York, 21 January 1997.

# 9

## Domination, Quiescence and War Crimes

*John Braithwaite*

One of the generalizations that seems mostly true from my reading of the criminological literature is that domination engenders crime. As a generalization, "domination engenders crime" is not always true and when it is, it is often true in a complex rather than a direct way. For example, the direct relationship is that women tend both to be more dominated than men do and to commit *less* crime than men do. Yet, empirical criminology in the feminist tradition demonstrates a variety of ways in which the domination by men of women engenders crime.

"Domination engenders crime" is a generalization with force from the most micro to the most macro of contexts. At the micro end, relationships based on domination in the schoolyard engender the violence that we call bullying.[1] Domination in families engenders family violence. At the macro end, structures of national economies that dominate or exclude fractions of the population are criminogenic. Inequality of wealth and power fosters crime not only by creating an underclass that are dominated, but also by creating an upper class that dominate. Both need and greed are implicated in different kinds of crime.[2] Some economies bring about greater extremes of need and greed than others. Need motivates the accumulation of goods for use, greed the accumulation of goods for exchange. More specifically, greed motivates unaccountable accumulation and nonstationary accumulation— fast money. Hence, greed militates against the kinds of investments that might alleviate need—investment that creates decent jobs for those in need. The other reciprocal relationship here is that when large, segregated sections of a population are in need, they are easy prey for the greed of the fast money set. They are prey both as consumers and suppliers of goods like heroin and as consumers and suppliers of services like loan-sharking, as suppliers of prostitution, and so on.

All this is why Edwin Sutherland was so theoretically muddled when he said that "If it can be shown that white-collar crimes are frequent, a general theory that crime is due to poverty is shown to be invalid."[3] Sutherland failed to see that both need and greed are criminogenic, that the political economy of need is causally dependent on the political economy of greed, inversely that the political economy of greed preys on the economy of need. The economy of need creates market niches for greed.

In the debate over inequality and crime, some criminologists point to selected time-series studies which find that crime rates do not go up when unemployment goes up. These criminologists also fail to see the whole picture of the evidence we have. At the empirical level, most time-series studies, especially those that include more recent years, do support an association between unemployment and crime.[4] Secondly, some recessions actually hit the rich harder than the poor, reducing income inequality in the economy.[5] Since the criminological theory at issue is not about unemployment per se, but about inequality and poverty, studies of the effect of income inequality on crime are the theoretically relevant ones. And more often than not, income inequality is a stronger predictor of crime than the unemployment rate.

Time-series studies of unemployment could be more theoretically relevant by measuring the volume of long-term unemployment and the average length of long-term unemployment. The criminologically important effect is not year to year variation in short-term unemployment, it is the longer term impact of whole generations of truly disadvantaged people, year after year, bereft of hope, giving up on their own future and that of their children. So I am more persuaded by the fact that most people in prison were unemployed for a long time before they were arrested than I am by the less powerful associations in time-series studies. A further reason for the time-series association of unemployment and crime being weaker than other inequality-crime relationships is that there are other criminological theories which also contain truth and which predict a rise in employment will increase crime. An implication of the routine activities perspective is that more employment means more homes unguarded during the day when both adults go out to work. More employment; more burglary.

Finally, we now know that the relationship between unemployment and crime is complex in a patriarchal society where women are expected to be guardians of children and housekeeping. For example, we know that patriarchy as an ideology entails men feeling humiliation at the suggestion that their wife could be equal or superior to them on as critical a dimension of male dominance as breadwinning. This is why you get a result such as that of Gartner and McCarthy that employed women married to an unemployed husband had six times the homicide victimization one would expect, given the proportion of the population in this group.[6] Just as such facts complicate the direct employment-crime nexus, they affirm the more general underlying proposition that domination engenders crime. In short, there are half a dozen reasons why the time-series unemployment-crime association is weaker than other kinds of associations between inequality and crime. None of them cast into doubt the claim that domination engenders crime.

This proposition continues to have explanatory power at the supranational level. Consider the crime of genocide. Much persuasive historiography has shown how the domination of the Allied powers at Versailles was used to humiliate Germany. Tom Scheff has argued how the appeal of *Mein Kampf* was an appeal to a humiliated people. Hitler's rhetorical calculation was to foster a shame-rage spiral. Each page of *Mein Kampf*, according to Scheff, bristles with shame and rage. Similarly, U.S. and British hegemony in Asia and the Pacific between the wars, and the way it was used to crush Japanese expansion through trade, was actively read by Japanese ultra-nationalists as the white man's humiliation of Japan. Some of the extraordinary crimes of the Japanese during World War II can be understood in part as a rage against what they saw as white oppressors. My father was a victim of one of those war crimes. He was one of six out of 2,500 Australians and British who survived the Sandakan Death March. My mother's first husband also perished on the Death March.

Why do I interpret this crime as a shame-rage spiral? Well, there are a lot of circumstantial things about it. There were some of the death marches themselves—rituals of public display to local Asian peoples of the literal collapse of white masters. There were more specific incidents along the way such as local prostitutes encouraged by Japanese guards to urinate on the men from the balconies of the buildings where they worked. There was the fact that when the commandant of my father's camp was hung, he bit the hangman's hand, drawing blood, and would not let go. Such anger in playing out an evil that one might have thought should have commanded remorse. The righteous anger, I surmise from his statements, of a man engulfed by the humiliation of his people, determined to resist to the end the idea of white men being masters over Asians. My father recalled him saying near the end: "We may lose this war. But if it takes one hundred years, one day we will be your masters."

As a young man I hated Emperor Hirohito of Japan. The Emperor, unlike the militarists, had been brought up in a culture of civility. He knew about the war crimes and I felt he commanded the respect in Japan to do something to stop them. I also have no affection for General MacArthur who vetoed an Australian Operation to rescue survivors of the camps in 1945. But it was MacArthur who resisted pressure from Australia and elsewhere to hang the Emperor. This was an act of great wisdom. It was a profoundly important gesture of reintegration to the Japanese people. Not only in Japan but also in Germany, the United States showed that it had learnt the lessons of Versailles. The Marshall Plan was the finest moment of the American century. The politics of retribution and humiliation of Versailles were replaced by the politics of reintegration.

Desert theorists have to say that justice was corrupted by leaving the Emperor unpunished. I have to say, notwithstanding my anger, that social justice was advanced by MacArthur's act of grace. It was where just deserts *were* administered, on the lesser minions of the Japanese army who were hung, that justice was corrupted. Some of them were set up as scapegoats by more corrupt men than themselves. My father could not face up to giving evidence at the war crimes trials. He was excused on medical grounds. He was, after all, barely alive. Only one stronger survivor was willing and able to attend throughout as a witness. That man was stronger because the Japanese fed him better than the other prisoners. I do not want to taint the memory of that long-dead man unfairly. We cannot be at all sure; there is no proof; but it was the openly expressed suspicion of more than one survivor that this man was a collaborator. If this is true, the testimony that decided who would hang and who would go back to their families was tainted testimony. Another Australian survivor admitted before he died that he had testified falsely against one certainly brutal guard who was hung for a murder he did not commit.

It is typical when crimes of the powerful do come to justice that there is scapegoating, that power is used to buy collaboration. Rats tend to turn in a way that submits mice to the greatest vilification. I have referred to this as a theorem of retributive justice: *where desert is greatest, punishment will be least*. In a fundamental sense, I therefore see the philosophy of retribution as an enemy of social justice in any world where unequal power puts some in a much better position than others to cover up their crimes.[7] That means any world. Mercy is a more plausible instrument of justice.

Mercy for Emperor Hirohito helped interrupt a vicious circle of humiliation and violence; mercy for an apprehended school bully can open his mind to the idea that there are better ways to fight fire than with fire; mercy for an Australian Aboriginal offender can interrupt the accumulation of lived injustice that Aborigines experience and resent in their dealings with the criminal justice system; and yes, mercy for a wife beater can interrupt the spurious righteousness of his anger with a space for dialogue, a space where righteousness might be supplanted by an understanding of the consequences of domination, where problem solving, empowerment and redress for victims can occur. By eschewing *punitive* justice, we can often, though not always, give *social* justice a better chance in the long run.

If "domination engenders crime" is of general explanatory import, is there anything of general import we can say about how criminologists might engage with struggles against domination at each of these levels—the micro contexts of schools and families, the macro context of the nation state and beyond to global struggles against domination? Yes, I think so. The most productive general answer I can give is a civic republican one—engagement with the institutions of civil society, those institutions that are intermediate between the individual and the state that will support survivors of domination.[8]

At the macro level, I have argued elsewhere that in Australia family violence, drunk driving and corporate crime are our deepest crime problems in terms of loss of property and injury to persons.[9] They have become our deepest crime problems because their perpetrators have been shielded from shame by certain realities of power in Australian society. For that very reason those crime problems are profoundly susceptible to social movement politics —family violence to shamefulness constituted by an active women's movement, environmental crimes to shamefulness constituted by greens. At the macro level, through social movement politics, we have made real progress in beginning to mobilize community disapproval against our deepest crime problems. Yet domination gets played out in micro arenas. After two hundred years of social movement politics against corruption, bribery is regarded almost universally as a bad thing in Western democracies. But politicians, police chiefs, and business leaders continue to give and take bribes because they continue to dominate the micro contexts in which they do business in a way that shields them from shame. They dominate those micro-contexts to ensure that their bribery is never defined as bribery. So we need to complement a vigorous social movement politics with micro strategies for infusing the disapproval of civil society into dominated micro spaces. That requires a creative interplay between state power and local community dialogue. Without that, we will never come to grips with the fact that the shielding of powerful men from both formal and informal sanction is a practical political accomplishment transacted in a very micro context.

So how do we help civil society to communicate its disapproval of a school bully who is shielded from confronting community disapproval by his reign of fear in the schoolyard? Progress in the micro context of schools has been particularly encouraging in recent years. There has been a proliferation of anti-bullying programs, some seemingly quite successful. The best known is the Norwegian Ministry of Education program that reduced the prevalence of victimization by 50 percent.[10] It involved a school conference day on the bullying problem, establishing new monitoring policies for quick decisive interventions and social milieu development groups, among other elements of a whole school approach.

In the context of both schools and families, many of us have learned from New Zealand traditions of justice as institutionalized in the family group conference. Schools, churches, Aboriginal communities and welfare agencies as well as the police themselves are running these conferences in New Zealand and Australia as an alternative to reporting offences to the police and prosecuting them through the courts. A facilitator invites to the conference both the offender and the individuals who care most about the offender, who enjoy most respect from the offender. The victim and victim supporters are also invited. These two communities of care engage in a dialogue that both brings out the consequences of the crime and comes up with a plan of action to restore victims and prevent recurrence. Conferences can empower citizens affected by a crime to engage in problem solving in relation to it, can provide a politically practical alternative to the politics of punitiveness, and they can structure both shame and reintegration into a ritual that seems just and sensible to ordinary citizens. In a South Australian study, 90 percent of a small sample of 71 victims surveyed reported that participation had been "helpful" for them.[11] Preliminary evidence on their effect on recidivism is encouraging.[12]

Conferences are controversial when used for offenses like domestic violence, rape, armed robbery, attempted murder and serious white-collar crime, all of which have been conferenced in Australia or New Zealand. The controversy is about imbalance of power between offenders and victims for these kinds of offenses. There is not time here for the detailed exposition of how community conferences can solve some of the problems traditionally associated with Alternative Dispute Resolution or Peoples' Courts. Given my theme, however, let me at least illustrate the difference between traditional victim-offender mediation and conferences on the imbalance of power issue.

The problem with dyadic victim-offender mediation is that you have an imbalance of power if the offender is the school bully and the victim is a nerd; if the offender is a child, the victim an adult; the offender a man, the victim a woman. Worse, we have had conferences where the offender is a transnational insurance colossus like Norwich Union and the victim a young illiterate Aboriginal woman. What is different about a conference is that it is a meeting of two communities of care, both of which contain men and women, children and adults, the cool and the uncool, the organized (like an Aboriginal Community Council in the Norwich Union case) and the unorganized. To illustrate formally the significance of these cross-cutting matrices of power imbalance, let us assign the arbitrary quantum of power 4 to an adult and 1 to a child. The adult has four times as much power as the child in a dyadic victim-offender mediation. Add to both sides of the dialogue two other adults and one other child. The imbalance of power falls from 4 to 1 to 1.3 to 1.

The examples of whole school approaches to bullying and community conferences highlight how we must discover in criminology more productive ways of thinking about the interface between the state and civil society. We can reconceive the role of the state as one of enabling and empowering community problem solving rather than enfeebling it. The history of criminal justice across the world in the last two centuries has been one of enfeebling community problem solving because of fear of private vengeance combined with the political appeal of centralized law and order politics. I have argued that this centralized state law and order strategy no longer works politically in extending the use-by dates of political leaders, if ever it did.[13] This is why a new package based on restorative conferencing and crime prevention is already beginning to prove a political winner in some parts of the world.

The philosophy I have espoused is a responsive regulatory strategy. Occasionally we will encounter individuals who are so beyond shame or deterrence that they will have to be incapacitated by incarceration. Or companies (like the Bank of Commerce and Credit International) so beyond shame and deterrence that they must be incapacitated by withdrawing their license to engage in an activity like banking. Corporate capital punishment is occasionally necessary. The theory of a responsive regulatory pyramid (see figure 9.1) is that the capacity to escalate to state deterrent and then incapacitative remedies is displayed, not threatened but displayed, in a way that

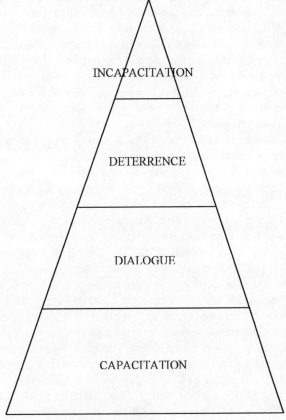

**Figure 9.1. A Reponsive Regulatory Pyramid**

motivates dialogic control, shame-based and preventive control at the base of the pyramid.[14] The most important form of preventive crime control is the obverse of incapacitation. It is capacitation.

The best way to prevent environmental crime is to capacitate firms with pollution control technologies and management techniques. This capacitation is best mediated through institutions of civil society such as the engineering profession, environmental auditing professionalization, universities and green social movements. The best way to capacitate the poor is with jobs and decent education: good old Cloward and Ohlin,[15] legitimate opportunity structures that render resort to illegitimate opportunity structures less appealing. Some criminologists in Australia have been active in persuading our government to promise a job compact with the Australian people. A compact that no Australian will be allowed to continue in long term unemployment without being offered either a job or placement in a paid retraining program. The compact in the former Keating government's White Paper on Employment was much more feeble on the implementation detail than we would have liked, but at least it was a framework of state commitment to a compact into which we might have injected more content in future years. Moreover, it did reinvent the state as nourishing institutions of civil society rather than supplanting them. So our Commonwealth Employment Service was partially privatized by a Labor government. Citizens are still guaranteed access to state funded job placement services. But if they prefer, they can get those services from regulated private or NGO providers of job placement and training services.[16]

In the contemporary world, state capacitation of civil society to be active in job creation or environmental protection quickly runs up against severe constraints. In Australia we lost the political battle for tax increases that would have seen corporate Australia and individuals with jobs pay a jobs levy to fund a grander Jobs Compact than the version we got. In addition to the politics of greed, the argument that defeated us was that tax increases would make us less internationally competitive and therefore would cost more jobs than would be created. While this argument is overblown (strong welfare states can compete), it cannot be dismissed.

What follows is that as criminologists we should become interested in global capacitation, because it is important for crime prevention. This means global cooperation to restore declining revenues that threaten employment-enabling and environment-protecting welfare state policies. A global carbon tax is one promising option, and here the European Union is showing some leadership toward a pan-European carbon tax. The other promising option is the Tobin tax named after its inventor, Nobel Laureate in Economics, James Tobin.[17] The Tobin tax is a global uniform tax on trades involving foreign exchange. If the Group of 7 agreed to a global uniform tax on foreign exchange transactions, the temptation for smaller economies to join them would be enormous because the revenue from such a tax in a world where fast money can shift from one currency to others many times a day would be stupendous even if it were applied at a very low rate. The other attraction of Tobin's idea is that it would buffer vulnerable currencies by acting, in the words of Keynes, "to mitigate the predominance of speculation over enterprise." And remember as criminologists we should be interested in that reciprocal relationship between the political economy of need and the political economy of greed. We should be interested in how we can reduce both crime in the streets and crime in the suites by shifting investment from fast money speculation to slow money job creation.

At the 1995 Social Development Summit in Copenhagen, activists attempted to work through civil society more so than states with these ideas, through the International Council of Social Welfare, the World Council of Churches, the International Confederation of Free Trade Unions, Oxfam and so on. The fact that long-term transformative struggles can be more cumulative within civil society than within states is well illustrated by the little victories we did have with states in Copenhagen. We persuaded the Australian delegation to support the idea of a Tobin tax at the Summit. But our Deputy Prime Minister, who pushed this through, stepped down last month. President Mitterand spoke in favor of the Tobin tax. But now he has been replaced by M. Chirac.

Weak social movements of course suffer constant defeats on such issues. Yet weak social movements are learning how better to harness the power of the strong in the world system. A good example is the remarkable accomplishments of the Montreal Protocol on Ozone Depleting Substances. The green movement substantially prevailed over transnational business in that campaign because it divided them. First, the U.S. environment movement won legislative victories on the phasing out of ozone-depleting substances in the U.S. Congress. Then U.S. business became an ally of the global green movement against European and Japanese business because U.S. business did not want to suffer a competitive disadvantage at their hands.

There is every reason to be optimistic about engagement with social movement politics. As my family made its tiny contribution to the vigil outside the French Embassy in Canberra in 1995 concerning the French nuclear testing in the Pacific, I did feel pessimistic about stopping the French from the crime they are contemplating which would cause such loss of life from increased cancer among the people of the Pacific. But I felt optimistic that, through all our little contributions to Greenpeace, we will teach the French people that their President had made a political mistake and France will never do this to us again. The voices of global civil society also put a break on the considerable momentum that had built up for a resumption of nuclear testing by the UK and the United States. Just as global civil society has stopped atmospheric testing, so shall it soon stop underground testing. The Nuclear Non-Proliferation regime is an incredible accomplishment when you put it in historical context. Thirty-five years ago President Kennedy was saying that it was inevitable that within two decades there would be more than twenty nuclear powers. That inevitability never went close to realization, and at this moment the number of nuclear weapon states is being reduced. What enabled this implausible accomplishment was a global peace movement that harnessed U.S. hegemony and U.S. satellite monitoring technology to its cause.

My message in this chapter is that the way to resist the dominations that engender crime is by building democratic institutions that nurture a propensity to speak up against violence and exploitation. At the most macro level that means global social movement politics. At the meso level it means rethinking interfaces between the state and civil society so that the state is enabling and empowering of civil society rather than enfeebling of it. For example, that means a regulatory agency enabling an Aboriginal Community Council to negotiate alongside Aboriginal victims of the fraud of an insurance multinational. At the micro level, it means simple, practical institutional changes that enable a deeper sense of democracy in workplaces, families and school grounds. Community accountability conferences are an example.

To prevent the kind of war crime I have discussed, we need to build a genocide-preventive community through the institutions of civil society, not just through Amnesty, but through more mundane institutions as well. On this I commend to you a paper by one of my Ph.D. students, Jennifer Balint.[18] Civility means for Jennifer a community commitment to dialogue as the preferred means of social decision. It means "processes of public dialogue through which individuals come to an understanding of the sufferings, miseries and humiliations..[she adds, hopes and dreams] of those fellow citizens who are quite unlike themselves."

Why not leave the miseries of the past behind, critics say? One answer is that reminiscence constitutes the shamefulness of war crimes to new generations. My mother is old and wise. She comprehends the history of why she and her two husbands suffered as victims of the Sandakan Death March. Her government during and after World War II did not speak out against the war crimes of the Japanese for three basic reasons. Early in the war, the Australian government did not speak out against the Japanese brutality in Manchuria because of an implicit racism: "an incredulous smugness . . . an unshakable belief that it would not, could not happen to white people."[19] After the murder of British soldiers and rape of captured white nurses in Hong Kong, the Australian government wanted to mobilize national and international outrage against the atrocities. They were prevented from doing so by their imperial masters in Britain and then the United States. MacArthur was clear in orders that the Australian Prime Minister was too weak to resist:

1. The Commander-in Chief has laid down the policy that news material discussing atrocities performed by the Japanese upon prisoners in their hands should be suppressed.

2. The reason for this is purely military. These stories are known to be having a bad effect on the morale of Allied airmen. The fear of mistreatment by the enemy in case they are forced to land in enemy territory cannot but have a bad effect upon the morale of the air forces.[20]

After the war the Australian government continued to cover up its weakness in failing to prevent further atrocities that it might have prevented by speaking out and by giving higher priority to the rescue of prisoners. The influential Returned Servicemen's League continued to support this policy until 1950 on grounds that the gruesome facts would "cause distress to families." It is easy to understand why the Allies suppressed their own crimes in the Pacific War, terrible as they were. And now recent historical research also helps us to understand why we suppressed public distress at Japanese crimes as well.

My mother understands that distress from evil cannot be avoided by refraining from speaking of evil. She grasps the importance of the older generation engaging in a public dialogue about the evils of their generation so that the next generation is educated to confront those who dominate. I commend her testimony to you.

## NOTES

This chapter is the edited text of a Plenary address to the British Criminology Conference, Loughborough, 19 July 1995.

1. See, for example, David P. Farrington, "Understanding and Preventing Bullying," in M. Tonry, ed., *Crime and Justice: Annual Review of Research*, vol. 17, (Chicago: University of Chicago Press 1993); Dan Olweus "Annotation: Bullying at School: Basic Facts and Effects of a School Based Intervention Program," *Journal of Child Psychology and Psychiatry* 35, 1994: 1171–1190.

2. See John Braithwaite, "Poverty, Power and White-Collar Crime: From Sutherland to the 1990s," in K. Schlegel and D. Weisburd, eds. *White-Collar Crime Reconsidered*. (Boston: Northeastern University Press, 1992).

3. Edwin H. Sutherland, *White Collar Crime: The Uncut Version*. (New Haven: Yale University Press, 1983), 7.

4. T. G. Chiricos, "Rates of Crime and Unemployment: An Analysis of Aggregate Research Evidence," *Social Problems* 34, 1987: 187–212.

5. H. Mendershausen, *Changes in Income Distribution During the Great Depression*. (New York: National Bureau of Economic Research, 1946).

6. Rosemary Gartner and Bill McCarthy, "The Social Distribution of Femicide in Urban Canada, 1921–1988," *Law and Society Review* 25, 1991: 287–312.

7. See John Braithwaite and Philip Pettit, *Not Just Deserts: A Republican Theory of Criminal Justice*. (Oxford: Oxford University Press, 1990), chapter 9.

8. See John Braithwaite, "Inequality and Republican Criminology," in J. Hagan and R. D. Peterson, eds. *Crime and Inequality*, (Stanford: Stanford University Press, 1995).

9. Braithwaite, "Inequality and Republican Criminology."

10. Dan Olweus, "Annotation: Bullying at School: Basic Facts and Effects of a School Based Intervention Program," *Journal of Child Psychology and Psychiatry* 35, 1994: 1171–1190. See also John Pitts and Philip Smith, "Preventing School Bullying," *Police Research Group: Crime Detection and Prevention Series Paper 63* (London: Home Office, 1995).

11. Timothy Goodes, *Victims and Family Conferences: Juvenile Justice in South Australia.* (Adelaide: Family Conferencing Team, 1995).

12. See John Braithwaite (forthcoming), *Restorative Justice and Responsive Regulation* (New York: Oxford University Press), chapter 3.

13. John Braithwaite, *Law and Order Politics*, The Media and Building the Safer Society. Address to the Australian National Press Club, Canberra, 1 June, 1995.

14. Ian Ayres and John Braithwaite, *Responsive Regulation: Transcending the Deregulation Debate* (New York: Oxford University Press, 1992).

15. R. A. Cloward and L. E. Ohlin, *Delinquency and Opportunity: A Theory of Delinquent Gangs* (Glencoe, Ill.: Free Press, 1960).

16. Since the time of this address in July 1995, a new conservative Australian government has dismantled most aspects of the job Compact except the privatization of job placement services, which it has accelerated!

17. See James Tobin, "A Proposal for International Monetary Reform," *Eastern Economic Journal* 4, 1978: 153–58. For an illuminating current discussion of the Tobin tax, see David Felix "Suggestions for International Collaboration to Reduce Destabilizing Effects of International Capital Mobility on the developing Countries," in UNCTAD, *International Monetary and Financial Issues for the 1990s*, volume 3, 1993.

18. Jennifer Balint, "Towards the Creation of an Anti-Genocide Community: The Role of Law," *Australian Journal of Human Rights* 1, 1994: 12–43.

19. Norman Abjorensen, "Biting the Lip on War Crime," *Canberra Times*, 23 September 1995, C2.

20. Abjorensen, "Biting the Lip on War Crime."

# REFERENCES

Abjorensen, Norman. 1995. "Biting the Lip on War Crime." *Canberra Times*, 23 September: C2.

Ayres, Ian and John Braithwaite. 1992. *Responsive Regulation: Transcending the Deregulation Debate.* New York: Oxford University Press.

Balint, Jennifer. 1994. "Towards the Creation of an Anti-Genocide Community: The Role of Law." *Australian Journal of Human Rights* 1: 12–43.

Braithwaite, John. 1992. "Poverty, Power and White-Collar Crime: From Sutherland to the 1990s," in *White-Collar Crime Reconsidered*, edited by K. Schlegel and D. Weisburd. Boston: Northeastern University Press, 1992.

———. 1995. "Inequality and Republican Criminology," in *Crime and Inequality*, edited by J. Hagan and R. D. Peterson. Stanford: Stanford University Press, 1995.

———. 1995. Law and Order Politics, The Media and Building the Safer Society. Address to the Australian National Press Club, Canberra, 1 June.

———. Forthcoming. *Restorative Justice and Responsive Regulation.* New York: Oxford University Press.

Braithwaite, John and Philip Pettit. 1990. *Not Just Deserts: A Republican Theory of Criminal Justice.* Oxford: Oxford University Press.

Chiricos, T. G. 1987. "Rates of Crime and Unemployment: An Analysis of Aggregate Research Evidence." *Social Problems* 34: 187–212.

Cloward, R. A. and L. E. Ohlin. 1960. *Delinquency and Opportunity: A Theory of Delinquent Gangs.* Glencoe, Ill.: Free Press.

Felix, David. 1993. "Suggestions for International Collaboration to Reduce Destabilizing Effects of International Capital Mobility on the Developing Countries," in UNCTAD, *International Monetary and Financial Issues for the 1990s*, vol. 3.

Gartner, Rosemary and Bill McCarthy. 1991. "The Social Distribution of Femicide in Urban Canada, 1921–1988." *Law and Society Review* 25: 287–312.

Goodes, Timothy. 1995. *Victims and Family Conferences: Juvenile Justice in South Australia.* Adelaide: Family Conferencing Team.

Mendershausen, H. 1946. *Changes in Income Distribution during the Great Depression.* New York: National Bureau of Economic Research.

Moore, David with Lubica Forsaythe. 1995. *A New Approach to Juvenile Justice: An Evaluation of Family Conferencing in Wagga Wagga: A Report to the Criminology Research Council.* Center for Rural Social Research, Charles Stuart University.

Olweus, Dan. 1994. "Annotation: Bullying at School: Basic Facts and Effects of a School Based Intervention Program." *Journal of Child Psychology and Psychiatry* 35: 1171–1190.

Pitts, John and Philip Smith. 1995. "Preventing School Bullying." *Police Research Group: Crime Detection and Prevention Series Paper 63.* London: Home Office.

Sutherland, Edwin H. 1983. *White Collar Crime: The Uncut Version.* New Haven: Yale University Press.

Tobin, James. 1978. "A Proposal for International Monetary Reform." *Eastern Economic Journal* 4: 153–58.

# 10

# The Threat of Terrorist Exploitation of Nuclear Smuggling

*Gavin Cameron*

## NUCLEAR SMUGGLING

Concern about nuclear terrorism, in various forms, is not new. It can be traced back to the 1940s, almost to the birth of atomic energy itself. However, in the past, the focus was on state use of such weapons as an international issue, and on substate nuclear terrorism as a predominantly domestic issue, since attacks on reactors seemed the most immediate threat. In the last ten years, but especially since the end of the Cold War, this preoccupation has had to be changed somewhat, as the threat posed by other forms of nuclear terrorism has become increasingly pressing. Nonproliferation has increasingly had to encompass the micro as well as the macro level, to the extent that the most immediate, if not the gravest, nonconventional threat to the developed world today may come from substate use of such weaponry.

The reasons for this change are well known. The threat has risen with easier access to fissile material, largely a result of the collapse of the former Soviet Union and the growth of nuclear trafficking that has stemmed from it. As Graham Allison has noted: "Russia is a state in revolution. . . . This revolution is shredding the fabric of a command and control society, in a state that houses a superpower nuclear arsenal and a superpower nuclear enterprise."(Allison 1995) Reliable estimates put the Russian inventory at between 150 and 165 metric tons of weapons grade plutonium, and 1,000 and 1,300 metric tons of enriched uranium. (Williams and Woessner 1995: 211–212; Potter 1995: 12) However, poor accounting procedures mean that such figures are really little more than educated guesswork. The proliferation problem stems, at least in part, from the fact that in the Soviet Union, nuclear security was dependent on the existence of a closed society that re-tained strict controls over foreign travel by its citizens. Internal security was strict, discipline was rigidly enforced when controls were violated, and there was simply no black market for nuclear materials. Personnel were tightly screened and closely supervised by members of the security services. Usually, nuclear material could be accessed only in a three-man team: two technicians and a member of the security services.

Clearly, such procedures are no longer feasible in the new Russia and members of the security services are now as likely to be responsible for nu-clear diversion as anyone else. (U.S. General Accounting Office 1996: 18–19) Much of the theft is insider crime: staff employed within the indus-try making the most of their access to nuclear material. Furthermore, the amounts of material available for theft will only increase in the near future. Russian-American arms reduction agreements mean that Russia will cut its number of nuclear warheads from about 15,000 to 5,000 by the year 2007, increasing its supplies of highly enriched uranium (HEU) by hundreds of tons and of plutonium by tens of tons. Currently there is a considerable de-bate on what should be done with the additional material: using it as part of a closed fuel cycle is the most probable option. However, whatever is de-cided seems certain to take time to implement, adding to the risk of the ma-terial falling into the wrong hands.

The problem of micro-proliferation is not limited to Russia; there have been seizures or leakage of material, of varying grades, in states as diverse as the Ukraine, Kazakhstan, the Baltic states, South Africa, Sweden, Switzer-land, Poland, Turkey, Romania, Hungary, Bulgaria, the Czech Republic, Aus-tria, Belgium, Italy and India. However, Russia remains the main threat, if only because the amounts of nuclear material available for embezzlement are so much greater there than anywhere else.

It has been suggested that the market that may exist is composed almost exclusively of non-weapons grade material. There is little doubt that traf-ficking in low-grade material has continued, while the weapons-grade mate-rial seizures have been limited to half a dozen incidents, between 1992 and 1994. (Woessner 1997: 114–209) However, it is also important to note that it is only in building a nuclear-yield weapon that the quality of fissile material is key: most other forms of nuclear terrorism would be just as effective using industrial-grade material as weapons-grade. Furthermore, it is increasingly evident that there are several more conduits into the West which have grown in significance, as the profile of the German one has risen and thus de-creased its usefulness to nuclear smugglers. It seems clear that progressively more and more material is being brought through southern routes such as the Balkans or Turkey, rather than through Eastern Europe. In many cases, traditional routes for smuggling a range of other goods are being utilized for the nuclear traffic. As John Deutch, has argued:

The countries of Central Asia and the Caucasus—Kazakhstan, Armenia, Azer-
baijan, Kyrgyzstan, and Uzbekistan—form transit links between Asia and the
West, and the Middle East and the West. The break-up of the Soviet Union has
resulted in the breakdown of the institutions that kept many smugglers and
questionable traders out of this region. The pervasive controls once exerted by
a combination of the Soviet KGB, the Soviet military, and the Soviet border
guards no longer exist. Even before the break-up, however, some of the southern borders, especially with Afghanistan, were penetrable. According to anecdotal information from recent travelers to these areas, anything can go across
the borders in these countries for a minimal price. (Deutch 1996)

The extent of this so-called gray market is much debated: the March 1996
General Accounting Office report linked lax control over fissile materials to
several nuclear thefts and the threat of nuclear blackmail, but found no direct evidence of a market operating within the former Soviet Union. While
this would suggest that the trade is still in its infancy and has yet to be firmly
established, that it is still a series of opportunistic bilateral deals, in fact, there
has yet to be a single unequivacated example of stolen nuclear materials
reaching a *bona fide* customer. (Ford 1996) Of 278 radioactive theft incidents
recorded by the Russian MVD between January 1992 and December 1995,
only eight involved a purchase, in each case to a middleman. (Lee 1996: 21)
That there have been no unequivocal cases of a transaction involving stolen
fissile material may be as much a reflection of our ability to apprehend these
smugglers as the absence of such a market. There clearly are states (and
maybe substate actors), such as Iran, that would be willing buyers for such
material. Equally, there is solid evidence of individuals, in many cases complete amateurs, who have been able to obtain such material, but who have
little contact with buyers. It is these individuals that have been caught as they
tried to find a market for their product. The real risk, in terms of a market developing, comes from middlemen who are willing to exploit an individual's
access to sources of material and also have contacts with buyers. The obvious candidates for such a role would be the military or organized crime in
Russia.

The main buyers for weapons-grade nuclear material are almost certainly
pariah states eager to take a shortcut towards nuclear programs of their
own. There is currently little hard evidence to decisively prove the existence
of this market, but that is possibly more a reflection of the fact that the opportunities stemming from the collapse of the former Soviet Union are still
so relatively new. It would be rash to wholly exclude the possibility that this
may increase the likelihood of state-sponsored nuclear terrorism: the former
Director General of Britain's domestic security agency, MI5, has said that,
"Some two dozen governments are currently trying to obtain such technology. A number of these countries sponsor or even practice terrorism, and
we cannot rule out the possibility that these weapons could be used for that

purpose."(Rimington 1994: 9) However, in view of the evident risks associated with permitting a client group access to nuclear weapons (the difficulty
of state control and the need to ensure that any terrorist action cannot be
traced back to the sponsor are both key ones), it makes more sense to suggest that, having obtained such material, a state would use its own agencies
to exploit the situation. This is particularly so since, by and large, states
seem to seek membership of "the nuclear club" for the prestige and the
leverage that it conveys on a regional and global level, rather than for
the overt intention of imminently using the new capability. It is worth noting, as an analogue, that while there are a number of states that sponsor terrorism and have a chemical or biological weapons capability, there is little
evidence that there has been biological or chemical terrorism by substate
actors as a result.

While state-sponsored groups potentially have many advantages in terms of
resources, the real danger from an intelligence and incident aversion perspective probably comes from groups such as Aum Shinrikyo or loosely-affiliated
splinters of larger organizations, such as the alleged bombers of the Murrah
Building in Oklahoma, because they come from nowhere. Aum "just weren't
on anyone's radar screens." While "[w]e currently have no evidence that any
terrorist organization has obtained contraband nuclear materials" (Deutch
1996), if the flow of nuclear materials out of Russia continues, it is probably
only a matter of time before a well-resourced organization is able to become a
purchaser. Such a group need not be state-sponsored: the Aum Shinrikyo cult
had a billion dollars and 40,000 members spread worldwide. If terrorists were
intent on building a nuclear-yield device, their biggest technical difficulty remains the acquisition of fissile material. This is especially the case if the assumption is that terrorists are content with a crude nuclear weapon, of variable
and uncertain yield. It could be built by a small group, using the open literature, and without requiring testing of components or a great deal of technological equipment, the cost of which need only be a fraction of a million dollars. (International Physicians for the Prevention of Nuclear War 1996: 6–10)

## NUCLEAR AND RADIOLOGICAL TERRORISM

Given the ostensible lack of weapons-grade material being smuggled, then,
the immediate threat comes from radiological terrorism. This is especially so
since it seems unlikely that most terrorist organizations would seek to enrich
material for a yield-producing device: it is simply too complex and requires
considerable expertise and unnecessary cost to achieve. The more telling argument against it, though, is that enrichment would be unnecessary in many
cases: a crude nuclear-yield bomb can be made with material that is not
weapons-grade and even low-grade fissile material would have considerable

utility as the basis for a radiological device. Materials in this category can be more easily stolen from nuclear, industrial and research facilities than can weapons-grade material (Freeh 1994: 62). Since such a radiological device would be extremely easy to construct (it need only be an aerosol can or a bomb with a radioactive coating or with a container of radioactive material next to it), and since the materials for it are so widely available (cesium-137, for example, is commonly used in hospitals for X-rays), it is by far the most likely form of nuclear device, as well as the least catastrophic. However, it would still have considerable value as a terrorist weapon, since the mere fact of being "nuclear" would almost certainly ensure that it had a considerable impact on the public's imagination and fear, and thus on a governmental response. For the same reason, being "nuclear," it conveys added prestige and status on the perpetrators. Radiological terrorism therefore sets terrorists apart from other groups, in a way that even the use of biological or chemical weapons does not.

There are, however, problems associated with radiological weapons from the terrorist's perspective. The most critical of these is that of handling the materials. Both cobalt-60 and cesium-137, the materials most often mentioned in connection with radiological terrorism, are, potentially, highly dangerous and consequently require extremely careful handling. This point is supported, to some extent, by the several cases that have occurred of nuclear smugglers fatally irradiating themselves as a result of their contact with the materials. Furthermore, both cobalt-60 and cesium-137 would require a fierce fire to effectively disperse them, ensuring a widespread effect. It is questionable whether placing the material close to conventional explosives or even wrapping them around the explosive would generate a sufficiently fierce fire. Some analysts have suggested that these factors may mean that effective radiological terrorism is not significantly easier than building a nuclear-yield device. (Barnaby 1998) This may be true, but in both cases, radiological and nuclear-yield terrorism, acquiring the requisite material is the main problem. In the case of radiological terrorism, due to the greater availability of the material, the extent of this difficulty is considerably below that for constructing a nuclear-yield device. Certainly, the examples of radiological terrorism, some of which are outlined below, suggest that it is entirely feasible. While there have been no instances of terrorists contaminating wide areas using a radiological device, many of these examples have, because of their "nuclear" nature, nonetheless received widespread publicity. Furthermore, if widespread contamination was the objective of a group, they could mix high explosives with incendiary material to create the necessary fire to disperse the radiological material. Such a firebomb is, technologically, well within the reach of many terrorist organizations.

It is almost impossible to generalize on the extent of the risk to the public from a radiological dispersal device: it depends so much on the material used, the means of dispersal, population density, weather conditions and the period of time that the public is exposed to it. However, the IPPNW, in their publication on crude nuclear weapons, argue that:

> [T]he consequences of a radiological weapon using plutonium in amounts that are potentially available for a terrorist attack are very largely long-term in nature: primarily increased cancer incidence, particularly of lung, bone, and liver cancer . . . Thus in health effect terms, the impact of such a weapon would be hidden for several decades, and probably would not be dramatic. However, given the public aversion to cancer risk, and the fears engendered by plutonium as a potential carcinogen, there are likely to be immediate and dramatic responses by the emergency services. (International Physicians for the Prevention of Nuclear War 1996: 38)

To a very large extent, though, the effects of a radiological weapon are dependent on the type of material used: while weapons-grade plutonium might cause limited damage, other elements such as cesium or even radioactive waste are potentially lethal very rapidly. In 1987, in Goiana, Brazil, two adults broke open a cesium source found abandoned in a clinic and allowed children to play with the glowing material inside. Within days, four people died and 249 others were contaminated. There was public hysteria and thousands of cubic meters of soil had to be removed for decontamination (Sopko 1996: 7–8)

While radiological devices are not ideal for creating mass casualties, and certainly not in the short-term, they would have vast impact and could, potentially, pose a considerable problem for an extended period. Once aware of the problem, it would probably be possible to clean up the radiological effects of a device, but restoring public confidence would be very difficult. Suppose that terrorists put radioactive material in the main ventilation system of a building such as the World Trade Center or of the New York subway. Even if all of the material was successfully removed and the contamination dealt with, how easy would it be to persuade people to return to work in the WTC or to use the subway again? Clearly, the disruption would be immense and somewhat similar to the situation in Tokyo on April 15, 1995, when the Aum cult threatened fresh attacks on the subway, causing the entire city to come to a grinding halt for the day and an estimated third of Japan's police force to be mobilized to defend the city. Commuters simply refused to take the risk of being the victim of another sarin attack, and so stayed at home. The decision as to whether or not to use a nuclear-yield device, or a radiological weapon, or neither, must be largely dependent not only on the type of terrorist group concerned, but also on the type of target selected. An attack requiring the destruction of an enormous area, such as an army base, or the death of as many people as possible, might conceivably justify the use of a full-scale nuclear weapon. However, in terms of destructive capability, a radiological device is unlikely to improve significantly on conventional weapons. This, then, leads to the question: why would one use such a weapon, since it would require so much more effort, especially in acquiring fissile material, than would conventional terrorism? Part of the answer must lie in its publicity value, and the fear it is capable of engendering. At the moment, it is still possible to argue that massive conventional attacks attract just as much coverage as previous nonconventional actions: the publicity around the WTC and Oklahoma attacks or the assault on the Marine Barracks in Beirut or the destruction of Pan-Am 103 was just as intense as that surrounding the sarin attack in Tokyo by Aum. It is no less so for the fact that there have now been several such devastating attacks in the past fifteen years. Perversely, given the immense destructiveness associated with nuclear weapons, radiological terrorism offers terrorists the opportunity to obtain vast publicity *without* necessarily having to kill many people, at least not visibly or immediately. However, the sorts of groups that might consider this an advantage are those whose strategy is based on an element of rationality, those that do have an earthly objective, and therefore those that are likely to be reluctant to potentially commit themselves to being considered responsible for continuing to kill people decades after the attack.

The use of lower-grade nuclear material for terrorism or extortion is already a fact. There can be no doubt that there is a fascination that exists with nuclear weapons which is starting to have an impact on the tactical decisions of would-be attackers. Three New Yorkers were arrested in June 1996 for plotting to kill the chief investigator for Brookhaven and two officials of the local Republican Party by planting radioactive material in their food and in their cars. Rather than trying to use the five cases of radium that they stole from a defense contractor, it would have been far more straightforward and effective to rely on conventional means for the assault (McQuiston 1996). In addition, the Russian mafia killed a Moscow businessman in 1995, using gamma-ray-emitting pellets, placed in his office. (Williams and Woessner 1996: 30) The CIA are also concerned that non-fissile, radioactive materials could be used in a terrorist device designed to create psychological or economic trauma or to contaminate buildings or localized areas. The concern is that the proliferation of fissile material out of the former USSR will result, not in a terrorist nuclear bomb, but in a nuclear-enriched conventional explosion. Such a bomb would cause panic and could make whole areas no-go zones without requiring the cost, difficulty or risk that is entailed by a nuclear-yield device.

In the past, there have been a few isolated incidents of radiological poisoning, but it does seem to be becoming a more widespread phenomenon, and one that, whereas in the past, was largely the province of disaffected workers able to exploit their access to nuclear material, is increasingly the tactic of attackers with a political motive for their actions. Earlier cases of use (rather than threats, of which there are dozens) of radiological weapons include: a mentally ill Austrian with little political agenda who contaminated a railway coach with non-lethal quantities of Iodine 131 and, the following week, Indium 113-M in Vienna in April 1974. There was an attempt by a disaffected worker to kill his supervisor using three highly irradiated pieces of magnesium placed under the driver's seat of the foreman's car. The pair worked at the French Atomic Energy Commission's nuclear waste reprocessing plant at La Hague in Normandy and the worker was able to simply walk out of the plant with the material. The supervisor was exposed, between August and November 1978, to many times the recommended level of radiation, but appeared to suffer no ill effects beyond fatigue. In 1982, two university laboratory researchers at Brown University, Rhode Island, were apparently deliberately contaminated with a small amount of radioactive phosphorous, when the material was used to poison their food. Authorities asserted that it was impossible for this contamination to have occurred accidentally. In 1985, plutonium tri-chloride was put in reservoirs serving New York by a man demanding that murder charges be dropped against Bernard Goetz, who shot four black youths allegedly attempting to mug him on the subway. The danger posed by this attack was small: plutonium is largely insoluble, and so is a highly ineffective means of contaminating water supplies. (Hibbs 1995: 13)

## THE CHANGING NATURE OF TERRORISM

It might be possible to dismiss the Moscow and the Brookhaven examples as part of the same phenomenon: of malcontents exploiting their ready access to nuclear material. However, in both cases, the perpetrators went out of their way to use radiological material, even when it would have been more convenient and effective to use conventional means. Both are examples of a wider trend: the resort to mass-destructive weaponry for political purposes. Although there have been earlier incidents, such as the followers of Baghwan Shree Rajneesh debilitating residents of a small Oregon town with salmonella bacteria or the 1984 White Supremacist plot to pollute municipal water supplies in Arkansas with cyanide, such occurrences have, in recent years, become increasingly common. Examples include not only Aum Shinrikyo's attack, using sarin, on the Tokyo subway, but also White Supremacists Thomas Lewis Lavy, who attempted to smuggle 130 grams of *ricin* (a nerve agent) into Canada from Alaska, and Larry Wayne Harris, arrested in 1995 for ordering bubonic plague from the American Type Culture Collection and, in 1998, for possession of anthrax. (Sopko 1996: 4–6)

The most important substate use of radiological material occurred on November 23, 1995, when Chechen guerrilla leader, Shamyl Basayev, informed the Russian television network, NTV, that four cases of radioactive cesium had been hidden around Moscow. NTV discovered the 32-kilo case, wrapped in a yellow plastic bag and giving off 310 times the background level of radioactivity in Ismailovo Park. Basayev had repeatedly threatened to attack Moscow with nuclear or chemical weapons, and had already proved his ability to create "terrorist spectaculars" by taking 1500 people hostage in Budennovsk in June. Both Russian and international officials largely dismissed the nuclear threat. However, the truth about the Chechens' nuclear capability is less important than the credibility, shown by the precautions the Russian authorities took, sending emergency search teams out around the city with Geiger counters. If the Chechens had sought to inflict harm on the city's residents, they could have left the container open and allowed the contents to disseminate through the park. Dzhohar Dudayev, then Chechen leader, did claim that there were conventional explosives with the nuclear material, threatening radiological dispersal, but this was a hoax. Basayev was intent on displaying capability and in ensuring that his threats to launch further attacks against Moscow, unless Russia withdrew from Chechnya, were taken seriously. His warning was plausible because the state of the Russian nuclear industry made it impossible to rule out that the Chechens had acquired fissile material.

The truism that terrorists do not use weapons of mass destruction has had to be dramatically reassessed in the wake of events such as Aum's attack in Tokyo. Where once it was possible to argue that secular terrorists are purely instrumentalists, not interested in killing many people, fearing the counterproductive consequences, now even traditional types of groups, such as nationalist-separatists like the Chechens, may be more willing to at least credibly threaten mass destructive terrorism. Still, religious-inspired terrorism tends to be more violent than the secular type. For example, between 1982 and 1992, Shia Muslims were responsible for 8 percent of international terrorist attacks, but nearly 28 percent of fatalities from such attacks. (Hoffman 1994: 10) This problem of religious-inspired violence is even greater now, as the millennium approaches and the numbers of millenarian groups increase. Whereas most religions are prepared to take a passive role, for some religions, it is possible to facilitate redemption, "to force the end." Not all messianic belief results in terrorism. Messianic groups are not essentially or inherently violent; indeed, most of them must be pushed before they resort to such extremes of action. Aum saw their mission as saving mankind after Armageddon, and when a vast earthquake struck the city of Kobe on January 17, 1995, it served only to confirm their beliefs that the end was near. However, by that time, Asahara and Aum, feeling rejected, increasingly disaffected and bent on revenge, had already decided that the world as a whole was irredeemable, and therefore needed to be destroyed.

The greatest threat of mass-destructive terrorism currently comes from such nontraditional types of groups, of which Aum Shinrikyo is just one example. Acting Director of Central Intelligence, William Studeman, testified in April 1995 that:

> These groups—often ad hoc—are even more dangerous in some ways than the traditional groups because they do not have a well established organizational identity and they tend to decentralize and compartment their activities. They also are capable of producing and using more sophisticated conventional weapons as well as chemical and biological agents. They are less restrained by state sponsors or other benefactors than are the traditional groups. These groups appear disinclined to negotiate, but instead seek to take revenge on the United States and Western countries by inflicting heavy civilian casualties. (Studeman 1995)

There has been a significant growth in organizations that fit this pattern, inspired by a range of motivations, from a desire to visit an apocalyptic vision on the World, to a wish to punish a government or even an entire culture. In many cases amateur organizations are willing to use improvised weaponry, but, unbound by the constraints of public opinion, they are also willing to contemplate the use of nonconventional weaponry. Undoubtedly, they aspire to higher levels of violence than has been the case with other, more traditional terrorist organizations. Although, like most terrorist organizations, these groups base their tactical decisions on a largely rational combination of feasibility and necessity, they are also willing to regard mass terrorism as justifiable. The way that they achieve that may depend only on the availability of the different types of raw material. As the supply of non-weapons grade material increases, radiological terrorism will become a growing threat, one that, although unlikely to compare with a nuclear-yield device, has the potential to inflict considerable damage, on people, on property and on confidence. Such a risk has to be taken seriously and averted by rigorous and comprehensive protection of all nuclear material, not just that which is usable in a yield device.

## GOVERNMENTAL RESPONSES

Some measures are being undertaken to improve the situation: the problem of material proliferation from the former Soviet Union has two core elements: money and the lack of a culture of nuclear safety. The Russians have accepted U.S. assistance in upgrading equipment, training and procedures to remedy faults in their security programs. It is a slow process, but safety cultures are being built and there is some prioritization in allocating money to the most sensitive areas. Joint U.S.-Russian cooperation on improving material protection, control, and accountability (MPCandA) is also a reality. (Oehler 1996) Almost $2 billion is being spent to install video cameras, locks, alarm systems, electronic fences, and gates at over 25 civilian and military nuclear sites within Russia.

In April 1994, the U.S. Department of Energy initiated the lab-to-lab program, cooperating with Russian laboratory personnel in bringing MPCandA improvements to Russian nuclear facilities. (U.S. General Accounting Office 1996: 16) This is probably the most effective part of the upgrade program. The 1992 Cooperative Threat Reduction program (the Nunn-Lugar program) provides American financial assistance for the safe transport of weapons from the former-Soviet republics to storage sites within Russia, the destruction of the weapons and the alternative employment in Russia of ex-Soviet nuclear scientists. The effectiveness of these U.S.-sponsored measures is debatable; on the one hand, there has not been an incident of weapons-grade material smuggling since 1994, but that may only reflect that none have been discovered rather than that none have occurred. On the other hand, Russian military pay and morale remains poor, and the situation is actually worsening, although it is the civilian side that remains the main proliferation concern. Furthermore, there continue to be numerous incidents of non-weapons-grade fissile material, much of it useable for radiological terrorism, being smuggled. (Woessner 1997: 114-209) The Nunn-Lugar-Domenici amendment to the 1997 Defense Authorization Act, passed at the end of the 104th Congress in 1996, goes further towards trying to solve the problem, not only of avoiding nuclear leakage from the former Soviet Union, but of improving the U.S. domestic response to a nuclear incident. It provides training and advice to local officials likely to be first on the scene of any incident and improves cooperation between federal and local authorities in responding to an incident involving WMD. It provides funds for both United States and Russian customs officials to buy equipment that would ease their task of detecting materials crossing their borders. It provides funds for MPCA programs in the U.S. Departments of Energy and Defense and extends and improves the Cooperative Threat Reduction program within the former Soviet Union. Finally, it creates a presidentially appointed national co-coordinator to oversee U.S. policy and countermeasures against proliferation of WMD and related materials and technologies. (Sopko 1996: 16–20)

Although the current focus of attention is the proliferation problem from the former Soviet Union, in a few years the problem could be equally great from another source. It is impossible to accurately predict the future, so it is important that there are nonproliferation measures that extend beyond safeguarding material in Russia now. Essentially, what is needed is an effective two-tier system. The priority needs to be on control at the source; but there also have to be export controls and effective nonproliferation regimes, especially since, at the moment, dual-use goods are poorly protected at the source. (Spector 1996) While they contain a number of helpful provisions and certainly continue to have an important role in nonproliferation, especially in establishing the norms of a state's nuclear-related activities, providing "a moral and legal framework for practical mechanisms to deter and detect violations of international treaties" (Nunn 1996), the Non-Proliferation Treaty (NPT) may be of only limited effectiveness in countering the acquisition of WMD by terrorists. The problem of dual-usage is less acute for weapons-grade nuclear material, but is considerable for material such as cesium-137 or cobalt-60 which could be used for a terrorist "dirty" bomb. It is hard to envisage how a regime such as the NPT could successfully close these loopholes and therefore genuinely control access to these necessary materials that are nonetheless exploitable for terrorist use (Oehler 1996). There are similar problems with dual-use machinery and instruments. Agreements, such as the NPT, may slow the transfer of relevant technologies and materials but they remain most unlikely to stop them (Deutch 1996). This remains particularly the case since, under Article IV of the NPT, the nondiscriminatory dissemination of nuclear technology for peaceful purposes is encouraged. Unfortunately, even nuclear technology intended for peaceful use is helpful in developing weapons. Micro-proliferation may be intimately connected with macro-proliferation, at the very least, the opportunities for the former will increase with the latter, so a consistent and unified policy by governments on nuclear proliferation as a whole remains crucial to avoiding nuclear terrorism.

The government's response to the threat of nuclear terrorism is also important. Particularly in democratic states, there is a problem balancing the need for security against the core values of social justice and civil liberties that are essential to the existence of such states as democracies. While a full-scale military response against the terrorist group is not inconceivable, a less extreme series of measures remains a more likely answer unless the crisis was to be perceived to be out of control. The precedents for emergency powers short of military authority are manifold: the Canadian government's 1970 *War Measures Act* and the UK *Prevention of Terrorism (Temporary Provisions) Act* are two examples. The nature of any emergency powers is likely to be in proportion to the extent of the threat. State priorities are likely to be geared towards survival and that may lead it to over-ride the norms of democratic countries temporarily. Whether such measures could be preserved in the long-term, if for example, there was a heightened risk of nuclear terrorism but no specific threat, is more debatable.

Contingency planning for nuclear emergencies, including terrorist incidents, is vital to an effective response. As well as civic response plans, the United States also has the NEST, a government agency with 1000 volunteers mostly taken from within the nuclear power industry. They operate in teams to search for nuclear devices using radiation detectors, and have been placed on alert over 110 times and mobilized 30 times, although always for what turned out to be a hoax. (Bone 1996: 9) Other states have equivalent organizations: Canada has a Special Threat Assessment Group (STAG), comprising medics and scientists, to assess, prevent, contain or assist in the response to terrorist threats and incidents involving nonconventional weaponry. (Purver 1995)

A proactive response to the problem is difficult. By making it as difficult as possible for terrorists either to acquire fissile material or use it for terrorism, it may be possible to deflect most potential terrorists onto other tactics and targets. It will probably not deter the most determined and most resourceful groups. Effective intelligence does offer some protection, but even this is limited. Democratic societies rightly protect the liberties of the individual, making it hard for intelligence agencies to track groups and individuals, protected by freedoms of speech, travel and religion, unless there is clear proof of the intent and ability to commit an offence. Aum was, under Japanese law, strongly protected as a religious movement, severely limiting the extent to which Japanese law-enforcement agencies were willing to investigate their activities. As well as the legal difficulties in such an approach is the sheer magnitude of the task: even focusing on one type of group in one country, the militias in the United States, is a massive task. Effective defense will realistically mean concentrating on scores of different types of organizations in dozens of states. (Institute For National Security Studies 1996)

## CONCLUSIONS

Since the collapse of the former Soviet Union and the increased smuggling of nuclear materials, both weapons-grade and non-weapons-grade, that has followed it, the threat of radiological terrorism has risen exponentially. Although there were several such incidents before the end of the Cold War, in many cases using locally obtained material, the increased access to material from the former Soviet Union, combined with the increasingly absolutist and violent nature of terrorism and the increasingly frequent uses of nonconventional weapons for political ends has meant that, for some groups, nuclear terrorism is an attractive option. Radiological terrorism offers, to its perpetrators, some of the advantages in publicity and leverage of a nuclear-yield device, without the difficulty or risk in acquiring the necessary material and building the weapon. Although the consequences of an incident of radiological terrorism are unlikely to be as severe as for a nuclear-yield device, it is nonetheless a potent threat that should be taken seriously by governments, especially since it is far more likely to occur.

Efforts to combat nuclear terrorism should therefore have three elements: "deterrence, interdiction and consequence mitigation."(Nunn 1996) Since intelligence and effective policing may only partially deal with the problem, the most effective policy to prevent nuclear terrorism is likely to continue to be one of international cooperation encompassing risk minimization schemes such as the Cooperative Threat Reduction program, strong export controls, the preservation of international regimes such as the NPT, and target-hardening measures designed to deter potential terrorists as much as possible, along with vigorous police and intelligence efforts to detect and intercept possible terrorist attacks and incidents of nuclear smuggling. Finally, if these policies fail to deflect an incident of nuclear terrorism, there should be an effective emergency response that provides a fully trained and prepared, multi-agency effort that minimizes the results of such an act. This three-pronged approach to nuclear terrorism, as a whole, cannot guarantee that there will never be such an act, but it can go some way to making it difficult to achieve and ensuring that its repercussions are mitigated as far as possible. While not ideal, it is the best, most realistically available solution.

## REFERENCES

Allison, Graham T. 1995. *Testimony to the Senate Committee on Foreign Relations Subcommittee on European Affairs.* August 23.

Barnaby, Frank. 1998. Discussions with the Author. January 19, 1998.

Bone, James. 1996. "American Nuclear 'Swat' Team Emerges from The Shadows." *The Times,* January 2, 9.

Deutch, John. 1996. *Testimony before the Permanent Subcommittee on Investigations of the Senate Committee on Government Affairs by the Director of Central Intelligence,* March 20.

Ford, James. 1996. "Nuclear Smuggling: How Serious a Threat?" *Strategic Forum No. 59,* Institute for National Strategic Studies, January.

Freeh, Louis. 1994. Testimony to U.S. Congress, 103rd Congress, 2nd Session, "International Organized Crime and its Impact on The United States." *U.S. Senate Governmental Affairs Committee, Permanent Subcommittee On Investigations,* May 25.

Hibbs, Mark. 1996. "Plutonium Thieves Pose No Threat to Drinking Water, LLNL Reports." *Nucleonics Week* 36(6), February 9.

Hoffman, Bruce. 1994. "Responding To Terrorism Across The Technological Spectrum." *RAND.* April.

*Institute for National Security Studies.* 1996. Center for Strategic Leadership, "Report of the Executive Seminar on Special Material Smuggling," September 13.

*International Physicians for the Prevention of Nuclear War.* 1996. "Crude Nuclear Weapons: Proliferation and the Terrorist Threat." IPPNW Global Health Watch, Report No. 1.

Lee, Rensselaer. 1996. Address to the *Institute for National Security Studies,* Center for Strategic Leadership, "Report of the Executive Seminar on Special Material Smuggling." September 13.

McQuiston, James. 1996. "Third Man Held in Plot to Use Radium to Kill N.Y. Officials." *New York Times*, June 14, B2.

Nunn, Sam. 1996. *Congressional Record—Senate*. September 28, S11755.

Oehler, Gordon C. 1996. "The Continuing Threat from Weapons of Mass Destruction." *Testimony to the Senate Armed Services Committee*, March: 27.

Potter, William. 1995. "Before the Deluge? Assessing the Threat of Nuclear Leakage from the Post–Soviet States." *Arms Control Today* October: 9–16.

Purver, Ron. 1995. "The Threat of Chemical/Biological Terrorism." Canadian Security Intelligence Service, *Commentary* 60, August.

Rimington, Stella. 1994. "Security and Democracy—Is There a Conflict?" The Richard Dimbleby Lecture, *BBC Educational Developments*.

Sopko, John F. 1996–1997. "The Changing Proliferation Threat." *Foreign Policy* 105, Winter.

Spector, Leonard. 1996. Director, Nuclear Non-Proliferation Project, Carnegie Endowment for International Peace, Washington D.C., *Interview with Author*, November 15.

Studeman, William. 1995. *Testimony of the Acting Director of Central Intelligence to the House Judiciary Committee Hearings on the Omnibus Counterterrorism Act of 1995*, April 6.

*U.S. General Accounting Office*. 1996. "Nuclear Nonproliferation: Status of U.S. Efforts to Improve Nuclear Material Controls in Newly Independent States." March.

Williams, Phil and Paul N. Woessner. 1995. "Nuclear Material Trafficking: An Interim Assessment." *Transnational Organized Crime* 1(2) Summer: 206–38.

Williams, Phil and Paul N. Woessner. 1996. "The Real Threat of Nuclear Smuggling." *Scientific American* 274(1) January: 26–30.

Woessner, Paul N. 1997. "Chronology of Radioactive and Nuclear Smuggling Incidents: July 1991–June 1997." *Transnational Organized Crime* 3(1) Spring: 114–209.

# VI

## INTERNATIONAL LAW
## AND ORDER

# 11

# International Legal Harmonization: Peace, Prosperity, and Democracy?

*Jarrod Wiener*

Advanced industrialized states are engaged in an accelerated pace of public policy coordination, regulatory cooperation, and legal harmonization. The Organization for Economic Cooperation and Development (OECD) has identified some 227 policy areas now on the international agenda, as diverse as competition, biotechnology, health and safety, and the environment.[1] This has attracted the attention of scholars from a number of fields, ranging from public policy,[2] economics,[3] law,[4] and international relations.[5] It is not only the increased amount of policy cooperation, but also its scope (range of policy areas involved) that has sparked interest. Equally interesting is the "depth," or intensity of policy harmonization—the degree to which international coordination requires domestic adaptation to systems of legislation.

The majority of policy areas now on the international agenda used to be conceived, until relatively recently, as being largely within the domain of domestic concern, with the majority of a state's choices about modes of internal regulation believed to have little international implication, and conversely, international activity perceived to have little direct impact on modes of domestic organization. As states become enmeshed in complex webs of trade, credit, production, and information systems, it seems reasonable to argue that heightened levels of interdependence are responsible for a growing number of *international* governance issues increasingly to concern the further harmonization of *domestic* regulatory regimes, national policies, and domestic legal systems. It is also reasonable to suggest that due to interdependence the continued efficacy of some domestic policies of a state depends on other states adapting their domestic policies to achieve the same aims and objectives. After all, the idea that international interdependence can lead to increased conflict, but also to heightened pressure for cooperative solutions to

common problems through mutual adjustment, is neither empirically nor theoretically novel.[6] Indeed, so firmly entrenched is the "interdependence explanation" that some scholars, such as Robert Gilpin, state "it is obvious that
increasing interdependence of national economies has made legal, policy,
and structural differences among national societies both more important and
frequently also a source of conflict."[7]

The difficulty with this explanation for the internationalization of domestic practices is that it is equally reasonable to suggest on the weight of econometric analyses that the post–World War II international economy is only
now approaching the levels of integration characteristic of the late 1800s and
early 1900s.[8] The latter part of the 1800s certainly did witness a phenomenal
increase in the number of international organizations and the scope of their
work, including the coordination of post, telegrams, shipping, and other issues. The agenda of the League of Nations included trade, finance, organized
crime, the drugs trade, and a number of issues that remain on the international agenda.[9] Moreover, it is difficult to imagine any issue in political economy that is "purely" international in the sense that it does not either grow out
of domestic policy, or require domestic adaptation of some form to meet international commitments. However, the idea that several hundred domestic
practices of states affect negatively the international opportunities, or domestic objectives, of other states did not influence the international agenda
to the same extent as today. One could argue that were it not for the interruption of two global wars that agenda might have evolved to include more
issues, all other things being equal, but that would be a counterfactual claim.
Moreover, as this chapter argues, the agenda for international cooperation—
what is deemed to be legitimately an issue for international consideration—
depends heavily on the guiding philosophy about the relationship between
politics, society and the economy, that is, the ideology of governance.

Thus, while it may be "obvious" that interdependence is a necessary condition for policy harmonization, it is far from obvious that interdependence is a
*sufficient* explanation. *Why* is further progress in liberalizing international trade
and foreign direct investment perceived to require that a range of domestic
policies come on the international agenda? *Why* do transnational risks—like organized crime, money laundering, the drugs trade, international banking—
need to be met by harmonizing domestic practices and laws to a common standard? One need not strain the imagination to conceive of alternative
mechanisms of international governance, possibly equally viable, and possibly
more efficient. While interdependence can be part of an explanation, we need
to look elsewhere for an understanding of the deeper processes underlying the
exponential internationalization of domestic policies, regulations, practices,
and laws. Underlying the project of harmonization, I argue, is a particular view
of what the economy is, its "proper" relationship to society, the role of the state
in mediating between the two, and how public policy "ought" to function.

I argue that there is a process of socialization into the idea that noninterference in the economic and social affairs of states is perceived to be outmoded. There is increasingly little force to the chapter 2.7 equivalent for domestic economic and social governance. Interestingly, while this change among advanced industrialized economies in the OECD is accompanied by conflict over issues ranging from growth hormones to vehicle emissions, the process of conflict resolution and policy adaptation is occurring in a manner that shows a high degree of consensus on the mode through which cooperation ought to occur—domestic regulatory harmonization.[10] Conflict does not in itself demonstrate fundamental divergence of goals: not all conflict is dysfunctional and a good deal of it is part of a process of cooperation.

This chapter begins by noting that while modern patterns of economic cooperation have been established through multilateral forums since the Second World War, the focus of objectives has shifted considerably from negotiating internationally acceptable border measures to achieving internationally acceptable domestic policies. This illustrates substantive change, but does not necessarily demonstrate change to patterns of cooperation. I argue that to understand the shift in the focus of objectives it is necessary to look to impressionist explanations for change, and particularly to perceptions of what domestic practices are deemed legitimately to be international, and indeed what is the perceived location of authority in the international economic system.

Underlying all of that, I argue, is a neo-liberal understanding of public policy regulation buttressed by a structural understanding of the market among advanced industrialized states. That understanding is that the market is universal, determinist, and which is perceived to foreclose alternatives. The neo-liberalism that has achieved prominence as a mode of economic management since the early 1980s but particularly since the early 1990s is such that it ascribes to the market economy an intrinsic, universal logic, and to individuals the capacity rationally to discover those structural imperatives and be guided by them. Thus, the "science" of the *market* is prioritized over the peculiar, contingent, socially constructed, and therefore "non-rational" *political* and *social* practices of states that interfere with the efficient functioning of the international market. I therefore prioritize in this chapter the role of dominant ideology that prescribes "normality": the structural understanding of the market is a basis on which legitimacy is ascribed to some policies, regulations, and processes of achieving cooperation, and others are de-legitimized.

Following a brief section that sketches the evolution of change in policy harmonization, I describe the structural understanding of the economy implicit within neo-liberalism, or the "strong thesis" of globalization. I then relate that discussion to my understanding of what an expanded scope, scale, and intensity of policy and legal harmonization means for the themes of this volume—peace, prosperity, and democracy.

## EVOLUTION OF HARMONIZATION

International harmonization of policy and law is designed to mitigate differences between national systems in order to achieve conformity with a common standard.[11] Harmonization cannot overcome vast differences; it presupposes an existing degree of convergence. At a basic level, market economies require market-based legal systems and market-societies, meaning fundamental organizing principles that include conceptions of property, rights, the role of capital, state-society and market-society complexes—all of which have been normalized through processes of capitalist development.[12] It is not surprising that the demise of radial alternatives to capitalism in Eastern Europe and elsewhere prompted a good deal of literature on the "globalization" of a mode of economic governance and its policy norms and regulatory standards.[13] For, a certain convergence of legal and regulatory systems is a prerequisite for interdependence.[14] Neither is it surprising that recent explanations for the lack of economic growth in less developed states should go back to fundamentals to point out the absence of a market-sustaining legal system in those economies.[15] As John R. Commons pointed out insightfully,[16] capitalism requires essential legal norms and policies in order for it to function—one might say they are structural prerequisites. Harmonization is therefore an enterprise of fine-tuning laws and regulations to reduce the differentiation among domestic institutions that arises as a result of the contingent and the peculiar—that is, social practices that are the result of culture and history.

While convergence on essentials is necessary for international harmonization, it is of course not sufficient. Harmonization requires a political determination to achieve common objectives; all harmonization is enabling and reinforces state-capacity. This is no less true of the harmonization that occurred under the highly nationalized governance system of Bretton Woods than it is of the current harmonization under neo-liberal economic management. However, there are important differences. Instrumentally, these differences concern "depth" and conceptions of "space." Current harmonization that accompanies neo-liberal economic management is "deeper" as it involves a greater intensity of domestic readjustment. "Space" refers to the geographical scope in which the market is believed to operate.

Both of these instrumental differences are due to a more fundamental difference about what the economy is deemed to be *for*. The Bretton Woods system was essentially a project of nationalizing liberalism by prioritizing state control of the market, and coordinating multilateral economic management through the use of border measures. Neo-liberal globalization, on the other hand, is the reverse: the economy is believed to operate at a structural level independent of, and "de-linked" from, the territorial state, and which determines to various degrees what appropriate government policy should be if a state is to be a successful actor in the market.

Just as capitalism in a domestic context is predicated on market-based laws, so the idea implicit in neo-liberalism is that "global" capitalism—in the sense that it is not contained by a territorial state—requires states to assimilate at a "deeper" level legal and regulatory systems on a concomitant geographical space.

## "Depth," "Space," and "Discipline"

Bretton Woods was a system of elaborate economic border controls that implied limited domestic re-organization (though it certainly involved some). It was based on a consensus of goals, norms, and principles that should guide market-society relations, which John Gerrard Ruggie coined as the "compromise of embedded liberalism."[17] That consensus among industrialized economies was characterized by shared expectations of economic growth that would be achieved through a liberal international economy, but growth that would not be damaging to societal stability, expressed principally in terms of social welfare. It reflected a shared assumption about the standard of appropriateness in balancing growth with social purpose in the market-society relationship. It permitted states to pursue shared objectives of increasing transborder commercial transactions, while maintaining domestic priorities on which there was broad international consensus, as well as providing conflict-avoidance and conflict-resolving mechanisms.

That consensus served as a foundation on which policy convergence—from which followed a range of regulatory and legal harmonization—was achieved through the international economic organizations of the General Agreement on Tariffs and Trade (GATT) and the International Monetary Fund (IMF), in particular. The state pursued an active role in mediating, therefore, between society and the economy. Elaborate sets of border-controls, principally the tariff and capital controls (but ancillary related policies as well), were harmonized in issue-specific normative systems in which there would be competition on rules, not competition of rules. Post-war harmonization was therefore based on the multilateral nationalization of liberalism, in which states attempted to control the economy and determine the pace and extent of international market integration.

The post-war international economic institutions also served to initiate a structure of cooperation[18] both in terms of multilateralism, and also in terms of international agreements being transposed and implemented in the domestic realm. Therefore, patterns of socialization into cooperation and modes of governance occurred both "horizontally" at the international level among states and "vertically" where both domestic and international management were contingent on each other.[19]

The Bretton Woods consensus has changed, of course, with a neo-liberal agenda that began arguably with the turmoil of the fixed-exchange system in the early 1970s, the rapid internationalization of production, and technolog-ical change.[20] Neo-liberalism is associated with privatization, and freedom of action for market actors based on a more orthodox neo-classical view of market efficiency and rational allocation. It implies "minimal" govern-ment, that empowers both market- and civil-society actors as participants in governance through deregulated or mixed public-private networks of inter-nal and transnational governance ("new public management").[21] This sec-tion explains briefly the change that occurred in the international trade and finance regimes accompanying the change in intellectual climate about ap-propriate modes of economic governance.

### International Trade

By the 1970s, there were fewer formalized state controls at the border for trade—quotas had gone early except notably for agriculture, and industrial tariffs were brought to very low levels following the implementation of the Tokyo Round of the GATT (1973–1979), save for the most politically sensi-tive sectors. The 1970s ushered a period in which there was great concern over the specter of "new protectionism": it was feared that some political "law of constant protectionism" would relocate protectionist pressures to a range of non-tariff barriers (NTBs) as the tariff became a severely circum-scribed device under international legal control.[22] NTBs included a wide range of categories from "administrative" protectionism (anti-dumping and countervailing duty actions) to domestic market and social regulatory poli-cies, including subsidies, health and safety rules, technical standards, and government procurement practices. In fact, the U.S. government identified some 800 domestic policies, laws, and regulatory practices as potential NTBs in the early 1970s.[23]

It is not necessary to dispute the extent to which there was greater re-course to NTBs for protectionist purposes, however it is certainly also the case that domestic policies came on the international agenda for a number of other reasons.[24] They became more "visible" as tariffs were eliminated. Technology had advanced such that the growth sectors of advanced economies were no longer industry but "new" sectors like services and in-tellectual property. Multinational corporations became the primary partici-pants in international trade and encountered a different and more elaborate range of barriers to commerce than did traditional exporters moored in a par-ticular territorial state. And, perhaps institutionally there was also a political need to put "something" on the international agenda to rescue the faltering GATT. For whatever combination of reasons, the international trade agenda including and since the Uruguay Round (1986–1994) included a greater host of "barriers" to trade that concern "market access" rather than border mea-sures.

The governance of international trade now principally concerns directly the harmonization of domestic regulations and laws, rather than domestic harmonization being mediated, as before, through the international control of border measures. Such is the climate of international trade that some observers note harmonization of domestic legislation to be an accepted and necessary "side effect" of free trade.[25] This implies a deeper domestic reorganization, both in terms of the types of laws affected and the range of actors involved—politicization of the issues of biotechnology, cinematographic films, and intellectual property rights for pharmaceutical products are only some examples.

It is also important to note that new trade-regulatory harmonization remains "enabling" and contributes to state governance capacity of OECD states. Governments in many ways have become more involved in international trade issues, both because the agenda has grown, and because more government departments and agencies are necessarily involved in any given issue. Health and safety issues, for instance, can involve Agriculture, Commerce, Labor, as well as the "traditional" trade representative office and the legislature. Issues like electronic commerce are such that an inter-agency task force of up to ten branches of government can be involved, along with a broad consultation or active participation of the private sector, both market actors and increasingly civil society. It is not necessarily the case that neo-liberalism means "minimal government," nor that more liberalization means less government intervention, less heavy regulation, or fewer laws—trade agreements now run to the tens of thousands of pages, and statute books are getting heavier.[26]

Indeed, the weight of regulation is related directly to the shift that is occurring in its form. Functionally, while the state retains control, internationally negotiated regulation takes on a more "disciplinary" function.[27] It disciplines government by more stipulatively prescribing appropriate actions and proscribing ones deemed less appropriate in its domestic governance role. Some agreements, like the Agreement on Trade-Related Aspects of Intellectual Property Rights (TRIPS) are quite specific, mandating the intellectual creations that will be deemed private property in national systems of legislation, and the manner and duration for which they will be protected by law. In some cases, such as in the Agreements on Technical Barriers to Trade or the Agreement on Sanitary and Phytosanitary Measures, there is vague reference to "scientific evidence," which defers the battle of science to the Dispute Settlement Mechanism but which nevertheless constrains government actions to scientific rationalism (and to the skill of legal representation). However, new market-access regulation also permits governments to exercise a greater and more precise disciplinary function over private actors—principally of market actors, but increasingly of civil society as well. Market actors under new public management style governance may be offered the alchemist's stone of a greater degree of freedom through self-regulation or loose mixed public-private governance networks, but they are severely disciplined by the boundaries of mandated "appropriate" action, and in many ways are empowered in their own self-regulation by being required to internalize norms and a raft of self-monitoring and reporting procedures. "Minimal" government often means governments do not get involved in the routine auditing; market actors audit and discipline themselves by being required to internalize regulation, but governments retain the role of supervisor and final coercive arbiter.

## International Finance

In the international finance system, capital controls were dismantled from 1971–1976 as the fixed exchange system of the IMF broke down, with rapid domestic policy re-adjustment occurring in OECD states in the early 1980s. The deregulation of international finance both shifted the monetary system from one that was government-led to one that became market-led, and privatized the international credit system by making private banks principal sources of international liquidity. Such has been the phenomenal growth of private international capital movements that international finance has been referred to as a "stateless" system that is "de-linked" in fundamental ways from the control and oversight of states.[28] However, privatized systems not only require regulation, they require *greater* domestic and international regulation as well as greater degrees of international regulatory harmonization than which pertained under the Bretton Woods system. Under the latter, national systems were essentially compartmentalized from each other through capital controls that acted as "fire-walls" to destabilizing activity occurring outside. This is no longer the case.

The shift to privatized international finance increased the scope and potential scale of risks that inhere in privatized credit. The principal difficulties of management today are primarily, and briefly, as follows.[29] First, there is "excess" international liquidity provided by private lending. The size of the international inter-bank lending market stands at nearly $8 trillion.[30] This can lead, and has led, to competition among banks and other non-bank financial institutions, resulting in imprudent lending and overexposure. Second, the speed of inter-bank electronic clearing systems is such that an estimated $6 trillion passes daily through international payments and settlement networks, which increases the speed at which mistakes can be transmitted across borders, increasing the specter of both contagion and systemic risk. Banking regulation was a national prerogative under Bretton Woods (and indeed earlier), though as the consequences of shock today can be transmitted widely throughout the system such that the imprudence of a banker in one state is cause for international concern, increased regulatory harmonization is found necessary.

The states of the OECD, in which is concentrated some 80 percent of international banking, welcome the increase in private liquidity, and competition in the financial market is seen as desirable to rationalize the efficiency of financial institutions and to create a competitive credit sector. These states have agreed that governance of the market-led system requires international cooperation through harmonized systems of national regulation and laws. States have agreed that banks, including transborder branches, are subject to the laws of the state in which they operate (rather, than, for instance, institutionalizing a global regulator). The state therefore retains supervisory jurisdiction, and is forced to "domesticate" risks of transnational capital flows through domestic law. Choosing domestic law as the medium for control has also led to a concomitant "deepening" of regulatory cooperation and to the harmonization of national legislation. As contagion risk does not respect political borders, the objective of cooperation has been to ensure that similar legislation prevails in the states that are highly integrated into the system, lest there be a "weak link" that can harbor pockets of instability that can spread to the rest and frustrate the efforts of those states which do maintain prudential supervision.

National regulators, primarily through the Basle Committee on Banking Regulation and Supervisory Practices of the Bank for International Settlements, coordinate the supervision of international banking.[31] The Basle Committee enunciates concordats that states transpose into legislation. The objective of regulation is, again, "discipline": discipline of private banks by regulators to ensure they behave prudently, and of national regulators disciplining each other. There have been a series of concordats and capital adequacy accords that establish the risk-adjusted minimum reserves that banks are required to hold, and the internal auditing records that banks should maintain, as well as the manner in which regulators will supervise banks, and the ways in which national regulators will share information with each other.

Of particular relevance is the principle of "consolidated supervision" under the Basle Committee's Minimum Standards. This mandates that host-country regulators of foreign banks must first determine that the bank operates prudentially, meaning it has sufficient capital and risk-management procedures, before it permits the establishment of that bank on its territory. The interesting part is that the host regulator must also determine whether the home country has given its permission to the establishment of the cross-border operation, and whether the home country has the capacity to exercise consolidated supervision—that is, oversight of the amalgamated position of the bank's global activities—prior to permitting the bank to establish in its jurisdiction. If the bank regulators are not satisfied, they should prevent the establishment of the bank in its jurisdiction.[32] Therefore, as cross-border branches of international banks weave the international finance system into an integrated web, the international banking regulations permits national bank regulators to assess the capacities of each other, on the basis of internationally harmonized regulatory norms.

## Summary

Substantively, the form of international cooperation in these issue areas has evolved from a system of negotiated "border controls"—principally tariffs and quotas for trade, and capital controls for finance—into a system that focuses on "market access" and domestic regulatory and legal regimes. The choice of policy instruments for economic management grows out of international consensus on what domestic governance priorities should be. Thus, border control measures are to the "Keynesian compromise" what "market access" rules through domestic regulatory and legal harmonization are to neo-liberalism. Market access rules, like border control measures, are domestic regulations that serve both internal, domestic governance functions as well as international governance functions. There is little point making a functional distinction between the two. However, my point has been that there are obvious qualitative differences that involve much deeper levels of domestic assimilation under neo-liberal modes of economic governance. As internationally oriented measures, domestic regulation and laws act as semipermeable membranes that permit goods and services into a state, in the same way that tariffs and capital controls do, but they are distinguished by their selectivity of those goods and services that meet domestic standards that are internationalized—internationally agreed and harmonized across domestic spaces. What is a regulation on the "inside" of the state is therefore melding into regulation on the "outside," and visa-versa.

The process of domestic internationalization has also undergone qualitative change. Unlike under the Bretton Woods system, domestic institutional, regulatory, and legal arrangements are no longer mediated exclusively through agreements made at the "edges" of states through border measures, where domestic harmonization was a consequence of negotiated border controls. Domestic laws and regulations now go directly on the table, which opens up the range of what hitherto has been considered "domestic" to international consideration. This is to a great extent due to the fact that neo-liberal governance mandates different kinds of regulation than that which pertained under Keynesian and Fordist economies of the early post-war era. As I expand in the next section, domestic harmonization of regulations and laws grows out of the domestic re-configuration of economic governance across OECD states.

Domestic regulations are also no longer mediated exclusively through formal international institutions. The focus of the agenda of the GATT changed particularly through the Uruguay Round, and requires greater cooperation with other organizations, such as the World Intellectual Property Organization (WIPO) for intellectual property issues; the International Labor Organization (ILO) for workers' rights issues. Trade issues also involve increasingly the international cooperation of specialized government departments. Similarly, the function of the IMF is now only part of the process of financial regulation—the Basle Committee is another important part.[33]

Both the change in substance and form of international economic governance constitute the "deeper" regulatory cooperation to which I referred. While neo-liberal theory implies deregulation and privatization that ostensibly requires "less" government intervention, re-regulation means a different, but no less active, role for government. Yet, interestingly, the "strong" thesis of globalization argues that states are increasingly "losing control" over transnational capitalism.[34] This might be because of an implicit—and erroneous— assumption, particularly in the discipline of International Relations, that the principal mechanisms of sovereign control of international affairs lie at the borders. If anything, more parts of national governments are involved in more aspects of international governance, and indeed, more of the state, market, and civil society have become internationalized as well: what used to be considered "sheltered" or "exclusive" domestic policies are now considered legitimately to be on the international agenda.

## EXPLAINING AND UNDERSTANDING HARMONIZATION

Technological determinism is often cited as one reason for the increasing disembedding of the domestic into the international. United States Federal Communications Chairman Michael Powell recently made a characteristic statement on this reasoning about the "necessity" of harmonized rules between the United States and the European Union. Because "technology is agnostic to borders," he suggested, it is necessary to seek a greater degree of "harmonization" across the Atlantic.[35] Similar explanations have been offered as regards the Internet: because Internet communications cross borders with seeming impunity, it is "necessary" to seek harmonization of rules for e-commerce, for instance, that include the range of consumer rights and seller responsibilities, and to standardize commercial contracts for easier dispute-settlement.

This technological determinist explanation is as simplistic as the "interdependence" explanation outlined earlier. These explanations assume too much, are *ex post facto*, and are partly tautological. There is a range of prior questions that they do not engage. If collective decisions about appropriate domestic laws have become transnationalized, we need first to inquire about the nature of the underlying ideological and inter-subjective understandings of purpose and interests that shape the market. Just as the Bretton Woods system was founded on the "compromise of embedded liberalism" we need to begin with the contemporary alternative. Dominant ideologies—like Keynesianism and neo-liberalism—structure the manner in which problems are framed, the manner in which the present is perceived and normalized, and the manner in which the future is conceived.

Governance *can* be conceived as the purposive project of providing stability through coercive devices and consensual steering mechanisms. However, governance can also be conceived of as the normative stability that arises from the clustering of values, the inter-subjective understandings of the "rules of the game" without there necessarily being a putative center of power.[36] Rather, power is located in the crystallization of an ideological center, the core of values, purpose, and interests *served by* the instrumental mechanisms of power. Those functional mechanisms can be Bretton Woods institutions, just as they can be harmonization of domestic legal systems. The important point is that all institutions that manage interdependence are necessarily founded on "ideological hegemony"[37] that underlies and informs modes of governance and provides the necessary normative foundation and reference points for collective decision making.

We need therefore to investigate how current normative consensus is constructed and legitimized at the international level. And, we need to examine the shifts in power and influence that have underlain decisions to transfer certain issues from exclusive domestic decision making to the international agenda. Clearly these are big questions and cannot be addressed fully in the space remaining in this chapter, but I can expose the issues that I believe need to be problematized but which are not addressed adequately by other explanations.

Such questions can be answered only through a political economy approach that begins with an appreciation that market activity is founded on shared ideas that provide a normative foundation for the practice—what the economy is *for*. The dominant ideology among the OECD states is neo-liberalism that accords greater freedom of action for market actors to compete with each other across borders, and therefore to have greater opportunities for market penetration, as competition is deemed to be desirable and beneficial. That the market is best operated by private individuals under deregulated competition expresses a neo-classical faith that it contains an intrinsic rationality such that it operates efficiently if there is competition and government role is limited to providing legal stability. Importantly, and contentiously, such a view is founded on a structural understanding of the nature of the market that posits that the market is "exogenous": it operates according to a logic that is given, and intrinsic to itself.

Social structures can be conceived as arising broadly in two ways.[38] The first is a "hard," or "strong" thesis. This posits that there exists an objective structure composed of market imperatives that operates according to an autonomous logic that exists independent from our understanding of it. Ontologically, it sees the market as prior to our discovery of its principles. Thus, becoming efficient and benefiting from economic activity is reduced to a scientific rationalism whereby those principles can be discovered—a view not unlike neo-classical orthodoxy that dates from the French Physiocrats, if not perhaps earlier. There is little scope for change to the logic of the market; rather, to benefit from the market requires change to political and social forms of organization. The task of government policy is to attempt to orient economic regulation and laws to those principles in order to derive the most benefit.

If the market is perceived to be determining of government policy, then there is within this understanding both a process—whereby actors adjust continually their behavior to the mandates of the market and to each other—and also an end-point—a "perfect" market that unfolds from the culmination of actors' behavioral adjustments over time.

As for process, this understanding points to the inevitability of the collapse of the Bretton Woods compromise: the market cannot be constrained, reigned-in, nationalized, atomized, or otherwise tamed by governments for very long. Indeed, writers of this ilk delight in pointing out that Bretton Woods, New Hampshire, that lent its name to the famous "compromise" between an international market and domestic social prerogatives does not even exist. Rather, it is the name of a conference center at the foot of Mount Deception,[39] and governments were "deluding" themselves by the belief that the market could be constrained by them to serve any nonmarket objectives, social or otherwise.

As regards end-points, competitive systems like the market force the adoption of policy that is "good," or consistent with the market, and they also force emulation of "winners." Conversely, the market structure punishes actors who adopt "bad" policy, or policy that is inconsistent with the market, through fewer rewards. On this line of reasoning, states have little alternative but to emulate the most efficient form of organization in a structurally functional sense. The "vulgar" expression of this was Karl Marx and Friedrich Engels declaring that capitalism "compels all nations, on pain of extinction. . . to become bourgeois themselves. . . . it creates the world after its own image."[40] The structural functionalist reasoning may have its roots in Emile Durkheim and was employed to great effect to understand international relations by Keneth Waltz. Phil Cerny has also applied it to economic globalization and convergence insightfully.[41]

The second conception of social structures is that they are constructed by human belief in them, which characterizes the neo-Gramscian approach to globalization of Robert Cox and others.[42] On this understanding, there is little that is "given" or objective prior to human subjectivity bringing it into the realm of concrete reasoning. Inter-subjectively shared understandings

of the rules of the game create structures. Following this, the idea that globalization contributes to diminished state capacity for governance constitutes a "myth" that is used by politicians who find it politically expedient
either to blame amorphous external forces for policy failure or to declare a
lack of alternatives to justify policies that have been adopted. Linda Weiss
has called this the "political construction of helplessness," and Ian Robert
Douglas has suggested that the very rhetoric of "globalization" constitutes
the "episteme of contemporary governance."[43]

For present purposes, while noting that these different ontologies of globalization differ radically in their understandings of the genesis of structures
and in the potential for change—positivist versus critical—it is sufficient for
the argument developed here to underline that neither dispute that a structure of the market is perceived to exist and that it is perceived to constrain
and shape policy by delimiting parameters for appropriate action. Both approaches to market structure also offer a convincing explanation of the
changed convergence of interest from the Keynesian compromise to neo-
liberalism, and of an inherent belief in the "expanse" or "scope" of the market that operates in a plane that is autonomous and conceptually "above"
the actors—bounded territorial states. It is this belief in the inherent "ex-
pansiveness" of the market that involves a process of deeper reconfiguration
of societal matrixes of which harmonized regulation and laws is part.
Stephen Gill has called this a "neo-liberal market civilization," based on an
ideological hegemony that normalizes, and therefore re-produces, a particular conception of society-market complexes, and which like any ideology,
marginalizes alternatives.[44]

In Gill's words, neo-liberalism is characterized by the, "spatial expansion
and social deepening of liberal definitions of social purpose." Just as John R.
Commons described the necessary requisites for the legal foundations for
capitalism in a bounded territorial state, so "globalization" is writing willy-
nilly the rules for the transnational assimilation of legal and regulatory policy
prerogatives for a neo-liberal market civilization that is conceived to be unbounded by the territorial state. Just as the market requires as a structural
prerequisite a market-based legal system, so highly evolved and highly-
interdependent transnational markets are seen to require a deeper level of
convergence and harmonization of a range of practices from product standards to sanitary and phytosanitary inspection systems, health and safety
rules, banking supervision, the transnational control of money laundering,
and so on. From the neo-liberal idea that the "scope" of the market is naturally uninterrupted by borders, it follows that it ought not be interrupted by
differential regulations embedded within different domestic spaces. This
places domestic regulations and laws on the international agenda as legitimate foci for attention, and turns domestic regulatory and legal harmonization into a mechanism for the management of the neo-liberal international

market in the same way that the formal Bretton Woods organizations served as institutions to govern the relations between highly atomized and nationalized economies that were seen to be "contained" by borders. My point: the belief in the unbounded market as a structure can and is rationalizing the normalizing and homogenizing processes that discipline government policy and which translate that discipline to the composition of society.

The "interdependence explanation" is therefore incomplete. It also contributes to the rationalization and reproduction of the logic of the process by failing to question its underlying assumptions. Without adequate understanding that international mechanisms of cooperation grow out of hegemonic constructs of the economy, explanations that take a given form of system-level governance for granted cannot appreciate adequately that the "deepening" of economic governance into society and the expanding "scope" of governance through harmonization are both part of a single process. Harmonization of regulation and law expands the "scope" of neo-liberal governance concomitant with both the perceived scope of the market that it follows, and it also follows the "deepening" of international/domestic regulation intrinsic to neo-liberal economic management. The strategy of harmonized law in neo-liberal governance is therefore the *consequence* of a deeper rationalization of dominant ideology and domestic societal-organizational transformation among advanced industrial states.

## PEACE, PROSPERITY, AND DEMOCRACY?

This critical understanding of the market structure does not answer the question of *whose* regulatory and legal standards should prevail. Nor should it be expected to. Such is the stuff of politics at actor-level, the outcome of which depends on power, skill, and scientific and normative justification. My analysis above offers an explanation for *why* there should be increasingly harmonized regulations and law by outlining the normative foundation on which collective decision making takes place. But, it is little surprise that the politics associated with it should be fierce, both at interstate level and at the level of civil society. In this concluding section, I relate regulatory and legal harmonization to the themes of this book. Indeed, the normative implications of the process of domestic internationalization in general, and regulatory and legal harmonization in particular, are profound.

It is not long ago that interest in issues relating to the GATT was confined principally to specialist lawyers and political economists, and industry groups that had a direct stake in the outcome of negotiations. Members of civil society might have taken note if they happened to find excitement in things like watching paint dry, and perhaps the General Agreement was seen as a necessary bedside item for insomniacs. Even eminent trade layers like

John Jackson joked that the GATT was the "boiler room" of international relations. This was by design. One of the primary purposes of the drafters of Bretton Woods was to de-politicize economic issues following the experience of the 1929–1939 Depression. It was also a function of the foundation ideals of a system in which state borders should serve to shelter domestic societies from the international economy. Social stability and nonmarket values were a matter of domestic concern, and there was a clear realization that the economy should serve the society, mindful of Karl Polanyi's warning about unbridled liberalism being capable of destroying the social and political foundations on which it depends.[45]

Yet, by the Uruguay round, farmers on both sides of the Atlantic were dumping very foul things on the streets and burning effigies of trade representatives, and cinematographers in Europe in more intellectual ways related the issue of trade in audio-visual services to the loss of political identity. By the late 1990s the World Trade Organization, and the IMF and World Bank became the focus for a clustering of a variety of international civil society groups, and violent mass social protest became a regular feature of meetings of the international economic institutions.[46] Indeed, the disembedding of the domestic into the international has raised fears about nothing less than the maintenance of domestic autonomy, the protection of national difference, and retaining the right democratically to choose ways in which a community decides to live.

The disjuncture between the economy and society under neo-liberalism has been explained in Polanyian terms by a number of writers.[47] It points to states located within an international market structure that forecloses government policy options, while on the other hand there is a civil society contained within the state, holding to a self-conception as a bounded community of meaning that prioritizes nonmarket values that are socially-constructed, and that increasingly looks to the state for protection from international market forces. In brief, the state is constrained by a market structure that requires of it policies that are transnationally oriented, and suffers a crisis of legitimacy because it is unable to meet domestic expectations. Such crises of legitimacy may be seen clearly on the streets outside international economic meetings—to the extent that one can see clearly through tear gas. As applied to the present discussion, the disjunction is between states negotiating domestic systems of regulation that increasingly mitigate difference for economic purposes, while society's conceptions of regulation that is appropriate for the community is based on peculiarity that is a product of contingent factors such as culture, history, and identity.

Through international cooperation there is normally a trade-off between different facets of sovereignty. By reaching agreement on a standard, states give up autonomy, including the potential for difference, in exchange for the increased capacity to control. Harmonization of domestic laws, similarly, is undertaken as a means to increase the capacity to control, to mitigate risk unleashed by deregulation, and indeed to exert sovereign powers of coercion over transnational market actors. Yet, this act of sovereignty constrains autonomy for future decisions, possibly creates path-dependence that undermines choice among a range of possible policy options, and diminishes the freedom to undertake alternative decisions.

However, harmonization of domestic law as a means of international governance raises distinct issues within this general framework of tradeoffs between autonomy and control, and these concern essentially the extent of transnational domestic integration. Indeed, there is a "rooting" effect whereby one piece of harmonized law, like dominoes, impacts upon a range of other laws, forcing a deeper uniformity. There is a "Trojan horse" here of deeper societal integration across borders, and it raises fundamental issues of democratic choice.

Domestic regulations and laws cannot be seen in isolation, either from other laws, or from the social and cultural practices that give rise to, and are expressed by, legal systems. Legal systems are organic self-referential wholes; each principle relates to others and each rule is based on a further set of rules.[48] A change to one part of a legal system implies change to other parts of the system and possibly to the deeper foundations—legal norms and rules—on which the legal system is founded. Harmonizing one aspect of legislation to a core international standard necessarily involves as a "harmonization by-product" a range of further adjustments that mitigate difference still further. For instance, the adoption by Switzerland of the reporting mechanism for banks in the policing of money laundering caused quite a serious disjuncture to occur in the civil liability of banks for the breach of banker-customer confidentiality.[49] The harmonization of environmental standards and the approval requirements for pharmaceutical products similarly illustrated the "spill-over" effect of harmonization, as efforts that began with minimum guidelines for approval procedures for drugs quickly extended to the medical technology used by regulatory agencies and the standards for electronic data transmission.[50] The growth of private standards as mechanisms of regulation within the EU by implication "spillover" and "leads to an indirect integration of European private law"[51] in the areas of environmental protection, public education standards, and supervision of banks and insurance companies.

My point is that it is difficult if not impossible simply to harmonize one regulation or law without entailing a knock-on change to a range of laws, and very often to the "upstream" legal rules and principles—such as "duty," as in the example of money laundering—that inform those laws. It is also the case that harmonization of money laundering laws, for instance, mean little unless states also decide to "criminalize" the same things that give rise to "illegitimate" money.[52] Harmonizing laws for copyrights entails the upstream harmonization of principles such as "property right," the definition of "rights holders" and of "copying." Law is not simply a command structure that seeks to determine the behavior of individuals by forcing compliance through a system of coercion. A sociological conception of law views legal systems as giving expression to the collective will of a community; indeed, law is the expression of socially constructed ethical norms and frameworks of justice and the "good" that are held by a community of shared meaning. Harmonization therefore implies not only changes to systems of legal rules and principles, but also the mitigation of those differences that are peculiar, socially constructed, and contingently formed by culture and history.

It is largely for these reasons that the project of harmonization has been subject to a good deal of controversy and criticism, from both economic and legal perspectives. Some economists have argued, on the basis of efficiency, that standards that are formulated outside a state and applied in the national context do not always lead to optimal outcomes.[53] Lawyers that adopt a sociological view of law also question the effectiveness of applying in one social context laws that have been formulated in another.[54] The meaning and purpose of laws can be understood only with reference to the constellation of other laws, rules, and norms embedded within a society's social and legal universe.[55] Leading legal scholars, like Gunther Teubner, have gone so far as to suggest that the "legal transplant" from one jurisdiction to another is better described as a "legal irritant."[56]

Legal harmonization therefore raises key normative issues, and they lie behind—and for the most part, away—from the scenes of fury outside the meetings of the international economic institutions. From the perspective of economics and law, such questions involve the appropriateness and efficacy of foreign practices and concepts being transposed to a different legal-social system. From a political perspective, the harmonization of laws in the neoliberal project points to greater depths of domestic assimilation and the loss of autonomy at levels much more deeply embedded in societies than "traditional" institutional cooperation at the state's "edges." It also raises the issue of "path dependence," in the sense that greater convergence of domestic legal systems could be self-enforcing, as previous convergence shapes the ground-work on which in collective decisions—both internationally *and* domestic—about domestic laws will be taken, and in that way structures future outcomes. From the perspective of International Relations, the incremental mitigations of difference at such deep levels of market-society and society-law matrixes can raise serious questions about the normative foundations of the Westphalian order founded on compartmentalization, atomization, and of territorial states as "containers of difference." Without question, the harmonization of laws raises issues for democracy, because at stake is nothing less than the rules by which societies decide to live, yet the process of arriving at them seems increasingly to take place in international negotiations by states, rather than by civil society, by choice.

# NOTES

1. The OECD also maintains a database of regulatory policies of member states in a wide range of areas. On what the OECD called the "emerging multi-governmental regulatory system," see OECD, "International Regulatory Cooperation," OECD, Paris, at www.oecd.org//puma/regref/coopern.htm.

2. Diane Stone, "Learning Lessons and Transferring Policy across Time, Space and Disciplines," *Politics* 19(1) 1999: 51–59. See also, M. Evans and J. Davies, "Understanding Policy Transfer: A Multi-Level, Multi-Disciplinary Perspective," *Public Administration* 77(2) 1999: 361–85.

3. S. Berger and R. Dore, ed., *National Diversity and Global Capitalism* (Ithaca, N.Y.: Cornell University Press, 1996); Colin Crouch and Wolfgang Streek, *Political Economy of Modern Capitalism* (London: Sage, 1997); Hollingsworth, Schmitter, and Streek, eds., *Governing Capitalist Economies,* (Oxford: Oxford University Press, 1994); Jagdish Bhagwati and Robert Hudec, *Fair Trade and Harmonization: Prerequisites for Free Trade?* (Cambridge: MIT Press, 1996).

4. William Twinning, *Globalisation and Legal Theory* (London: Butterworths, 2000). See also the contributions to the specialist journal, the *Indiana Journal of Global Legal Studies*, at www.law. indiana.edu/glsj.

5. Jarrod Wiener, *Globalization and the Harmonization of Law* (London: Pinter, 1999).

6. See, for instance: Robert Axelrod, *The Evolution of Cooperation* (New York: Basic Books, 1984); David Baldwin, *Neorealism and Neoliberalism: New Directions in World Politics* (New York: Columbia University Press, 1993); John A. C. Conybeare, *Trade Wars: The Theory and Practice of International Commercial Rivalry* (New York: Columbia University Press, 1987); Robert Keohane, *International Institutions and State Power: Essays in International Relations Theory* (London: Westview Press, 1989); Robert Keohane and Joseph Nye, *Power and Interdependence* 2nd ed. (Harper-Collins, 1989); and Kenneth Oye, ed., *Cooperation Under Anarchy* (Princeton, N.J.: Princeton University Press, 1985).

7. Robert Gilpin, *Global Political Economy* (Princeton, N.J.: Princeton University Press, 2001), 195.

8. Vincent Cable, "The Diminished Nation-State: A Study of the Loss of Economic Power," *Daedalus* 124(2) 1995; Paul Hirst and Grahame Thompson, *Globalisation in Question* (Cambridge: Polity Press, 1996).

9. See AJR Groom, "The Advent of International Organisation," in Paul Taylor and AJR Groom, eds., *International Institutions at Work* (London: Pinter, 1988), 3–19; and F. S. Northedge, *The League of Nations: Its Life and Times, 1920–1946* (Holmes and Meier, 1986).

10. In this chapter, I confine my analysis to the highly integrated states of the OECD. There is another caveat: the matter of domestic institutions raises a different set of questions than I raise here about regulatory policies and laws. Recent literature on "globalization" as "homogenization" has raised a variant of "convergence theory" on which the jury is still deliberating. The process is disputed by for instance Berger and Dore, *op. cit.*, Crouch and Streek, *op. cit.*, and Hollingsworth, Schmitter and Streek, *op. cit.* On the other hand, writers such as Asia Sassed pointed out, "a large number of national states have had to become deeply involved in the

implementation of the global economic system and have, in this process, experienced transformations of various aspects of their institutional structure." See Saskia Sassen, "Embedding the Global in the National," in David Smith, Dorothy Solinger, and Steven Topik, eds., *States and Sovereignty in the Global Economy* (London: Routledge, 1999), 159. See also Sassen, *Losing Control? Sovereignty in an Age of Globalisation* (New York: Columbia University Press, 1996).

11. See A. J. R. Groom and Alexis Heralds, "Integration and Disintegration," in Margot Light and A. J. R. Groom, eds., *International Relations: A Handbook of Current Theory* (London: Pinter, 1985), 177; and R. J. Harrison and Stuart Mungall, "Harmonization," in A. J. R Groom and Paul Taylor, eds., *Frameworks for International Cooperation* (London: Pinter, 1990); and Robert Cox, ed., *International Organisation: World Politics* (London: Macmillan, 1969).

12. Karl Polanyi, *The Great Transformation* (London: Beacon Press, 1986).

13. For an early example, see Leah A. Haus, *Globalizing the GATT: The Soviet Union's Successor States, Eastern Europe, and the International Trading System* (Washington, D.C.: Brookings Institution, 1992).

14. See Aseem Prakash and Jeffrey A. Hart, "Globalization and Governance: An Introduction," in Prakash and Hart, eds, *Globalization and Governance* (London: Routledge, 1999).

15. See Hernando de Soto, *The Mystery of Capital: Why Capitalism Triumphs in the West and Fails Everywhere Else* (New York: Basic Books, 2001). Note, that the idea that capitalism requires a market-based legal system was studied in depth by John R. Commons (if not two hundred years earlier by Jeremy Betham).

16. John R. Commons, *The Legal Foundations of Capitalism* (Madison, Wis.: University of Wisconsin Press, 1957).

17. John Gerrard Ruggie, "International Regimes, Transactions, and Change: Embedded Liberalism in the Postwar Economic Order," in Stephen D. Krasner, ed., *International Regimes* (Ithaca: Cornell University Press, 1983), 195–232.

18. See T. Baumgartner and T. R. Burns, "The Structuring of International Economic Relations," *International Studies Quarterly* 19, 1979.

19. On establishing socialization and patterns of cooperation, see Michael Mann, "The Social Cohesion of Liberal Democracy," *American Sociological Review* 35(3) 1970: 423–39; and as applied to international regimes, see John G. Ikenberry and Charles Kupchan, "Socialization and Hegemonic Power," *International Organization* 44(3) 1990: 283–315.

20. The story has been rehearsed elsewhere. See, for instance, Richard O'Brien, *Global Financial Deregulation: The End of Geography* (London: Pinter, 1990); Kenichi Ohmae, *The Borderless World: Power and Strategy in the Interlinked Economy* (London: Fontana, 1990); Malcolm Waters, *Globalisation* (London: Routledge, 1995); Susan Strange, *The Retreat of the State* (Cambridge: Cambridge University Press, 1996).

21. R. A. W. Rhodes, *Understanding Governance: Policy Networks, Governance, Reflexivity and Accountability* (London: Open University Press, 1997); John Shields and Mitchell Evans, *Shrinking the State: Globalization and Public Administration "Reform"* (Halifax: Fernwood Publishing, 1998); and Phil Cerny, "Paradoxes of the Competition State: The Dynamics of Political Globalization," *Government and Opposition* 32(2) 1997: 251–74. .

22. The "law" belongs to Bhagwati. See *Protectionism* (London: MIT Press, 1988); and Bhagwati, *The World Trading System at Risk* (London: Harvester Wheatsheaf, 1991).

23. See Gardner Patterson, Robert Baldwin, U.S. Department of Commerce, and U.S. Department of State, *United States International Economic Policy in an Interdependent World: Papers Submitted to the Commission on International Trade and Investment and Published in Conjunction with the Commission's Report to the President* (Compendium of Papers, vol.1, U.S. Government Printing Office, Washington, D.C , 1971).

24. See Jarrod Wiener, "Transatlantic Trade: Economic Security, Agriculture, and the Politics of Technology," in J. Wiener, ed., *The Transatlantic Relationship* (London: McMillan/St. Martins, 1996).

25. See, for instance, Stephen Zamora, who addressed this issue in "NAFTA and the Harmonization of Domestic Legal Systems: The Side Effects of Free Trade," *Arizona Journal of International and Comparative Law* 12(1): 401–27.

26. The regulatory involvement required of government frustrates the capacity of states with fewer human and capital resources, particularly developing countries. They have already raised the sheer administrative weight of trade agreements as an issue in Geneva. A similar situation occurs as regards the manpower required adequately to supervise international banks, discussed below.

27. I use "discipline" in the sense that Foucault understood it when he described the subtle mechanisms that government adopted to maintain social control as economic systems became more liberal and societies more open in eighteenth century Europe. See Michel Foucault, *Discipline and Punish: The Birth of the Prison* (New York: Vintage Books, 1995)

28. See Phil Cerny, "The Political Economy of International Finance," in Cerny, ed., *Finance and World Politics* (Aldershot, Australia: Edward Elgar, 1993); and Eric Helleiner, "States and the Future of Global Finance," *Review of International Studies* 18(1) 1992.

29. See: "Remarks by Chairman Alan Greenspan Before the 34th Annual Conference on Bank Structure and Competition of the Federal Reserve Bank of Chicago, May 7 1998," at www.federalreserve. gov/boarddocs/speeches/19980507.htm.

30. Bank for International Settlements, "The BIS Consolidated International Banking Statistics," Bank for International Settlements, Basle, Switzerland, www.bis.org/press/p010507.htm.

31. On the successive measures for international cooperation on these issues, see: Duncan E. Alford, "Basle Committee Minimum Standards: International Regulatory Response to the Failure of BCCI," *George Washington Journal of International Law and Economics* 26, 1992; Daniel M. Laiffer, "Putting the Super Back in the Supervision of International Banking, Post-BCCI," *Fordham Law Review* 60, 1990; Thomas F. McInerney III, "Towards the Next Phase in International Banking Regulation," *DePaul Business Law Journal* 7, 1994; and J. J. Norton, "The Work of the Basle Supervisors Committee on Bank Capital Adequacy and the July 1998; Report on 'International Convergence of Capital Measurements and Capital Standards,'" *International Lawyer* 23, 1989. For subsequent developments, such as the 16 January 2001 Capital Adequacy Accord, and the 1997 *Core Principles for Effective Banking Supervision,* at www.bis.org.

32. Note, for instance, the similarities between the United States Foreign Bank Supervision Enhancement Act, 1991 (FBSEA) and the European Council Directive 92/30 of 6 April 1992 on the Supervision of Credit Institutions on a Consolidated Basis, *Official Journal of the European Communities,* 1992 (L110), 52.

33. For a fuller treatment of complex global governance, see Aseem Prakash and Jeffrey A. Hart, eds., *Globalization and Governance* (London: Routledge, 1999); James Rosenau, "Governance in the Twenty-First Century," *Global Governance: Review of Multilateral and International Organization* 1(1) 1995: 13–43; Martin Hewson and Timothy Sinclair, eds., *Approaches to Global Governance Theory* (Albany: State University of New York Press, 1999); and Raimo Vayrynen, ed., *Globalization and Global Governance* (Oxford: Rowman and Littlefield, 1999).

34. For instance O'Brien, *op. cit.*; Waters, *op. cit.;* and especially Thomas L. Friedman, *The Lexus and the Olive Tree* (New York: Farrar, Straus and Giroux, 1999).

35. Interview with U.S. Federal Communications Chairman Michael Powell, CNN Europe, Friday 25 May 2001.

36. See Rhodes, *op. cit.*

37. This is a particular form of power that fits "between material power, ideology, and institutions . . . [which] frames thought and thereby circumscribes action." Robert Cox, "Multilateralism and World Order," *Review of International Studies* 18, 1992: 179. See also Cox, "Gramsci, Hegemony and International Relations: An Essay in Method," *Millennium: Journal of International Relations* 12(2) 1983.

38. Of course, there are many permutations of these. See, for instance, Gil Friedman and Harvey Starr, *Agency, Structure, and International Politics: From Ontology to Empirical Enquiry* (London: Routledge, 1997).

39. This story is told by Gregory J. Millman, *Around the World on a Trillion Dollars a Day: How Rebel Currency Traders Destroy Banks and Defy Governments* (London: Bantam Press, 1995). The "hard" structural ontology underlies such works as Ohmae, *op. cit.*, and Friedman, *op. cit.*

40. Marx and Engels, *The Manifesto of the Communist Party*, 1948.

41. Emile Durkheim, *The Rules of Sociological Method* (New York: Free Press, 1964). Waltz, "Reflections on Theory of International Politics: A Response to My Critics," in Robert O. Keohane, ed., *Neorealism and Its Critics* (New York: Columbia University Press, 1986), 323–26; Philip Cerny, "Globalization, Governance, and Complexity" in Prakash and Hart, *op. cit.* , esp. 193–96. (Note that Cerny might disagree with the thesis that I am advancing here.) See also Fred Halliday, "International Society as Homogeneity: Burke, Mark, Fukuyama," *Millennium: Journal of International Studies* 21(3) 1992: 435–61.

42. See Robert W. Cox, "Towards a Post-Hegemonic Conceptualisation of World Order: Reflections on the Relevancy of Ibn Khaldun," in Robert W. Cox and Timothy J. Sinclair, eds., *Approaches to World Order* (Cambridge: Cambridge University Press, 1996).

43. Linda Weiss, *The Myth of the Powerless State: Governing the Economy in a Global Era* (Cambridge: Polity Press, 1998); Ian R. Douglas, "Globalization *as* Governance" Toward an Archaeology of Contemporary Political Reason," in Prakash and Hart, *op. cit.*, 134–61. See also Michael Veseth, *Selling Globalization* (New York: Lynne Reinner, 1991).

44. Stephen Gill, "Globalisation, Market Civilisation, and Disciplinary Neoliberalism," *Millennium: Journal of International Studies* 24(3) 1995: 399.

45. Karl Polanyi, *op. cit.*

46. See Robert O'Brien, Anne Marie Goetz, Jan Aart Scholte, and Marc Williams, *Contesting Global Governance: Multilateral Economic Institutions and Global Social Movements* (Cambridge: Cambridge University Press, 2000).

47. An interesting discussion of many of these is Hannes Lacher, "The Politics of the Market: Re-reading Karl Polanyi," *Global Society: Journal of Interdisciplinary International Relations* 13(3) 1999: 313–26.

48. I am adopting a sociological conception of law here. See Max Weber, *Max Weber on Law in Economy and Society*; Edward Shils and Max Rheinstein, eds. (Cambridge: Harvard University Press, 1954); and Niklas Luhmann, *A Sociological Theory of Law*, (trans. Elizabeth King and Martin Albrow, Martin Albrow, ed.), (London: Routledge, 1985).

49. Rebecca G. Peters, "Money Laundering and its Current Status in Switzerland: New Disincentives for Financial Tourism," *Journal of International Law and Business* 11, 1990: 104–39; and Kanwar M. Singh, "Nowhere to Hide: Judicial Assistance in Piercing the Veil of Swiss Banking Secrecy," *Boston University Law Review* 71, November 1991: 847–61.

50. David Vogel, *Trading Up: Consumer and Environmental Regulation in a Global Economy* (Cambridge: Harvard University Press, 1995); and Vogel, "The Globalization of Pharmaceutical Regulation," *Governance: An International Journal of Policy and Administration* 11(1) 1998: 1–22.

51. Gerald Spindler, "Market Processes, Standardisation, and Tort Law," *European Law Journal* 4(3) 1998: 316–36, at p. 317.

52. Most treaties for mutual assistance contain the requirement for "dual criminality," but it is important to note that recent measures to tighten the anti-money laundering legislation in the United Kingdom, will leave it to the prosecuting authority to define what is a "crime" that gives rise to illicit money. See "Through the Ringer," *The Economist*, 12 April 2001.

53. Bhagwati and Srinavasan, *op. cit.*

54. See Twining, *op. cit.*, 152.

55. See Hugh Collins, "European Private Law and the Cultural Identity of States," *European Review of Private Law* 3, 1995.

56. Gunther Teubner, "Legal Irritants: Good Faith in British Law or How Unifying Law Ends Up in Divergencies," *Modern Law Review* 61(1) 1998: 11–32.

# 12

# Lawyers as a Commodity in International Trade

*Timothy J. O'Neill*

Three decades ago it made little sense to speak about a worldwide legal profession. There were many different legal professions, each comfortable within its national borders, each with its own special rules and professional organizations. There was little need to harmonize rules or to consider what effect changes in the rules of one nation's legal profession would have on the pattern of practice in other countries. The political and professional map has since changed. The North American Free Trade Area (NAFTA) and the most recent GATT agreement include legal services as part of business services, opening law practice to international trade and commerce. The European Union, the Mercosul countries of South America (Brazil, Argentina, Paraguay, and Uruguay), and the trade agreements along the Pacific Rim have lowered regional trade barriers and transformed law from a national into a transnational profession.

This essay is part of a project that seeks to identify the factors affecting the development of a transnational legal profession. The project asks how the rise in an international commerce of legal services may affect not only legal practices and doctrines but also the role of lawyers as carriers and sustainers of national interests and values and as a distinct profession. Efforts by attorneys and firms to develop their transnational legal practice may encourage a convergence among legal doctrines and processes. No longer will national boundaries offer a convenient and sensible way to divide what lawyers and courts "do." A transnational legal practice may transform national bar associations into a transnational legal profession.[1]

My object in this essay is narrowed to the issue of what it means to be a profession in a changing world. What changes will be wrought in the profession's self-image as a changing legal market challenges its authority over professional affairs? How is the emerging world market in legal services affecting the set of norms, traditions, and practices that lawyers have constructed to establish and maintain their identities as professionals and their jurisdiction over legal work? How do legal professions cope with the individual and collective forces that are reshaping the market within which their members must compete, the workplace in which they must labor, and the profession within which they secure their status in society?[2]

I offer a simple model of the political economy of the legal profession and draw upon a sample of interviews with over ninety European lawyers in four nations in order to examine how attorneys in the European Union are responding as professionals to the opening up of law as a commodity service to international trade. My interviews were conducted during the summer and fall of 1995 and the summers of 1996 and 1997 with bar officials and attorneys in Germany, France, Great Britain, and Belgium. The data do not represent a random sample of the national bars of these four nations but depend upon a grapevine sample, one constructed by asking informants to suggest prominent members in their legal communities active in transnational legal practice. I selected these four nations because they possess four different legal cultures (common law and three variants of the civil law system) and because Germany and France grant lawyers a monopoly in providing legal service while Great Britain or Belgium do not. Their legal professions differ significantly because of their differing judicial cultures and restrictions on legal counseling. If a transnational legal practice is corroding the old national distinctions defining what it means to be a legal professional, than these four nations, with their differing legal traditions and practices, offer a reasonable basis for making qualified generalizations about the phenomenon.

This data is supplemented by interviews with officials of and access to the files of the Council of Bars and Law Societies of Europe (the "Comité Consultatif des Barreaux Européens," or CCBE). The CCBE consists of national delegations from the European Union and the European Free Trade Association. It represents the legal profession before the EU and other transnational bodies when they consider changes affecting the profession. Recent CCBE meetings have discussed multinational partnerships, the GATT round, and alternative dispute resolution.

Data drawn from the CCBE meeting and the interviews permit identifying emerging patterns of practices among lawyers in Europe. It may also provide clues as to the development of legal practices in the United States as the United States becomes more open to the international commerce in legal services. For example, CCBE's 1988 code of ethics for EU attorneys is the basis for the Model Rules for Foreign Legal Consultants adopted by the American

Bar Association in August 1993. However, this essay focuses exclusively on the European Union.[3]

## THE POLITICAL ECONOMY OF THE LEGAL PROFESSION

The literature seeking to define what constitutes a profession is extensive and contradictory. One summary found over twenty-three distinct characteristics associated with professionalism in twenty-one separate studies. No one characteristic was found in all twenty-one studies, and none of the studies agreed on what blend of characteristics determined a profession (Waddington 1985: 650–51). The problem with the checklist approach is that the checklist itself presumes a theory of what distinguishes a profession from other forms of human association. The search for defining criteria presupposes a theory distinguishing what are the organizing features of a profession from those characteristics of other human associations.

Alternative approaches include Weberian, economic, Marxist, and structural-functionalist. Marxist approaches stress the unifying thread of class conflict and find it difficult to assimilate professions into the analytical framework without considerable twisting of key concepts. The structural-functionalist approach accepts that a profession exists and analyzes it in terms of its purported role in assuaging human and social needs. The Weberian stresses the power of expertise in a legal-rational age.[4] While these approaches have their value, none is well adapted to a study of professional responses to market changes.

The following model is based on economic theories of how professions organize themselves in a market economy. It accepts that lawyers are actors in an imperfectly competitive market. It asks that we imagine attorneys as firms dealing in commodities—the goods and services labeled "legal" by law and custom. Picture clients as consumers, trying to decide if the price of the goods is right. As with all markets, the legal market is characteristically a competition amongst suppliers, suggesting division within the profession, and a competition with suppliers of alternative goods and services, in this case other professions laying claim to authority over individual and group conflicts (medicine, accounting, religion, science, and bureaucracy). Law is cumbersome, expensive, and unreliable. Other mechanisms of social control compete with law for the allegiances and support of clients. Finally, the model expects attorneys to act to lessen the uncertainties accompanying competition. They seek predictability by creating market-limiting arrangements—in brief, a protected market.

As players in a marketplace, lawyers offer their special goods and services in exchange for wealth and status. To be effective sellers in a marketplace, lawyers must offer a commodity that is perceived as uniquely theirs to offer and that is valued by consumers. For a service to be valued, lawyers must satisfy not only consumers' appetites for the service but the consumer's confidence in the quality of the service provided. Services are not as fungible as many products are; the standardization of services does not ensure consistent quality in the same way as the standardization of products can. The quality of a legal service can thus be gauged only after it has been consumed. Professions exist at least in part to offer reliable surrogates for the quality of its members' services through credentialing and regulatory requirements.

The underlying ideology of a free market insists on relative autonomy from government control. Professions argue for a restricted market precisely because, in their minds, a free market will lower the quality of professional services. Being a profession is not only a matter of regulating entry into the market. A profession is self-regulating. Only experts can supervise experts, professionals insist, and so the profession needs independence both from the state and from the client if it is to meet its mission.

The nature of the distinctive goods and services offered by lawyers differ from nation to nation. The civilian law's notary is a prominent legal actor, unlike the less prestigious notary in the Anglo-American tradition, a role that is not even a legal professional one. However, it is a mistake to emphasize unduly the specific formal roles and restrictions for different classes of attorneys in different nations. What most attorneys do in most nations is only mildly related to the formal depiction of legal tasks found in official or popular presentations. Most attorneys, even those such as the English barrister who is formally excluded from direct client contact, depend less on their technical skills than on common sense advising. Their role is more mediational than adversarial (Macaulay 1979: 117; Spedding 1987: 93).

Whatever the legal cultural role, however, attorneys differ from many other suppliers of key services by offering legal advice and expertise. Lawyers are not mere go-betweens, distributing a commodity produced elsewhere. They are makers of law and the processes by which law is interpreted, applied, and directed.[5] As Maureen Cain (1994) and others have pointed out, lawyers create the systems of meaning that are the law and the profession, and these systems in turn mold the behavior and practices of legal actors. Legal practice is constitutive as well as constituted by the law. Moreover, attorneys are "important retailers of ideology" (Sugarman 1994: 199). Consumer's needs for the law are thus more than a product of individual aspirations or cultural or economic norms. The political and especially the legal cultures also help form consumer needs.

Lawyers deal with the uncertainties of a competitive market by organizing themselves into the distinctive economic association called a cartel. Like all cartels, the profession characteristically seeks to limit entry into the market for the services it provides. The profession is thus one form of lawful cartel, existing under the umbrella of governmental approval and regulation, empowered by the authority of the state to restrict competition and entry. Not only does the state authorize the profession's restrictive practices concerning who can offer legal advice and who can be admitted to the bar, the state also subsidizes legal practice with near exclusive access to courts of law.

Cartel is the proper label because the legal profession is neither a single dominant firm (a monopoly) nor is it a tight cluster of a few major firms (an oligopoly). A monopoly requires one seller, but the profession is not so monolithic that it can operate like a single firm. Nor is it an oligopoly. An oligopoly creates entry barriers imposing a cost on potential entrants into the market that do not affect the oligopoly itself.

As a cartel the profession must struggle with the problems that afflict all cartels. It is easier to effectively collude in a rising market than in a stagnant or declining one. When consumers become scarce or disinterested, cartels tend to turn in on themselves, the collegiality of mutual interest displaced by the antagonism of competing interests. Thus like all cartels, a profession struggles with members' incentives to cheat on each other. Competition among service providers generates conflicts over the constraints that limit the members' actions, affecting the prices and profits that the profession can extract from the market. As Michael Powell (1985) demonstrates, major changes within the American legal profession dealing with advertising, discipline, and ethical conduct are largely the result of competing groups within the profession rather than reformist efforts from outside it. Cartels must cope with the high costs of group decision making. These costs rise as the number in the group increases. The larger and more varied the membership, the more difficult it is to resolve conflicts within the profession over what are the appropriate practices of the profession.

Since private collusive agreements are hard to sustain, and incentives to cheat are high, cartels are inherently unstable, constantly threatening to disintegrate absent an external agent's intervention. In the search for predictability and control in its environment, a profession must turn to the support of the coercive authority of the state. Finally, cartels are most effective when they supply many small buyers rather than one or a few big buyers. Large buyers have an incentive to undermine collusion among sellers by offering inducements to sellers who will lower prices in expectation of high volume sales.

This purely economic understanding of a profession is insufficient to capture the dynamic of the legal profession as it actually is. It may fail to grasp the role of cultural expectations and institutional processes that affect both the needs that the profession satisfies and the processes by which the profession creates its commodities. Markets require needs and the capacity to meet those needs. But needs such as legal services do not have an objective existence apart from the culture within which the market operates. Needs are human desires, and the specific forms of such desires are largely learned, not inborn. The emergence of a transnational legal profession in the EU thus has ramifications that go beyond the way in which legal work is organized and provided. Legal practice embodies values and ideals that may conflict with the fundamental precepts of a society. Just as a commodity such as pesticides is a mixed blessing, costs accompanying the benefits of its use, so too the specific forms of legal practice pose threats as well as rewards to the cultures within which they are practiced. However, a simple economic model does offer insight into the emerging world market in legal services and how national bars are adapting or falling to it.

## TOWARD A "EUROPEAN" PROFESSION?

The 1957 Treaty of Rome compelled lawyers and bar associations in the European Union to struggle with the transformation wrought by lowered barriers to legal trading. Article 3 (c) calls for the abolition of obstacles to the free movement of services among EU member states and prohibits discrimination based upon nationality. Article 52 specifically requires removing restrictions on professional activities. Article 59 establishes the right to cross-border practices. Articles 54 and 57 (2) mandate that the Council of Ministers of the (now) European Union issues directives dealing with the recognition of credentials, degrees, and other qualifications for the professions. However, it was not until 1977 that the then European Community adopted the Lawyers' Services Directive (77/2491 EEC) permitting lawyers to offer cross-border services including legal advice on law in nations other than their own.

The major impetus to lowering barriers to transnational legal practice within the EU has come from the European Court of Justice (ECJ). The ECJ struck down restrictions on professional practices during the 1970s and early 1980s.[6] The passage of the Single European Act of 1986 added Article 8 (a) to the Treaty of Rome, set December 31, 1992, as the deadline for an internal market for goods and services within the Community. The Council of Ministers adopted the Directive on the Recognition of Higher Education Diplomas in 1989 (89/48/EEC, OJ 1989, L 19/16), establishing the universal recognition of professional qualifications. The so-called Diplomas Directive stipulated that a member of one member state bar must be admitted to another state bar without an examination if the legal systems in both states are similar. Attorneys from member-states with different legal systems must be admitted to the bar after taking a shortened version of the bar examination. In 1988 the CCBE adopted a common code of conduct applying to all cross-border legal practices in the EC.[7]

EU directives, court decisions and professional codes create the opportunity for a single market in legal services to develop. But pressures towards a single market go well beyond the borders of the EU. There are three international trends (following and adapting Abel 1994: 739–40) that help explain why transnational legal practice is growing and why it may be eroding the authority of traditional legal professions.

*1. Global companies demand new kinds of lawyering*

The development of the European Union creates a single market transforming the economics of legal practice. Multinational corporations find it convenient to work with the same legal firm on a European-wide basis. Corporations search for easy communication, uniform standards of service, and reliable quality. As legal and financial issues transcend borders, legal firms are forced to cross them as well.

*2. Supranational governments accompany supranational markets*

The emergence of "[s]upranational government generates a need to influence, interpret, and evade its regulatory grasp" (Abel 1994: 740). The actions of the EU government have profound and continuing impact on the market. EU regulations affect matters as diverse as insurance, consumer protection, the environment, and social issues. This has stimulated an informal bar specializing in EU law. EU regulations also affect domestic law as the member-states revise their own regulations. This additional layer of government creates new opportunities for attorneys to practice their special skills of interpretation, consultation, and litigation.

*3. Competitive domestic markets for legal services stimulate expansion into cross-border markets*

As competition intensifies within a domestic market, law firms are pushed to form national alliances. The new economies of scale and the access to volume litigation encourage national law firms to exploit their advantages by expanding into cross-border practice, where such advantages provide opportunities for financial gain.

European law firms have aggressively exploited new market opportunities by expanding into new localities either by establishing new branches or by mergers, joint ventures, or alliances with law firms in other nations. And it is characteristically the larger law firms that have reaped the greatest benefit from these alliances. A more competitive environment encourages bigness in law firms. The transnational practice of law stresses the expertise of firms, not of individual practitioners. Few individuals have the range of expertise to practice in multiple legal jurisdictions. A large law firm, on the other hand, can provide the broad range of expertise demanded by the sophisticated consumer.

The imperative of a free market is to compete or die. Some national bars have been more eager to exploit the new market for cross-border legal services than others, creating two classes, one "exporters" and the other "importers" of legal services. England and the Netherlands have been the most notable "exporters" in the EU. The ease with which these two sets of attorneys moved into the emerging market can be explained by precedent and management style. English attorneys were already familiar with structuring certain kinds of international commercial arrangements, given London's preeminence as the international financial center. The Dutch had The Hague and a century-long acquaintance with international public law to draw upon. But the Belgians, despite hosting the headquarters of the Union, were not as quick to adapt. Familiarity with transnational legal activities is not enough; special structures are needed to deal with the complexities of cross-border legal counsel. The English and the Dutch law firms adopted the American model of a large law firm with the resources to exploit the emerging market.

Market pressures are now prompting "importers"—nations who host more foreign attorneys than they export (Godfrey 1995: 13)—to liberalize their practices. Initially, France, Germany and Belgium responded to aggressive penetration of their home courts by protectionism. While the legal profession has a legitimate interest in protecting the public from incompetent lawyers, such an interest may mask a less legitimate motive to protect native industries from foreign competition. When the European Court of Justice and Commission pushed to open domestic markets to cross-border practice, Germany responded by insisting that the legal profession is "intimately involved" in the exercise of official authority and is therefore exempt under Article 55 of the Treaty of Rome from the demand for free market access. France passed legislation forbidding anyone not otherwise qualified as an attorney in France to provide legal advice even on EU law or the law of other nations. Even the English, despite their advocacy of a free market paradigm in cross-border practices, sought their own special exemptions. English solicitors are the sole administrators of estates and control transactions involving transfers of property in England. The English Law Society won an exemption of these activities from cross-border practice.

Persistent demands for liberalization, rising both from the EU and from important clients, eventually began to overcome these protectionist barriers. Belgium law firms were permitted to form joint ventures and cost-sharing alliances with foreign law firms in the late 1980s. In 1989 Germany permitted its attorneys to practice abroad, and during the early 1990s there was a rash of law firm mergers, the establishment of branches in several cities, and the approval of joint venture associations with foreign firms. In 1991 France officially merged its two separate legal professions, a reform that had been delayed by two decades of wrangling within the French professions.

Protectionist restrictions may be misguided and unnecessary. They may simply provide an opportunity for some breathing space, a short-term adjustment, permitting the national bars to adapt to the new market pressures. The real barrier to extensive cross-border practice is not restrictive regulations but how many attorneys actually are capable and willing to take up such practice. Few attorneys appear interested in taking advantage of the opportunities to become fully admitted members of legal associations other than their own.

Unless an attorney plans to spend the better part of his or her career in a foreign nation, few will seek full assimilation in their host country.

Significant barriers to a fully open European market in legal services persist. Some are practical barriers. Despite the convergence of some doctrines and practices, the four legal cultures of England, France, Belgium, and Germany continue to have profoundly different ways of thinking and learning about the law. The English emphasize legal history in the education of their attorneys, the French and German stress economics and public management. Each system has different substantive rules and procedures, different ways in which the law is argued and analyzed. To learn the law of a new nation is literally to learn a new language with its distinctive vocabulary, grammar, and underlying cultural preoccupations. The principal barriers are thus linguistic as well as legalistic.

These real and important differences have served to support a final barrier to the easy emergence of a free market in law—cultural nationalism. The argument that free trade in legal services fosters economic efficiency and growth has placed the national bars on the defensive. More damning, in the light of modern sensibilities about cultural integrity, members of legal professions in three of the four nations studied—Belgium, Germany, and France—argue that the law as a profession is different from other professions. They argue that engineering and, less persuasively, medicine rely upon universal physical principles that do not vary from culture to culture. The law, on the other hand, is a cultural artifact, made by and in turn molding a culture. The movement to a "European" lawyer, as opposed to a French, German, or Belgian one, is a misinformed one, some fear, because it rips attorneys from the cultural matrix that gives their profession form, substance, and authority.

Despite these differences, there are equally profound similarities in values, especially the respect for the rule of law, which can form the connective tissue of a transnational legal practice. Moreover, the member-states of the EU are largely advanced industrial democracies, capitalist in their economies, parliamentarian in their politics. These common fibers of economics and politics helped to bring about the fusion of the EU and may unite the legal professions within it.

## A CARTEL IMPERILED? IMPLICATIONS FOR THE PROFESSION

The impact of a single market on Europe has been significant. There have been strong pressures to harmonize national laws, either as a result of the promulgation of EU regulations and directives, or simply the effort by member-states to bring their laws into some rational relationship with their principal trading partners. There has been considerable loosening of bar regulations dealing with joint ventures, limited partnerships, and the establishment of branches, hitherto forbidden in most nations in the EU. And finally there has been increased litigation. Especially in areas such as consumer protection and environment, there has been a growth in EU legislative activity and, at the same time, plans to increase access to the courts by widening the availability of class and group action suits. The 1968 Brussels Convention on the Mutual Enforcement of Judgments has already introduced a measure of forum shopping. This inevitably leads to much greater cross-border consideration being required in litigation and eventually the need for coordination of litigation and regulatory action on a European scale.

The legal profession in the European Union confronts two major perils in this emerging single market: the threat of lost market shares to other professions and the threat of a deprofessionalized legal profession. Not only is the European single market encouraging competition among legal professionals, it is also attracting competition from other professions willing to offer legal services. Paralegals, accountants, bank officials, and tax advisers can use their expertise to insert themselves into activities currently controlled by attorneys. Accountants are especially threatening, since they are further along than lawyers are in the internationalization of their profession.

The second peril threatens not simply the income but the identity of the profession. As the market for legal services opens up to attorneys from throughout the Union, there is the possibility of deprofessionalization. An open market makes it difficult to monitor the behavior of professionals offering legal services. There exists no effective organization to monitor the competence or ethics of lawyers other than the current national bars. But domestic regulation is ineffective when dealing with cross-border transactions. If any nation is too demanding in its practices or ethical expectations, it faces the probability that firms or clients may move to jurisdictions less restrictive and better able to satisfy them. Even such a boundary-spanning institution as the CCBE, founded to coordinate national bar and legal societies' responses to the single market, has largely been ineffective in establishing monitoring mechanisms to enforce its 1988 common code of conduct or its 1992 directive on the right of establishment (see Godfrey 1995: 17–27). There is then an impetus toward the standardization of norms and services across the EU without a corresponding professional organization to monitor and regulate those norms and services.

The most profound changes may not simply be to dissolve national boundaries among legal professions, but to dissolve distinctions within the national bars themselves. France has removed the distinction between *avocats* and *conseils juridiques*. The English are discussing removing the distinction between solicitors and barristers. The German principle of localization of law practice is unlikely to persist since it handicaps German lawyers who can only appear before their local courts while EU attorneys are free to practice in any German court.

A final reason for deprofessionalization is that the legal profession is under pressure to become more overtly involved in politics. Legal professions have always sought the support of the state to buttress their authority and jurisdiction. But the ideology of professions, the argument that their claim to regulate themselves and to monitor the supply and quality of legal services in the marketplace, resists overtly politicized activities. The hallmark of a profession is independence from government and client. To become too closely identified with an explicit political agenda, to become too clearly a self-interested actor in the political process, threatens this hard-won independence. The dangers of attempts to re-impose strong professional associations through governmental rather than through market forces are that the defeat of deprofessionalization may bring with it the rise of a more politicized bar.

Pressures toward deprofessionalization come from outside as well as from within the profession. The transnational market supports a multinational corporate system. The presence of such big buyers offers incentives for cartels to cheat, especially since multinationals often operate on the presumption of economies of scale. The normal asymmetries of information and expertise that characterize law practice and which justify government regulation of doctors and lawyers are minimized in a large market. No longer do clients necessarily lack the knowledge or expertise to assess the quality of a specialist's services. Where in a small market consumers purchase services one at a time and lack the clout of organized consumption, in a large market large buyers can match the sellers in their expertise and organized power.

A transnational market generates sophisticated and informed consumers, well acquainted with the services they want and with definite expectations about their price and quality. This threatens the legal profession's cartel since big buyers' advantage is their routine involvement in similar transactions. Simply expanding the cartel so as to match big buyers with big (organized) sellers may not work. Bigness exacerbates the two key problems of cartel cohesion: group decision making costs and the presence of big buyers. The easy solution, expanding or consolidating national bars into a "supra" or transnational bar, may not work.

## CONCLUSIONS

We are still far from a truly global legal profession, at least in part because significant barriers still stand to an unfettered international trade in legal services. Transnational legal practice is not simply a matter of extending practices once confined to a nation's borders into other settings, nor is it a simple process of harmonizing divergent national practices. But the evidence from my interviews suggests that a transnational legal profession is emerging in the EU, but one sharply reduced in its capacity to control the market in legal services.

The competition to provide cross-border legal counsel had advantaged large, multinational law firms at the expense of small firms and solo practitioners. This is partially explained by the dominance of multinational corporations in the single market. National cartels are disrupted by the presence of big, well-informed and financed buyers. But large corporations are not the only consumers of transnational services. An English woman widowed by the passing of her Italian husband is obliged to settle an estate in two very different jurisdictions. A deprofessionalized transnational bar may not be able to protect a client's interest in such a situation. As larger buyers benefit from changes in the form and practice of legal services in the EU, smaller ones may be put at risk.

What is the future of the legal profession in the EU? Three patterns seem evident: the European attorney of tomorrow will confront a more fragmented profession, one with a greater stress on the commercial aspects of legal practice, in which greater breadth in training will be expected. Fragmentation is the expected product of a continuing struggle within and among legal bars over what ought to be the content and form of legal practice. Big buyers will stress economic rather than professional definitions of quality, further encouraging the contemporary shift from traditional professionalism to commercialism. As cross-border considerations loom larger in the everyday practice of law, attorneys will need to master more than the law of their home states. A single market will place a premium on specialization within the framework of versatility. Since few individual attorneys will be able to provide such breadth and depth by themselves, there will be a continued movement toward law firm mergers, joint agreements, and voluntary alliances.

The law profession's future in the EU is one of potential fraught with danger. As the EU promotes rights and trade across borders, national boundaries are likely to be less significant. Boundaries marking professional activity are also under assault. An attorney's authority depends in part on an attorney's capacity to lend authority to certain kinds of rights-claims. Changes in the market for legal services will inevitably affect the authority of attorneys and change the kinds of claims that are seen as authoritative.

## NOTES

1. Abel (1994: 738) notes that "transnational law practice is *numerically* [sic] a trivial component of all national legal professions. . ." However, Lonbay (1993: 410) reports that 98 percent of law firms on England's Law Society list undertook some kind

of transnational commercial work in 1992. The small number of attorneys actually engaged in such practice may misrepresent the extent to which such practice has affected the profession.

2. This chapter specifically excludes judges, law professors, and law students from its analysis.

3. How the United States will respond to this emerging transnational legal commerce is an important question. In 1965 only two U.S. law firms had offices in London. By 1992, more than half of the 100 largest U.S. firms had offices there. However, states such as Texas obstruct practice by foreign attorneys by requiring indemnity insurance that is almost impossible to obtain. This may explain why there is only one foreign attorney registered in Texas in 1993 as compared to over 170 in New York.

4. See Abel (1989: chapter 2) and Nelson and Trubek (1992: 15–17, 177–214) for a brief discussion of the Marxist, Weberian, and the structural functionalist approaches.

5. It is characteristic of a profession that it is more than a retailer of goods and services. Professions make as well as reflect and transmit the organizing values of their discipline. This is one way in which a scientist differs from a bricklayer. Each works with physical materials, but the scientist remakes the context and meaning of the materials of her discipline as an integral part of her tasks. A bricklayer can simply lay bricks along a pre-set pattern.

6. The key cases were *Jean Reyners v. The Belgian State* [1974] ECR 631, [1974] 2 CMLR 305; *Johannes Henricus Maria van Binsbergen v. Bestuur van de Bedrijfsvereniging voor de Metaalnijverheid* [1974] ECR 1299, [1975] 1 CMLR 298; *Jean Thieffry v. Conseil de l'ordre des avocats a la cour de Paris* [1977] ECR 765, [1977] 2 CMLR 373; *Van Ameyde v. UCI* [1977] ECR 1041; and *Ordre des Avocats au Barreau de Paris v. Onno Klopp* [1984] ECR 2971, [1985] 1 CMLR 99.

7. The full text of the "Code of Conduct for Lawyers in the European Community of October 28, 1988" can be found in the appendix to Toulmin (1992: 673).

# REFERENCES

Abel, Richard L. 1994. *American Lawyers*. New York: Oxford University Press, 1989.

———. "Transnational Legal Practice." *Case Western Reserve Law Review* 44(2) Winter: 737–870.

Berlant, Jeffrey L. 1975. *Profession and Monopoly: A Study of Medicine in the United States and Great Britain*. Berkeley: University of California Press.

Cain, Maureen. 1994. "The Symbol Traders," in *Lawyers in a Postmodern World: Translation and Transgression*, Maureen Cain and Christine B. Harrington. eds. New York: New York University Press, 15–48.

Godfrey, Edwin. 1995. "The European Union," in *Law Without Frontiers: A Comparative Survey of the Rules of Professional Ethics Applicable to the Cross-Border Practice of Law*, Edwin Godfrey, ed. London: Kluwer Law International, 12–27.

Larson, Magali S. 1977. *The Rise of Professionalism: A Sociological Analysis*. Berkeley: University of California Press.

Lasok, D. and J. W. Bridge. 1991. *Law and Institutions of the European Community*. 5th ed. London: Butterworth.

Lonbay, Julian. 1993. "Basic Competence in EC Law for All Lawyers." *European Law Review* 10(5) October: 408–16.

Macaulay, Stewart. 1979. "Lawyers and Consumer Protection Laws." *Law and Society Review* 14: 115–71.

Nelson, Robert L. and David M. Trubek. 1992. "New Problems and Paradigms in Studies of the Legal Profession" and "Arenas of Professionalism: The Professional Ideologies of Lawyers in Context," in *Lawyers' Ideals/Lawyers' Practices*, Robert L. Nelson, David M. Trubek, and Rayman L. Solomon, eds. Ithaca, N.Y.: Cornell University Press, 1–28, 177–214.

Powell, Michael. 1985. "Developments in the Regulation of Lawyers: Competing Segments and Market, Client and Government Control." *Social Forces* 64: 281–305.

Spedding, Linda S. 1987. *Transnational Legal Practice in the EEC and the United States*. Dobbs Ferry: International Publications.

Sugarman, David. 1994. "Blurred Boundaries: The Overlapping Worlds of Law, Business and Politics," in Maureen Cain and Christine B. Harrington, eds., *Lawyers in a Postmodern World: Translation and Transgression*. New York: New York University Press, 105–23.

Toulmin, John.1992. "A Worldwide Common Code of Professional Ethics." *Fordham International Law Journal* 15(3) Spring.

Waddington, I. 1985. "Professions," in *The Social Science Encyclopedia*, Adam and Jessica Kuper, eds. London: Routledge and Kegan Paul, 1985.

Weber, Max. 1978. *Economy and Society*. Berkeley: University of California Press.

# VII

## PEACE, PROSPERITY, AND DEMOCRACY

# 13

# Violent Conflict, Security, and Development

*Yannis A. Stivachtis*

The relationship between violent conflict, security, and development did not appear as an independent item on the research agenda until the end of the Cold War. Up to then the subject had come up most indirectly during the consideration of other issues, notably the North-South relations. In the 1960s and 1970s, the North-South debate was about the effects of neo-colonialism and neo-imperialism. Later, the North-South dialogue aimed at defining the bases of the New International Economic Order.[1] An issue that was regularly touched upon during these years was the effect which defense expenditures had on economic growth.

From the early 1970s onwards, a new debate appeared regarding the advisability of expanding the term "security" to include political, economic, societal, and environmental components, while discussion about conflict led to the broadening of the concepts of "violence" (structural violence) and "peace" (positive rather than negative peace). In the 1980s, two ideas gained prominence in international thinking about development: that of "sustainable development" and that of the "right to development." The former has become particularly fashionable since its use in the Brundtland Report (1987), and the latter received its formal launch in the United Nations *Declaration on the Right to Development* (1986).

Despite its current importance, the relationship between violent conflict, security, and development has not been adequately examined. The purpose of this study is, therefore, to investigate how these concepts are related to one another. It seeks to answer questions like: are security and development similar, identical, or different concepts? If they are not identical then, what are the differences between them? When we speak of security and development, whose security and development do we refer to? To those of the state and its élites, or to those of the individuals who compose it? Does development imply necessarily the absence of violent conflict or under certain conditions, may it lead to violent conflict instead of preventing it? What lessons can be drawn from the relationship between violent conflict, security and development?

## VIOLENT CONFLICT, SECURITY, AND DEVELOPMENT IN THE POST–COLD WAR ERA

The threat of nuclear war between the two superpowers and their respective allies dominated the international security agenda during the Cold War. Although there was always a potential for a direct military confrontation between East and West, no such conflict actually took place. However, there was an actual and indirect battleground in the Third World where military conflict took the form of the so-called proxy wars.[2]

Although the Soviet/Russian-American confrontation has ended or, as some believe, temporarily suspended, the Third World has experienced a new wave of collective violence, not so much between but within states. Domestic conflicts, like those of Afghanistan, Angola, Liberia, Rwanda, Somalia, Sri Lanka, Sudan, and the former Zaire, have severely damaged the physical and institutional bases of those states and deeply divided their indigenous societies. Beyond death and destruction, these conflicts have left behind a legacy of deep and enduring social, political, and psychological wounds, and impeded future development.

Often such events are described as ethnic or religious conflicts. However, there are ethnic groups with far more substantial cultural differences who have been living together peacefully for years. It is true that ethnicity, culture, and religion can be important factors in the mobilization of political violence. But factors of a quite different nature can also increase a country's susceptibility to conflict. Such factors are related to economics; to politics; to the rule of law; to the role of the military and the police; to questions regarding refugees and internally displaced persons; and the history of earlier inter- and intra-state violence.

In current intra-state violence there is a common factor of a striking nature: almost all of these conflicts are taking place in the developing countries of the Third World.[3] On the other hand, armed conflicts, both inter- and intra-state, have been almost absent in the so-called "First" or "Industrialized World." How can this difference be explained? Current international political thinking concerning conflict, peace, and security focuses on political, social, and economic development as a means of preventing, managing, and resolving both inter- and intra-state conflict in the Third World.

## STUDYING THE THIRD WORLD: THEORETICAL PROBLEMS

The main problem in theorizing about security and development in the Third World is that the states that are included in this category have widely divergent social, economic, and political attributes.[4] This diversity has important implications for policy making in Third World countries because it implies the absence of a unique policy formula that could apply without distinction to any Third World state.

There are three difficulties related to this theorization.[5] First, it is the lack of agreement and precision in respect to the attributes that define the Third World. In other words, by what criteria are states assigned to this category? It is argued that traditional society, rather than being conceptualized in its own right, and thereby giving traditional states something in common by definition, is treated as a residual category.[6] Thus any society that is not modern is called traditional. This creates a diverse category of systems that do not necessarily share anything in common other than the fact that they do not belong to the other category. In fact, many Third World states operate with political forms associated with the absence of modernity, while possessing a modern industrial base and advanced technology.[7] Problems related to the traditional/modern dichotomy have been further enhanced by the failure of the relevant literature to distinguish the social, economic, and political dimensions of modernity.[8]

A second difficulty is the invalidity of the assumption that any or all of the dimensions mentioned above constitute mutually exclusive dichotomies in the sense that states are either purely modern or purely traditional by one of these criteria. Actually, all states possess some elements of traditionalism and some elements of modernity, and are more modern along some dimensions than along others. Similarly, it has been suggested that traditional societies are characterized by the lack of integration and of a united communication system.[9] But sociopolitical segmentation characterizes a number of Western states like Belgium and Canada. Moreover, it has been shown that the process of assimilation into a general culture is imperfect in any system.[10] Finally, it has been asserted that traditional systems have a more ideological political style.[11] Although this may be true, rather than the dichotomy of modern versus traditional, more scholars prefer to think of this dimension as a continuum of more or less modern.

A third difficulty is the confusion created by the distinct yet related dimensions of the development process. Although it is difficult to dispute the idea that the distinction between development and modernization is difficult to justify, the distinction between political development or modernization, social development, and economic development is important.[12] This distinction will be examined in detail later on.

## THE CONCEPT OF "VIOLENT CONFLICT"

In examining the relationship between violent conflict, security, and development, a methodological problem arises that concerns the definition of the term "conflict." If the concept is defined as a difference of opinion with regard to the allocation of values within a particular society, then the concept is anything but objectionable. In fact, conflict is an important element of any democratic system. Thus, in this study, conflict will be related to the use of violence as a means for imposing a particular type of political order and the values associated with it.

But having opted for this approach, it must be then decided whether violent conflict is confined to large-scale violence (wars), or even to smaller explosions of violence. Indeed, one of the major issues in conflict research is the question of whether the causes of limited conflicts differ from those of larger ones, and whether it would be true to say that any limited conflict may be expected to escalate. In this study, violent conflict will encompass both large- and small-scale violent disputes. The reason for this is that in the Third World the absence or weaknesses of state institutions to manage tensions within society can easily provide the fertile ground for the escalation of a small-scale dispute to a large-scale violent conflict.

Finally, another choice that must be made concerns the advisability of concentrating exclusively on violence orchestrated by organized groupings against one another. In everyday political discourse, genocide, and communal violence are more and more often mentioned in the same breath as war and civil war. Due to the nature of the Third World state, violent conflict will refer to all types of violent disputes orchestrated either by organized groups or by the governments themselves.

Obviously, violent conflict works both against development and security. But if the relationship between violent conflict on the one hand, and security and development on the other, is easy to understand, the same does not apply to the complex relationship between security and development. The primary cause of this complexity is the way in which the terms "security" and "development" are defined. Because both concepts appear to be catchall terms, they are open to a wide variety of interpretations. Thus searching for relationships between them is a difficult and complicated task. For understanding these relationships, however, the examination of each of these concepts is imperative.

## DEFINING SECURITY

The answer to what makes something a security problem has been a subject of academic debate for almost thirty years.[13] In fact, there are two main views about security: the new one of the wideners and the old military and state-centered view of the traditionalists.[14] The former grew out of dissatisfaction with the narrowing of the field of security studies imposed by the military logic of the Cold War. It has been, therefore, argued that concerns about military security traditionally masked underlying issues of political, economic, and societal threats.[15] Although military threats remain important for security thinking, other types of threats have risen in importance. At the same time, higher density of human activity and interaction has increased both interdependence and awareness of events worldwide.[16]

To make justice, however, to the above views of security a third and more provocative one should be added; that of critical theory and postmodernism that is rooted in a distinct philosophical tradition that intends to challenge established outlooks.[17] For critical theory and postmodernism, all politics, including international politics, is open-ended and based on ethics. This stands in sharp contrast to the limited horizons and claimed objectivity of Realism.[18] Critical theory and postmodernism, therefore, seek to move the theory and practice of security out of the traditional realist grip into the different philosophical and operational camp. The highest value of these theoretical approaches is emancipation. The latter will lead to significantly different policies from those associated with power and order. This implies that the security problematique should be re-thought. The aim is to undertake political action to extend the moral communities with which individuals identify in the modern world. Although critical theory and postmodernism come theoretically closer to the wider view of security, they do not identify themselves with it. Hence they should be treated as a distinctive theoretical approach.

Most recently, a comprehensive framework for security analysis has been constructed and advocated by Barry Buzan and his colleagues. It is based on the wider security agenda and incorporates both the traditionalist position and some theoretical elements associated with critical theory and postmodernism.[19] It is on this approach that the present study is based.

In the traditional military-political understanding of the concept, security is about survival. As Buzan argues, security questions arise when issues are presented as posing existential threats to a designated referent object such as the state or a particular government.[20] Whatever the referent object is, the special nature of security threats justifies the use of extraordinary measures to handle them. Existential threat, according to the wider security agenda, can only be understood in relation to the particular character of the referent object in question. In other words, the wideners do not accept the existence of a universal standard based on what threatens individual human life.

For Buzan, the precondition for understanding security requires a wide-ranging understanding of the major levels of analysis and issue sectors that comprise the field of International Relations. Although the term security suggests a phenomenon on the state level, the connections between that level and the individual and international system levels are too numerous and too strong to deny. Similarly, although security suggests a focus in the political and military sectors, where the state is most strongly established, the idea cannot be properly comprehended without bringing in the actors and dynamics from the societal, economic, and environmental sectors.[21] According to Buzan, the concept of security binds together these levels and sectors so closely that it demands to be treated in an integrative perspective. Attempts to treat security as if it was confined to any single level or any single sector invite serious distortions of understanding.[22]

According to the comprehensive security perspective, the dynamics of national security are highly relational and interdependent between states.[23] This implies that individual national securities can be only fully understood when considered in relation both to each other, and to larger patterns of relations in the international system as a whole. The tension and interplay between anarchy and interdependence are major elements in the conditions that define international security. As Buzan suggests, the prospects for international security "have to be located within the complex dialectic which results from the dividing tendencies of anarchy interacting with the binding ones of interdependence."[24]

The logics of anarchy and interdependence are both at work in the international system. The logic of anarchy focuses on the competitive nature of the anarchic international system and claims that states have to look after themselves and that their security is their highest priority. On the other hand, interdependence focuses attention to the specific conditions that shape the way in which states interact with each other. It points to issues where international linkages are so strong that independent action by one state cannot avoid engaging the concern of the others.[25]

According to Buzan, the principal driving force behind interdependence is the rising density of the interaction networks that tie the international system together.[26] The principal political impact of rising density is to increase the levels of interdependence among states across a broad spectrum. In the economic sphere, states depend for their prosperity on complex patterns of access to markets, resources, and credit. In the environmental sphere, they increasingly depend on each other to adopt restraint towards environmentally damaging activities.[27] In the societal level, they are aware of the fact that their actions may pose threats to patterns of communal identity and culture within or beyond their borders.

The rising density of the international system creates a very powerful interplay between anarchy and interdependence. The linkage between the structure of political fragmentation on the one hand, and the rising tide of mutually consequential activities in several sectors on the other, create common fates and security interdependencies across a wide range of issues. In this respect, the national security problem turns out to be a systemic security problem in which individuals, states, and the international system all play a part, and in which economic, societal, and environmental factors are as important as political and military ones.

### Security for Whom?

According to Buzan, security at the state level is defined both internally and externally. This means that a state can be threatened equally from within and outside. Although external security can be quite easily understood, internal security requires more clarification. Focusing on internal security, Buzan asserts that the sociopolitical cohesion of states is extremely significant for understanding their insecurity.[28] In so doing, he introduces the notion of "weak" state. Whether a state is weak or strong in terms of its sociopolitical cohesion has little to do with whether it is weak or strong as a power.[29]

According to Buzan's framework, state security can be identified at two different though inter-related levels: the regime and the strategic or international levels. Security at the regime level is defined in terms of the capacity of a government to protect itself from domestic disorder or revolt. A state can be threatened from below (by individualistic or organizational pressures on the regime) and from above (by oppressive or threatening governmental initiative, policy or action). Strategic security, on the other hand, is identified as the ability of the state to defend itself from external coercion, attack or invasion.[30] Thus when we speak of security we refer not only to the security of the state and its government, but also to the security of the individuals who compose it.

Due to their sociopolitical cohesion, weak states face great insecurity at the regime level. This implies that the degree of a state's political, societal and economic development is an important determinant of its domestic security. As a consequence, a first link between security and development is established.

Whether weak states face insecurity at the regime level is not only crucial to their own security, but also to that of the regions within which they are located. The international anarchy is a decentralized system of order and, therefore, depends for its stability on the stability of its components units (states). Weak states are problematic for international order because their internal politics are often violent, and their domestic insecurity often spills over to disrupt the security of the neighboring states. Moreover, weak states can easily attract competitive outside intervention, as well as serve as targets to opportunistic aggressors. Thus states' sociopolitical cohesion is a fundamental factor because it shows whether they are capable of dealing with or are vulnerable to domestic and international pressures resulting from the inter-play between anarchy and interdependence.

## Types of Security Problems

Buzan has identified five security sectors: military, political, economic, so-cietal and environmental.[31] In the military sector, the referent object is mainly the state. Military action usually threatens all the components of state. It can, for instance, repress the idea of state, subject its physical base to strain and damage and destroy its various national institutions. According to Buzan, military actions not only strike the state's basic protective functions, but also threatens damage deep down through the layers of social and individual in-terest that underlie, and are more permanent than, the state's superstruc-tures.[32] Human achievements can be threatened, while a defeated society is in the mercy of the conqueror's power. Thus military insecurity can jeopard-ize any development process, and this is the reason for which military threats are traditionally accorded the highest priority in national security concerns.

While in the military sector threats are mainly external to the state, in the political sector a state may be threatened both internally and externally. In-ternal threats may arise as a result of governmental actions that pose major threats to individual citizens or groups. Resistance to the government, efforts to overthrow it or movements aimed at autonomy or independence all threaten state stability and enhance state insecurity. Since political develop-ment is an important determinant for the internal security of the state, the linkage between security and development is confirmed.

External threats, on the other hand, are traditionally defined in terms of the constituting principle, that is sovereignty, but it is also possible to be defined in terms of the ideology of the state. Political threats are aimed at the orga-nizational stability of the state. Their purpose varies from pressuring the gov-ernment on a particular issue to disrupting the political functions of the state so as to weaken it prior to military attack.

The idea of state, particularly its national identity and organizing ideology, and the institutions that express it, are the usual targets of political threats. The latter stem from the great diversity of ideas and traditions. Because con-tradictions in ideologies are basic, states of one persuasion may well feel threatened by the ideas represented by others. Threats to national identity, for instance, may involve attempts to heighten the separate ethno-cultural identities of groups within the target-state. Thus an external threat can be transformed into an internal one.

Political threats may be intentional or may arise structurally from the im-pact of foreign alternatives on the legitimacy of the state. Such threats may come into existence when the organizing principles of two states contradict each other in a context where the states cannot ignore each other's existence. In other words, where the achievements of one state automatically erodes the political stature of another, this often leads to more intentional forms of political threats. Since the state is an essentially political entity, political threats may be as much feared as military ones. However, the degree to which external political threats can be successfully applied is determined by a state's political development.

In the economic sector, the referent objects and existential threats are more difficult to pin down.[33] The main problem with the idea of economic security is that the normal condition of actors in a market economy is one of risk, competition and uncertainty. In today's world, the market stands as the dominant model for sound economic practice. In order to function efficiently, however, markets must impose continuous threats of failure. In other words, the actors in the market economy have to be insecure if the system as a whole is to operate effectively. But if actors must be insecure then what does economic security mean in the market context?

Within the market system, therefore, a significant number of economic threats exist which cannot reasonably be construed as threats to national security. Although national economy as a whole may serve as an alternative reference object and may thus have a greater claim to survival, only rarely can a threat to that survival actually arise. However, when the consequences of economic threat reach beyond the strictly economic sector, into military and political spheres, then three somewhat clearer national security issues can emerge. The linkages involved are between economic capability on the one hand, and military capability, power and sociopolitical stability on the other.[34]

A state's military capability rests both on the supply of key strategic materials and the possession of an industrial base capable of supporting the armed forces. When strategic materials must be obtained outside the state, threat to security of supply can be seen as a national security issue. Similarly, an economic decline of basic industries raises questions about the ability of the state to support independent military production. The desire to maintain or acquire production capability in key militarily related industries may easily insert a national security requirement into the management of the national economy. The process can also work in the other direction when the pursuit of military research and development prevents investment in the civil economy.[35]

Economic threats may also enhance domestic instability, especially when states pursue economic strategies based on maximization of wealth through excessive trade. Where complex patterns of interdependence exist, many states will be vulnerable to disruptions in the flows of trade and finance.[36] The link between economy and political stability generates a set of questions about development that could be seen as national security issues. For developed states, for instance, the concern is that because socioeconomic structures have come to depend on sustained growth rates and functional

specialization, domestic political stability may be undermined by distur-
bances in the economic systems as a whole. Less developed states, on the
other hand, because they are less efficient producers, may find themselves
locked into a cycle of poverty and underdevelopment from which there is
no obvious escape. For example, Third World governments may find themselves having to choose between meeting their debt payments at the expense of lowering the already very low living standards. This points to another strong relationship between security on the one side, and political and
economic development on the other.

Economic threats may be also viewed as an attack on the state, in the
sense that conscious external actions by other states result in material loss,
strain on various institutions of the state, and even substantial damage to the
health and longevity of the population. In this context, economic threats
raise concerns about the overall power of the state within the international
system. If the economy declines, then the state's power also declines.[37]

Finally, economic threats raise the dilemma of distinguishing between domestic politics and national security. In other words, are other actors or the
economic system as a whole to blame, or do the causes of weak economic
performance lie more within states and societies? If the answer is domestic,
then it raises questions of whether organizing ideologies are being improperly
implemented, or they are basically flawed and their modification is required
as a response. This question is also raised with reference to development.

In the societal sector, the referent object is collective identities that can
function independent of the state, such as religions and nations. In relations
between states, significant external threats on the societal level are often part
of a larger package of military and political threats, such as those faced by Israel from the Arab states. Therefore, societal threats can be difficult to disen-
tangle from political or military ones. At lower levels of intensity, even the
interplay of ideas and communication may produce politically significant societal and cultural threats, as illustrated by the reaction of Islamic fundamen-
talists to the penetration of Western ideas. Language, religion, and local cultural tradition all play their part in the idea of state, and may need to be
defended or protected against cultural imports. If the local culture is weak,
even the unintended side effects of casual contact could prove disruptive
and politically charged.[38]

As in the political sector, threats in the societal sector may arise from the internal or external environment of the state, while an internal threat may be
transformed into an external one and *vice versa*. Moreover, if societal security
is about the sustainability of traditional patterns of language, culture, and religious and ethnic identity and custom, then threats to these values come much
more frequently from within the states than outside them. The state-nation
building process often aims at suppressing, or at least homogenizing, substate social identities as many examples suggest. As a result, internal societal

threats may precipitate conflict between states if the latter wish to protect groups of people with whom they have close affinities and who find themselves in a state that suppresses their rights. However, it is the level of their political and economic development that determines the extent to which states are vulnerable to societal threats. A state that is economically and politically advanced is less likely to face societal threats than a less developed state. Thus another link is established between security and development.

In the environmental sector, the range of possible referent objects is large. The basic concerns, however, are how human beings and the rest of the biosphere are related, and whether this relationship can be sustained without risking a collapse of the achieved levels of civilization and/or the disruption of the planet's biological legacy.[39] Environmental threats to national security, like military and economic ones, can damage the physical base of the state, perhaps to a sufficient extent to threaten its idea and institutions. Some environmental threats, for instance, such as pollution, water distribution and deforestation, link activities within one state to effects in another. Traditionally, such threats have been seen more as matter of fate than a national security issue.

However, the increase of human activity is beginning visibly to affect the conditions for life on the planet. This puts environmental issues more and more into the political arena. At the same time, a linkage between environmental security and development is established whenever the development process affects positively or negatively the environment.

## THE CONCEPT OF "DEVELOPMENT"

Because the very concept of development is a site of struggle there is a variety of definitions and interpretations. The Western concept of development, for example, is often used as a synonym for modernization. Used in this way, development theory can be seen as an intellectual outgrowth of the idea of progress. Very often development also receives negative definitions.[40] Underdevelopment is present in a society in which a number of mutually reinforcing evils are present, such as high rates of infant mortality, low rates of productivity, poor provision of health care and educational opportunities, and poverty. In this context, development implies efforts to move away from this cycle of evils.

Different disciplines also provide different interpretations of development. Economists, for example, emphasize changes in patterns of production and distribution, consumption, and investment. Various economic conceptual schemes place countries on a developmental continuum, classifying them according to a level of economic development or prevailing mode of production. Different economic studies share the assumption that economic development

leads to physical well being derived from the increasingly efficient organization and mechanization of production. This process is usually viewed as in-
separable from social and political modernization.[41]

Anthropologists and sociologists stress sociocultural aspects of development such as values, beliefs, taboos, attitudes and orientations and focus on
interpersonal and group relations. They believe that economic development
reflects a state of mind that it is essentially psychological and cultural.[42] They
suggest that personality structures conditioned by social and cultural norms
must change from within for development to be possible. Thus the solution
to the problem of underdevelopment lies in changing the psychology and
the culture of the society, as well as its political rules. To induce such
changes, these theorists often call for stepped-up foreign aid, trade and investment, and the introduction of modern technology.[43] A country that
absorbs Western products and capital will modernize not only its means of
production but also its consumption patterns and lifestyle. Greater popular
participation is likely to follow. This, in turn, will both galvanize the society
and spur the government to higher standards of performance.

Dealing with development, various disciplines, ranging from the traditional philosophy to modern behavioral sciences, have shed light on the
phenomenon of political development. The latter, however, means different
things to different people. One reason is that concepts of development often
conceal normative assumptions and assertions. Normative theorists, for instance, make moral choices: freedom over order, equality over liberty and so
on. On the basis of these choices, they prescribe developmental models and
policies designed to produce the type of society they prefer. Political systems
that manifest the traits they value most highly are labeled progressive or developed; regimes that display the opposite traits may be labeled traditional,
primitive, regressive, despotic, or reactionary.

Plato, for example, believed that a state constructed along the lines he proposed in *The Republic* would be perfect, and therefore any change or political development would be change for worse—regressive than progressive.
Some of Plato's ideas have been useful to founders of new states. For example, Plato's ideal society was predicated on a myth that Plato preferred to call
a "noble lie."[44] Plato understood that, without such a myth, it would not be
possible to preserve and perpetuate his ideal society. But just as Plato con-
templated the use of a noble lie to prevent development, the leaders of developing countries often use an emotionally appealing oversimplification,
such as anti-colonialism, nationalism, and pan-Arabism, to "promote" development.

Recently, Plato's ideas are re-advocated by Steven Chilton who posits the
evolution of a universal moral philosophy.[45] In his view, as people mature,
their capacity to engage in abstract moral reasoning increases. Some individuals, however, have a greater ability to engage in such reasoning than

others do. Political systems that manage to put these gifted individuals into leadership and policy-making positions are most likely to develop in accordance with universal moral values.

Finally, development has been an important subject for political scientists and political economists. The former focuses mainly on changes in patterns of power and authority. As societies develop, how do power relationships change? What new institutions emerge? What old ones disappear? What is gained and what is lost? How is political stability affected? What is the relationship between political development and economic development? Are certain kinds of government more suitable for developing societies than others? Is there a close correlation between regime type and economic development?

For political economists, politics and economics are viewed as two sides of the same coin. They therefore combine the disciplines of economics and political science and their respective analytical tools. The study of political economy is logical because global and national markets are never free of state intervention and regulation.

From the perspective of political economy, economic inequality among states and regions is a stark fact of international political life. The systemic causes for underdevelopment are more difficult to identify and more controversial. [46] The International Monetary Fund (IMF) has pointed to structural problems within many of the debtor nations' economies (hyperinflation, chronic budget deficits, high arms spending, capital flight, and a porous tax collections system). The traditional Third World perspective stands in sharp contrast to that of IMF. It is a mixture of ideas drawn from the writings of Marx and Lenin and more recent works by scholars who subscribe to a school of thought known as dependency theory.

Dependency theorists start with the proposition that the world has finite resources. The world, they contend, is divided into three basic classes: the industrial core, the semi-periphery and the periphery. The states of periphery and semi-periphery are dependent on the industrial core for markets, capital, and technology. The industrial states have a vested interest in perpetuating this state of dependency and keeping the periphery and semi-periphery underdeveloped.

The dependency system has several salient features. First, the core states produce expensive manufactured goods, and the peripheral states supply cheap raw materials. The price structure is manipulated by the dominant economic powers. The terms of trade thus heavily favor the core states. Commodity prices fluctuate widely and many developing countries are dependent on the export of one or two commodities. Thus export revenues are extremely sensitive to price fluctuations beyond the control of the exporting countries. But the developing countries must continue to import and must pay for imports with hard currency (foreign reserves). Often they must borrow, with no option but to pay whatever interest rates international financiers in the core states choose to charge. Further, if they seek foreign aid, they are forced to accept all the strings attached. Finally, in a crisis, they are left with little choice but to accept the conditions imposed by the IMF for short-term loans. Called "conditionality," this practice of imposing austerity measures has been a major bone of contention in the North-South conflict.

An especially insidious aspect of this whole system is the collusion between capitalists in the core states and a small economic élite in the peripheral states. This élite typically profits enormously from the arrangement, but it is mutually beneficial: the core states back regimes, which maintain order and stability and ensure access to domestic markets. Grants of military and economic aid, seen in this light, are payoffs and props that reap larger dividends for the donor states than for the recipients in part because corrupt rulers often siphon most of the funds.

However, not all political economists embrace dependency theory. Particularly in the West, development scholars tend to blame the developing nations themselves for most of their problems and argue that these states must find their own solutions. They stress that weak institutions, corrupt or incompetent leaders, and chronic sociopolitical instability have plagued many developing states. Hence the path to economic development is essentially political.

Political instability is thus regarded as the bane of economic health and social progress. Instability takes a variety of forms, including military coups, riots, and insurgencies. Its economic consequences are numerous, including disruption of communications and transport, diversion of scarce resources to internal security needs, and large-scale capital flight. Instability is anathema to investors. Political failure leads to economic failure, but the reverse is also true. Poverty begets instability by undermining economic development.

## Development for Whom?

Traditionally, political theorists have usually assumed that sovereign states are here to stay. They have therefore embraced ideas that have far-reaching implications for theories of political development. Thomas Hobbes, for instance, believed that life in the state of nature would be "solitary, poor, nasty, brutish and short."[47] An imposing state was thus necessary to "overawe" the masses and maintain order and stability. Societies that lacked such a strong state were, by definition, politically underdeveloped. Likewise, Friedrich Hegel argued that the nation-state represented the highest stage of development in world history. His famous dictum that "what is real is rational and only the rational is real" has a special relevance here. Hegel thought that the nation-state most closely approached true reality because it was the most rational organization.[48]

Not surprisingly, therefore, the modern state provides the framework for most models of development. Thus the latter has been equated with the economic improvement of the state, and the way to achieve economic growth has been through modernization (industrialization, advanced technology, and modern bureaucratic and economic mechanisms). This implies two things. First, the concept of development applies mainly to the state in general and its élites and not to the total sum of its citizens. And second, development does not, in principle, apply to the international level though it may be conditioned by international developments.

However, not all political theorists regarded the existence of state as a prerequisite for development. Indeed, Rousseau took exactly the opposite view: that the modern state represented political degeneracy, not progress. "Man is born free," he declared, and "everywhere he is in chains." Rousseau believed that human beings are also born innocent but are soon corrupted by society. He decried the institution of private property and viewed political systems as elaborate devices for perpetuating inequality based on property ownership. For Rousseau, the removal of the political and social props that both support the existing system and create a culture of greed and self-aggrandizement is necessary in order for the natural goodness of human beings to blossom.

Karl Marx provided the basis for another theory of political development. His concept of the "withering away of the state" holds that, as societies evolve, government will eventually become superfluous. The need for coercive political institutions to control society will disappear. Under socialism, society's members will internalize collective values rather than the individualistic values associated with capitalism. What we know as government will be replaced by the "administration of things."

A contemporary version of this idea has been espoused by sociologist James Davies.[49] In his view, the best-developed societies are those whose members most universally and thoroughly internalize rules associated with sharing and fair play. He argues that governments arose to combat anarchy and will be replaced by mere administration as societies evolve to a level where everyone internalizes the rules.

More recently, John Herz has propounded the theory that political units expand in response to the changing security needs of society.[50] When these needs could be satisfied by the family, clan, or tribe, there was no need for the modern state. But when traditional forms of sociopolitical organization were no longer adequate for protection, they were replaced by the modern nation-state. Herz has argued that the nation-state is now inadequate because of such new threats as nuclear war and ecological disaster and that only world government can deal effectively with these new challenges. Hence the next major stage of political development must go beyond the nation-state to establish a new global order.

However, one can question whether world government is in fact necessary. Evidence is mounting that nation-states are becoming increasingly interdependent. Evidence also suggests that the most plausible alternative to the nation-state may be regional rather than global government. Thus the success of the European Union is expected to spur intensified efforts at regional integration elsewhere. In any case, progress and development are no longer automatically set in the context of the modern state.

The ease of superpower relations in the second half of the 1980s and the subsequent end of the Cold War have allowed the identification of development with human security.[51] For instance, the *Declaration on the Right to Development* asserts that all human beings have a human right to development and that "development is a comprehensive economic, social, cultural and political process, which aims at the constant improvement of the well-being of the entire population and of all its individuals on the basis of their active, free and meaningful participation in development and in the fair distribution of benefits resulting therefrom."[52] Development is therefore viewed as encompassing those processes of change which result in an increase in life chances, notably life expectancy and quality of life, and thus give more and more people the opportunity to live a decent life.

Development has been consequently subdivided into several sectors, such as political security, economic security, environmental security, societal security, individual security, etc.[53] This has two important implications. First, development, like security, is subdivided into several sectors, many of which are identical with the respective security sectors. This means that security and development can, to a great extent, be operationalized in the same way.[54] And second, development refers not to states in general but most importantly, to the sum of the individuals who compose them. In this context, development can be defined as "the increasing capacity to make rational use of natural and human resources for social ends."[55] The focus on human development has made it possible to speak both about intra-state and international development.

If the economic gap separating rich and poor states is unbridgeable, does this mean that development is an unreachable target for 80 percent of humanity? Or is a more broadening understanding of development needed to move beyond the classical materialistic definition of it as accumulation of wealth?

It has been recognized that development cannot be simply about economic growth. For there are countries in which economic growth occurs and the Gross National Product (GNP) increases, but certain other things do not occur, like improvements for the very poor, or maintenance of civil liberties and democratic freedoms. Moreover, evidence shows that the human dimension of security is often much brighter than the economic. The fact that the gap in human disparity between North and South has narrowed, even as the economic gap between them has widened, points to the need for an establishment of a much wider understanding of development.

## Aspects of Development

Although it gained prominence in the second half of the 1980s, the human dimension of development first gained attention in the 1970s, partly in response to the growing popularity of dependency theory. To address the root structural causes of underdevelopment by reducing the dominance-dependence relationship between rich and poor states, the World Bank and foreign aid donors sought ways for foreign aid recipients to improve the lives of their citizens. Advocates of a "basic human needs" approach argue that the effects predicted by classical economic development theory have failed to materialize because of official corruption and other barriers to growth.

The "basic human needs" perspective required new ways to measure development beyond those focusing exclusively on economic indicators. Eventually the United Nations Development Programme (UNDP) constructed a human development index (HDI) to measure states' comparative ability to provide for citizens' well being. Successive *Human Development Reports* have provoked fresh debate about the meaning of human development in national and international forums including the 1992 UN Conference on Environment and Development, the 1994 UN Conference on Population and Development, and the 1995 World Summit for Social Development. The UNDP's human development index refers not only to economic factors but also environment, politics, and social welfare. Although growth is not viewed as the end of development, the absence of growth often is.

Under these conditions, the fertile ground for the redefinition of the concept of development and the examination of its relation with the concept of security was provided.

Political scientists have attempted to evaluate and compare the performance of different political systems by looking at goal-attainment capabilities and success in extracting and distributing resources or regulating social, economic, and political activity. Societies are often proclaimed to be developed and modern to the degree that they are able to perform such functions. Political instability and economic stagnation are therefore often cited as evidence that Third World states are underdeveloped and therefore incapable of managing society so as to extract and distribute resources efficiently.[56]

Thus political scientists stress the political prerequisites for economic development—political order and stability—which are in turn a function of viable institutions and enforceable rules. According to input-output theory, the political system receives inputs in the form of public demands and supports, as well as pressure from its various environments, and converts them into outputs expressed as policies, programs, and priorities.[57] This view holds that institutionalization of the functions of the political system will create a climate conductive to domestic peace and prosperity. Development thus entails an increase of capability of the political system to expand the range of individual freedoms, opportunities and choices.[58]

From the political science perspective there are two types of relationships. First, a relationship among the political, social, economic, and environmental aspects of development to the extent that changes in one sector may affect—negatively or positively—other sectors. For example, political underdevelopment may jeopardize societal and economic development. Second, there is a very close relationship between the development sectors and the respective security ones. In fact, they may, to a certain extent, be seen as identical or mutually reinforcing. This implies that changes in a development sector may affect—negatively or positively—a security sector and *vice versa*. For instance, in a country facing political underdevelopment, economic development may lead to domestic instability and the outbreak of violent conflict thereby jeopardizing economic and societal security.

## VIOLENT CONFLICT, SECURITY, AND DEVELOPMENT

Due to the tight connection between security and development, it may be argued that their relationship to violent conflict is a two-way one. Security and development are affected by the outbreak of violent conflict while the latter is conditioned by the level of a state's security and development. Specifically, violent conflict breaks out first, due to the inability of governments to promote economic development and create sustainable and effective welfare mechanisms. Second, violent conflict occurs due to the oppressive policies initiated and actions undertaken by regimes in order to safeguard their power and privileges. Third, violent conflict erupts as a result of the hostile actions undertaken by particular social groups against other social groups, as well as due to corruption and absence of social justice. Fourth, violent conflict occurs as a result of the efforts of national authorities to suppress riots, insurgency and secessionist and independence movements. Fifth, and very important, violent conflict starts due to the inability of governments to manage social and political change in a period of rapid economic growth.[59]

Actually, the record of instability and violence contradicts the conventional wisdom that the way to avoid revolution and instability is to stimulate development and industrialization. Empirical research shows that whatever the long-term benefits of modernization, its short-term impact tends to be more instability and violence. Research findings suggest that violence and instability are most likely to occur during a period of rapid change.

Actually, it is suggested that social revolutions occur in a period of rising prosperity and an improvement in the conditions that are the focus of the revolutionary movements. Specifically, it is asserted that when the satisfactions produced by an industrializing economy and society begin to increase, the expectations of the population also begin to increase. However, there are limits to how much and how long the material outputs and satisfactions produced by any regime can continue to increase. Such limits are imposed by the scarcity of resources or by cultural factors among other reasons. Eventually the increase in material outputs begins to level off, while expectations continue to rise at a rapid rate. Around this point, where the gap between expectations and satisfactions produces systemic frustration the likelihood of violence increases.[60]

In sum, it may be safely argued that social and political tensions are inevitable in the process of economic development. Although prolonged economic decline can be a potential source of conflict, economic growth alone does not prevent or resolve violent conflict, and may sometimes intensify tensions within society. The possible escalation of these tensions into open confrontation and violence can be a major obstacle to development. Thus discussion about development has emphasized political development; meaning the need of the establishment of institutions capable of managing sociopolitical tensions and preventing their escalation into violence that may threaten the security of the state and its citizens.

## CONCLUSION

A number of conclusions and policy recommendations may be drawn from the above analysis. First, Third World states have widely divergent social, economic, and political attributes. This diversity implies the absence of a unique policy formula that could apply without distinction to any Third World state. Thus policy makers should treat Third World states on an individual basis.

Second, security and development are not identical but very similar concepts. They are not identical because there is not a development sector identical to that of military security and they are similar because they have the same political, societal, economic, and environmental sectors that are, in fact, mutually reinforcing. This means that neither development can be achieved without security nor security without development. Policy makers should be aware of this relationship in planning their policies and strategies.

Third, with reference to the military sector, security and development are interrelated for two reasons. First, development enhances state power and capabilities as well as national and individual security. On the other hand, security provides the fertile ground for development. National security allows the individuals to participate in political and economic processes associated with development. Any threats to security ultimately affect development.

Underdevelopment, on the other hand, increases the vulnerability of the state and makes it subject to violent conflict which in turn further enhances its insecurity. Thus in regions which are susceptible to inter-state conflict, national/military security is a prerequisite for development. This leads to the paradox that while military spending affects development by using resources that would be otherwise used for social and economic purposes, it nevertheless provides the ground for it since external threats can prevent or disrupt development. Policy makers, however, should be very careful in the allocation of resources so to create a balance between military and social spending in order to avoid undermining national security from within.

Moreover, socioeconomic development and military security cannot be divorced from one another. Opting for the strategy of integration into the world market presupposes that certain conditions in the political-military sector have been met. In the area of security, the development of the market requires three things. First, that state control over the means of violence is separate from control over the means of production. Second, government officials do not make use of violence to enrich themselves through "theft." And third, the government, which in effect has a monopoly on the possession and use of arms, is responsible for safeguarding the individual rights of its subjects.

A fourth conclusion is that when we speak of security and development, we do not refer only to the security and development of the state and its élites, but most importantly, to the security and development of all individuals who compose it. Because the two concepts are mutually reinforcing, for a state to be secured and developed, security and development should apply to all its citizens and not only to a privileged class within it.

Fifth, the relationship between and among the development and security sectors is so strongly related that changes in one sector may affect—positively or negatively—another sector. For example, economic development may affect environmental security. Thus policy makers should pay special attention to the control of the effects stemming from such changes.

Sixth, there is a very close relationship between economic and political development. Economic development alleviates some causes of instability, but it also creates new stresses and strains. The dislocations (urbanization, unemployment, and so on) that accompany economic development give rise to social conflict as well as to feelings of personal alienation. Governments must be able to mediate between and among new social groups, accommodate competing demands, and manage conflicts. This requires the establishment of relevant institutions charged with this duty. Political development is therefore necessary to prevent conflicts that arise due to societal and economic reasons. Thus political development can serve both national security and the other forms of development and thus special attention should be paid to it.

Seventh, development does not imply necessarily the absence of violent conflict. In the absence of political development, for example, economic development may work against security. Violent conflict, security, and development are thus strongly interconnected. Conflict may be an important driving force behind processes of change and development. Violent conflicts, however, both between and within states, cause immense human suffering and both material and cultural damage, reducing the level of life chances which countries and communities are able to offer their people. In this sense, violent conflict works both against development and security. This implies that alongside development-oriented processes of change, mechanisms and institutions must be built or strengthened which promote the peaceful resolution of potential conflicts; that is political development.

Eighth, the capacities to mobilize resources and manage social conflict are necessary (but probably not sufficient) conditions of economic development. Although no developing state is immune to political instability, some governments are more capable of coping with conflict than others. Industrial democracies also experience occasional unrest but domestic tension rarely even strains the capacity of political institutions to accommodate conflict.

There is therefore a correlation between regime type and economic development. Some types of regimes are more willing than others at implementing policies aimed at rapid economic development. Common sense and experience both suggest that regimes in which power and authority are centralized or concentrated are more effective at mobilizing society and dealing with conflict (most often by crushing opposition). Such regimes are sometimes called "mobilization systems." They may be authoritarian or totalitarian in form. If the leadership fastens on to economic development as its supreme goal, a mobilization regime, by definition, is well equipped to do the job. By the same token, if the leaders set some other goal, such as military conquest or international prestige, they can also divert resources to postpone purely economic priorities indefinitely.

Democratic governments, on the other hand, place social harmony, personal liberty, and political compromise above rapid economic development. They try to accommodate rather than repress competing interest groups. Public policy is the result of compromises cobbled together on an *ad hoc* basis rather than of rational plans predicated on clearly articulated goals. The pace and direction of economic growth depends heavily on consumer choice. Regimes of this type are called "reconciliation systems."

In the early stages of economic development, mobilization regimes can accomplish rapid growth. But beyond a certain point, reconciliation regimes now appear to be the more successful and more sustainable of the two. Whatever the type of regime in power, its leadership will face a dilemma. What is needed to ensure stability in the long run is a prosperous society in which the benefits of economic growth are widely enjoyed. The austerity policies that often are urged on developing states are aimed at achieving this result. These policies, however, are often at odds with the leaders' short-run objectives of staying in power. Moreover, such policies may invite destabilizing and disruptive social conflict. In some countries where the government has taken such steps, massive food riots have erupted, and austerity measures have had to be softened or rescinded to quell the unrest.

Hence time is not always on the side of economic development. In poverty-stricken developing countries, immediate needs are likely to take precedence over longer-range goals and objectives. If the government decides to cut short-term consumption when many citizens live on the edge of starvation, the moral and political consequences are dire. But if the government takes care of basic needs, there may be little or nothing left over for long-term investment. And even in affluent countries, high-consumption policies are always more popular than high-investment policies. These realities should be taken into account not only by national governments, but also by international financial institutions and foreign aid donors in formulating their policies towards states facing grave economic difficulties.

Ninth, policy makers should pay the appropriate attention to political factors that impinge on the pace and direction of economic development. These factors include the quality of leadership, the capabilities of existing political structures, the availability of necessary resources, the quality of the citizenry, and the threats and opportunities presented by a changing regional and international environment.

Leadership quality is reflected in the attitudes and attributes of political élites. Are they progressive or traditionally bound? Do they want economic development even if it is accompanied by other changes that might be destabilizing? Are they more concerned about income distribution or economic growth? Do they value social justice, or are they interested only in feathering their own nests? Beyond moral character, of key importance are the skills and abilities of political élites. Do these élites understand basic principles of economics? Are they familiar with appropriate technologies? Do they have administrative experience and skills?

The concept of institutional capacity is particularly important because it is related to political development that is a prerequisite for security and other forms of development. Are variable institutions already in place, or do they have to be built from scratch? Can these institutions perform essential functions? Can they facilitate the processes of controlling, extracting, and mobilizing human and material resources?

As for the availability of resources is concerned, one needs to distinguish between potential and actual resources. Some political systems are more effective than others at extracting and developing resources. A state with oil reserves will not benefit from this resource until the oil has been discovered and the financial and technological where withal to develop it have been obtained. In addition, the infrastructure must be built. Clearly such an effort requires a great deal of planning, coordination and expertise. Equally important, human resources must be developed. Education and training is essential; so is the fulfillment of basic human needs such as food, shelter, and medical care. Otherwise, human resources will be wasted, and population growth will become a liability.

The quality of citizens is reflected in their values, attitudes, and behaviors, which can help or hinder economic growth, social harmony, and political stability. Are people highly motivated? Do people feel a sense of responsibility to the state and society, or are they sullen and cynical?

Finally, the regional and international environment gives rise to certain political possibilities and constraints. The ability to coordinate foreign policies regionally so as to present a united front to the rest of the world can be critical. The efforts of debtor states in Latin America to devise a common strategy show the costs of failing at policy coordination. Constraints arise in various forms, but nationalism is the most prevalent and persistent manifestation. Citizens and leaders continue to identify primarily with national ideals, symbols, interests and causes even though awareness is growing that regional and global action is needed to solve or alleviate many common problems.

## NOTES

1. Robert Tucker, *The Inequality of Nations* (London: Martin Roberts, 1977) and Hans W. Singer and Ansari A. Javed, *Rich and Poor Countries: Consequences of International Economic Disorder*, 4th edition (London: Unwin Hyman, 1988).

2. A. Gavshon, *Crisis in Africa: Battleground of East and West* (Harmondsworth: Penguin, 1981).

3. It has been suggested that after the demise of the Soviet Union, its successor states as well as some of its political satellites are also included in the Third World.

4. Christopher Clapham, *Third World Politics* (London: Routledge, 1985); A. D. Smith, *States and Nations in the Third World* (Brighton: Harvester Press, 1983) and Caroline Thomas, *In Search for Security* (Boulder, Colo.: Lynne Rienner, 1987).

5. Lawrence C. Mayer, John H. Burnett and Suzanne Ogden, *Comparative Politics: Nations and Theories in a Changing World*, 2nd edition (Upper Saddle River, N.J.: Prentice Hall, 1996), 321–27.

6. Samuel Huntington, *Political Order in Changing Societies* (New Haven, Conn.: Yale University Press, 1968), chapter 1.

7. Lucien Pye, "The Non-Western Political Process." *Journal of Politics* 20(3) August 1958, 468–86.

8. Lucien Pye, *Aspects of Political Development* (Boston: Little Brown, 1966), 45–46.

9. Pye, *Aspects of Political Development,* 46.

10. Michael Novack, *The Rise of Unmeltable Ethics* (New York: Macmillan, 1972).

11. C. Young, *Ideology and Development in Africa* (New Haven, Conn.: Yale University Press, 1982).

12. Vicky Randal and Robin Theobald, *Political Change and Underdevelopment* (Durham, N.C.: Duke University Press, 1985), 30.

13. Joseph S. Nye Jr. and Sean M. Lynn-Jones, "International Security Studies: A Report of a Conference on the State of the Field," *International Security* 12(4): 5–27.

14. Barry Buzan, *People, States and Fear: An Agenda for International Security Studies in the Post–Cold War Era,* 2nd edition (London: Harvester Wheatscheaf, 1991), introduction.

15. Barry Buzan et al., *The European Security Order Recast: Scenarios for the Post–Cold War Era* (London: Pinter, 1990).

16. Barry Buzan, "Is International Security Possible?" in *New Thinking about Strategy and International Security*, Kenneth Booth, ed. (London: HarperCollins, 1991), 34.

17. Mark Hoffman, "Critical Theory and the Inter-paradigm Debate," *Millennium: Journal of International Studies* 16(2): 231–49; Andrew Linklater, *Beyond Realism and Marxism: A Critical Theory of International Relations* (London: Macmillan, 1990); James Der Derian, *On Diplomacy: A Genealogy of Western Enstrangement* (Oxford: Blackwell, 1987); David Campbell, *Writing Security* (Manchester: Manchester University Press, 1992).

18. Richard K. Ashley, "The Poverty of Neo-Realism," *International Organization* 38(2): 225–61.

19. Barry Buzan, Ole Waever and Jaap de Wilde, *Security: A New Framework for Analysis* (London: Lynne Rienner, 1998).

20. Buzan, Waever and de Wilde, *Security A New Framework for Analysis*, 21.

21. Buzan, *People, States and Fear*, 363.

22. Buzan, *People, States and Fear*, 363.

23. Buzan, "Is International Security Possible?" 34.

24. Buzan, "Is International Security Possible?" 44.

25. Kalevi J. Holsti, "A New International Relations? Diplomacy in Complex Interdependence," *International Organization* 32(2) 1978: 513–30.

26. Buzan, "Is International Security Possible?" 41.

27. Thomas F. Homer-Dixon, "Global Environmental Change and International Security," in *Building a New Global Order*, David Dewitt, David Haglund and John Kirton, eds. (Oxford: Oxford University Press, 1993).

28. Buzan, "Is International Security Possible?" 45–46 and *People, States and Fear*, 96–107.

29. Joel S. Migdal, *Strong Societies and Weak States* (Princeton, N.J.: Princeton University Press, 1988).

30. Nazli Choucri, Janet Welsh Brown and Peter M. Haas, "Dimensions of National Security," in *In the U.S. Interest: Resources, Growth and Security in the Developing World*, Janet Welsh Brown, ed. (Boulder, Colo.: Westview Press, 1990) and Robert C. North, *War, Peace, Survival* (Boulder, Colo.: Westview Press, 1990).

31. Buzan, *People, States and Fear*, 116–34.

32. Buzan, *People, States and Fear*, 117.

33. Klaus Knorr, *The Power of Nations: The Political Economy of International Relations* (New York: Basic Books, 1975) and Klaus Knorr and Frank N. Trager, eds., *Economic Issues and National Security* (Lawrence: Regents Press of Kansas, 1977).

34. Buzan, *People, States and Fear*, 126.

35. Barry Buzan and Gautam Sen, "The impact of military research and development priorities on the evolution of the civil economy in capitalist states," *Review of International Studies* 16(4) 1990.

36. Robert O. Keohane and Joseph S. Nye Jr., *Power and Interdependence* (Boston: Little, Brown, 1977), chapters 1 and 2.

37. Paul Kennedy, *The Rise and Fall of the Great Powers* (London: Fontana, 1988) and James R. Schlessinger, "Economic Growth and National Security," in *The Theory and Practice of International Relations*, F. A. Sonderman, W.C. Olson and T.S. McLennan, eds. (Englewood Cliffs, N.J.: Prentice-Hall, 1970), 155–64.

38. Kalevi J. Holsti, *Why Nations Realign* (London: Allen and Unwin, 1982).

39. Nazli Choucri, ed., *Global Accord: Environmental Challenges and International Responses* (Cambridge, Mass.: MIT Press, 1993).

40. Nigel Dower, "Sustainability and the Right to Development," in *International Justice and the Third World*, Robin Attfield and Barry Wilkins, eds. (London: Routledge, 1992), 97.

41. W. W. Rostow, *The Stages of Economic Growth* (Cambridge: Cambridge University Press, 1966) and A. F. K. Organski, *The Stages of Political Development* (New York: Knopf, 1967).

42. Talcott Parsons, *The Social System* (New York: Free Press, 1964); Amitai Etzioni, *The Active Society* (New York: Free Press, 1968); Daniel Lerner, *The Passing of Traditional Society* (New York: Free Press, 1958), and David C. McClelland, *The Achieving Society* (New York: Halstead Press, 1976).

43. Huntington, *Political Order in Changing Societies*.

44. Plato, *The Republic*, Francis MacDonald Cornford, trans. (London: Oxford University Press, 1945), 106.

45. Stephen Chilton, *Grounding Political Development* (Boulder, Colo.: Lynne Reinner, 1988).

46. Thomas M. Magstadt, *Nations and Governments*, 3rd edition (New York: St. Martin's Press, 1998), 49–50.

47. Thomas Hobbes, *Leviathan* (London: Everyman's Library, 1953), 55–56.

48. Friedrich Hegel, *The Philosophy of Right*, T. M. Knox, trans. (Oxford: Clarendon Press, 1942).

49. Monte Palmer, *Dilemmas of Political Development*, 4th edition (Itasca, Ill.: Peacock, 1989), 10.

50. John H. Herz, *International Politics in the Atomic Age* (New York: Columbia University Press, 1959).

51. United Nations Development Programme (UNDP), *Human Development Report 1993* (Oxford: Oxford University Press, 1993), 2.

52. *Declaration on the Right to Development*, United Nations, December 1986, 41/128, preamble paragraph 2.

53. United Nations Development Programme (UNDP), *Human Development Report 1994* (Oxford: Oxford University Press, 1994), 24–40.

54. Jan Geert Siccama, "Intra-state Conflicts and Development," in *Internal Conflicts, Security and Development*, Bas de Gaay Fortman and Marijke Veldhuis, eds. RAWOO Lectures and Seminars, no. 14, 15.

55. James H. Mittleman, *Out from Underdevelopment: Prospects for the Third World* (New York: St. Martin's Press, 1988), 22.

56. Robert A. Nisbet, *Social Change and History: Aspects of Western Theory of Development* (New York: Oxford University Press, 1969).

57. David Easton, *The Political System* (New York: Knopf, 1977).

58. Gabriel Almond and James Coleman, *The Politics of Developing Areas* (Princeton, N.J.: Princeton University Press, 1960) and Gabriel Almond and G. Bingham Powell, *Comparative Politics: A Development Approach* (Boston: Little, Brown, 1966).

59. Mancur Olsen, "Rapid Growth as a Destabilising Force," *Journal of Economic History* 3(4) December 1963: 529–52.

60. James Davies, "Toward a Theory of Revolution," *American Sociological Review* 27(1) February 1962: 5–19; Ivo Feierabend, Rosalind Feierabend, and Betty Nesvold, "Systemic Conditions of Political Violence," *Journal of Conflict Resolution* 10(3) September 1966: 249–71 and Theda Skocpol, *Social Revolutions in the Modern World* (Cambridge: Cambridge University Press, 1994).

# 14

## Democracy, Diversion, and the News Media

*Douglas A. Van Belle*

The premise of the democratic peace, where nations with high levels of open domestic political competition do not go to war with one another, appears on the face to be at odds with the diversionary theory of war, where domestic political competition and unrest leads to increased external conflict. This apparent conflict has not been resolved by empirical analysis because empirical support can be found for both theories. The goal of this article is to explore the nature of these two seemingly contradictory theories and show that they are *not* contradictory. Further, by proposing mechanisms within the domestic politics of democracies that can generate both phenomena, it appears both may be a result of the domestic political competition to shape the content of news media coverage. Diversionary conflicts function by providing the leader the opportunity to dominate the sources of news considered to be legitimate and allowing him or her to generate a flood of news media coverage that reflects favorably upon his or her performance. This is compatible with the interdemocratic peace findings because the flow of information between the free presses of democracies reduces the leader's expectations that s/he will be able to dominate the legitimate sources of news and information concerning the conflict and reduces the likelihood that s/he will be able to sustain a predominantly positive image in the tide of coverage generated by a dramatic conflict.

On the surface, the diversionary theory of war and the Kantian proposition of the democratic peace appear to contradict one another. The diversionary theory of war uses propositions, such as those presented by Coser (1956),[1] concerning the effect intergroup conflict on the dynamics of relationships within groups to argue that domestic political conflict will be externalized. Intergroup conflicts such as war are expected to strengthen group identity and increase the centralization of decision making power. Both of these dynamics benefit the leader of the group; thus, it seems reasonable that leaders facing domestic challenges might engage in conflicts in order to obtain these benefits. Such a foreign policy choice leads to international conflict that "diverts" attention from domestic disputes and tends to enhance the leader's position in domestic political conflicts.

Kant (1991 [1795]), on the other hand, argued that democracies would be less war prone *because* of the constant and high levels of open domestic political conflict within them and the consistent threat this generated for the leader's tenure. Constant domestic political competition for the leadership positions within democracies creates a dynamic of public accountability that allows the public at large, who must bear the brunt of the costs of war, to punish leaders who choose war without good reason. Presumably this public would punish leaders who choose to wage frivolous wars, such as those simply diverting attention from domestic troubles. This mechanism should then prevent democracies from engaging in diversionary wars. There is empirical evidence supporting both perspectives, but how can domestic political competition both lead to war and prevent war?

This article attempts to address this apparent contradiction and show that the current depictions of these two theoretical perspectives are not only compatible, but they can both arise out of the same mechanism of domestic political competition within democracies. Most of the empirical muddle can be cleared up by simply focusing on the levels of analysis used in the operationalization and empirical exploration of these two perspectives. There is no real contradiction between the empirical results since the diversionary theory of war finds its modest support at the monadic level, while the democratic theory of war finds its strongest support at the dyadic level, but relatively little at the monadic level. It should come as no surprise to those familiar with the democratic peace literature that diversionary uses of force by democracies always occur against nondemocracies.

Examining the progression of research findings and explanatory focus over time demonstrates that both areas of research have moved toward a more theoretically rich focus on the threats and benefits that motivate the leaders making the foreign policy decisions. This can all be brought together to show that, at a conceptual level, the two areas of research are not incompatible. The high level of constant domestic political conflict within democracies is part of the normal process and does not represent the same level of threat to the leader that a similar level of domestic political conflict would create for a nondemocratic leader. It is only when domestic political competition represents a greater threat than usual for the leader that diversionary foreign policies become a reasonable possibility.

Further, by examining the specific mechanisms within democracies that drive diversionary conflict and asking why democracies always engage in diversionary wars against nondemocracies, it can be argued that both diversionary war and the interdemocratic peace are a result of the same democratic political dynamic of competition to shape the content of the domestic news media. The latter half of this article explores this possibility in depth and uses aspects of the Gulf War, the Cod War, and the crisis that preceded the Falklands/Malvinas, to provide examples of how these two phenomena might arise from the same theoretical foundation.

## EXISTING RESEARCH ON DEMOCRACY, WAR, AND DIVERSION

There are a few things that are clear about the question of democracies and international conflict. At a monadic level, where just the characteristics of an individual state are considered, the thesis that public accountability will make democracies less likely to engage in war is not well supported by the available evidence (Small and Singer 1976; Zinnes 1980; Chan 1984; Weede 1984; Vincent 1987; Domke 1988; Maoz and Abdolali 1989; Maoz and Russett 1992, 1993). Most of the modest support there is at the monadic level is found for the proposition that democracies might be less violent overall, indicated by the finding that they suffer fewer casualties in wars (Rummel 1983, 1995), though sophisticated statistical methods have recently revealed a slightly lower propensity for war involvement (Benoit 1996). However, at the dyadic level, where the characteristics of both nations involved in the conflict are considered, the empirical evidence clearly demonstrates that democracies do not appear to fight one another (Small and Singer 1976; Zinnes 1980; Chan 1984; Weede 1984; Vincent 1987; Domke 1988; Maoz and Abdolali 1989; Bremer 1992; Weede 1992; Maoz and Russett 1992, 1993; Russett 1993; Gleditsch 1995; Rousseau et al. 1996).[2]

It is made amply clear in almost all of the studies, across differing time frames and different levels of violent conflict, that democratic dyads are far less likely to go to war than nondemocratic and mixed dyads. It is also clear that the subject of democracy and war, as well as the questions surrounding it, are the focus of an inordinate amount of study. Morgan and Campbell (1991) attribute the scholarly interest to the persuasiveness of the Kantian thesis, the persuasiveness of those who support it, the normative appeal of the thesis, and the intellectual dissatisfaction with different levels of analysis producing completely opposing results. This disparity between the different levels of analysis also becomes highly significant in how the two theoretical perspectives can coexist both conceptually and empirically.

The literature on the diversionary theory of war has some equally interesting aspects. The theoretical expositions supporting it, particularly those by Coser (1956) are well articulated and intellectually compelling. It also reflects a long conceptual tradition. Machiavelli proposed that wars should be used as a means to quell domestic unrest, and the admonition to "never make war on a revolution" had long been a common axiom of conduct among leaders, generals, and diplomats. Further, the anecdotal evidence supporting the theory is strong to the point being almost undeniable. Just noting that the final decision to invade Grenada was made a few short hours after President Reagan was informed of the devastating bombing of the U.S. Marine Barracks in Beirut (Adkin 1989; Schoenhals and Melanson 1985:141), makes it almost impossible to explain the U.S. invasion of Grenada as anything other than a diversionary conflict. Translating this compelling theory and anecdotal evidence into an analysis that generates solid empirical support, however, has proven to be a difficult task.

Early examinations of linkages between internal and external conflict provided little or no support for the hypothesis. Neither Rummel's initial analysis (1963) with its factor analysis of internal conflicts leading to external conflict nor the attempts to replicate the study (Tanter 1966; Haas 1968; Wilkenfeld 1972; and Kegley, Richardson, and Richter 1978) found anything beyond very weak results. More sophisticated efforts that control for aspects of the domestic political and social environment initially found slight support (Wilkenfeld 1968; Zinnes and Wilkenfeld 1971; Hazelwood 1973) and more recent analysis that focus more carefully on the threat to the leader's hold on power have found more robust connections. An examination of increases of domestic conflict, which indicate an increased threat to the leader's tenure (James 1987), demonstrated that rising domestic conflict increases the likelihood that crises will result in war. Studies that have analyzed the level of domestic support for the President as one of multiple factors that could have contributed to the decision to employ force have found diversion to be a significant factor in U.S. uses of force (Ostrom and Job 1986; James and Oneal 1991). Morgan and Bicker's (1992) recent analysis indicated that threats to the support from the leader's ruling coalition are related to an increased likelihood of external conflict. This focus on the domestic aspects of the regime has culminated in the study by Miller (1995) which controlled for the nature of the domestic political regime and found the strongest statistical results to date. These studies are still modest in their explanatory power as indicated by a more recent analysis (Meernik and Waterman 1996) which concludes that there is no evidence of diversionary wars.

Though this shift to a more sophisticated operationalization of the diversionary theory appears to have improved the results and appears to have made the analyses more representative of the theoretical foundation, all of the work has been at the monadic level. The nature of the opposing regime is not considered. This is a notable contrast to the democracy and war findings where the strongest results are at the dyadic level.

## THE MONADIC LEVEL

The key to interpreting the monadic level empirical findings for both theoretical perspectives is provided by James (1987), who uses changes in levels of domestic conflict as his primary independent variable. His justification
for doing so is that the diversionary theory of war assumes that leaders are
responding to threats to their own personal power. Leaders and institutions
adapt to, or grow accustomed to persistent levels of conflict and it is only in
the increases in levels of conflict that a reasonable indicator can be found
for the threat that the internal conflict poses to the leader's hold on power.
Thus, in democracies, the overall high-levels of conflict are normal and do
not reflect the same immediate threat to the leader's power that similar absolute levels of conflict would pose in a totalitarian state.

The frequent marches on Washington, D.C., even those that claim a million participants, are seldom seen as a threat to the President's hold on
power. In fact, they have become almost mundane and no one would expect
them to lead to a diversionary war. There is actually a park next to the White
House that is a designated protest area where the participants in these
protests gather. However, the simple acts of protest in Tiananmen Square,
minor in comparison to some of the protests in the United States, were
viewed as a serious threat to the Chinese leadership's hold on power, and
many would agree that they easily could have lead to a diversionary conflict
if the opportunity had arisen. During the Tiananmen Square protests an
open concern expressed by the United States was the possibility of an increased Chinese threat to Taiwan.

What should be the analytical focus for the diversionary theory of war is
not the level of conflict, but the level of threat to the leader's hold on power.
Domestic conflict is just an indicator of such a motivation and it must be operationalized carefully to reflect the dynamics of domestic political competition and the underlying threat to the leader as closely as possible.[3] The empirical results at the monadic levels of analysis of the diversionary theory of
war support this contention that the focus should be on the threat to the
leader instead of the level of conflict. Early analysis that used raw levels of
internal and external conflict found no relationship. However later analyses
that tried to address the actual threat to the leader's hold on power by looking at approval levels of U.S. presidents (Ostrom and Job 1986; James and
Oneal 1991) looking at changes in the levels of domestic conflict (James
1987), or threats to the support of the ruling coalition (Morgan and Bickers
1992) all demonstrated modest, but positive results.

Similarly, the monadic-level democracy and war findings need to be operationalized and reinterpreted on the basis of the threat or benefit to the leader
and his or her ability to remain in office. The fact that democracies suffer
fewer casualties in war, might suggest that democratic leaders are avoiding

long or particularly deadly conflicts whenever possible because of the potential for a negative domestic political response. Diversionary wars by democracies would be ones where the leaders are seeking benefits and avoiding
costs, so they would more likely be clustered at the low casualty end of the
scale and they should probably be short in duration. Democratic engagement
in long and costly wars is likely to be motivated by other things and perhaps
some effort needs to be made to sort these out and analyze them separately.

## THE DYADIC LEVEL

At the dyadic level of analysis it is even easier to reconcile the empirical results.
There are no dyadic studies of the diversionary theory of war and the tremendous amount of work[4] on democracy and war has shown that at the dyadic
level, there is an overwhelming level of empirical evidence showing that
democracies do not fight one another. If democracies do not go to war with
one another, then it follows logically that they will not engage in diversionary
wars with one another. Thus, you would expect that all instances of diversionary uses of force by democratic countries would be against nondemocracies. Accordingly, in the data analyzed by James (1987) none of the crises between democracies with free presses[5] escalated into a war. If democracies do
engage in diversionary conflicts, yet they do not engage in those conflicts with
one another, there must be some reason, some aspect of how democracies interact, that allows leaders to make domestic political gains from war with nondemocracies, but prevents those gains from being made in conflicts with
democracies.

The peace between democratic dyads is generally explained through either the shared culture and resulting externalized norms developed between
democracies (Doyle 1986; Maoz and Russett 1993), or through the mutual
constraints on the leadership that reduce the probability of conflict so low
that it practically never occurs (Domke 1988; Bueno de Mesquita and Lalman
1990; Morgan and Campbell 1991). Morgan and Schwebach (1991) summarize these perspectives and comparatively test the explanatory power of
both. Their results are mixed and inconclusive, though they do appear to
slightly favor the structural constraints explanation. Other studies present
modest findings that lean more toward the cultural explanation. Dixon's
(1993) analysis of regime type and conflict resolution demonstrates that
democracies engaged in a dispute are more likely to turn to nonviolent forms
of resolution such as arbitration, thus, suggesting that the cultural, shared
norms explanation has merit.

Morgan and Bickers (1991) categorize regimes, including nondemocratic
regimes, by the constraints imposed upon leadership by the domestic political structure and find modest but positive results at the monadic level of

analysis indicating that constraints upon the leadership reduce slightly the regime's propensity to participate in international conflict. This suggests that careful attention to accurately representing the concepts through operationalization is a point of concern.

The focus on constraints arises naturally from the original thesis. Kant (1991 [1795]) made it clear that republican governments function through the enfranchised public's influence on the representative leadership that had to make decisions concerning peace and war. The public, which has to bear the brunt of the costs of war, is expected to punish its popularly elected leaders by removal from office if the leaders expose them to the costs associated with war without sufficient cause. Given the historical circumstances that Kant wrote from, it is not unsurprising that he focused on the constraints democracies imposed upon their leaders. He saw the unrestrained excesses of kings and princes as the primary cause of wars and he did not have the Spanish-American war, the Falklands/Malvinas war, or the U.S. invasion of Grenada to demonstrate how democratic political structures might also enable or even promote the choice of war. Notice, however, that the *mechanism* through which Kant expected the domestic political competition within republican democracies to generate the democratic peace is focused on the leader's ability to hold on to power. Expanding upon the foundation laid by Kant to include both sides of the effort to hold on to power, the motivating effect of potential gains as well as the restraining effect of potential punishment provides some insights into regime types and war.

The focus on both threats and benefits to the leader is reflected in recent efforts to explain the fact that democracies do not fight with one another. Hermann and Kegley (1996) argue for a more theoretically detailed focus on leadership and the leader. Mintz and Geva (1993) argue that for the democratic leader the "Use of force against a democracy is considered by the public as a *failure* of foreign policy" (Mintz and Geva 1993: 489; emphasis in original). As a result, the leader can expect no benefits and only costs from engaging in conflict with a democracy. This argument is supported by experimental evidence showing that when judging a hypothetical situation, the study participants in both Israel and the United States are more likely to approve of the use of force option when the target state is a nondemocracy (Mintz and Geva 1993).

Of note is how the study of the interdemocratic peace has moved to a closer focus on the mechanisms driving the leader's choice, a focus on the threats and potential benefits to the leader's domestic political position. This mirrors the shift that has occurred in the study of diversionary conflict. It is interesting, however, that they converge on this focus even though they were driven by exactly opposite difficulties. For the study of democracy and war, the change was driven by strong empirical results coupled with contradictory anecdotal evidence and relatively weak explanatory theories. The same shift in the study of the diversionary theory of war was driven by weak empirical results contrasting with strong anecdotal evidence and a strong explanatory theory.

In the section below, the argument is put forth that it is the domestic political competition to shape news coverage within a democracy, combined with the nature of international news flow, that can provide an explanation for both the peace between democracies and the diversionary use of force by democracies. It must be pointed out that in this discussion any notion that the domestic news media is a monolithic entity with a coherent political agenda, unified position, or single voice is explicitly *rejected*. Rather, the news media is depicted as a diverse arena in which elites compete against one another in an attempt to shape the overall coverage to reflect favorably upon themselves or negatively upon their opponents. The media strategies of political elites, including the Chief Executive, center primarily around providing material, such as research, comments, policy actions or staged events, to the press which reflect favorably upon themselves and which they hope will result in coverage. The provision of these resources for coverage is tailored to meet the needs of the reporters and the economic/entertainment imperatives of the news outlets (See for example Smoller 1990; Hess 1981; Cook 1989). Incumbents can use the resources of their position, (e.g. the White House press secretary) to facilitate their efforts. The executive struggles to influence coverage to his or her benefit while his or her opponents simultaneously try to influence it to theirs.

## DEMOCRACY, THE NEWS MEDIA, AND DIVERSION

The focus on leaders and the benefits they seek has benefited both areas of research. It has led to stronger empirical findings for the study of diversionary theory of war and it is a common aspect of the recent efforts to explain the democratic peace. If we can look to rally events as a representation of the benefit democratic leaders are pursuing through diversion, then, understanding how international conflicts become rally events lends insight into the specific mechanisms within democracies driving domestic political benefits from conflicts. The research literature on rally events is relatively extensive (Mueller 1970, 1973; Lee 1977; Kernell 1978; Erikson, Luttbeg, and Tedin 1980; Sigelman and Johnston-Conover 1981; MacKuen 1983; Brody 1984; Ostrom and Simon 1985; Russett 1990; Brody 1991; Oneal and Bryan 1995). Most of this literature, like much of the democracy and war literature and much of the diversionary use of force literature, focuses on empirical confirmation of a phenomena. However, more recent works have focused more heavily upon explanation. Brody (1991) provides the strongest explanation of how political events become rally events.

Brody (1991) argues that the difference between dramatic political events that become rally events and similar events that do not, lies in the news media coverage, specifically in what he calls opinion leaders. Opinion leaders are prominent individuals, such as political leaders, whose interpretation of events and actions are covered in the news media. The public then form their opinions from the information in this coverage. The key to rally events is the balance between the coverage obtained by supportive and critical opinion leaders. Successful rally events, when the leader experiences a short-term boost in approval ratings, occur when supportive opinion leaders dominate the news coverage. Events in which critical opinion leaders, such as challengers for the leadership position or prominent members of the opposing party, gain a significant portion of the news coverage, do not generate boosts in approval ratings.

The findings of Iyengar and Kinder (1987), specifically, that news coverage stimulates attention but does not alter opinions can easily be cited as evidence counter to this proposition. There are two aspects that are critical. First, the stimulus in the Iyengar and Kinder (1987) and subsequent studies is too small. Brody's use of the term, "dominating" in describing how leaders use media coverage to generate rally events, is critical. The leader has to dominate, has to create a nearly overwhelming positive surge of news media coverage, to generate a rally event. In the Gulf War case examined below, it took almost a month of the Gulf War capturing well over half of the total network television broadcasts and almost all of the politically relevant content, to generate a rally of just 20 percent. It appears to take a massive stimulus to alter mass opinion, however, the experimental studies of the effect of news media coverage on opinion alter just a few stories. Also, rally events are commonly just a few percentage points, with the average somewhere between 5 and 7 points (Oneal and Bryan 1995: 380). Even if the small stimulus in the experimental studies could change opinion, the N is really not large enough to measure a change in just 7 out of one hundred subjects. The assumption here is that attention is fleeting but opinions are stable. People invest effort into forming opinions and are reluctant to change them. In order for news coverage to change opinions in a broad, aggregate way, it must be overwhelming, or it must be constant and long term, effectively eroding held opinions.

Generalizing the finding of Brody suggests that democratic leaders, who have to periodically reaffirm a majority level of public support, and who's personal power is to at least some degree related to their domestic political standing, should not only be aware of the relationship between their standing and the supportive/critical balance of coverage in the news media, they should also use it as part of their decision making calculus. If leaders do use conflict to direct attention away from domestic political difficulties then it is reasonable to expect that the arena in which a significant portion of the domestic political competition within democracies occurs, the news media, should be an important factor in rally events. U.S. Presidents do appear to respond to negative coverage in a general sense. Within a crisis, leaders seem to respond to surges in negative news coverage. Clinton's policy actions towards Haiti consistently occurred after surges in negative coverage (Van Belle 1995). Further, low and falling standing is empirically correlated to the use of force by U.S. presidents (James and Oneal 1991), but it can also be shown that uses of force that occur when the President's approval rating is low and falling tend to be more dramatic, capturing greater news coverage, than when the leader's standing is high or at least stable (Van Belle 1996). This suggests that U.S. Presidents at least, are using foreign policy in the domestic political competition to shape the overall content of the news coverage. The question is: how?

It is doubtful that in an open society, such as the United States, a leader would be able to suppress directly, or lower forcefully, the salience of an already salient issue, but the salience of an issue can nonetheless be manipulated. There are always several issues in the domestic arena, all contending for a relatively finite amount of news media coverage. The amount of coverage that different issues receive can be thought of as a zero-sum, or more accurately a near-zero-sum,[6] relationship between several competing issues. The salience of any one issue can be manipulated downward by enhancing or bolstering the salience of one or more competing issues. From this perspective of domestic political competition within the news media, a diversionary use of force is a dramatic foreign policy action intended to generate salience and shift the public's attention away from a harmful issue or issues that are currently gaining coverage and harming the leader's standing. The leader can not or does not wish to deal with a troublesome issue directly and instead uses a foreign policy event that reflects favorably upon himself to redirect the attention of the domestic power bases[7] away from the troublesome issue.

Diversionary uses of force in democracies should ideally include the following characteristics:

1. The salience of a harmful issue, an issue gaining significant levels of coverage that is critical of the leader, should be very high.
2. The action chosen should be dramatic. Meaning it should have a high expected magnitude of domestic response so it captures the headlines in the media, or there should be a concerted effort by the leadership to enhance the magnitude of the response, or both.

For several reasons, diversionary uses of force in democracies should be fairly rare. There is the risk that the opponent will react much more forcefully or much more powerfully than expected. If the domestic response is cynical, there is the very real possibility of creating a second issue of high salience with significant levels of critical coverage where there was previously only one. There is also the possibility that a third issue will take the brunt of the zero-sum dynamic and the troublesome issue will be relatively unaffected by the diversionary action. A casual observation from the analysis of the Gulf War below suggests that when the economy is the troublesome issue, the latter is a very real concern. It was observed that the economy was the last issue pushed from the news by the Gulf War coverage and the first to return. The risks involved are the most important reason for expecting diversionary decisions to be rare. Though it is possible that the diversionary action will occur simply for the pursuit of gains, it is more likely that they will occur when the leader feels threatened and is apt to be more risk prone.

## THE GULF WAR AS A DIVERSIONARY WAR

The Gulf War is not usually depicted as a diversionary war. President Bush's standing was at a comfortable 60 percent when he first threatened Iraq and slightly higher just before the air war began. Yet it had the effect that diversionary wars are expected to have. It created, not just one, but two rally events for President Bush. The initial threat and then the beginning of the air war both drove the extremely troubling issue of the U.S. economy and federal budget from the news and reversed 20 point slides in his approval rating. Focusing on the initial threat that Bush made, it can be shown that the first rally coincided with both a tremendous jump in the coverage of Iraq and a statistically significant interruption in the news media coverage of the U.S. economic and budgetary woes.

The two months included in this analysis are also ideal for a brief exemplary case in that there are large swings in Bush's approval ratings, those swings occur at a time when the domestic political environment within the United States is relatively simple, and this simplicity makes news media coverage of political issues relatively easy to code. During this period the coverage of the U.S. economic woes was particularly harmful to Bush's domestic political standing. Its tone was extremely negative towards Bush, it labeled Bush's efforts to deal with the problem as ineffective or failing. It was also persistent and salient. It was a prominent issue for six months and during July 1990 it averaged four minutes of national television news coverage per night with peaks of over nine minutes per night. For several months prior to the initial threat towards Iraq, and throughout the duration of the conflict the coverage of the economy was uniformly negative. After the U.S. threat, the vast majority of the coverage of the confrontation with Iraq was positive towards Bush, depicting an image of decisive leadership.

President Bush's primary effort to deal directly with the budgetary crisis failed and there was no obvious policy alternatives available to deal directly with the issue. Bush's attempt at resolving the issue and derailing the steady train of negative coverage was the theme when the budget summit convened with leading members of congress. The effect of this conference, however, was less than beneficial to Bush. It accomplished little, it further increased the coverage of economic woes, and it raised the fear of higher taxes when Bush backtracked on his "No New Taxes" campaign pledge. It is unlikely that he could effectively deal directly with the issue.

If President Bush's actions toward Iraq were intended to drive down the level of media coverage that the economic problems confronting the United States had captured and replace it with a favorable issue, it was a tremendous success. Following the Iraqi invasion of Kuwait, the media coverage of the U.S. economy dropped off immediately and remained suppressed while being replaced by the overwhelmingly positive coverage of the U.S. confrontation with Iraq. This can be seen in table 14.1, which presents the coverage of the two issues as recorded in the Vanderbilt Television News Archives in the form of the percentage of political news they represented.

The significance of this change in the political content of the news media can be examined by applying an interrupted time series OLS regression to the data, with the date of Bush's coercive threat used as an interruption.[8] The results of this statistical analysis are striking.

The OLS analyses reported in table 14.1 confirm what is visually apparent in figure 14.1 and they show that there is a statistically significant drop in both the percentage of the politically relevant news devoted to the economy and the absolute levels of coverage of the economy. The shift variable rep-

**Table 14.1.  Results of Statistical Analysis in Coverage on the Economy**

**Economy as a percentage of political news**
Interrupted time series analysis

| Variable | B | SE B | Beta | T | Sig T |
|---|---|---|---|---|---|
| Shift | −56.106283 | 10.557021 | −.829885 | −5.315 | .0000 |
| Trend prior | .182729 | .400422 | .098309 | .456 | .6498 |
| Trend post | −.233669 | .580266 | −.070282 | −.403 | .6886 |
| (Constant) | 56.627647 | 7.224258 | | 7.839 | .0000 |

**Economy coverage in minutes per broadcast**
Interrupted time series analysis

| Variable | B | SE B | Beta | T | Sig T |
|---|---|---|---|---|---|
| Shift | −3.131071 | .767415 | −.796308 | −4.080 | .0001 |
| Trend prior | .050867 | .029108 | .470544 | 1.748 | .0857 |
| Trend post | −.061738 | .042181 | −.319285 | −1.464 | .1486 |
| (Constant) | 2.658617 | .525149 | | 5.063 | .0000 |

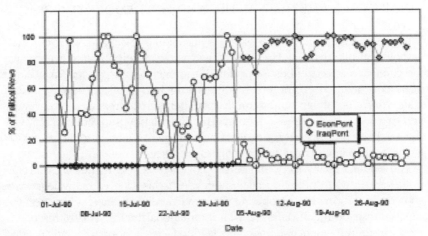

**Figure 14.1. Percentage of Political News: Economy and Iraq**

resents the change in the intercept, the immediate shift up or down at the point of the interruption independent of whatever changes are introduced by trends. At the point where Bush threatened Iraq, the proportion of the politically relevant news coverage that focused on the economy dropped by 56 percent. In absolute terms, the coverage of the economy dropped by 3.1 minutes per news broadcast. In both the proportional measure and the absolute measure, the trend in the coverage in the economy is not statistically significant. This indicates that it was not statistically distinguishable from a flat line, thus demonstrating that the coverage of the economy, though buffeted somewhat by random fluctuations, was holding a steady amount of coverage in the month before the interruption.

In the month after the interruption, it was again steady but the level of coverage was 3.1 minutes per broadcast less. The surge in coverage of the Gulf conflict and the drop in the coverage of the economy coincide with a jump in approval ratings from 60 percent on July 21, 1990 to 80 percent on August 10, 1990. Clearly, the confrontation with Iraq diverted domestic attention from the economic woes of the United States and generated a rally event for President Bush.

The next appropriate question is why divert with a foreign policy issue? There is no reason why the zero-sum mechanism must exclude domestic issues and policies. Presumably a dramatic domestic issue could drive other issues from the news media. There is however a profound difference between domestic and foreign policy issues in terms of the leader's ability to become a predominant source of news. Exploring how different conditions alter the Chief Executive's ability to act as a predominant source of news, also leads to an explanation for the peace between democracies that functions on the same mechanism of domestic political competition to shape the news media content.

## DEMOCRACY, THE NEWS MEDIA, AND THE DEMOCRATIC PEACE

Why are foreign policy events, such as diversionary wars, typically depicted as potential rally events? The best answer is that foreign policy events give the chief executive the best opportunity to generate a great deal of positive news coverage. Given the entertainment imperatives of the news, the dramatic nature of foreign policy conflicts can generate a great deal of coverage and capture a great deal of attention. The undeniable preponderance of war movies over parliamentary debate movies suggests international conflict is far more dramatic than domestic political conflict.

The leader's ability to dominate this coverage is also higher with foreign policy issues. On domestic issues the leader is just one of many legitimate sources of information competing for news media coverage. However, the situation can be much different with international issues. This difference is most profound when a democratic leader faces a nondemocratic leader. When a democracy faces a nondemocracy in international conflict, the democratic leader can expect to be the dominant source of "legitimate" information for the domestic news media.[9] Going into the conflict, a skillful democratic leader can expect to be reasonably successful at using the resources of his or her office, and branches of government subordinate to it, to influence the news content to his or her benefit. The press conferences, media briefings, combat information, and even intelligence reports that were made available to the press during the Persian Gulf War are all examples of the resources a leader can use to provide information leading to media coverage.

In most cases, domestic challengers do not have anywhere near the same resources as the leader to influence the coverage on foreign policy issues and barring unusual circumstances they are unlikely to carry the same weight of authority or legitimacy. The only real means domestic critics have of countering the President's dominance over the sources of news coverage is to rely on external sources. The difference between democratic external sources and nondemocratic external sources is the key to connecting diversionary war, rally events and the interdemocratic peace. The information reported from the government controlled media of nondemocratic regimes is reported as propaganda. It is readily dismissed by not only the news media, but also by domestic critics, challengers to the leader, and presumably the public at large. Again, using the Gulf War as a recent example, the Iraqi report that a baby milk factory had been bombed was treated as propaganda straight from Saddam Hussein. The U.S. intelligence report offered by the executive branch that that same building was a chemical weapons production plant was treated as credible by the U.S. press and widely reported as reliable despite the lack of any evidence to support either side's claim.[10]

In contrast, when two democracies come into conflict, the domestic news media on both sides share common norms of reporting responsibility, accuracy, and accountability. They accept each other as legitimate sources of information and reports travel relatively freely between the news gathering institutions in both states. As a result, neither leader can expect to dominate the "legitimate" sources of news to anywhere near the degree that they could in a conflict with the controlled media of nondemocratic regimes. Domestic critics will readily accept the information out of democratic regimes and employ it in their own domestic political struggles, something they are much less likely to do, and much less able to do, with the controlled media of non-democracies. Losing the near monopoly as a legitimate news source, any benefits the democratic leader might have expected to attain by dominating the sources of coverage have also diminished, if not disappeared.

Under these circumstances, the domestic costs of war that Kant based his model of a perpetual peace upon will almost certainly outweigh any domestic political benefits that spring from other sources such as the group dynamics discussed by Coser (1956). Thus, if a rational leader pursuing his or her own best interests is a reasonable depiction of the democratic foreign policy process, a controlled press on at least one side, is a necessary condition for violent international conflict. Results of recent analyses bear this expectation out. In terms of war involvement, press freedom, works just as well as democracy in predicting which dyads will or will not go to war with one another (Van Belle 1997a), and when the threshold of conflict is lowered to the infliction of casualties free-press performs much better as an indicator of which dyads engage in deadly international conflict (Van Belle 1997b).

This fits with recent experiences. Sticking with the Gulf War example, when the United States and Iraq faced off over Kuwait, news of protests broadcast by Iraqi television were treated as government organized propaganda and their content was dismissed. President Bush could expect that the crisis would provide him the opportunity to use the resources of the executive branch to dominate the news coverage and shape its content to his best advantage because the international opponent was effectively shut out. The information that did enter the U.S. media from Iraq was either from the United States or other free press sources, such as CNN whose reporters made a point of saying that their broadcasts were censored,[11] or it was simply dismissed as propaganda and was rejected, even by domestic critics and contenders for the leadership positions.

When the United States and France faced off over trade issues, the protests of farmers broadcast by French television were treated as indicators of the pressures and limitations the French government faced. In this instance President Bush could not expect to dominate the news in the same way because the U.S. news media accepted the French media coverage at face value and treated it as a legitimate source of news, often broadcasting images transmitted from the French television sources and providing unedited translations of French news reports. This allowed the French leader to compete with

Bush, albeit not on equal footing, for coverage in the U.S. news media. The coverage the French leader received gave him the opportunity to attempt to define the crisis and define the role of both participants. It also provided an information resource which, because of its perceived legitimacy, domestic critics could use to challenge the President.

Media management in international conflicts could be included as part of the leader's strategy to ensure at least temporary domination. Efforts to sanitize the news actually fit with the mechanism proposed here, because it is unlikely that any news management techniques that work when a democracy faces a nondemocracy, such as wartime censorship, would work when a democracy faces another democracy whose free press can provide an alternative channel for information considered legitimate. This alternative channel of legitimate information can serve to subvert many of the news control efforts that a democratic leader might employ to limit the flow of information to the public.

## EXAMINING HOW THE FREE PRESS MECHANISM FUNCTIONS: THE COLD WAR AND THE FALKLANDS CRISIS

This brief comparison focuses on the sources of news coverage in Britain during two conflicts, the Cold War with Iceland and the Falklands/Malvinas crisis with Argentina during the weeks prior to the Argentine Invasion of the Islands. In the Cod Wars, Britain was disputing Iceland's extension of its territorial waters and both sides eventually dispatched armed ships to the area. One thing that is immediately clear about the Cod War is that all of the sources and information about the motives and actions of both sides were reported in the British newspaper, *The Times*. Icelandic sources were relied upon by the British news media. In fact, Icelandic sources were very prominent sources of information for the British news media. In *The Times*, from October 1 of 1972 to November 9th 1973 when the conflict was resolved, just over 34 percent of the 1230 column inches of coverage were from Icelandic sources[12] compared to 57 percent from British sources (43 percent coming from British government and 14 percent coming from the British fishing industry). The remainder was unattributable or came from other foreign sources such as the UN, the Hague, and NATO. For a foreign power in an international conflict to capture one third of the domestic news coverage is remarkable. Thirty-four percent of the coverage is undoubtedly enough to provide an alternative source of information for domestic political opponents and prevent the British Prime Minister from thinking that s/he could dominate the coverage of an escalated conflict. In fact, the Icelandic Prime Minister received more direct quotes in *The Times* than the British Prime Minister.

The British news coverage during the 1982 conflict with Argentina, a country with a heavily restricted, but not completely controlled press, provides a sharp contrast.[13] The Falklands crisis during the period prior to the Argentine invasion of the island, when it was still considered a dispute, is remarkably similar to the case of the Cod Wars. It was a longstanding conflict over territorial claims in which negotiations were stalled. From the British perspective, in both cases the opposing government appeared to be using the conflict to shore up domestic political support and both opposing leaders faced a real threat of losing their position should they "lose" the conflict. In both cases the opponent initiated the threat of force and in both cases the opponent eventually used force first. Before the initial invasion, when Argentine sources had their most favorable level of coverage,[14] the news was overwhelmingly dominated by British sources. Seventy percent of the stories were from British sources, with just less than 5 percent from Argentine sources and most of the remainder divided between other foreign sources, such as the United States, and indistinct sources that appeared to be British but could not be identified with certainty. Shutting out the opponent does not mean that the leader will benefit, that depends on the leader's ability and skill at dominating the domestic news media. What it does do is deny the opponent the opportunity to prevent the democratic leader from dominating and thus preventing the opportunity for the democratic leader to achieve a rally.

The nature of the coverage also differs greatly. In the Cod Wars, Icelandic government sources were the *primary* source of factual information on the conflict. Collisions, harassment, trawler activity and gear cuttings were reported by the Icelandic Coast Guard and their reliability was not questioned. When disputes over these reports arose in the media, it was not over the factual content, but over the interpretation of motives, usually a question of whether or not one side was intentionally trying to ram the other. At the extreme, on October 17, 1973, *The Times* used Icelandic sources for the details of the negotiations held in London at #10 Downing Street. Throughout the conflict Icelandic sources were treated as reliable and the statements of the Icelandic government officials were treated on par with those of British government officials. Icelandic sources were often the basis of entire stories and were seldom interrupted. Ten uninterrupted column inches of Icelandic sources are common, occurring nine times during the conflict, sometimes including stretches as long as fifteen column inches. This demonstrates a reliable alternative channel of information, information that domestic opponents will be willing to use in their political struggles.

In the conflict with Argentina, the infrequent times when Argentine sources were used, they were treated as unreliable, interrupted with speculation concerning the true intent of the statement, or verified factually with other sources. This prevented domestic opponents from using what little came through for their own ends. For example the 1.5 inches of coverage that Argentine sources received on March 29, 1982 were split up into 3 one-half-column-inch single sentences each bracketed by confirmation or refutation by British sources. The longest uninterrupted Argentine source was a mere three column-inches and it came from a statement made in the United States, a free press country, not through the Argentine news media. All factual information in the conflict was reported from British sources.[15] In these conflicts the differences in the coverage of Icelandic sources, a free press country, and Argentine sources, a restricted press country, are remarkably different. The case of the Cod Wars provides some anecdotal evidence that leaders of free-press countries facing another free-press country in a conflict are unlikely to harbor expectations of being able to dominate the news coverage of the conflict in the same way that s/he might in a conflict against a restricted press country. This supports the plausibility that the free press is a crucial component of the democratic peace.

## CONCLUSIONS: DIVERSIONARY WAR, THE DEMOCRATIC PEACE, AND THE MEDIA

Obviously the cases and data presented above do not constitute a test of either the role of the media in diversionary wars or the role of shared free presses in the interdemocratic peace. The contribution of this article is probably best described as thick theoretical exposition. The goal is to explore the nature of these two seemingly contradictory theories on the choice to engage in international conflict, show that they are *not* at all contradictory and, by proposing the mechanisms that generate both phenomena, show that they might actually be related through the domestic political competition to shape the content of news media coverage in free-press democracies. The cases, data and analyses are intended to highlight or demonstrate aspects of the proposed mechanisms. In sum, diversionary conflicts and the rally benefits the democratic leader is seeking through them function by providing the leader the opportunity to generate a great deal of dramatic coverage that reflects favorably upon his or her performance. The leader is able to generate this coverage by dominating the sources of news considered to be legitimate and using the resources of the executive office to bolster coverage. This is compatible with the interdemocratic peace findings because the flow of information between the free presses of democracies reduces the leader's expectations that s/he will be able to dominate the legitimate sources of news related to the conflict and reduces the likelihood that s/he will be able to keep the coverage favorable. This significantly reduces the prospect of making domestic political gains through the conflict and increases the impact of the constraining forces proposed by Kant.

# NOTES

1. Though Coser is probably the first to state the theoretical propositions in a clear, organized, and applicable manner, he is not the first to articulate many of the propositions. Coser (1956) is a revision and refinement of Simmel (1955), and many of the concepts can be found in earlier works. For example, some of the dynamics of how international conflict can be used to help prevent or quell domestic unrest are specifically discussed by Machiavelli (1952 [1532]).

2. The criticisms Ray (1995: 1–47) makes concerning the empirical analyses of the democracy and war literature are relevant here. Specifically, since the dyadic democracy and war analyses examine roughly a universe of cases, tests of significance which rely on the statistics of sampling are of questionable value. Further, the cases are not all completely independent of one another. This latter problem could inflate the N and cause the significance measures to be inflated.

3. This suggests that at the very least, the concept of diversionary war should be operationalized differently for democratic and nondemocratic regimes.

4. Herman and Kegley (1995) list 111 references in their summary of hypotheses on regime type and war.

5. See Van Belle (1993) for a detailed explanation of why a free press is an important factor. Also, the significance of the free press will be made clear later in this chapter.

6. We can also look at in-group out-group conflict dynamics proposed by Coser (1956), because a shared free press also appears to prevent the formation of an extreme out-group image. (Van Belle 1997).

7. The term power base is simply being used as a generic term to refer to the individuals, groups, or organizations that exert influence in domestic politics. In a democracy this would typically include at least the voting electorate as a whole, elites from business, religions, or society, and other political actors.

8. The OLS interrupted times series technique is from Berry and Lewis-Beck (1986).

9. Not the sole source, but the dominant source.

10. In extended conflicts, such as the Vietnam War, domestic critics might be able to establish their own, reliable sources of information completely outside of the news media and government of the opposing country and challenge the leadership's dominance of the news sources.

11. Recall Peter Arnett's CNN reports from Baghdad during the Gulf War. Each was prefaced by the studio announcer reminding the audience that the reports were censored, and Arnett himself also constantly mentioned that he could only report what the Iraqi's decided to show him.

12. Two hundred two stories in *The Times* and *The Sunday Times* were coded by paragraph for the source of the information. Editorials (leading stories), and letters (correspondence) were excluded. This represents the entire universe of stories for this time period.

13. Presumably a completely restricted press would demonstrate an even greater contrast.

14. Except for a fairly large story in the first issue following the invasion Argentine sources held about the same absolute level of coverage as they had before the invasion. British sources, however, exploded to cover entire pages pushing the Argentine percentage down to almost zero in relative measures.

15. Note that this is before the conflict erupted into a war. During the fighting, for all practical purposes, Argentine sources disappeared from *The Times*.

## REFERENCES

Adkin, Mark. 1989. *Urgent Fury: The Battle for Grenada*. Lexington, Mass.: Lexington Books.

Benoit, Kenneth. 1996. "Democracies Really Are More Pacific (in General): Reexamining Regime Type and War Involvement." *Journal of Conflict Resolution* 40: 636–57.

Berry, William, and Michael Lewis-Beck. 1986. *New Tools for Social Scientists: Advances and Applications in Research Methods*. Beverly Hills, Calif.: Sage.

Bremer, Stuart. 1992. "Dangerous Dyads: Conditions Affecting the Likelihood of Interstate War, 1816–1965." *Journal of Conflict Resolution* 36: 309–41.

Brody, Richard. 1984. "International Crises: A Rallying Point for the President?" *Public Opinion* 6: 41–43, 60.

———. 1991. *Assessing the President: The Media, Elite Opinion, and Public Support*. Stanford, Calif.: Stanford University Press.

Bueno de Mesquita, Bruce, and David Lalman. 1990. *War and Reason: Domestic and International Imperatives*. New Haven, Conn.: Yale University Press.

Chan, Steve. 1984. "Mirror, Mirror on the Wall . . . Are the Freer States More Pacific?" *Journal of Conflict Resolution* 28: 617–48.

Cook, Timothy E. 1989. *Making Laws and Making News: Media Strategies in the U.S. House Of Representatives*. Washington, D.C.: Brookings Institution.

Coser, Lewis. 1956. *The Functions of Social Conflict*. New York: Free Press.

Dixon, William. 1993. "Democracy and the Peaceful Settlement of International Conflict." *Journal of Conflict Resolution* 37: 42–68.

Domke. 1988. *War and the Changing Global System*. New Haven, Conn.: Yale University Press.

Doyle, Michael W. 1986. "Liberalism and World Politics." *American Political Science Review* 80: 1151–70.

Erikson, Robert, Norman Luttbeg, and Kent Tedin. 1980. *American Public Opinion* 2nd ed., New York: Wiley.

Gates, Scott, Torbjørn Knutsen, and Jonathon Moses. 1996. "Democracy and Peace: A More Skeptical View." *Journal of Peace Research* 33: 1–10.

Gleditsch, Nils Petter. 1995. "Geography, Democracy, and Peace." *International Interactions* 20: 297–323.

Gleditsch, Nils Petter, and Håvard Hegre. 1995. Peace and Democracy: Three Levels of Analysis. Unpublished manuscript.

Haas, Michael. 1968. "Social Change and National Aggressiveness, 1900–1960," in *Quantitative International Politics,* J. D. Singer, ed. New York: McGraw-Hill.

Hazelwood, Leo. 1973. "Externalizing Systemic Stress: International Conflict as Adaptive Behavior," in *Conflict Behavior and Linkage Politics,* J. Wilkenfeld, ed. New York: David McKay, 148–90.

Hermann, Margaret, and Charles Kegley. 1995. "Rethinking Democracy and International Peace: Perspectives from Political Psychology." *International Studies Quarterly* 39: 511–33.

Hess, Stephen. 1981. *The Washington Reporters: Newswork.* Washington, D.C.: Brookings Institution.

James, Patrick. 1987. "Externalization of Conflict: Testing a Crisis Based Model." *Canadian Journal of Political Science* 20: 573–98.

James, Patrick, and John O'Neal. 1991. "The Influence of Domestic and International Politics on the President's Use of Force." *Journal of Conflict Resolution* 35: 307–32.

Kant, Immanuel. *Political Writings.* 1991. Hans Reiss, ed. Cambridge: Cambridge University Press.

Kegley, Charles, Neil Richardson, and Gunter Richter. 1978. "Conflict at Home and Abroad." *Journal of Politics* 40: 742–52.

Kernell, Samuel. 1978. "Explaining Presidential Popularity." *American Political Science Review* 72: 506–22.

Lee, Jong R. 1977. "Rallying 'Round the Flag: Foreign Policy Events and Presidential Popularity." *Presidential Studies Quarterly* 7: 252–56.

Machiavelli, Niccolo. 1952. *The Prince.* Luigi Ricci, trans. New York: Mentor Books.

MacKuen, Michael. 1983. "Political Drama, Economic Conditions, and the Dynamics of Presidential Foreign Policy Choice." *American Journal of Political Science* 27: 165–92.

Maoz, Zeev, and Nasrin Abdolali. 1989. "Regime Types and International Conflict, 1816–1976." *Journal of Conflict Resolution* 33: 3–35.

Maoz, Zeev, and Bruce Russett. 1992. "Alliances, Contiguity, Wealth, and Political Stability: Is the Lack of Conflict among Democracies a Statistical Artifact?" *International Interactions* 17: 245–67

———. 1993. "Normative and Structural Causes of Democratic Peace 1946-1986." *American Political Science Review* 87: 624–38.

Meernik, James, and Peter Waterman. 1996. "The Myth of the Diversionary Use of Force by American Presidents." *Political Research Quarterly* 49: 573–91.

Miller, Ross A. 1995. "Domestic Structures and the Diversionary Use of Force." *American Journal of Political Science* 39: 760–85.

Mintz, Alex, and Nehemia Geva. 1993. "Why Don't Democracies Fight One Another? An Experimental Study." *Journal of Conflict Resolution* 37: 484–503.

Morgan, T. Clifton, and Sally Howard Campbell. 1991. "Domestic Structure, Decisional Constraints, and War: So Why Kant Democracies Fight?" *Journal of Conflict Resolution* 35: 187–211.

Morgan, T. Clifton, and Valerie L. Schwebach. 1992. "Take Two Democracies and Call Me in the Morning." *International Interaction* 17: 305–20.

Morgan, T. Clifton, and Kenneth Bickers. 1992. "Domestic Discontent and the External Use of Force." *Journal of Conflict Resolution* 36: 25–52.

Mueller, John. 1973. *War Presidents and Public Opinion.* New York: John Wiley.

———. 1970. "Presidential Popularity from Truman to Johnson." *American Political Science Review* 64: 18–34.

Oneal, John R. and Anna Lillian Bryan. 1995. "The Rally 'Round the Flag Effect in U.S. Foreign Policy Crises, 1950–1985." *Political Behavior* 17: 379–401.

Ostrom, Charles and Brian Job. 1986. "The President and the Political Use of Force." *American Political Science Review* 80: 541–66.

Ostrom, Charles and Dennis Simon. 1985. "Promise and Performance: A Dynamic Model of Presidential Popularity." *American Political Science Review* 70: 334–58.

Ray, James Lee. 1995. *Democracy and International Conflict: An Evaluation of the Democratic Peace Proposition.* Columbia, S.C.: University of South Carolina Press.

Rousseau, David L., Christopher Gelpi, Dan Reiter and Paul K. Huth. 1996. "Assessing the Dyadic Nature of the Democratic Peace, 1918–88." *American Political Science Review* 90, September: 512–33.

Rummel, R. J. 1995. "Democracies Are Less Warlike Than Other Regimes." *European Journal of International Relations* 1: 457–79.

———. 1963. "Dimensions of Conflict Behavior Within and Between Nations." *Yearbook of the Society for General Systems* 8: 1–50.

———. 1983. "Libertarianism and International Violence." *Journal of Conflict Resolution* 27: 27–71.

Russett, Bruce. 1990. "Economic Decline, Electoral Pressure, and the Initiation of International Conflict," in *Prisoners of War?* Charles Gochman and Alan Ned Sabrosky, eds. Lexington, Mass.: Lexington Books.

———. 1993. *Grasping the Democratic Peace: Principles for a Post–Cold War World.* Princeton, N.J.: Princeton University Press.

Schoenhals, Kai and Richard Melanson. 1985. *Revolution and Intervention in Grenada: The New Jewel Movement, the United States, and the Caribbean.* Boulder, Colo.: Westview.

Sigelman, Lee and Pamela Johnston-Conover. 1981. "The Dynamics of Presidential Support During International Conflict Situations." *Political Behavior* 3: 303–18.

Simmel, Georg. 1955. *Conflict.* Kurt H. Wolff, trans. Glencoe, Ill.: The Free Press.

Siverson, Randolph M. 1995. "Democracies and War Participation: In Defense of the Institutional Constraints Argument." *European Journal of International Relations* 1: 481–89.

Small, Melvin and David Singer. 1976. "The War Proneness of Democratic Regimes, 1816–1965." *Jerusalem Journal of International Relations* 1: 50–69.

Smoller, Fredric T. 1990. *The Six O'clock Presidency: A Theory of Presidential Press Relations in the Age of Television.* New York: Praeger.

Tanter. 1966. "Dimensions of Conflict Behavior Within and Between Nations, 1958–1960." *Journal of Conflict Resolution* 10: 41–64.

Van Belle, Douglas. 1996. *Domestic Political Support and Dramatic Uses of Force.* Unpublished Manuscript.

———. 1993. "Domestic Political Imperatives and Rational Models of Foreign Policy Decision Making," in *The Limits of State Autonomy: Societal Groups and Foreign Policy Formulation,* David Skidmore and Valerie M. Hudson, eds. Boulder, Colo.: Westview Press, 151–83.

———. 1995. Managing to Miss Opportunity: Domestic Political Imperatives and Clinton's Policy Towards Haiti. Presented at the 1995 American Political Science Association Annual Meeting, Chicago, Ill.

———. 1997. Press Freedom and the Democratic Peace, forthcoming *Journal of Peace Research.*

———. 1997. Free Press, Dehumanization, and the Limits of Interdemocratic Conflict. Presented at the 1997 International Studies Association Annual Meeting, Toronto.

Vincent, J. E. 1987. "Freedom and International Conflict: Another Look." *International Studies Quarterly* 31: 103–12.

Weede, Erich. 1984. "Democracy and War Involvement." *Journal of Conflict Resolution* 28: 649–64.

———. 1992. "Some Simple Calculations on Democracy and War Involvement." *Journal of Peace Research* 29: 377–83.

Wilkenfeld, Jonathan. 1968. "Domestic and Foreign Conflict Behavior of Nations." *Journal of Peace Research* 1: 56–69.

———. 1972. "Models for the Analysis of Foreign Conflict Behavior of States," in *Peace War and Numbers,* Bruce Russett, ed. Beverly Hills, Calif.: Sage.

Zinnes, Dina. 1980. "Why War? Evidence on the Outbreak of International Conflict," in *Handbook of Political Conflict,* T. R. Gurr, ed. New York: Free Press, 331–60.

Zinnes, Dina and Jonathan Wilkenfeld. 1971. "An Analysis of Foreign Conflict Behavior of Nations," in *Comparative Foreign Policy,* W Hanreider, ed. New York: David McKay.

# 15

## Institutional Constraints, Political Opposition, and Interstate Dispute Escalation: Evidence from Parliamentary Systems, 1946–1989

*Brandon C. Prins and Christopher Sprecher*

### ABSTRACT

Research on the 'democratic peace' has received considerable attention in the last few years. Democracies, though, are often thrown together when examining the propensity of different regime types to become engaged in international conflict. Yet, democratic governments vary dramatically across nation-states. Whether it be presidential versus parliamentary, or multiparty versus single-party, democratic states clearly differ in the structure of their governing institutions. This article examines the relationship between government type, domestic political opposition, and the threat, show or use of military force. The analysis finds that Western parliamentary governments are rarely involved in militarized interstate disputes, but when they are they tend to be the targets of aggression by non-democratic states. Furthermore, the evidence suggests that these democratic governments are much more likely to reciprocate disputes when their opponent is a non-democracy. Reciprocation, though, also tends to be influenced by the type of government in power during a dispute. Coalition democratic governments, rather than single-party governments, are much more likely to reciprocate militarized disputes. In fact, the findings suggest that coalition governments are more likely to reciprocate disputes in general, and particularly more likely to reciprocate with the actual use of military force. The results also suggest that the level of polarization of a parliamentary government tends to decrease the probability of dispute reciprocation.

## DEMOCRACIES AND THE DEMOCRATIC PEACE

Evidence increasingly demonstrates that the presence of two democratic states is a near sufficient condition for peaceful relations between them (Maoz and Russett 1993; Russett 1993; Maoz and Abdolali 1989; Raknerud and Hegre, 1997; Gleditsch and Hegre, 1997; Rousseau, et al., 1996). While these dyadic level findings have held up to rigorous empirical scrutiny, the evidence at the monadic level is less than consistent (Chan 1984; Weede 1984; Maoz and Abdolali 1989; Benoit 1996). Indeed, most studies have found politically free polities to be equally as conflict-prone as non-free polities. Maoz and Abdolali (1989: 20) concluded that "regime type is generally not an important predictor of national conflict involvement." This mixed dyad result is anomalous and continues to confound students of international politics.

The lack of monadic level findings, however, may be partly a result of methodological weaknesses (see Raknerud and Hegre 1997). Benoit (1996) reexamined the monadic level findings and his evidence provides support for the idea that freedom promotes pacific behavior (also see Hewitt and Wilkenfeld 1996). Furthermore, some recent research suggests that democracies are often targets of aggression by nondemocratic states, inflating their incidence of war-proneness (see Leeds and Davis 1997; Gowa 1998). Plus, Raknerud and Hegre (1997) found the incidence of conflict for democracies to be related to their propensity to come to the aid of other democratic states (also see Gleditsch and Hegre 1997).[1] Therefore, democratic conflict involvement appears to be higher than it should be due to war joining behavior rather than the actual initiation of conflict. It seems, then, that questions remain regarding the monadic level relationship between democracy and peace.

In this article, we extend two lines of inquiry into the democratic peace research program. First, we address foreign policy behavior that falls short of the threshold for war (see for example, Gowa 1998; Senese 1997). There is a need to better understand foreign policy decision making that involves lower levels of conflict. Are low levels of force prohibited between democratic governments, or are threats and shows of force common responses to dispute situations regardless of the regime type of the opponent? Indeed, a diversionary theory of conflict seems to imply that low-level disputes can potentially provide electoral rewards to those in power (see for example, Stoll 1984; Ostrom and Job 1986; Smith 1996).[2]

Second, we explore variation in foreign policy decision making within the democratic community. Such variation has received little empirical attention (exceptions include Hagan 1993; Schjølset 1996). However, Benoit (1996) insisted that the dichotomous categorization of regime type ignores important information with regards to government characteristics and foreign policy behavior. Certainly, one might guess that different institutional arrangements would have a differential impact on foreign policy decision making (see Risse-Kappen 1991). Waltz (1967), in his study of the foreign policies of Great Britain and the United States insisted that institutional differences between these two democratic states contributed to the influence domestic political forces had over foreign policy decision making and to the stability and success of those policies. We must not forget, then, that there are significant institutional differences even among the states of the democratic community. As such, attention needs to be given to how these differences affect foreign policy decisions.

## POLITICAL CONSTRAINTS

The conspicuous growth of democracy over the past two hundred years potentially constitutes a fundamental shift in world politics. Given that democratic countries rarely fight one another, the ascendancy of such regimes could be the path to global peace. Two arguments have been posited to account for the lack of conflict between democratic nations. The normative or cultural model insists that domestic decision processes tend to be externalized, establishing conflict resolution procedures between liberal states that are grounded in compromise and the rule of law (Maoz and Russett 1993; Gowa 1995). The normative model also implies that relations between democratic states and nondemocratic states will be dominated by the politics of the latter, forcing democratic leaders to remain wary of the promises and actions of authoritarian diplomats (Maoz and Russett 1993). The structural model, in contrast, grounds the pacific tendencies of democratic states in their domestic political institutions. Indeed, to successfully accomplish foreign policy objectives democratic leaders must secure support from multiple domestic groups (Bueno de Mesquita and Lalman 1992). Consequently, as Elman (1997: 12) wrote, "democratically elected leaders cannot easily commit the state to war."

Both the normative and structural models have received empirical support. It seems, though, that the former argument cannot explain variation found between different democratic states with regards to their conflict-proneness. However, if differences do exist, as we think they should, then institutional variation must be a critical factor. Maoz and Russett (1993) insisted that the structural argument necessarily implies that conflict behavior should vary across democratic systems. They wrote: "Presidential systems should be less constrained than parliamentary systems, in which the government is far more dependent on the support it gets from the legislature. Coalition governments or minority cabinets are far more constrained than are governments controlled by a single party (p. 626)." Frognier

(1993) similarly found the single-party/coalition distinction to account for a large portion of the variance in cabinet decision making. To date, however, there is little, if any, empirical support for Maoz and Russett's suppositions.

Schjølset (1996) is one of the few students of international politics to examine variation in conflict behavior within the democratic community. Similar to Morgan and Campbell (1993), Schjølset (1996) argued that institutional constraints should prevent leaders from engaging in potentially costly interstate conflicts. She investigated whether belligerency varied across different types of democratic systems, due to their different levels of institutional constraints. Majoritarian democracies, she argued, possess fewer constraints than consensus democracies and therefore should be more likely to engage in interstate conflict. Schjølset found that indeed majoritarian democracies are not only more war-prone than consensus democracies, but even more war-prone than nondemocracies. She also found centralized and parliamentary democracies to be more belligerent than federal and presidential democratic states.

According to Morgan and Campbell (1991), Morgan and Schwebach (1992), and Hagan (1993), institutional constraints have an important and substantial influence on a leader's foreign policy behavior. The need to secure political support from multiple domestic sources implies, according to Maoz and Russett (1993), that foreign policy decisions which involve the use of military force will often tend to be politically difficult to make. As a consequence, democratic leaders often move cautiously in order to avoid electoral punishment. The potential costs incurred by nondemocratic leaders for poor decision making are considerably fewer than democratic chief executives given the fact that the nondemocratic heads of state are generally accountable to a much smaller group of individuals. Furthermore, democratic institutions convey a visible sign of the political constraints these leaders face (Bueno de Mesquita and Lalman 1992), and therefore, according to Elman (1997:12), "serve as a useful indicator of a state's trustworthiness, legitimacy, and reliability."

Morgan and Campbell (1991) offered three sources of executive constraint. First, decisional constraints increase as both the heterogeneity of the electorate and the frequency of electoral selection increase. Second, the choices of leaders are constrained by political opposition.[3] Lastly, the use of force should respond inversely to the number of individuals and institutions required for such an authorization. Therefore, the dispersion of executive authority among institutions and individuals should inhibit the escalation of interstate disputes (Morgan and Schwebach 1992). In the United States, for example, competing demands among the foreign policy players, such as the State Department, the National Security Council, and the Pentagon, help restrain executive decision making in foreign affairs.

## EXPECTATIONS

When it comes to parliamentary systems, Maoz and Russett (1993), Hagan (1993), and Frognier (1993) all insisted that single-party governments should possess the greatest freedom in foreign policy decision making. This assumes, however, that the party is ideologically unified (see Hagan 1993). Disparate policy views within rank should increase the constraints on the cabinet and thus lead to inefficient leadership. Coalition governments, on the other hand, face numerous difficulties in policy decision making of any kind. Indeed, one of the main criticisms of proportional representation is that conflicts over policy objectives are not resolved prior to government formation. Therefore, such disagreements form an integral source of cabinet instability. Budge and Keman (1990) additionally suggested that concessions made by parties to successfully form a coalition government often lead to increased conflict among members of each party. Furthermore, in a coalition no single party has the ability to unilaterally direct foreign policy decision making, and there may not be enough of a shared interest between the coalition parties to generate and sustain a long term foreign policy objective (Hagan 1993: 72–73).[4]

Minority governments should demonstrate the least ability in developing and sustaining a coherent and stable foreign policy regardless of whether the minority cabinet consists of a single party or a coalition of parties. Frognier (1993) contended that minority cabinets possess the least amount of freedom in decision making because of the necessity of acquiring outside support to implement a policy option. Moreover, if minority governments are a result of fragmentation within the electorate at large, as Budge and Keman (1990) have argued, then executive decision making will seemingly tend to be fraught with confusion and uncertainty.[5] We hypothesize, then:

$H_1$: *Single-party governments will have the fewest decisional constraints and therefore the greatest freedom to reciprocate militarized disputes. These governments should then be the most willing to escalate disputes in which they have been targeted.*

$H_2$: *Coalition and minority governments will possess greater constraints on decision making and as a result the likelihood of reciprocation should decrease while these types of governments hold the reins of power.*

Interestingly, though, there exists considerable disagreement over the relationship between government type and decision making. Strøm (1990), in fact, argued that coalition governments may be less accountable and thus less constrained than single-party cabinets. And, Alesina and Rosenthal (1995) suggested that coalition governments may provide greater stability in certain policy areas than their single-party counterparts. Indeed, given that single-party governments often face opposition parties that intend to redirect public policy in a very different direction, they may act extremely cautiously to avoid providing political ammunition to the parties out of power. Furthermore, the relatively higher level of domestic uncertainty that surrounds coalition cabinets may, as Downs and Rocke (1995) have argued, encourage greater risk-taking behavior. With coalition governments, the voting public may be less able to attach responsibility to any one party for policy failures. Presumably, then, coalition leaders would have greater flexibility in their handling of foreign affairs. Therefore, two alternative hypotheses are posited:

> $H_3$: *Single-party governments will tend to avoid costly actions that could be seized upon by opposition groups. Therefore, these governments should be less likely to risk reciprocating militarized disputes.*
> $H_4$: *Coalition governments tend to be less accountable than single-party cabinets and as a result should be less constrained in decision making. These types of governments, then, should be more willing to reciprocate militarized disputes.*

Government type, however, only targets one dimension of potential constraint. We must not forget the parliament more generally in an examination of political constraints and executive action. The degree to which the legislature is splintered along partisan lines reflects to a certain extent the polarization of the electorate over the appropriate direction of government policy. Such disagreement should only exacerbate the difficulties governments face in arriving at and implementing government policies and programs. Seemingly, the more unified and homogenous an electorate the greater the ability of lawmakers to construct government policy. In particular, a strong political opposition manifest in the legislature should tend to inhibit executive decision making by threatening to expose deficiencies in government policies. This leads to the final hypothesis:

> $H_5$: *Higher levels of disagreement among political parties, and greater oppositional strength should both increase the decisional constraints on the executive body and consequently decrease the likelihood of dispute reciprocation.*

## RESEARCH DESIGN

In our opinion, the structure, composition, and ideological consensus of a cabinet indirectly provide important information with regards to foreign policy behavior. If cabinet structure influences government duration, as many scholars have shown, it seems logical to assume that such factors may additionally affect foreign policy decision making. To be sure, interstate disputes are relatively rare events, and they involve behavior that might deviate from more routine relations between nations. In fact, it is conceivable that the escalation of a dispute involves decision making within a government that avoids partisan and policy differences. If this were true, decision making at higher levels of conflict would tend to rely more on issues of national security. We argue that the threat, show, or use of force occupies a middle ground between common interstate relations and the more extreme behavior associated with crisis bargaining. Furthermore, as Chan (1993: 208) insisted, the international relations community needs to begin examining "whether democracies are less likely to engage in a variety of conflict behavior that falls short of the threshold of war." Indeed, this is precisely what we are attempting to do in the analysis that follows.

Unlike Morgan and Campbell (1991), we are concerned only with western parliamentary democracies and how they differentially respond to militarized dispute situations. Furthermore, we are not solely interested in disputes that escalate to war or no war, but include foreign policy decisions that involve both threats and shows of force. One of the difficulties in expanding the dependent variable in this fashion is that we are faced with a substantial number of disputes that involve low levels of violence. In fact, 77 percent of the disputes involved no casualties and 35 percent lasted no longer than a single day. So, although 40 percent of the disputes involved the use of force by at least one side, we are faced with the fact that these disputes often revolve around low levels of force, such as the seizure of fishing trawlers. To avoid these types of disputes, we concentrate on the reciprocation of militarized disputes, and the domestic political determinants of this decision.[6]

Morgan and Campbell (1991) included both democracies and nondemocracies in their study and measured constraints utilizing Gurr's Polity dataset (1974, 1978). The nations included in our study are all Western parliamentary democracies. Therefore, the variable they coded for executive selection is absent in our analysis. All 15 of the countries included here select their executive through competitive elections. Similarly with regards to decisional constraints and political opposition, the 15 governments drawn from Strøm demonstrate very little variation. Indeed, generally all possess legislative parity and all have institutionalized political opposition.[7] However, this is not to say that the 15 nations presented here do not demonstrate variation in institutional constraints. In fact, we hope to show that there exists such variation even among those countries which Morgan and Campbell (1991) coded as the most structurally inhibited.

If, as we argue, political leaders are constrained by institutional attributes and political competition, then variation should exist within the democratic community with regards to foreign policy decision making. Yet, we must acknowledge the importance of factors associated with a realpolitik vision of international relations. Thus, we propose here a modified realist model along the lines of Huth (1996).[8] First, militarized disputes take place because of some underlying issue of contention between one or more parties. As numerous authors (Holsti 1991; Vasquez 1993, 1995; Hensel 1994; Mitchell and Prins 1997) have demonstrated, territorial issues have been one of major points of contention between nations over the centuries. Even disputes between democratic governments appear to involve higher levels of violence when the issue in disagreement is territory (Mitchell and Prins 1997). Therefore, the parliamentary governments examined here should be more willing to reciprocate disputes that involve this kind of issue. In our model, then, we account for whether the dispute involves a question of territory, as coded by the MID datafile.

Second, realism has placed a great emphasis on the role of power and capabilities through the years. Indeed, the decision to escalate a dispute naturally involves a consideration of the capabilities of both sides. Therefore, we code both the military expenditures and military personnel for each of the states involved in a given dispute, at the start of each dispute. From these data, then, a ratio of military capabilities is constructed (i.e., a/a+b). For multilateral disputes, the capabilities of the states in each coalition are summed to produce the ratio. We argue that as the ratio of capabilities of a state increases, the probability of reciprocation increases.[9]

Third, we include a dummy variable for contiguity to control for the costs involved in projecting influence abroad.[10] Not only do borders present opportunities for states to interact, which inevitably leads to the rise of issues over which fundamental differences exist. But, states should be less willing to incur the political costs required to respond ardently to geographically distant disputes. Consequently, we would expect contiguous states to be more likely to reciprocate disputes. Vasquez (1993: 127), in fact, reported that war is 35 times more likely between contiguous states than noncontiguous ones.

Lastly, to help control for serial dependency, we include a variable that measures whether the disputes are temporally related. Drawing on Beck, Katz, and Tucker (1998), we count the number of months between disputes for each of our 15 countries. When a dispute was begun prior to the resolution of a previous one, the count was coded 0. Our months-peace variable is meant to coincide with their peace-years variable (see Beck, et al. 1998: 1276), and its inclusion is intended to help prevent misleading results as a result of temporal dependence.

## Empirical Beginnings

In our analysis, the unit of observation is international dispute involvement. Therefore, the Militarized Interstate Dispute (MID) data set provides an appropriate data source. Gochman and Maoz (1984: 587) defined a dispute as "a set of interactions between or among states involving threats to use military force, displays of military force, or actual uses of military force." Additionally they argued that the coded acts "must be explicit, overt, nonaccidental, and government sanctioned." While the MID dataset includes all instances involving the threat or use of force from 1816–1992, the dataset containing information on cabinet structure only codes from 1946 until 1989. Our analysis thus will be limited to the post–World War II era. Data for the independent variable—cabinet structure—come from Strøm (1990). Characteristics of fifteen Western parliamentary democracies are coded for approximately a 40-year period.[11] The relevant disputes are matched with the governments coded by Strøm, and the variables selected are designed to match the ones used by Morgan and Campbell (1991). Thus, nearly all disputes involving the fifteen democracies Strøm coded in his study have been paired with the governments that were in power at the time of the conflicts.

To be clear, then, our concern here is with the reciprocation of militarized disputes, and whether domestic political forces influence the decision by a government to respond to an act of aggression with a threat, show, or use of military force. So, given these democratic governments are targets in a dispute, are some governments more likely to reciprocate than others? Similar to Senese (1997), a dispute in which a target state responds with a two or greater on the MID hostility level scale is coded as reciprocal.[12] Drawing upon Strøm (1990) and Downs and Rocke (1995), then, we argue that single-party governments that face highly polarized legislatures and strong political opposition should be the most constrained in their decision making. In contrast, coalition governments with low polarization and weak political opposition should be the least constrained in their ability to respond to militarized disputes.

Table 15.1 presents the domestic political variables utilized in the following analysis and how they compare to the three categories established by Morgan and Campbell.[13] The decisional constraint measures are relatively straightforward. However, the two variables measuring general parliamentary instability are a bit more complex. Polarization refers to the proportion of legislative representation possessed by extremist political parties (see Powell 1982).[14] This

**Table 15.1. Domestic Political Variables Drawn from Strøm (1990)**

| Decisional Constraints | Political Opposition | General in Stability |
|---|---|---|
| 1. Single vs. multiparty | 1. Percentage of seats held by major opposition bloc | 1. Polarization |
| 2. Majority vs. minority | | |
| 3. Percentage of seats held by the government | | |
| 4. Number of parties in the coalition | | |

measure attempts to account for the extent of conflict and extremism within the legislature. According to Strøm (1990: 14), "such conflict adversely affects the a priori willingness of political parties to negotiate for government participation." Therefore, developing a consensus, forming coalitions and general cabinet decision making should be more difficult as the polarization of the legislature increases. The fractionalization variable is drawn from Rae (1967, 1971) and according to Strøm (1984: 207), "is a measure of the probability that two randomly selected legislators will belong to different parties." The measure is a function of the number and size of the political parties within the legislature. Strøm (1990: 13) wrote, "the more parties, and the more evenly they split the electorate, the greater the degree of fractionalization." In other words, Rae's measure suggests that as the number of political parties increases the greater the dispersion of interests. Strøm additionally cited Sartori (1976) and Dodd (1976) who agreed that high fractionalization leads to miscalculation and greater uncertainty for party leaders.

The final category—political opposition—involves an attempt to measure the strength of political opposition within the parliament (Strøm 1984: 219). This variable quite simply indicates the percentage of parliamentary seats held by the major opposition bloc. Conflict at home can be either a catalyst or a constraint to foreign policy adventurism. Diversionary theory would suggest the former, while a structural constraints argument may suggest the latter. In the literature there does not appear to be a clear consensus on this question. However, Gleditsch and Ward (1997) found the Polity democracy score to be predominantly influenced by executive constraints. Given the dearth of violent conflict between democracies, plus the recent monadic-level evidence presented by Benoit (1996), Gleditsch and Ward's (1997) finding suggests that constraints on the chief executive, such as an effective political opposition, may serve to inhibit diversionary uses of force.

## Targets of Aggression

Of the 291 disputes involving Strøm's 15 Western parliamentary democracies, over 85 percent of the opponents were nondemocracies.[15] Given that these democratic governments were also the targets of aggression in nearly 70 percent of the 291 disputes, the evidence supports the findings of Leeds and Davis (1997) and Rousseau, et al. (1996) that democracies are less likely to initiate disputes, and are often targeted by nondemocracies (also see Gleditsch and Hegre 1998).[16] Furthermore, our findings support the argument advanced by Lemke and Reed (1996) and Kacowicz (1995) that democracies tend to be satisfied with the international status quo. These democratic governments were classified as revisionist in only 57 (20 percent) of the 291 disputes they were involved in.

The democratic governments examined here also tended to respond to aggression much differently when they were targeted by a nondemocracy. Reciprocation was over 50 percent when a nondemocracy was the opponent, while less than 30 percent when targeted by another democratic government. A closer look reveals that this higher incidence of reciprocation in part has to do with the issues in contention. Thirty-five percent of the disputes involving a nondemocratic opponent were over territory. Territory, though, was the issue in dispute only 20 percent of the time when democratic states were the opponents. Moreover, the territorial disputes that involved democratic opponents were reciprocated only 45 percent of the time. In contrast, over 75 percent of the territorial disputes involving a nondemocratic opponent were reciprocated. So, the combination of territory and a nondemocratic opponent appears to incite a dispute response by Western parliamentary democracies. A democratic opponent, in contrast, appears to help restrain reciprocation, even when the issue in contention involves territory.

## Institutional Constraints and Political Opposition: Bivariate Results

Initial bivariate results suggest that certain domestic political forces influence the reciprocation of militarized disputes. Coalition governments, in particular, appear at first glance to be much more likely to reciprocate than single-party parliamentary governments (see table 15.2). This supports the argument we made above, however it does not support the contention made by Maoz and Russett (1993). They insisted that single-party cabinets should possess the greatest freedom in handling issues of foreign policy. Presumably, though, the direction of the relationship we find reflects strategic behavior on the part of the parties in power. Coalition governments may be more inclined to risk a foreign policy venture inasmuch as a failure cannot be attributed solely to one political faction. Indeed, the

**Table 15.2.   Parliamentary Government Type and the Reciprocation of Militarized Disputes (1946–1989)**

| Reciprocation? | Single party governments | Coalition governments | Total |
|---|---|---|---|
| No | 49 | 37 | 86 |
| Column % | 58% | 41% | |
| Yes | 36 | 54 | 90 |
| Column % | 42% | 59% | |
| Total | 85 | 91 | 176 |

n = 176
χ2 = 5.08 (p = .024)

*Note:* The data are drawn from Strøm (1990) and the Militarized Interstate Dispute dataset version 6.04 (1994).

responsibility is diffused through the coalition and therefore attaching blame to any one party becomes more difficult. Single-party governments may respond more cautiously because they recognize that the responsibility for any mistake will rest squarely on their shoulders alone (Waltz 1967).[17]

Political opposition, as well, seems to be related to reciprocation. The results of a bivariate logit model show the number of seats in the legislature held by the major opposition bloc to be inversely related to dispute reciprocation (p=.067). Political opposition, then, as we argued above, does appear to act as a constraint on the escalation of militarized disputes. Additional bivariate models show majority governments to be more likely to reciprocate disputes than minority governments, though this result remains rather questionable due to the small number of minority cabinets present in our sample. Lastly, both polarization and fractionalization appear to be generally unrelated to dispute reciprocation. Therefore, both political extremism and a dispersion of interests within the legislature do not seem to influence cabinet decision making in dispute situations.

### A Modified Domestic Model: Multivariate Results

Clearly, bivariate models can be very misleading. What is needed is a multivariate logistic model that controls for additional variables of import. In order to test the impact that domestic political structures have on dispute reciprocation, in this section we construct a modified realist model that incorporates both domestic considerations and realist concerns.

Table 15.3 presents the results of the model controlling for the realist factors indicated above.[18] While the three realist variables appear extremely relevant in the decision to reciprocate a dispute, two of the three domestic variables seem to be important, as well. In this multivariate model, coalition governments are once again much more likely to reciprocate disputes than single-party cabinets. Interestingly, polarization, which was insignificant in the bivariate analysis, now appears marginally significant, and the sign is in the hypothesized direction; greater instability tends to diminish the likelihood of reciprocation.

As is to be expected, disputes involving contiguous states are much more likely to be reciprocated, as well. Presumably the costs of projecting force or influence increase as the distance between two states increases. While economic or political interests may involve states in regions outside their own, it clearly becomes more difficult to respond to militarized dispute situations when distances are substantial. Interestingly, the regime type of an opponent is not significantly related to dispute reciprocation, although the sign does fall in the appropriate direction. This result may indicate that low-intensity conflicts are not prohibited among democratic states. Given a dispute, West-

**Table 15.3. Logit Estimation Results with the Effects of Domestic Political Variables on the Reciprocation of Militarized Disputes, Controlling for Realist Factors (1946–1989)[a]**

| Variable Type | Variable | Coefficient | Robust Standard | p- value |
|---|---|---|---|---|
| Decisional constraints | Single party/ coalition | 1.27 | .51 | .013 |
| Political opposition | % seats held by opposition block | 1.37 | 1.72 | .428 |
| Legislature instability | Polarization | –3.87 | 2.32 | .096 |
| Realist factor | Military expenditures | 1.48 | .68 | .030 |
| Realist factor | Territorial issue dummy | 1.60 | .44 | .000 |
| Control | Opponent type | –.61 | .62 | .32 |
| Control | Timing[b] | –.000 | .005 | .94 |
| Control/realist | Contiguity | 1.37 | .52 | .009 |
| | Constant | –4.43 | 1.41 | .002 |
| Log likelihood = –95.91 | Pseudo $R^2$ = .2135 | $\chi^2$ (8) = 39.58 (.0000) | N = 176 | |

*Notes:* Models estimated in Stata 5.0. Standard errors are robust. The data are drawn from Strøm (1990) and the Militarized Interstate Dispute dataset version 6.04 (1994).
a. % Predicted Correctly: 70.45%. Null Model: 51.14%.
b. Control for temporal dependence. See Beck et al. (1998).

ern parliamentary democratic governments appear equally willing to use threats and shows of force against other democratic governments as they are nondemocratic ones.

An alternative multivariate model was also run to assess potential differences between governments that reciprocate disputes with a threat or show of force, and governments that are willing to actually respond to aggression with the use of military force. A dichotomous dependent variable was constructed that was coded a 1 when one of Strøm's states reciprocated with a 4 or 5 on the MID hostility level scale, and a 0 otherwise. In the previous analysis, a threat or a display of force received a 1, as well. In this model, only three variables are related to reciprocation: territory, contiguity, and government type. Disputes involving issues of territory are much more likely to incite a response that involves the use of military force, rather than a mere threat or display of force. Similarly, reciprocation using force is much more likely when the opponent is contiguous. And, once again, coalition governments continue to show a greater propensity to reciprocate, but with the actual use of military force.[19]

## Predicted Probabilities

Due to the nonlinear nature of logistic regression coefficients, the influence of the explanatory variables on the probability of using force fluctuates. Using the logit formula to ascertain the predicted probabilities presents a more tractable method of evaluating the relative influence of each of the exogenous variables. What we find is that the average probability of reciprocation given dispute involvement is about 53 percent.[20] Using the logit formula, we find that coalition governments are over one and a half times more likely to reciprocate MIDs than single-party cabinets. Relative military expenditures and whether the issue in contention involves territory also have a substantial impact on the probability of reciprocation. When the ratio of military expenditures equals 0, the likelihood of reciprocation is 32 percent.[21] When the ratio equals 1.0, the likelihood of reciprocation is nearly 70 percent. Similarly, the likelihood of reciprocation is nearly two times greater for territorial issues than nonterritorial ones.

Polarization of the legislature additionally affects the likelihood of dispute reciprocation. When the variable is fluctuated from its empirical low (.00) to its empirical high (.43), the probability of reciprocation decreases from 62 percent to 23 percent. Finally, reciprocation tends to be, not surprisingly, much less likely when substantial distance exists between the dispute opponents. The likelihood of dispute reciprocation when the opponent is contiguous is 58 percent, while only 27 percent when the opponent is not contiguous.

The predicted probabilities demonstrate that both domestic and realist variables are having an influence on the reciprocation of militarized disputes. Indeed, when all variables are at their maximum values (and polarization and opponent are at their minimum values) the probability of reciprocating a militarized dispute is over 95 percent. This dramatically drops to less than 1 percent when all variables are at their minimum values (and polarization and opponent are at their maximum values). It additionally is evident that the realist variables are not driving the probability. Both cabinet composition and polarization are important factors in a government's decision to reciprocate an MID.

## Diagnostics

With a logistic model, an examination of the residuals generally involves evaluating the influence of each observation on the probability of Y. Such a robust technique provides insight into whether certain disputes are unduly affecting the overall logistic results. Diagnostic tests may also provide information regarding the influence of specific combinations of X values that may be shared by numerous observations. When a combination of exogenous values contradicts the general pattern estimated across the remaining disputes, it may have a substantial influence on the coefficient estimates.

Plotting the change in deviance versus predicted probability shows that a dispute between Italy and Iran does not fit the general pattern. The change in deviance measures the size of the poorly fit pattern's influence on the probability of Y. Figure 15.1 shows that not only does this dispute fit the overall pattern poorly, but it additionally appears to be highly influential in estimating the model coefficients. This dispute between Italy and Iran occurred in September of 1987 and involved a disagreement over government policy. The model predicts a low probability of reciprocation by Italy due to the nonterritorial nature of the dispute and the substantial distance that exists between the two nations. Furthermore, Italy was experiencing a highly polarized legislature at the time that also tends to decrease the likelihood of reciprocation. Despite the model's prediction, Italy responded to Iran's raid by deploying naval vessels in the area.

Three of the four remaining outlier disputes involve the Soviet Union; one with Sweden, one with Norway, and one with Italy. All three of these disputes involved a show of ships or a border violation by the USSR. Both Sweden and Norway reciprocated with a seizure even though the model predicted a small likelihood of reciprocation given the overwhelming military advantage held by the Soviets and the nonterritorial nature of the disputes.

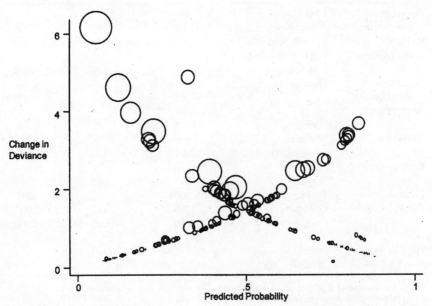

**Figure 15.1.** The Presence and Influence of Certain Outliers on the Probability of Dispute Reciprocation (1946–89)

Furthermore, both states had single-party cabinets and both faced only modest political opposition. Italy faced similar conditions and the model once again predicted only a small likelihood of reciprocation. Italy, though, met the Soviet border violation with a show of ships.

The final outlier case involved the UK against Argentina in 1976. British territory seems to have been occupied by the South American state and even though the UK held a substantial military advantage over Argentina, the British government in power at the time failed to reciprocate with even a threat of force. The dispute only lasted a week, and the overthrow of Argentina's President Isabel de Peron in 1976 may have contributed to the raid by Argentinian forces.

By removing these five poorly fit cases the model shows substantial improvement. The Pseudo $R^2$ increases from .21 to .29, the log likelihood value increases from –95.9 to –83.65, and the model now predicts 73.10 percent of the cases as opposed to 70.45 percent by the final model presented above. Removing these five cases, as table 15.4 demonstrates, additionally improves the significance of all eight of the variables considerably. Coalition govern-

**Table 15.4.[a]   Revised Logit Estimation Results with the Effects of Domestic Political Variables on the Reciprocation of Militarized Disputes, Controlling for Realist Factors and after Five Poorly Fit Cases Have Been Removed (1946–1989)[a]**

| Variable Type | Variable | Coefficient | Robust Standard | p- value |
|---|---|---|---|---|
| Decisional constraints | Single party/ coalition | 1.72 | .62 | .005 |
| Political opposition | % seats held by opposition block | 1.60 | 1.94 | .409 |
| Legislature instability | Polarization | –7.12 | 2.72 | .009 |
| Realist factor | Military expenditures | 2.39 | .77 | .002 |
| Realist factor | Territorial issue dummy | 2.01 | .50 | .000 |
| Control | Opponent type | –.62 | .69 | .364 |
| Control | Timing[b] | .004 | .006 | .517 |
| Control | Contiguity | 1.96 | .57 | .001 |
|  | Constant | –6.28 | 1.59 | .000 |
| Log likelihood = –83.65 | Pseudo $R^2$ = .2942 | $\chi^2$ (8) = 50.93 (.0000) | N = 171 |  |

*Notes:* Models estimated in Stata 5.0. Standard errors are robust. The data are drawn from Strøm (1990) and the Militarized Interstate Dispute dataset version 6.04 (1994).
a. % Predicted Correctly: 73.10%. Null Model: 50.30%.
b. Control for temporal dependence. See Beck, et al. (1998).

ments clearly show a greater propensity to reciprocate militarized disputes and polarization is now significant at an alpha level of .01. Political opposition continues to have only a slight impact on the decision to reciprocate, while relative military expenditures and the territory dummy remain highly significant. Lastly, proximity continues to exert a strong influence on these governments' decision to reciprocate MIDs, while the regime type of the opponent remains largely inconsequential.

Clearly removing these five cases to improve the statistical fit of the model is poor science. The diagnostic tools, though, do point out that a few disputes may deserve further attention. Indeed, the most appropriate course of action would be to theoretically and methodologically account for these deviant cases. Certainly further attention needs to be devoted to distinguishing foreign policy decision making when states are primary dispute actors versus those disputes in which states find themselves involved as third party participants. Furthermore, attention needs to be given to saliency of the issue under contention. Clearly nonterritorial issues can be equally as important as territorial ones to the states involved. This analysis, though, does demonstrate that domestic political variables have an influence on a government's decision to reciprocate a militarized dispute, and the effects of these variables are not confined to a few influential cases.

## CONCLUSION

Previous studies have demonstrated that domestic political constraints influence foreign policy decision making. However, most research has failed to examine variation within the democratic community. To be sure, realist factors, such as military capabilities and territorial concerns, continue to play a role in the foreign policy decisions made by parliamentary governments. Our results, though, indicate that domestic political differences among Western parliamentary governments also matter in the decision to reciprocate militarized disputes. Indeed, in the post–World War II era, among Western parliamentary democracies, coalition governments appear to be more likely to reciprocate when targeted in a MID. In fact, coalition governments are more likely to reciprocate disputes in general, and particularly more likely to reciprocate with the actual use of military force. This may be more a result of single-party governments avoiding the electoral risks involved in escalation, rather than a clear-cut active attempt by coalition governments to militarily engage dispute opponents.

Polarization, as well, tends to be strongly related to dispute reciprocation. Indeed, polarization is highly significant (p=.009) when the five poorly fit disputes are removed, and the variable appears to restrain the decision by a parliamentary government to reciprocate an MID. Given that polarization reflects domestic turmoil, governments presumably are attending to these domestic concerns rather than attempting to divert attention to foreign affairs. Interestingly, this latter result is not consistent with Hagan's (1986) findings. Hagan found political turmoil to decrease the number of cooperative foreign policy decisions, and to moderately increase the number of conflictual foreign policy actions. Our results, however, tend to show that domestic unrest decreases the likelihood of militarized responses to dispute situations.

Our results additionally illuminate the relationship between foreign policy decision making and the proximity of one's opponent. Clearly, contiguity matters in dyadic-level conflict initiation analyses. However, it additionally appears to affect even the projection of influence abroad. Even threats and shows of force are less likely as the distance between the two dispute opponents increases. Finally, it seems that low-intensity conflicts may not be prohibited among democratic states. No significant relationship was found between dispute reciprocation and the regime type of the opponent.

Admittedly, the results are only tentative, but the evidence is perhaps strong enough to warrant further theoretical and empirical attention. If variation does truly exist within the democratic community of nations this seemingly indicates the importance of domestic governing institutions and political opposition in determining foreign policy behavior. Indeed, only by examining domestic political factors more closely can we hope to fully understand the relationship between democracy and peace.

## NOTES

We would like to thank Kaare Strøm for generously providing us with his data. For helpful comments we thank Scott Gates, Nils Petter Gleditsch, Jim Granato, Gretchen Hower, Chris Butler, Sara McLaughlin, Bryan Marshall, Glenn Palmer, and three anonymous reviewers. Of course, we remain responsible for any remaining errors. The data can be obtained from the authors at www.msu.edu/~prinsbra/.

1. Evidence also suggests that democracies are rarely the targets of military intervention by other democratic states (see Hermann and Kegley 1996; Kegley and Hermann 1996).

2. The use of covert military force in one sense suggests that democracies are willing to engage other democracies militarily (Cohen 1994). In another sense, though, such actions, if fully disclosed, would not be welcomed by the general public and executives feel that undercover operations are the only way to achieve the desired political goals (see Elman 1997).

3. In the United States, for example, the Republican lead Congress presented a formidable political obstacle for the Clinton Administration in both domestic and foreign affairs. The military interventions in Somalia, Haiti, and Bosnia as well as relations

with Beijing all met with considerable disapproval from Republicans on Capitol Hill. Opposition such as this clearly constrains and inhibits executive action.

4. Hagan (1993) did admit that some coalition governments may succeed in securing a consensus that subsequently insulates the government from domestic opposition.

5. On the other hand, Strøm (1990: chapter 4) found minority governments to be nearly as durable as alternative cabinet types, therefore contesting the argument Budge and Keman (1990) have espoused, that such cabinets are a result of confusion and instability. Nonetheless, because these governments must seek support from outside parties the constraints they face tend to be greater than either single-party or coalition majority governments.

6. As an alternative means of dealing with the issue of low-violence MIDs, Gleditsch and Hegre (1998) restricted themselves to disputes with at least 25 casualties.

7. Only Spain, Portugal and Israel scored less than a 10 on the Polity III democracy scale. Spain scored an 8 or a 9; Portugal a 9 or a 10; and Israel scored a 9 or a 10. So, there is very little variation on the level of democracy scale.

8. Opportunity presents another problematic issue. Presumably large states with economies highly involved in the international arena will have a greater opportunity to become involved in disputes. Similar to Morgan and Campbell (1991), we define a dispute as an opportunity.

9. The ratio of military capabilities is measured in two different ways. One variable uses military personnel and the other uses military expenditures. Expenditures presented the best fit and therefore was chosen over personnel. High collinearity prevented both from being used.

10. The variable is coded a 1 if the states involved in the dispute share a land border or are separated by less than 150 miles of open water. France and Great Britain are considered great powers and therefore are coded here as contiguous to all of their opponents. Colonial disputes are not coded as contiguous, though we ran the analysis both ways and the results largely remain unchanged.

11. The fifteen nations include Belgium (1946–1988), Canada (1946–1989), Denmark (1946–1988), Finland (1946–1987), France IV (1946–1959), Iceland (1947–1988), Ireland (1948–1989), Israel (1949–1989), Italy (1946–1988), Netherlands (1946–1989), Norway (1946–1989), Portugal (1975–1987), Spain (1977–1986), Sweden (1946–1988), and United Kingdom (1946–1987).

12. We find that the parliamentary governments included in our analysis reciprocated their disputes 51 percent of the time. The other 49 percent were resolved in some manner short of militarized reciprocation.

13. The econometric models presented below only show the results of the final form of the model. Due to high pairwise correlation between some of the variables, all could not be run in the same model. However, the variables listed in table 15.1 were designed to provide different operationalizations of the three important domestic political variables.

14. Strøm (1984, 207) defines extremist parties as those parties that possess one or more of the following characteristics:
    1. A well-developed nondemocratic ideology.
    2. A proposal to break up or fundamentally alter the boundaries of the nation.
    3. Diffuse protest, alienation, and distrust of the existing political system.

15. In the logit analysis that follows, we concern ourselves with only the reciprocation of militarized disputes. Therefore, of the 291 MIDs, we selected out 193 where Strøm's governments were the targets of aggression in the disputes (i.e., side b in the MID dataset). This clearly prevents us from examining why democratic governments initiate, and subsequently escalate, disputes in the first place. However, we find that a substantial number of the disputes initiated by Strøm's governments involved minor incidents, many of them fishing disputes with other democratic states. Dropping these cases is not the ideal solution, but it effectively allows us to control for opportunity, and address the more narrowly defined question of why some parliamentary governments reciprocate disputes when targeted and why others do not. We were additionally forced to drop 17 of the 193 disputes because there were a number of disputes that spanned two or more governments. We were unable to ascertain which government made the decision to reciprocate.

16. Hewitt and Wilkenfeld (1996) found the level of violence to diminish as the proportion of democracies involved in a dispute increased. We find that although casualties were generally quite low in the disputes here, when these parliamentary democracies were the targets of aggression the number of casualties was on average over two times greater than when they initiated the disputes.

17. It may also be the case that these coalition governments are seizing opportunities in foreign affairs to demonstrate competence and leadership skill to constituents back home.

18. The logistic regression models were run with robust standard errors. Due to the difficulty in examining residuals, a robust estimator may provide more reliable estimates if model assumptions are potentially being violated. Particularly problematic in the analysis presented above is the assumption of independence of observations. A robust estimator, even with dependence, provides correct estimates of the standard errors of the coefficients. While the standard errors of the coefficients are nearly identical in both regressions, the small changes that do occur are systematically related to the variable type. The standard errors of the two realist variables, relative military capabilities and the territory issue dummy, become smaller using the robust estimator. The standard errors of the three domestic variables, plus the regime type of the opponent, on the other hand, all become slightly larger.

19. A reviewer suggested that the relationship between government type and dispute reciprocation may in fact be endogenous; in other words, coalition governments are formed because of the threat of attack. While the analysis here cannot conclusively answer this intriguing possibility, we do find that the duration and fatality level of disputes involving coalition versus single-party cabinets are not statistically different. The main difference is that the disputes involving coalition governments are much more likely to concern a question of territory. However, we control for this in the multivariate logistic model.

20. This is calculated by using the mean values of all the explanatory variables and plugging them in to the logit formula:

$P_i = E[Y=1|X_i] = [1/(1+ \exp{-(\beta_1 + \beta_2 X_i)})]$.

21. This point may seem a bit puzzling. As one reviewer queried, how can a state with no military capabilities reciprocate? However, both threats and shows of force also qualify as legitimate responses. Furthermore, even Iceland has the ability to seize foreign ships, which could be coded as a use of force by the MIDs.

# REFERENCES

Alesina, Alberto and Howard Rosenthal. 1995. *Partisan Politics, Divided Government, and the Economy.* Cambridge: Cambridge University Press.

Beck, Nathaniel, Jonathan N. Katz and Richard Tucker. 1998. "Taking Time Seriously: Time-Series—Cross-Section Analysis with a Binary Dependent Variable." *American Journal of Political Science,* 42(4): 1260–88.

Benoit, Kenneth. 1996. "Democracies Really Are More Pacific (in general): Reexamining Regime Type and War Involvement." *Journal of Conflict Resolution* 40(4): 636–58.

Budge, Ian. and Hans Keman. 1990. *Parties and Democracy : Coalition Formation and Government Functioning in Twenty States.* Oxford: Oxford University Press.

Bueno de Mesquita, Bruce and David Lalman. 1992. *War and Reason.* New Haven, Conn.: Yale University Press, 1992.

Chan, Steve. 1984. "Mirror, Mirror on the Wall: Are the Freer Countries More Pacific?" *Journal of Conflict Resolution* 28(4): 617–48.

———. 1993. "Democracy and War: Some Thoughts on Future Research Agenda." *International Interactions* 18(2): 205–13.

Cohen, Raymond. 1994. "Pacific Unions: A Reappraisal of the Theory that 'Democracies Do Not Got To War With Each Other.'" *Review of International Studies* 20(2): 207–23.

Dodd, Lawrence. *Coalitions in Parliamentary Government.* 1976. Princeton, N.J.: Princeton University Press.

Downs, George W. and David M. Rocke. *Optimal Imperfection? Domestic Uncertainty and Institutions in International Relations.* Princeton, N.J.: Princeton University Press.

Elman, Miriam, ed. 1997. *Paths to Peace: Is Democracy the Answer?* Cambridge, Mass.: MIT Press.

Frognier, Andre-Paul. 1993. "The Single Party/Coalition Distinction and Cabinet Decision-Making." In *Governing Together: The Extent and Limits of Joint Decision-Making in Western European Cabinets,* Jean Blondel and Ferdinand Muller-Rommel, eds. New York: St. Martin's Press, 1993, 133–49.

Gleditsch, Kristian S. and Michael D. Ward. 1997. "Double-Take: A Re-examination of Democracy and Autocracy in Modern Politics." *Journal of Conflict Resolution* 41(3): 361–83.

Gleditsch, Nils Petter and Håvard Hegre. 1997. "Peace and Democracy: Three Levels of Analysis." *Journal of Conflict Resolution* 41(2):283–310

———. 1998. "Hazardous States: The Democratic Peace at the Nation-State Level." Paper presented at the 39th Annual Conference of the International Studies Association, Minneapolis, Minnesota, 18–21 March 1998.

Gochman, Charles and Zeev Maoz. 1984. "Militarized International Disputes, 1816–1976: Procedures, Patterns, Insights." *Journal of Conflict Resolution* 28(4): 585–616.

Gowa, Joanne. 1995. "Democratic States and International Disputes." *International Organization* 49 (3): 511–22.

———. 998. "Politics at the Water's Edge: Parties, Voters, and the Use of Force Abroad." *International Organization* 52(2): 307–24.

Gurr, Ted Robert. 1974. "Persistence and Change in Political Systems, 1800–1971." *American Political Science Review* 48(4): 1482–1504.

———. 1978. *Polity Data Handbook.* Ann Arbor, MI: Inter-University Consortium for Political and Social Research.

Hagan, Joe D. 1986. "Domestic Political Conflict, Issue Areas, and Some Dimensions of Foreign Policy Behavior Other than Conflict." *International Interactions* 12(4): 291–313.

———. 1993. *Political Opposition and Foreign Policy in Comparative Perspective.* Boulder, Colo.: Lynne Reinner.

Hensel, Paul. 1994. "One Thing Leads to Another: Recurrent Militarized Disputes in Latin America, 1816–1986." *Journal of Peace Research* 31(3): 281–98.

Hermann, Margaret and Charles Kegley. 1996. "Ballots, a Barrier against the Use of Bullets and Bombs: Democratization and Military Intervention," *Journal of Conflict Resolution* 40(3): 436–60.

Hewitt, J. Joseph, and Jonathan Wilkenfeld. 1996. "Democracies in International Crisis." *International Interactions* 22(2): 123–42.

Holsti, Kalevi. 1991. *Peace and War: Armed Conflicts and International Order 1648–1989.* Cambridge: Cambridge University Press.

Huth, Paul. *Standing Your Ground.* 1996. Ann Arbor, Mich.: University of Michigan Press.

Kacowicz, Arie M. 1995. "Explaining Zones of Peace: Democracies as Satisfied Powers?" *Journal of Peace Research* 32(3): 265–76.

Kegley, Charles, and Margaret Hermann. 1996. "How Democracies Use Intervention: a Neglected Dimension in Studies of the Democratic Peace," *Journal of Peace Research* 33(3): 309–23.

Leeds, Brett Ashley, and David Davis. 1997. "Domestic Political Vulnerability and International Disputes." *Journal of Conflict Resolution* 41(6): 814–36.

Lemke, Douglas, and William Reed. 1996. "Regime Types and Status Quo Evaluations: Power Transition Theory and the Democratic Peace." *International Interactions* 22(2): 143–64.

Levy, Jack. 1988. "Domestic Politics and War." *Journal of Interdisciplinary History* 18(2): 653–77.

Maoz, Zeev and Nasrin Abdolali. 1989. "Regime Type and International Conflict." *Journal of Conflict Resolution* 33(1): 3–35.

Maoz, Zeev, and Bruce Russett. 1993. "Normative and Structural Causes of the Democratic Peace, 1946–1986." *American Political Science Review* 87(3): 624–38.

Mitchell, Sara M. and Brandon Prins. 1999. "Beyond Territorial Contiguity: An Examination of the Issues Underlying Democratic Interstate Disputes." *International Studies Quarterly,* (March).

Morgan, T. Clifton and Sally Campbell. 1991. "Domestic Structure, Decisional Constraints, and War." *Journal of Conflict Resolution* 35(2): 187–211.

Morgan, T. Clifton and Valerie Schwebach. 1992. "Take Two Democracies and Call Me in the Morning: A Prescription for Peace?" *International Interactions* 17(4): 305–20.

Mueller, John. 1973. *War, Presidents, and Public Opinion.* New York: John Wiley.

Nincic, Miroslav. 1992. *Democracy and Foreign Policy.* New York: Columbia University Press.

Ostrom, Charles and Brian Job. 1986. "The President and the Political Use of Force." *American Political Science Review* 80(2): 541–66.

Powell, G. Bingham. 1982. *Contemporary Democracies*. Cambridge, Mass.: Harvard University Press.

Rae, Douglas. 1971. *The Political Consequences of Electoral Laws*. New Haven, Conn.: Yale University Press.

Raknerud, Arvid and Håvard Hegre. 1997. "The Hazard of War: Reassessing the Evidence for the Democratic Peace." *Journal of Peace Research* 34(4): 385–404.

Risse-Kappen, Thomas. 1991. "Public Opinion, Domestic Structure, and Foreign Policy in Liberal Democracies." *World Politics* 43 (4): 479–512.

Rousseau, David L., Christopher Gelpi, Dan Reiter and Paul K. Huth. 1996. "Assessing the Dyadic Nature of the Democratic Peace, 1918–1988." *American Political Science Review* 90(3): 512–33.

Russett, Bruce. 1993. *Grasping the Democratic Peace*. New Haven, Conn.: Yale University Press.

Sartori, Giovanni. 1976. *Parties and Party Systems*. Cambridge: Cambridge University Press.

Schjølset, Anita. 1996. "Are Some Democracies More Peaceful than Others?" Paper prepared for the 1996 Annual Meeting of International Studies Association.

Senese, Paul D. 1997. "International Sources of Dispute Challenges and Reciprocation." *Journal of Conflict Resolution* 41(3): 407–27.

Smith, Alastair. 1996. "Diversionary Foreign Policy in Democratic Systems." *International Studies Quarterly* 40(1): 133–53.

Smoke, Richard. 1987. *National Security and the Nuclear Dilemma, 2nd Edition*. New York: Random House.

Stoll, Richard. 1984. "The Guns of November: Presidential Re-elections and the Use of Force." *Journal of Conflict Resolution* 19(2): 379–416.

Strøm, Kaare. 1984. "Minority Governments in Parliamentary Democracies: the Rationality of Nonwinning Cabinet Solutions." *Comparative Political Studies* 17(2): 199–227.

Strøm, Kaare. 1990. *Minority Government and Majority Rule*. Cambridge: Cambridge University Press.

Vasquez, John. 1993. *The War Puzzle*. Cambridge: Cambridge University Press.

———. 1995. "Why Do Neighbors Fight? Proximity, Interaction, and Territoriality." *Journal of Peace Research* 32(3): 277–93.

Waltz, Kenneth. 1967. *Foreign Policy and Democratic Politics: The American and British Experience*. Boston, Mass.: Little, Brown and Company.

Weede, Erich. 1984. "Democracy and War Involvement." *Journal of Conflict Resolution* 28(4): 649–64.

Wilkenfeld, Jonathan. 1968. "Domestic and Foreign Conflict Behavior of Nations." *Journal of Peace Research* 1(1): 56–69.

Wright, Quincy. 1965. *A Study of War*. Chicago: University of Chicago Press.

# Index

World Summit for Social Development, 301
World Trade Center (WTC), 232, 233
World Trade Organization, 260

Yugoslavian successor states, 166, 181–82; association incentives and disincentives, 184–86; breaking impasse, 186–88; current appraisal, 182–84; economy, 184, 185; humanitarian issues, 182–83, 187; nationalism, 185–88; "offices," 182–83; service sector, 184–85; Yugo-nostalgia, 181, 186–88
Yugoslav National Army, 182

Zhou-Enlai, 34n41
zones of peace/turmoil, 161, 162

# About the Contributors

**John Braithwaite** is Professor of Law and Political Science at the Australian National University in Canberra, Australia.

**Gavin Cameron** is a lecturer in the Department of Politics and Contemporary History at the University of Salford, Salford, UK.

**A.W. Harris** is Professor of Government and Politics at Humboldt State University, Arcata, California.

**Aaron Karp** is Senior Faculty Associate in the International Studies graduate program at Old Dominion University, Virginia.

**H. Peter Langille** is Adjunct Professor of Political Science at the University of Western Ontario, London, Ontario, Canada.

**Timothy J. O'Neill** is Professor of Political Science at Southwestern University, Georgetown, Texas.

The late **Stuart S. Nagel** was Emeritus Professor of Political Science at the University of Illinois at Urbana-Champaign.

**Brandon C. Prins** is Assistant Professor of Political Science at the University of New Orleans, Louisiana.

**Paul J. Rich** is President of the Policy Studies Organization. Active in Harvard alumni affairs, Dr. Rich was a consultant and professor in Saudi Arabia before serving for eleven years as head of training and development in the Arab sheikhdom of Qatar in the Gulf. A Fellow of the Hoover Institution at Stanford University, he is President of the Congress of the Americas and of Phi Beta Delta, the honor society for international education.

**Richard Saull** is a lecturer in International Relations at the School of Oriental and African Studies, University of London.

**James H. Seroka** is Professor in the Department of Political Science and the Center for Governmental Services, Auburn University, Alabama.

**Courtney B. Smith** is Professor at the School of Diplomacy and International Relations at Seton Hall University, South Orange, New Jersey.

**Christopher Sprecher** is a graduate student in Political Science at Michigan State University, Lansing, Michigan.

**John D. Stempel** is Professor of Political Science and Director of the Patterson School of Diplomacy and International Commerce at the University of Kentucky, Lexington.

**Yannis A. Stivachtis** is Assistant Professor of International Relations and Strategic Studies at Schiller International University, Lausanne, Switzerland and a Research Fellow at the UN Institute for Disarmament Research (UNIDIR).

**Douglas A. Van Belle** is Assistant Professor of Political Science at East Stroudsburg University, East Stroudsburg, Pennsylvania.

**Jarrod Wiener** is the Director of the Brussels School of International Studies at the University of Kent, UK.

**Jing-dong Yuan** is Senior Research Associate at the Institute of International Relations at the University of British Columbia, Vancouver, Canada.